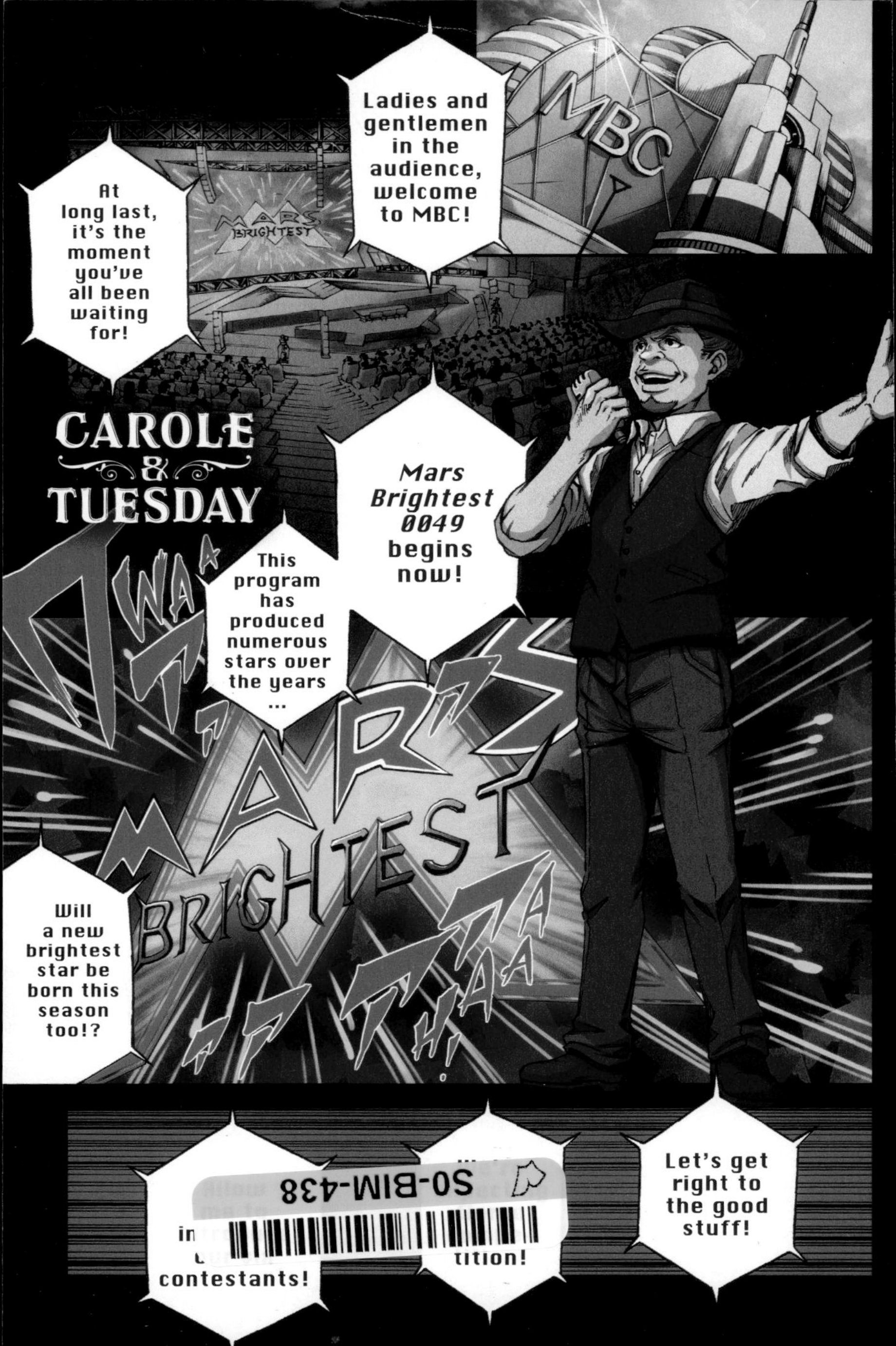

Ladies and gentlemen in the audience, welcome to MBC!
MBC
At long last, it's the moment you've all been waiting for!
MARS BRIGHTEST
CAROLE & TUESDAY
Mars Brightest 0049 begins now!
This program has produced numerous stars over the years...
MARS BRIGHTEST
Will a new brightest star be born this season too!?
Let's get right to the good stuff!
tition!
contestants!

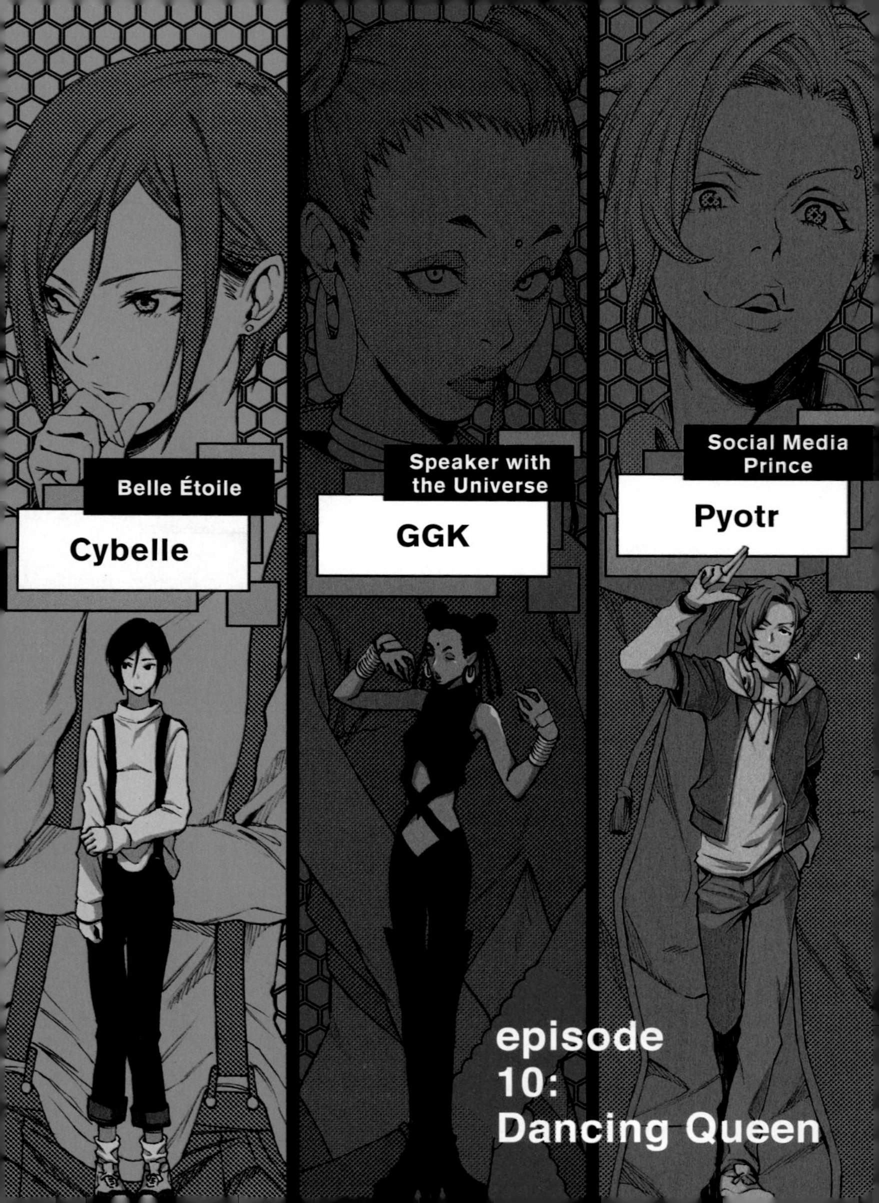
Social Media Prince
Pyotr
episode 10: Dancing Queen
Speaker with the Universe
GGK
Belle Étoile
Cybelle

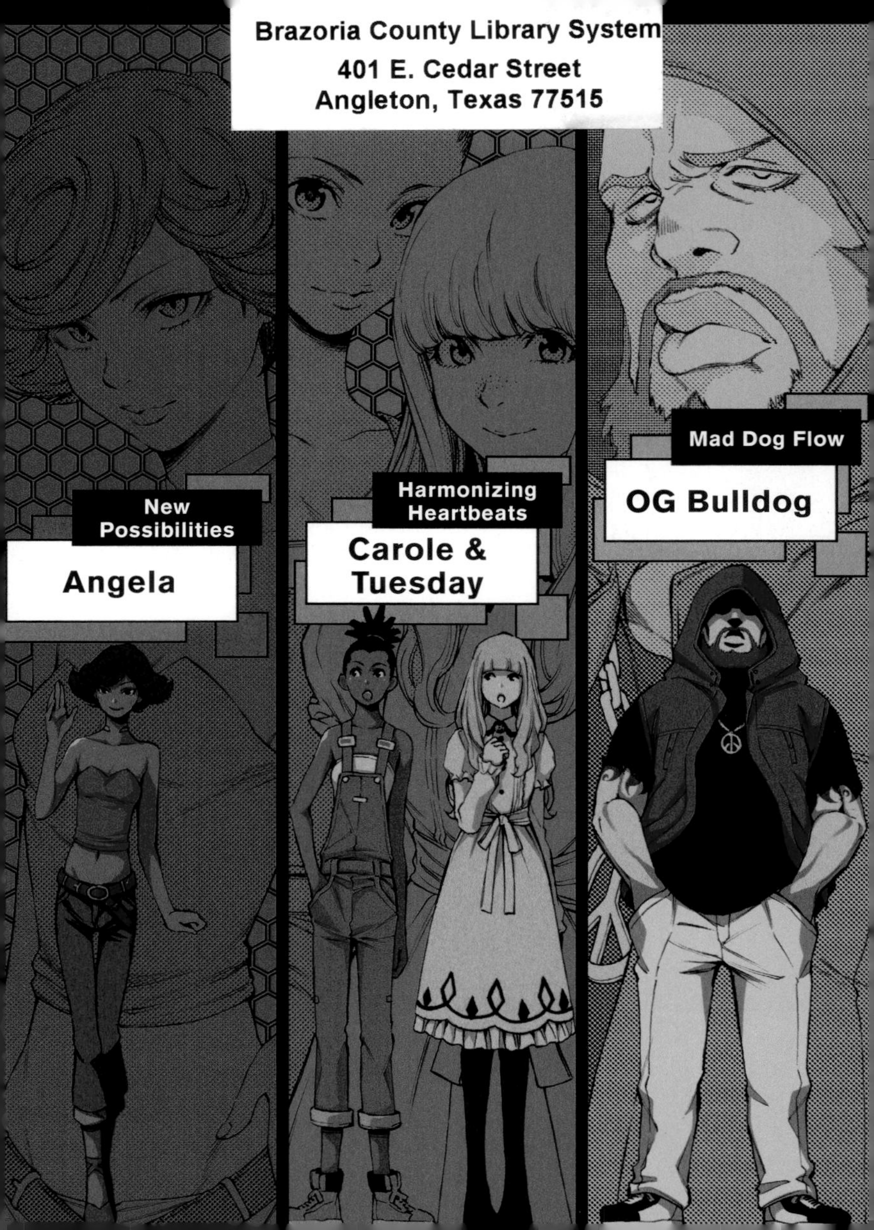
Mad Dog Flow
OG Bulldog
Harmonizing Heartbeats
Carole & Tuesday
New Possibilities
Angela

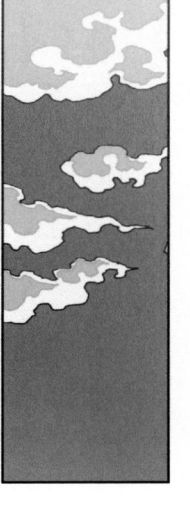

CONTENTS

CAROLE & TUESDAY

**Morito Yamataka
BONES, Shinichiro Watanabe**

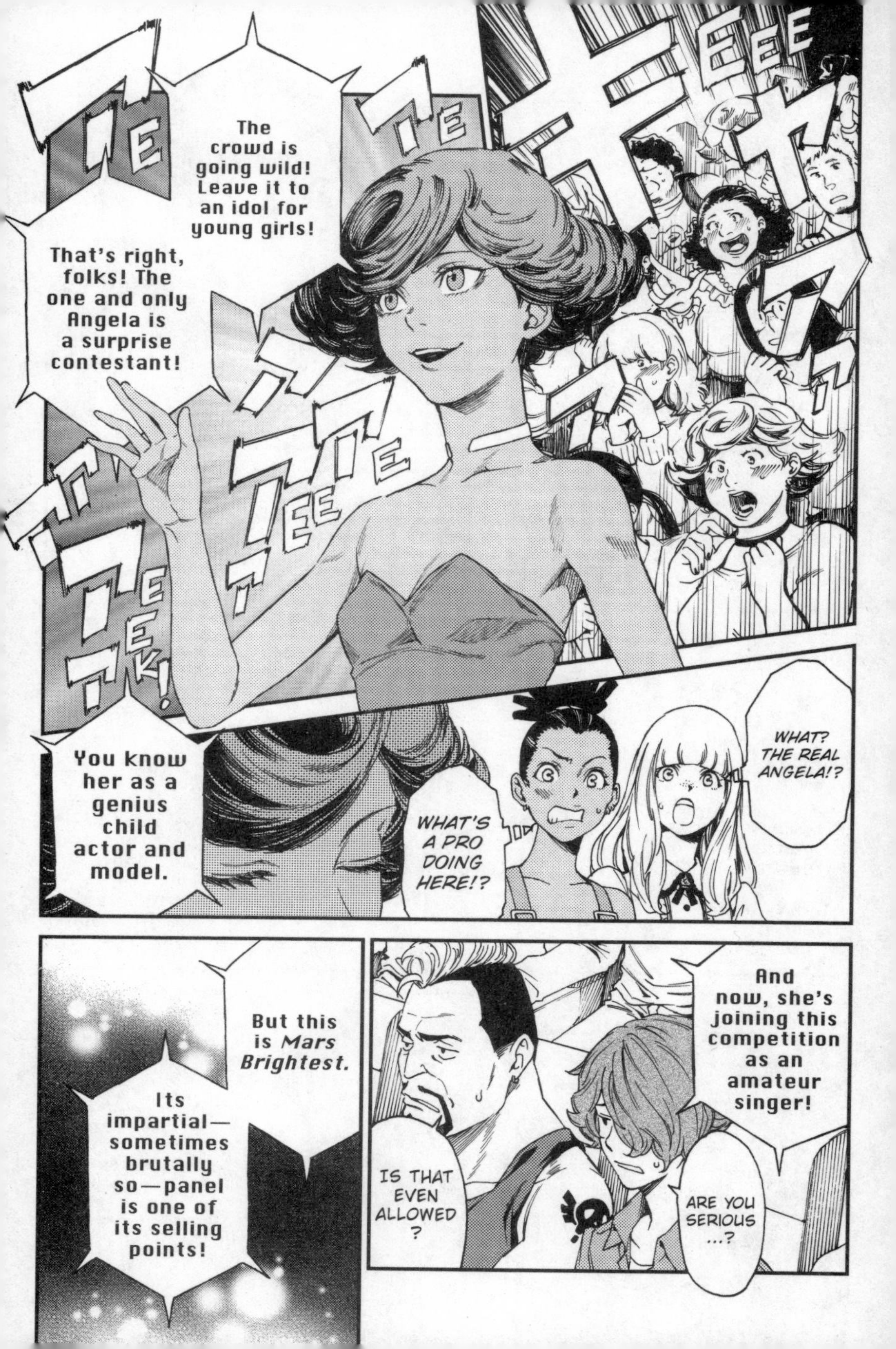
The crowd is going wild! Leave it to an idol for young girls!
That's right, folks! The one and only Angela is a surprise contestant!
WHAT? THE REAL ANGELA!?
WHAT'S A PRO DOING HERE!?
You know her as a genius child actor and model.
And now, she's joining this competition as an amateur singer!
ARE YOU SERIOUS ...?
IS THAT EVEN ALLOWED ?
But this is *Mars Brightest.*
Its impartial—sometimes brutally so—panel is one of its selling points!

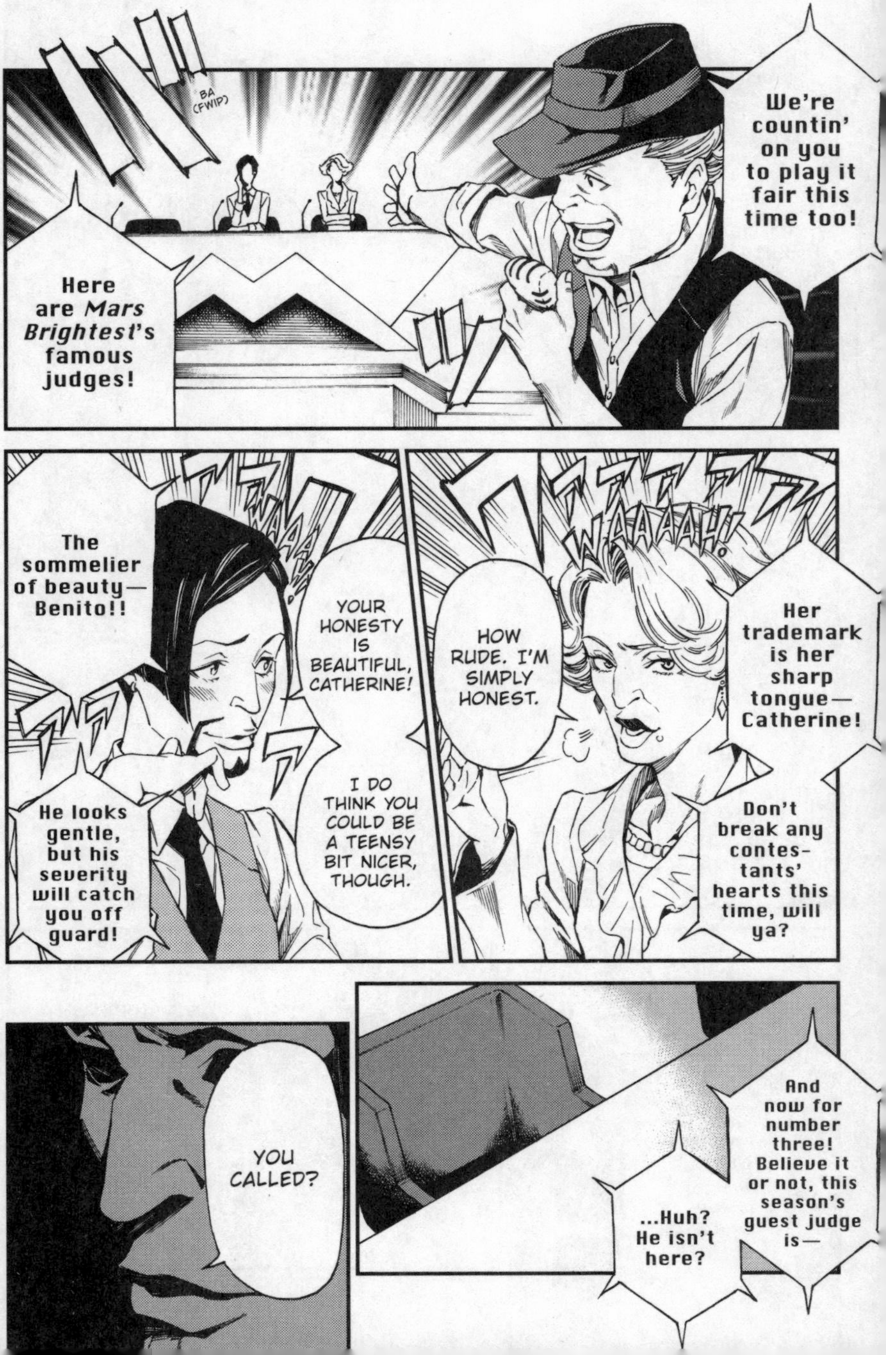
We're countin' on you to play it fair this time too!
BA (FWIP)
Here are *Mars Brightest*'s famous judges!
WAAAAH!
Her trademark is her sharp tongue—Catherine!
Don't break any contes-tants' hearts this time, will ya?
HOW RUDE. I'M SIMPLY HONEST.
WAAAH!
The sommelier of beauty—Benito!!
YOUR HONESTY IS BEAUTIFUL, CATHERINE!
I DO THINK YOU COULD BE A TEENSY BIT NICER, THOUGH.
He looks gentle, but his severity will catch you off guard!
And now for number three! Believe it or not, this season's guest judge is—
...Huh? He isn't here?
YOU CALLED?

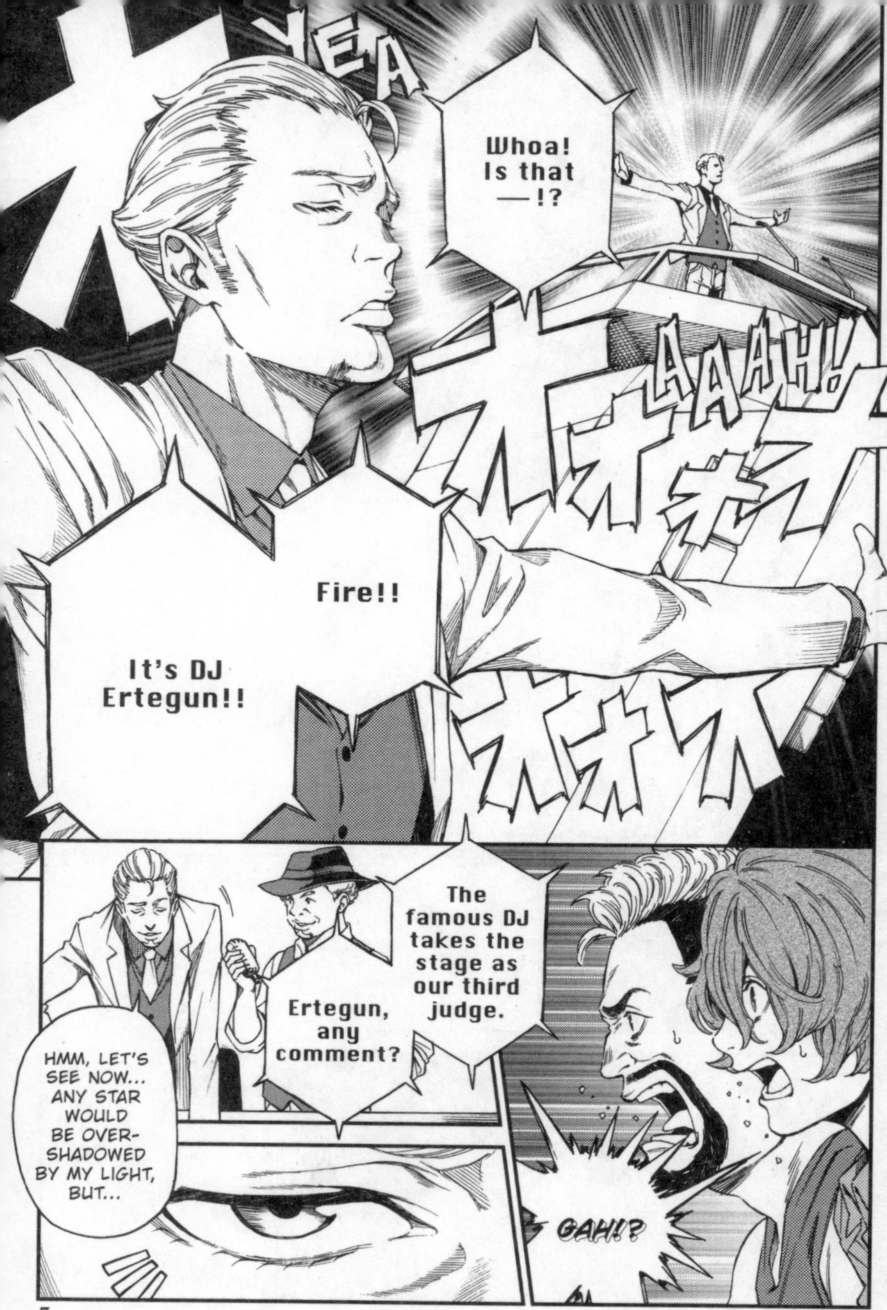
Whoa! Is that —!?
YEA
AAAH!
Fire!!
It's DJ Ertegun!!
The famous DJ takes the stage as our third judge.
GAH!?
Ertegun, any comment?
HMM, LET'S SEE NOW... ANY STAR WOULD BE OVER-SHADOWED BY MY LIGHT, BUT...

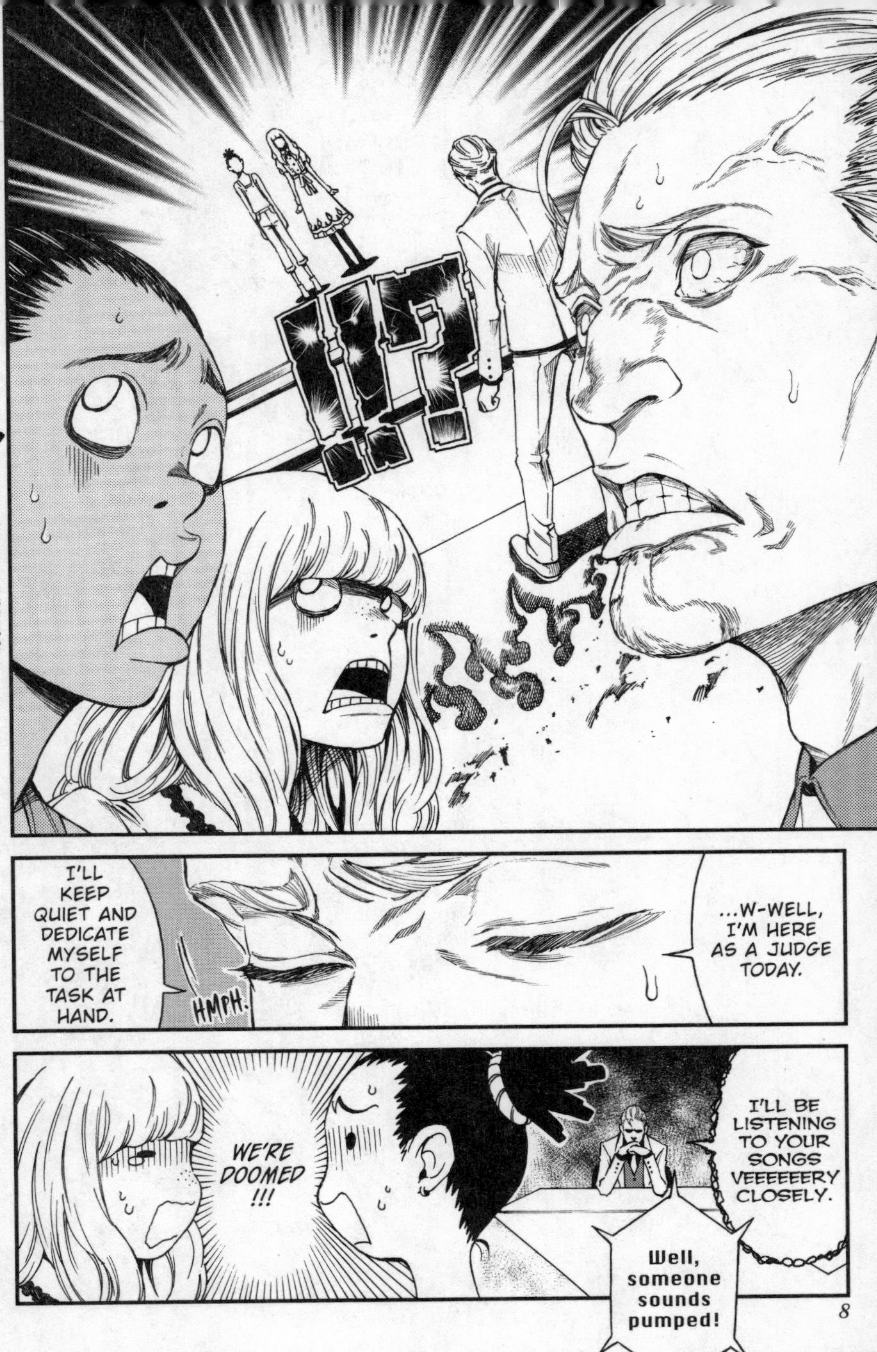
!!?
SUDDEN CHANGE IN EXPRESSION
...W-WELL, I'M HERE AS A JUDGE TODAY.
HMPH.
I'LL KEEP QUIET AND DEDICATE MYSELF TO THE TASK AT HAND.
I'LL BE LISTENING TO YOUR SONGS VEEEEEERY CLOSELY.
Well, someone sounds pumped!
WE'RE DOOMED!!!

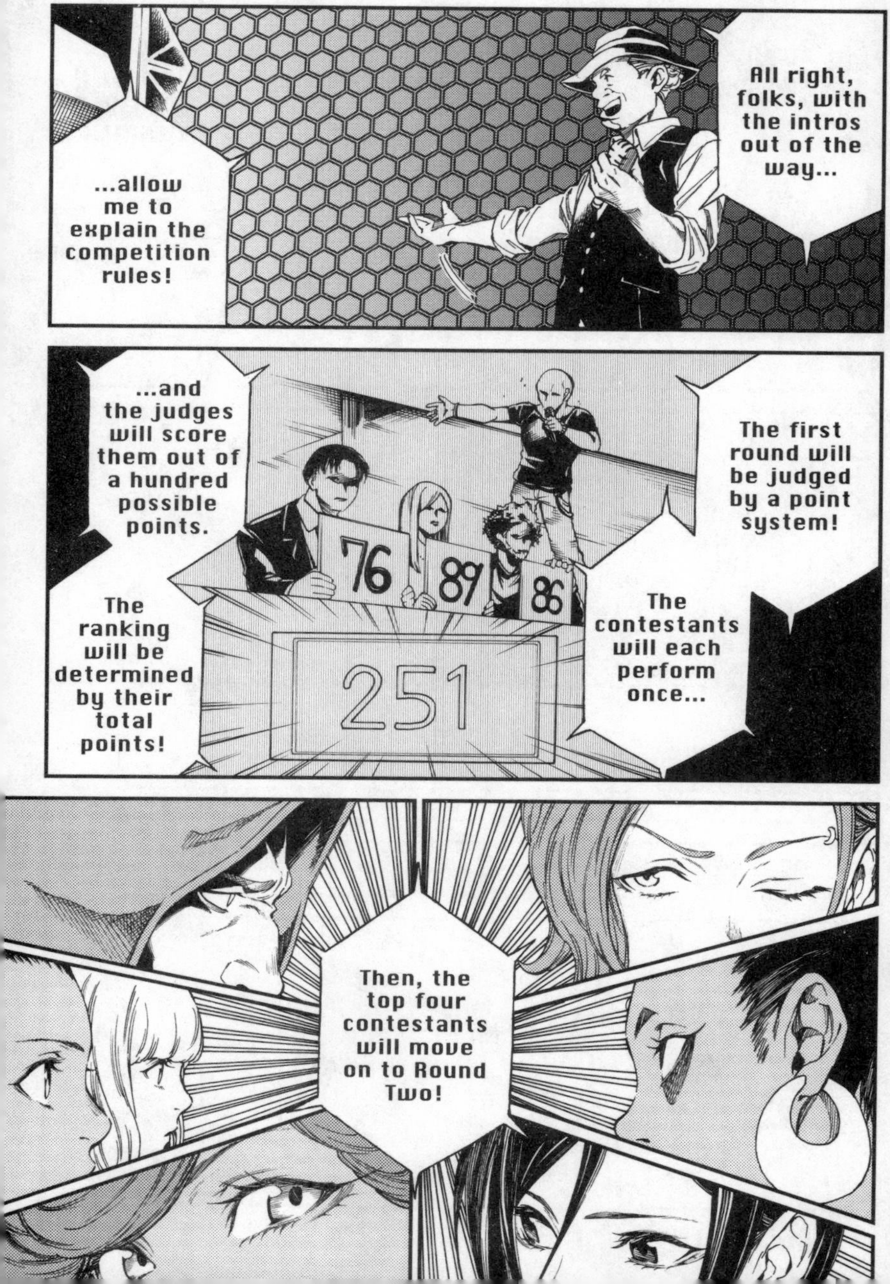
All right, folks, with the intros out of the way...
...allow me to explain the competition rules!
The first round will be judged by a point system!
...and the judges will score them out of a hundred possible points.
76
89
86
The contestants will each perform once...
251
The ranking will be determined by their total points!
Then, the top four contestants will move on to Round Two!

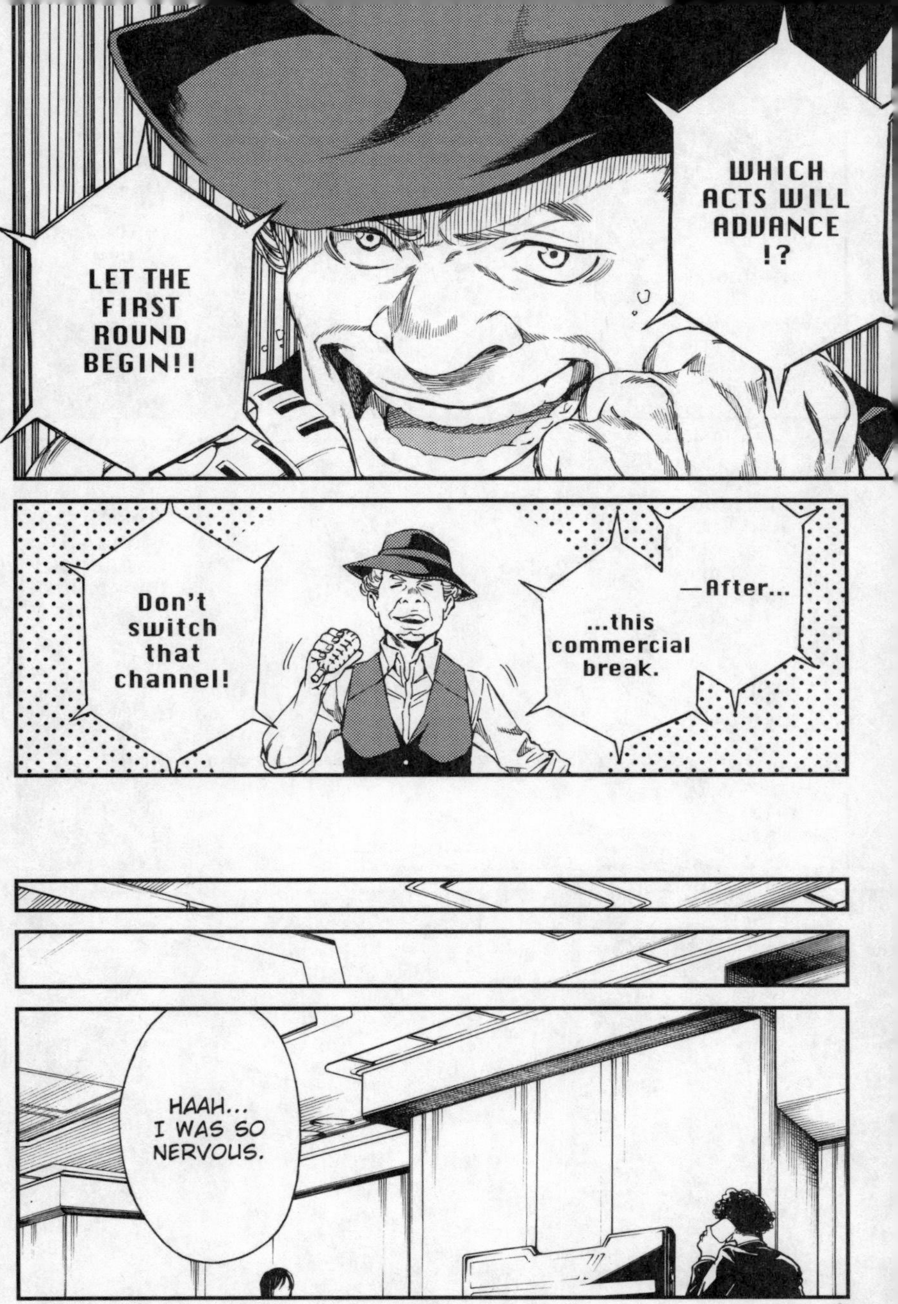
WHICH ACTS WILL ADVANCE !?
LET THE FIRST ROUND BEGIN!!
—After...
...this commercial break.
Don't switch that channel!
HAAH... I WAS SO NERVOUS.

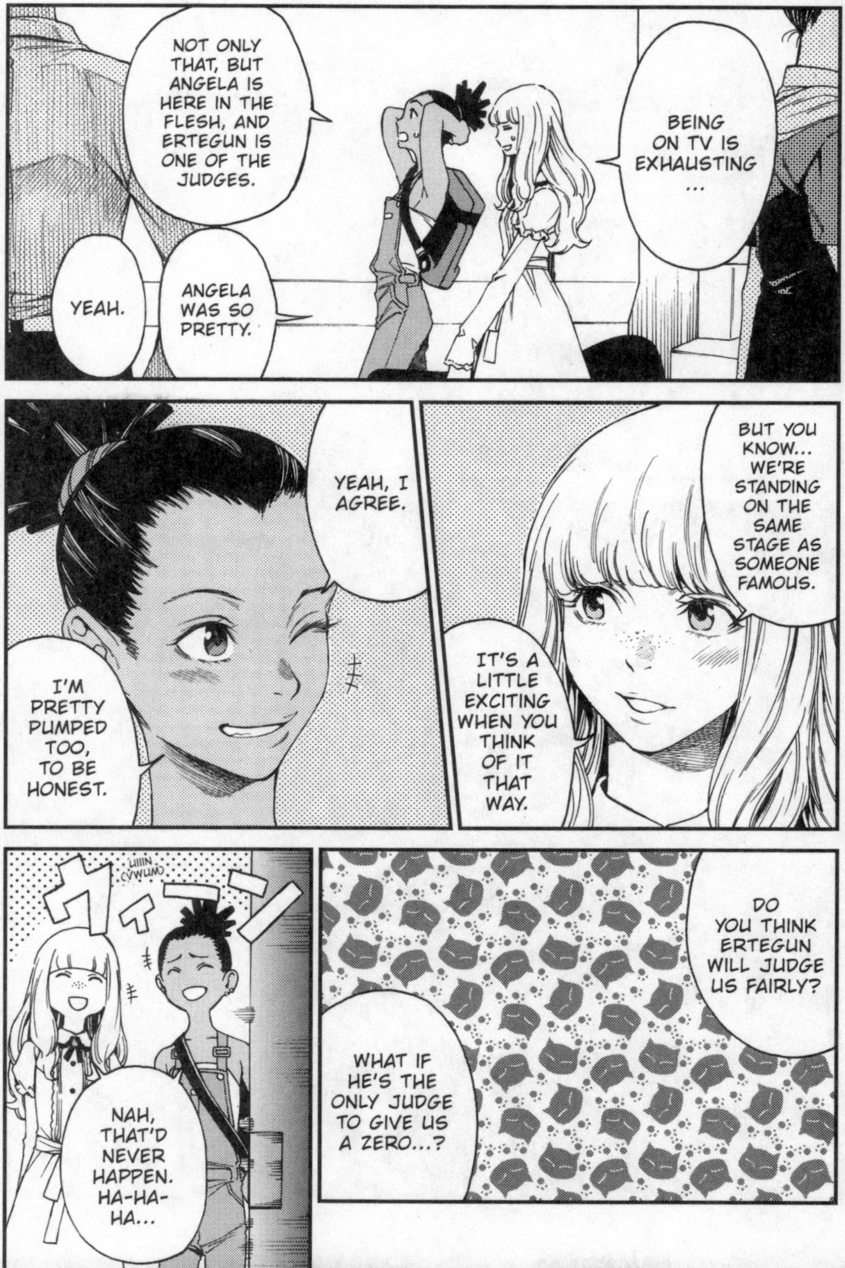
BEING ON TV IS EXHAUSTING ...
NOT ONLY THAT, BUT ANGELA IS HERE IN THE FLESH, AND ERTEGUN IS ONE OF THE JUDGES.
ANGELA WAS SO PRETTY.
YEAH.
BUT YOU KNOW... WE'RE STANDING ON THE SAME STAGE AS SOMEONE FAMOUS.
IT'S A LITTLE EXCITING WHEN YOU THINK OF IT THAT WAY.
YEAH, I AGREE.
I'M PRETTY PUMPED TOO, TO BE HONEST.
DO YOU THINK ERTEGUN WILL JUDGE US FAIRLY?
WHAT IF HE'S THE ONLY JUDGE TO GIVE US A ZERO...?
UIIIN (VWUM)
NAH, THAT'D NEVER HAPPEN. HA-HA-HA...

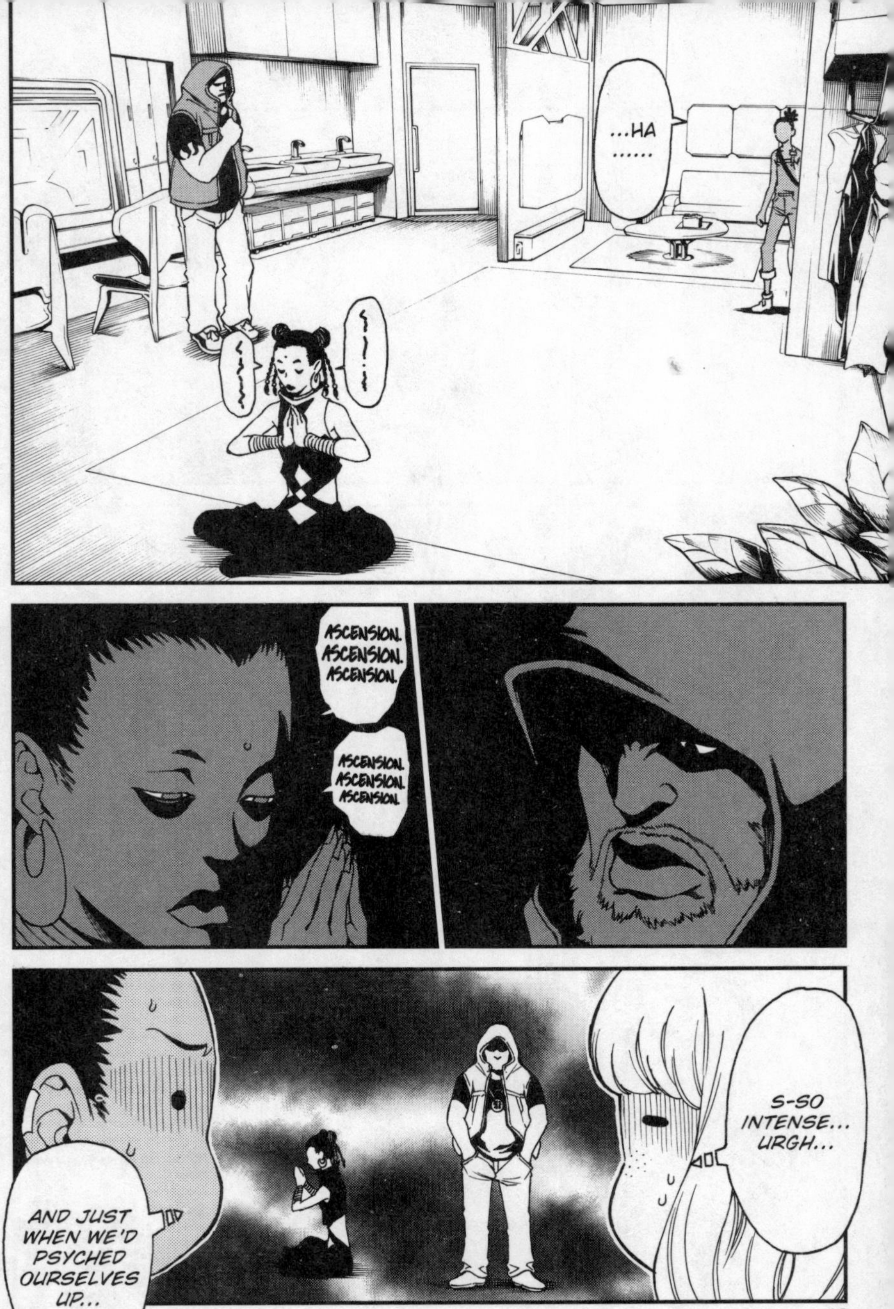

...HA ......
ASCENSION. ASCENSION. ASCENSION.
ASCENSION. ASCENSION. ASCENSION.
S-SO INTENSE... URGH...
AND JUST WHEN WE'D PSYCHED OURSELVES UP...

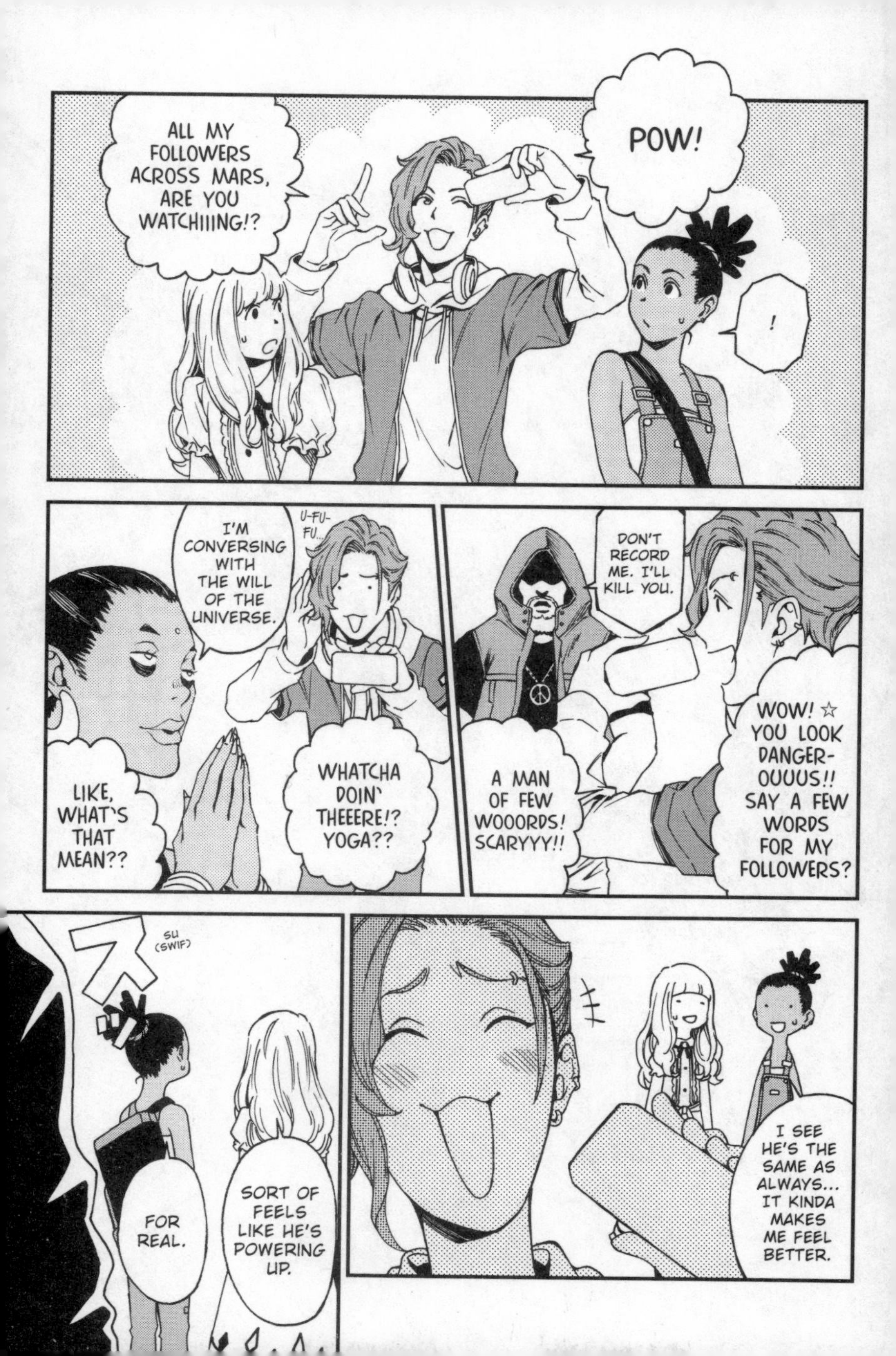
POW!
ALL MY FOLLOWERS ACROSS MARS, ARE YOU WATCHIIING!?
!
WOW! ☆ YOU LOOK DANGER-OUUUS!! SAY A FEW WORDS FOR MY FOLLOWERS?
DON'T RECORD ME. I'LL KILL YOU.
A MAN OF FEW WOOORDS! SCARYYY!!
U-FU-FU...
I'M CONVERSING WITH THE WILL OF THE UNIVERSE.
WHATCHA DOIN' THEEERE!? YOGA??
LIKE, WHAT'S THAT MEAN??
I SEE HE'S THE SAME AS ALWAYS... IT KINDA MAKES ME FEEL BETTER.
SU (SWIF)
SORT OF FEELS LIKE HE'S POWERING UP.
FOR REAL.

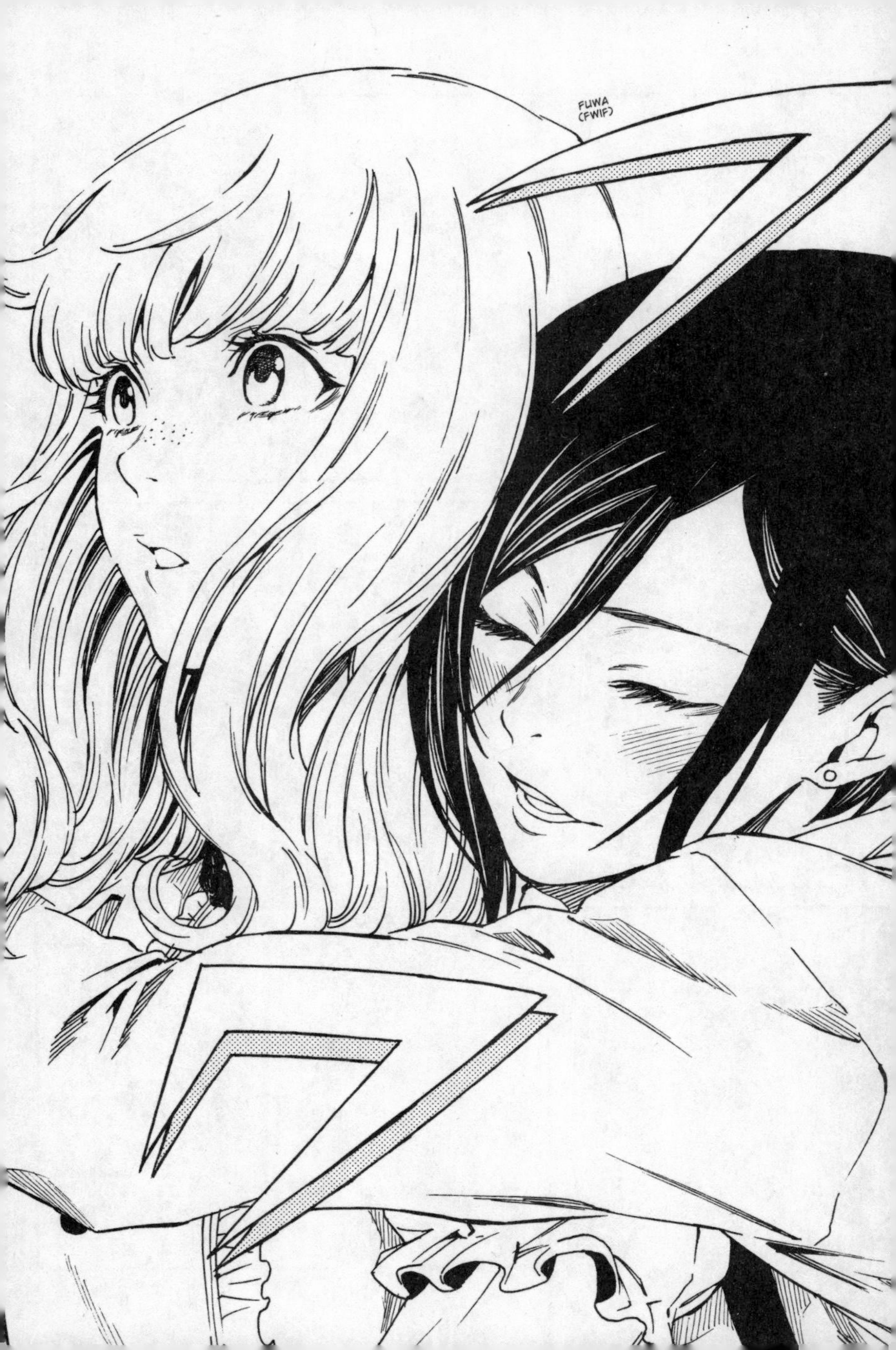
FUWA
(FWIF)

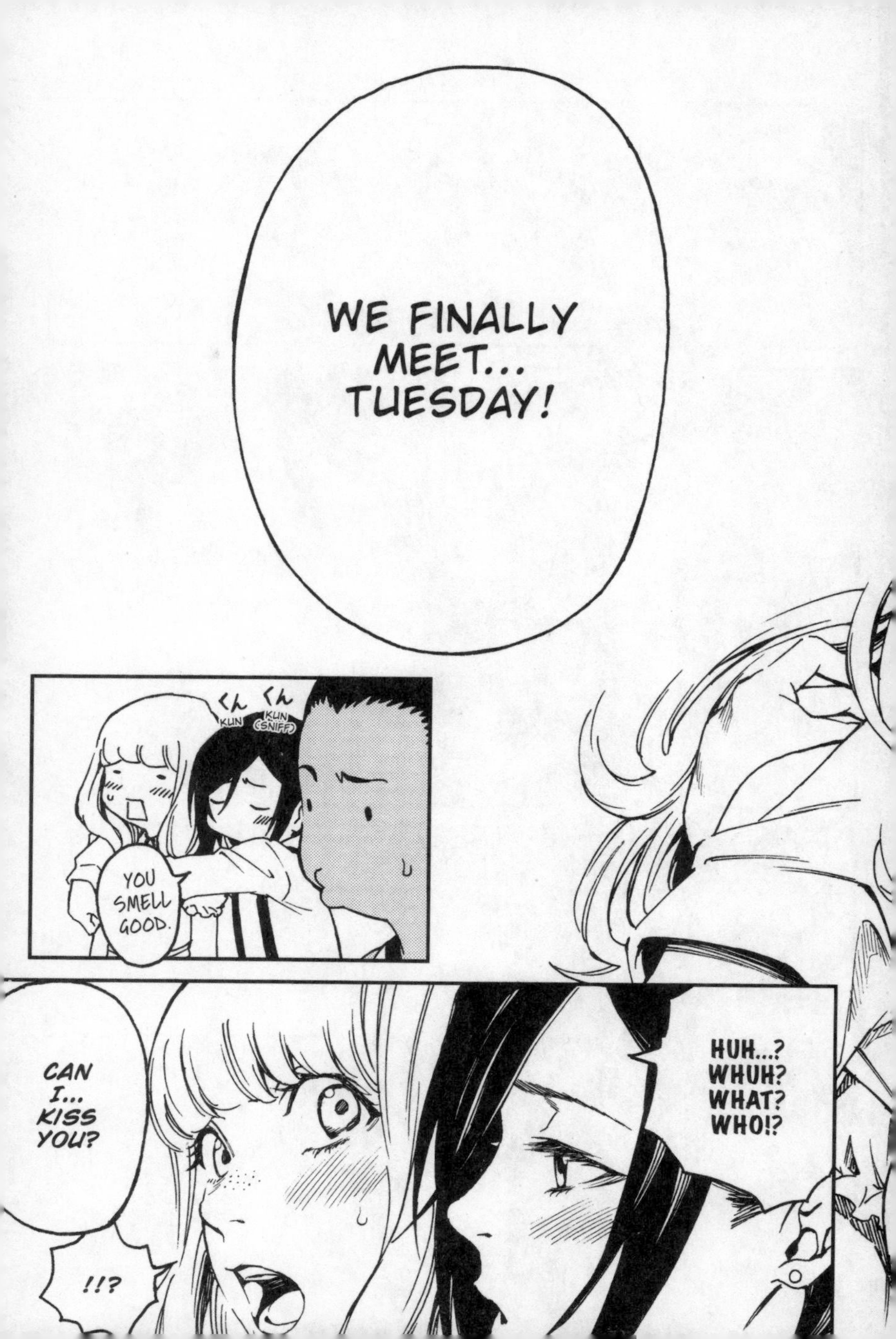
WE FINALLY MEET... TUESDAY!
くん くん
KUN KUN (SNIFF)
YOU SMELL GOOD.
HUH...? WHUH? WHAT? WHO!?
CAN I... KISS YOU?
!!?

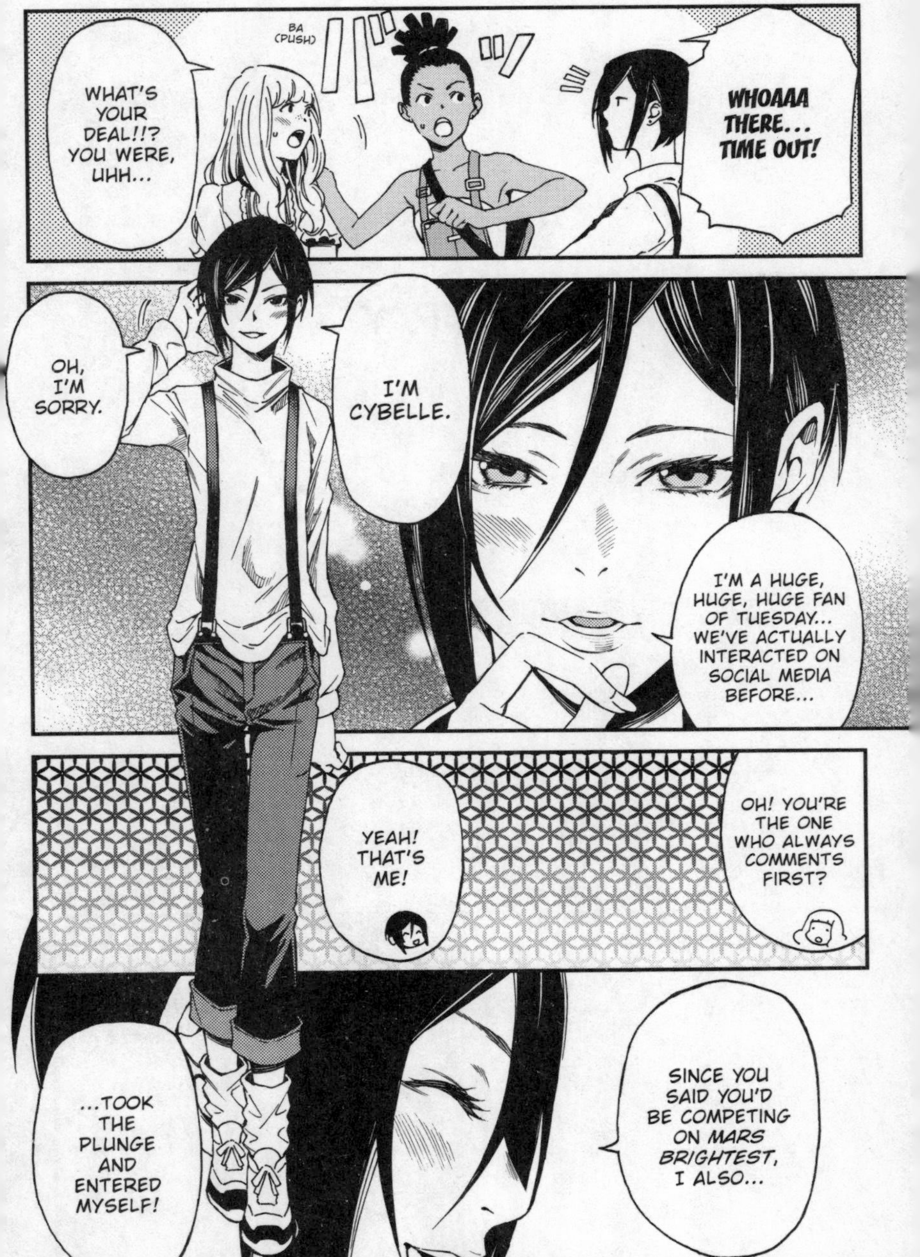
WHOAAA THERE... TIME OUT!
BA (PUSH)
WHAT'S YOUR DEAL!!? YOU WERE, UHH...
I'M A HUGE, HUGE, HUGE FAN OF TUESDAY... WE'VE ACTUALLY INTERACTED ON SOCIAL MEDIA BEFORE...
I'M CYBELLE.
OH, I'M SORRY.
OH! YOU'RE THE ONE WHO ALWAYS COMMENTS FIRST?
YEAH! THAT'S ME!
SINCE YOU SAID YOU'D BE COMPETING ON *MARS BRIGHTEST*, I ALSO...
...TOOK THE PLUNGE AND ENTERED MYSELF!

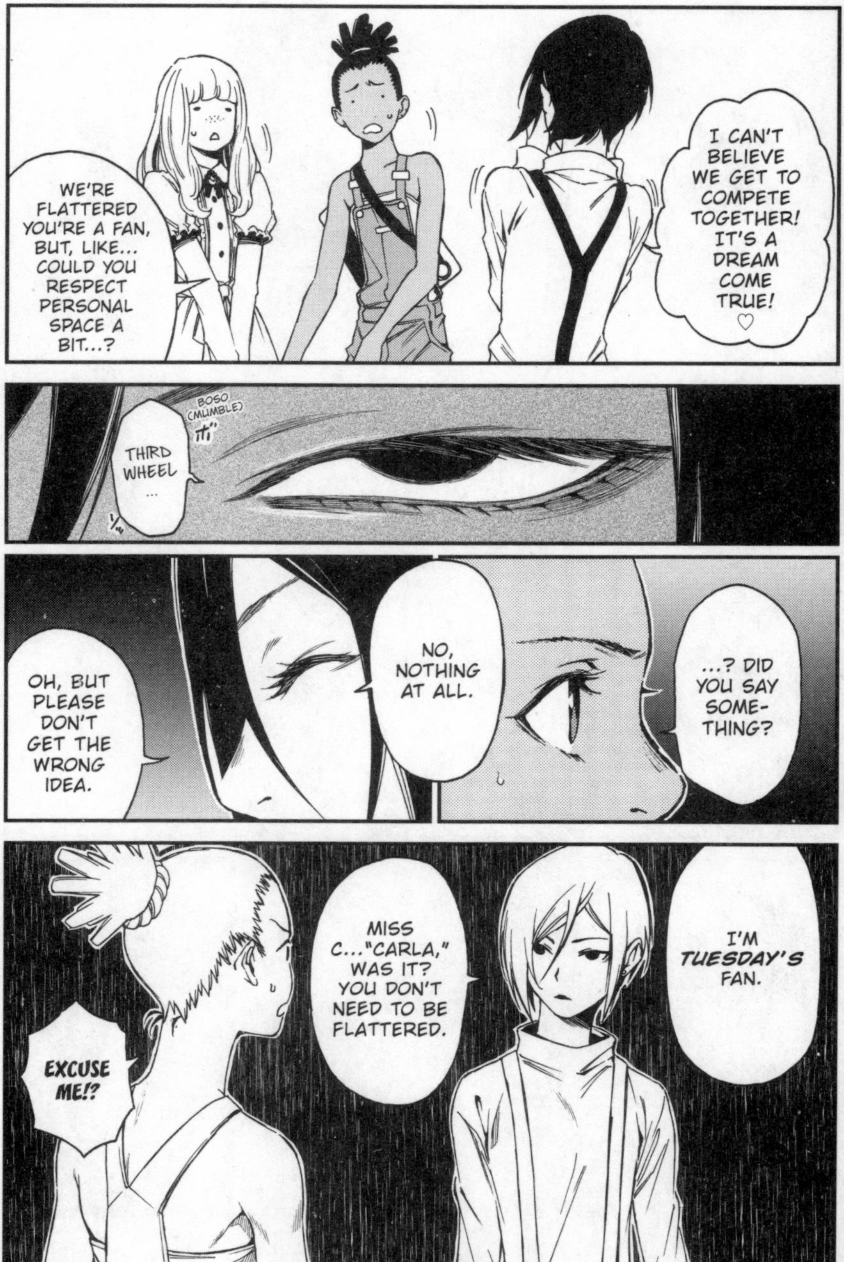
I CAN'T BELIEVE WE GET TO COMPETE TOGETHER! IT'S A DREAM COME TRUE! ♡
WE'RE FLATTERED YOU'RE A FAN, BUT, LIKE... COULD YOU RESPECT PERSONAL SPACE A BIT...?
BOSO (MUMBLE)
THIRD WHEEL ...
...? DID YOU SAY SOME-THING?
NO, NOTHING AT ALL.
OH, BUT PLEASE DON'T GET THE WRONG IDEA.
I'M *TUESDAY'S* FAN.
MISS C..."CARLA," WAS IT? YOU DON'T NEED TO BE FLATTERED.
EXCUSE ME!?

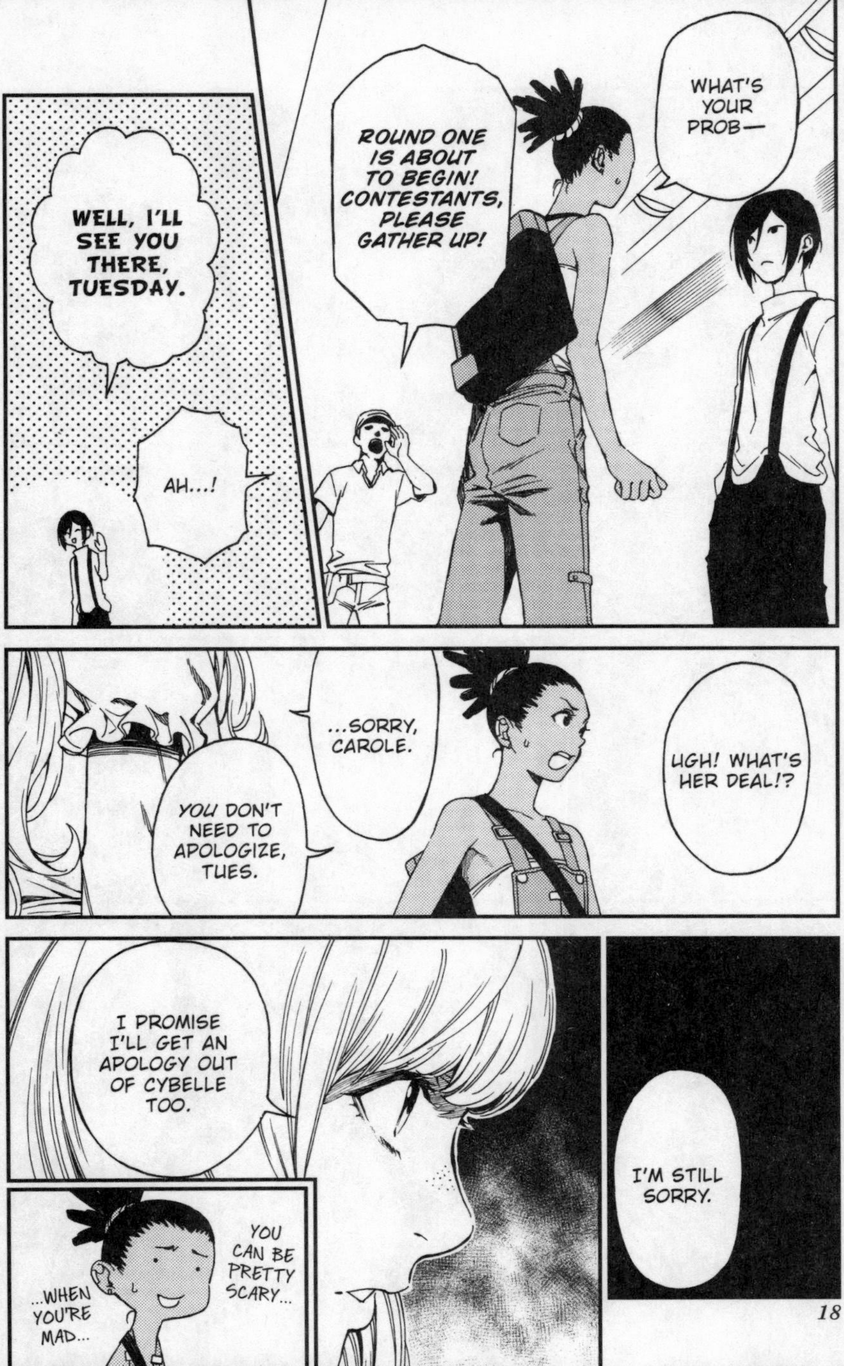
WHAT'S YOUR PROB—
ROUND ONE IS ABOUT TO BEGIN! CONTESTANTS, PLEASE GATHER UP!
WELL, I'LL SEE YOU THERE, TUESDAY.
AH...!
UGH! WHAT'S HER DEAL!?
...SORRY, CAROLE.
YOU DON'T NEED TO APOLOGIZE, TUES.
I'M STILL SORRY.
I PROMISE I'LL GET AN APOLOGY OUT OF CYBELLE TOO.
YOU CAN BE PRETTY SCARY...
...WHEN YOU'RE MAD...

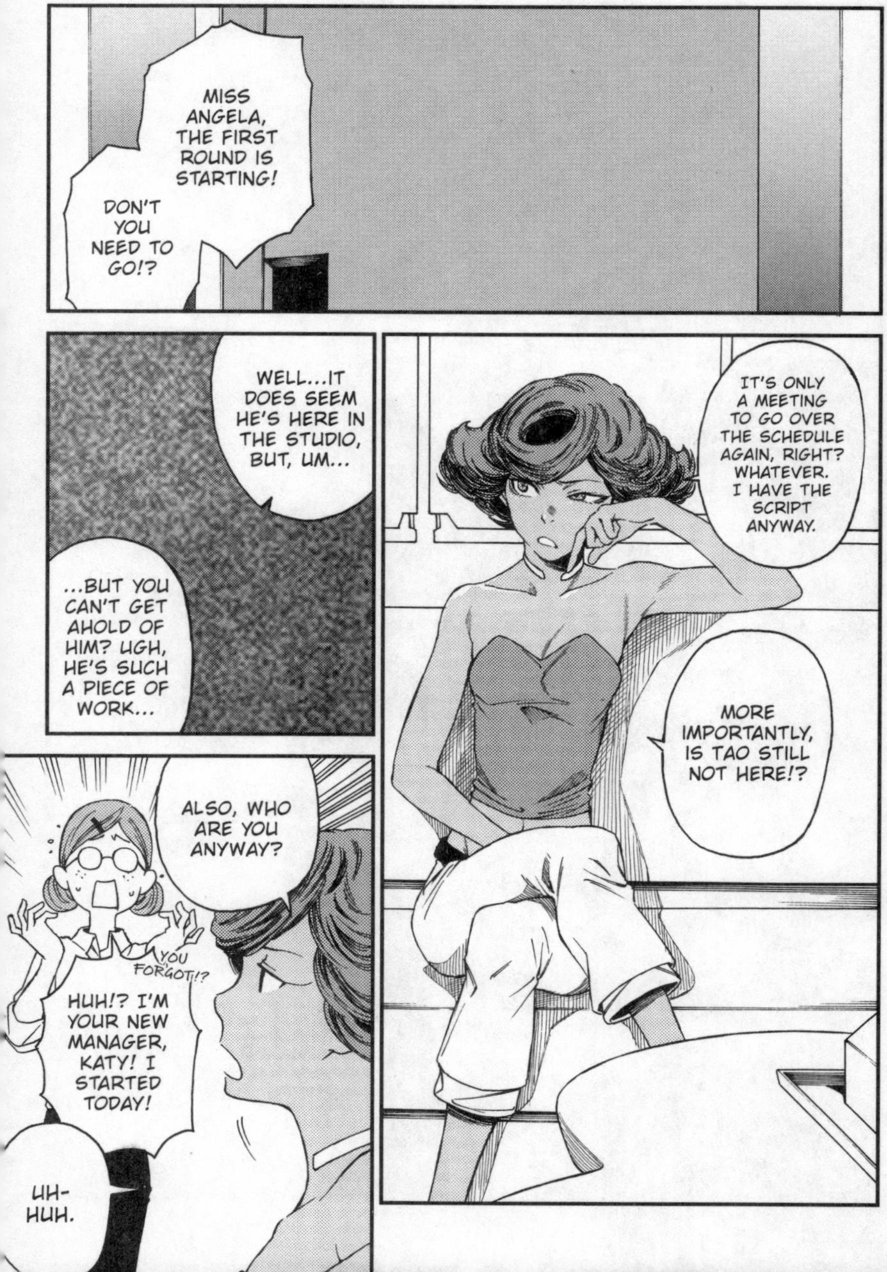
MISS ANGELA, THE FIRST ROUND IS STARTING!
DON'T YOU NEED TO GO!?
IT'S ONLY A MEETING TO GO OVER THE SCHEDULE AGAIN, RIGHT? WHATEVER. I HAVE THE SCRIPT ANYWAY.
MORE IMPORTANTLY, IS TAO STILL NOT HERE!?
WELL...IT DOES SEEM HE'S HERE IN THE STUDIO, BUT, UM...
...BUT YOU CAN'T GET AHOLD OF HIM? UGH, HE'S SUCH A PIECE OF WORK...
ALSO, WHO ARE YOU ANYWAY?
YOU FORGOT!?
HUH!? I'M YOUR NEW MANAGER, KATY! I STARTED TODAY!
UH-HUH.

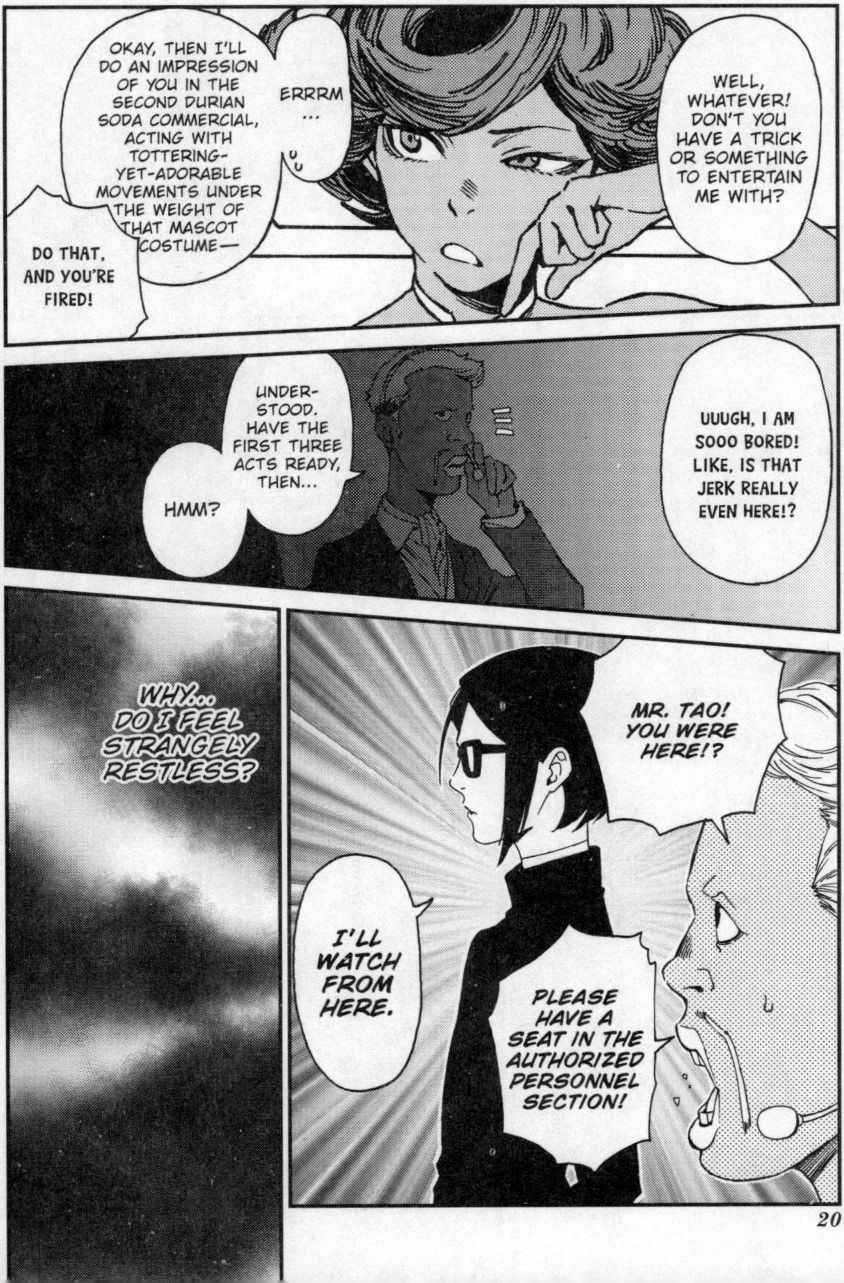
WELL, WHATEVER! DON'T YOU HAVE A TRICK OR SOMETHING TO ENTERTAIN ME WITH?
ERRRM ...
OKAY, THEN I'LL DO AN IMPRESSION OF YOU IN THE SECOND DURIAN SODA COMMERCIAL, ACTING WITH TOTTERING-YET-ADORABLE MOVEMENTS UNDER THE WEIGHT OF THAT MASCOT COSTUME—
DO THAT, AND YOU'RE FIRED!
UUUGH, I AM SOOO BORED! LIKE, IS THAT JERK REALLY EVEN HERE!?
UNDER-STOOD. HAVE THE FIRST THREE ACTS READY, THEN...
HMM?
MR. TAO! YOU WERE HERE!?
PLEASE HAVE A SEAT IN THE AUTHORIZED PERSONNEL SECTION!
I'LL WATCH FROM HERE.
WHY... DO I FEEL STRANGELY RESTLESS?

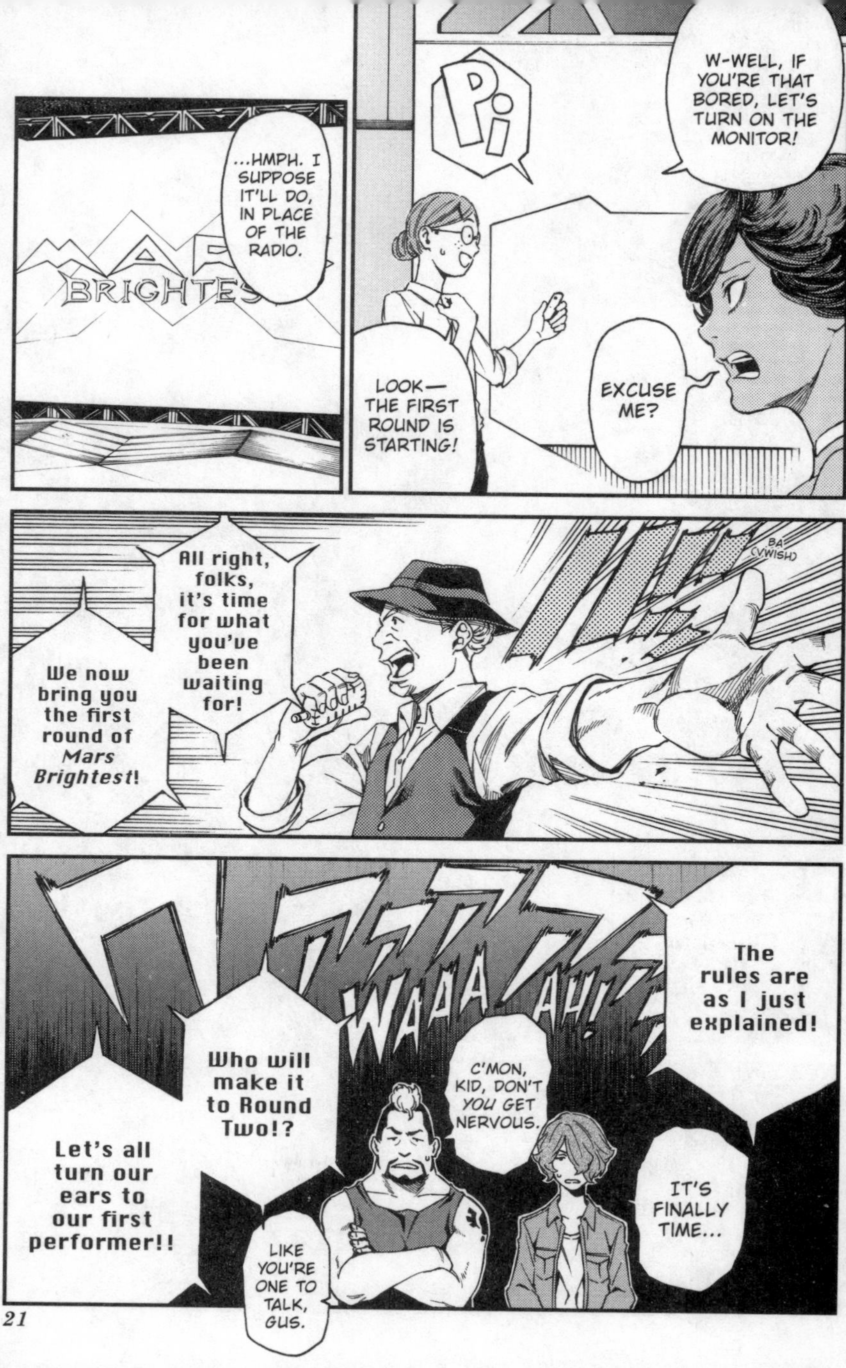
W-WELL, IF YOU'RE THAT BORED, LET'S TURN ON THE MONITOR!
Pi
EXCUSE ME?
LOOK— THE FIRST ROUND IS STARTING!
...HMPH. I SUPPOSE IT'LL DO, IN PLACE OF THE RADIO.
BRIGHTES
BA (VWISH)
All right, folks, it's time for what you've been waiting for!
We now bring you the first round of *Mars Brightest*!
The rules are as I just explained!
WAAA AH!
C'MON, KID, DON'T *YOU* GET NERVOUS.
Who will make it to Round Two!?
IT'S FINALLY TIME...
LIKE YOU'RE ONE TO TALK, GUS.
Let's all turn our ears to our first performer!!

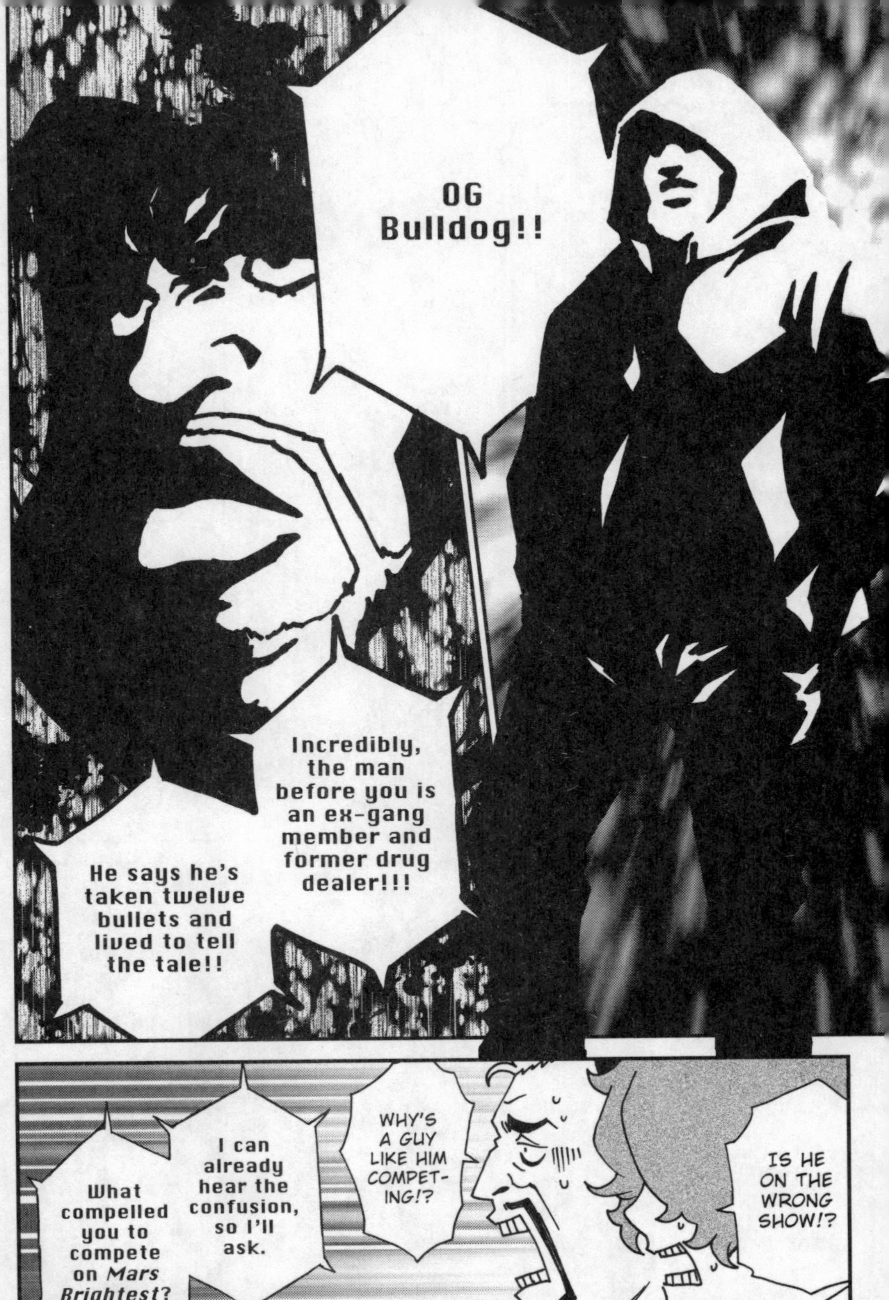
OG Bulldog!!
Incredibly, the man before you is an ex-gang member and former drug dealer!!!
He says he's taken twelve bullets and lived to tell the tale!!
IS HE ON THE WRONG SHOW!?
WHY'S A GUY LIKE HIM COMPET-ING!?
I can already hear the confusion, so I'll ask.
What compelled you to compete on *Mars Brightest*?

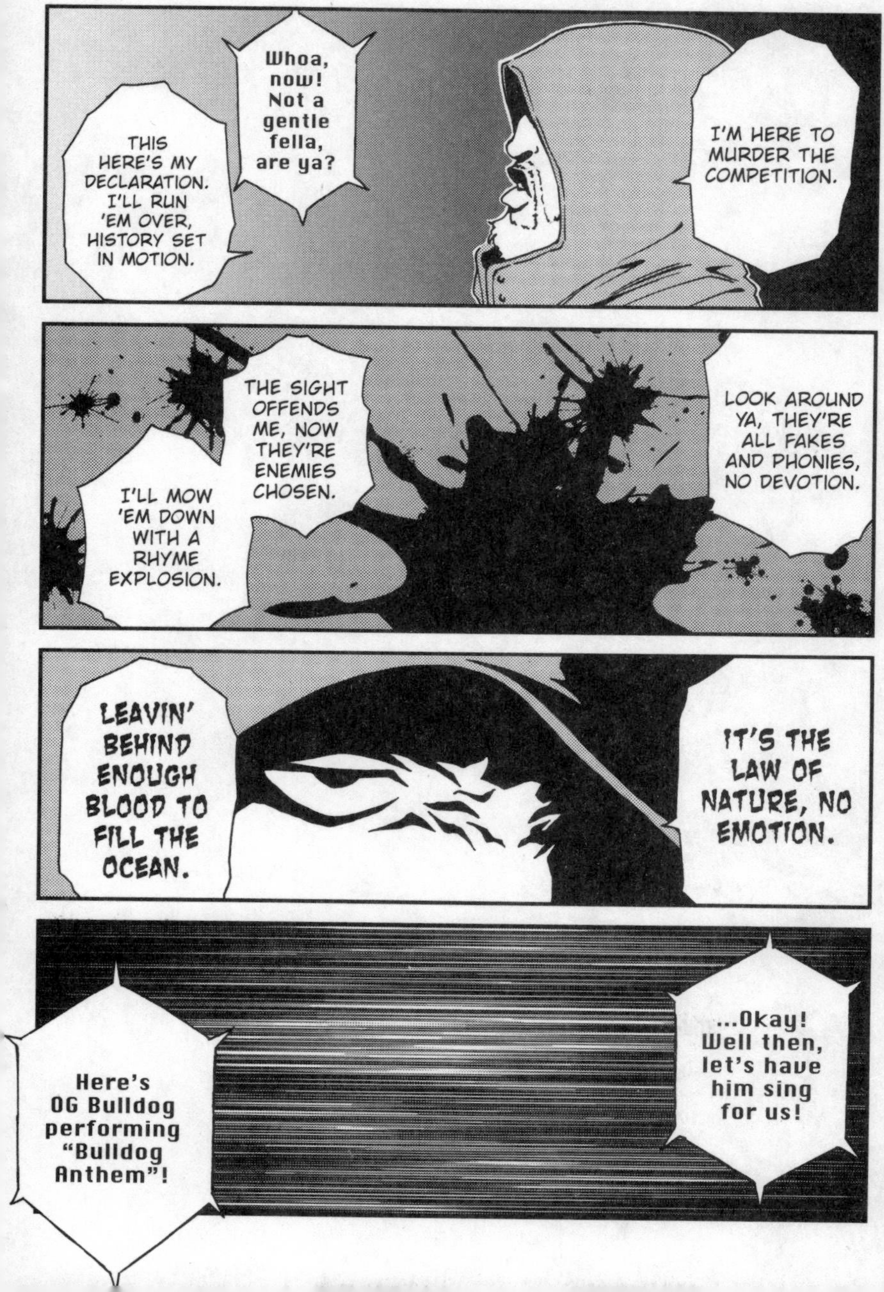
I'M HERE TO MURDER THE COMPETITION.
Whoa, now! Not a gentle fella, are ya?
THIS HERE'S MY DECLARATION. I'LL RUN 'EM OVER, HISTORY SET IN MOTION.
LOOK AROUND YA, THEY'RE ALL FAKES AND PHONIES, NO DEVOTION.
THE SIGHT OFFENDS ME, NOW THEY'RE ENEMIES CHOSEN.
I'LL MOW 'EM DOWN WITH A RHYME EXPLOSION.
IT'S THE LAW OF NATURE, NO EMOTION.
LEAVIN' BEHIND ENOUGH BLOOD TO FILL THE OCEAN.
...Okay! Well then, let's have him sing for us!
Here's OG Bulldog performing "Bulldog Anthem"!

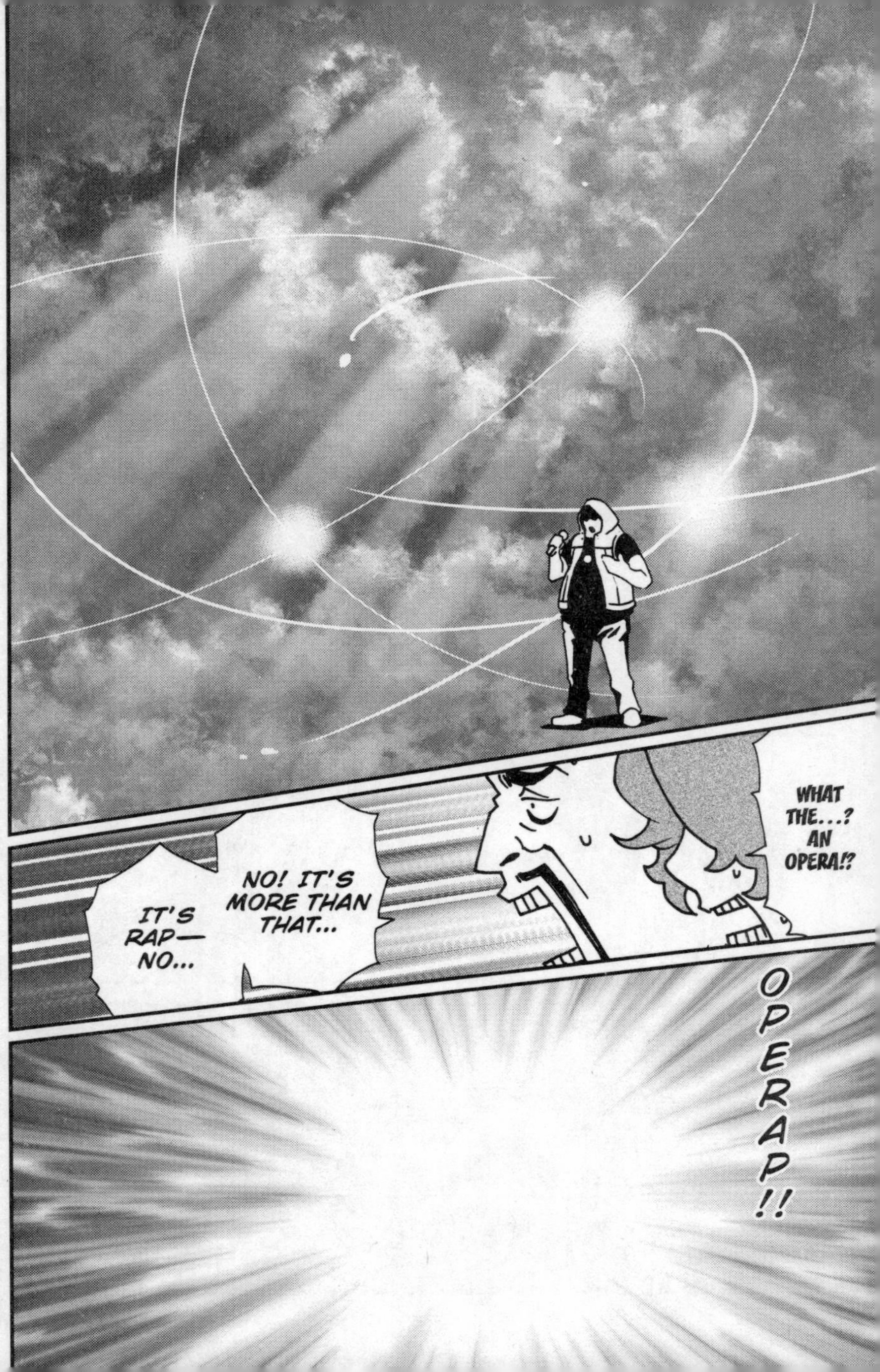
WHAT THE...? AN OPERA!?
NO! IT'S MORE THAN THAT...
IT'S RAP— NO...
OPERAP!!

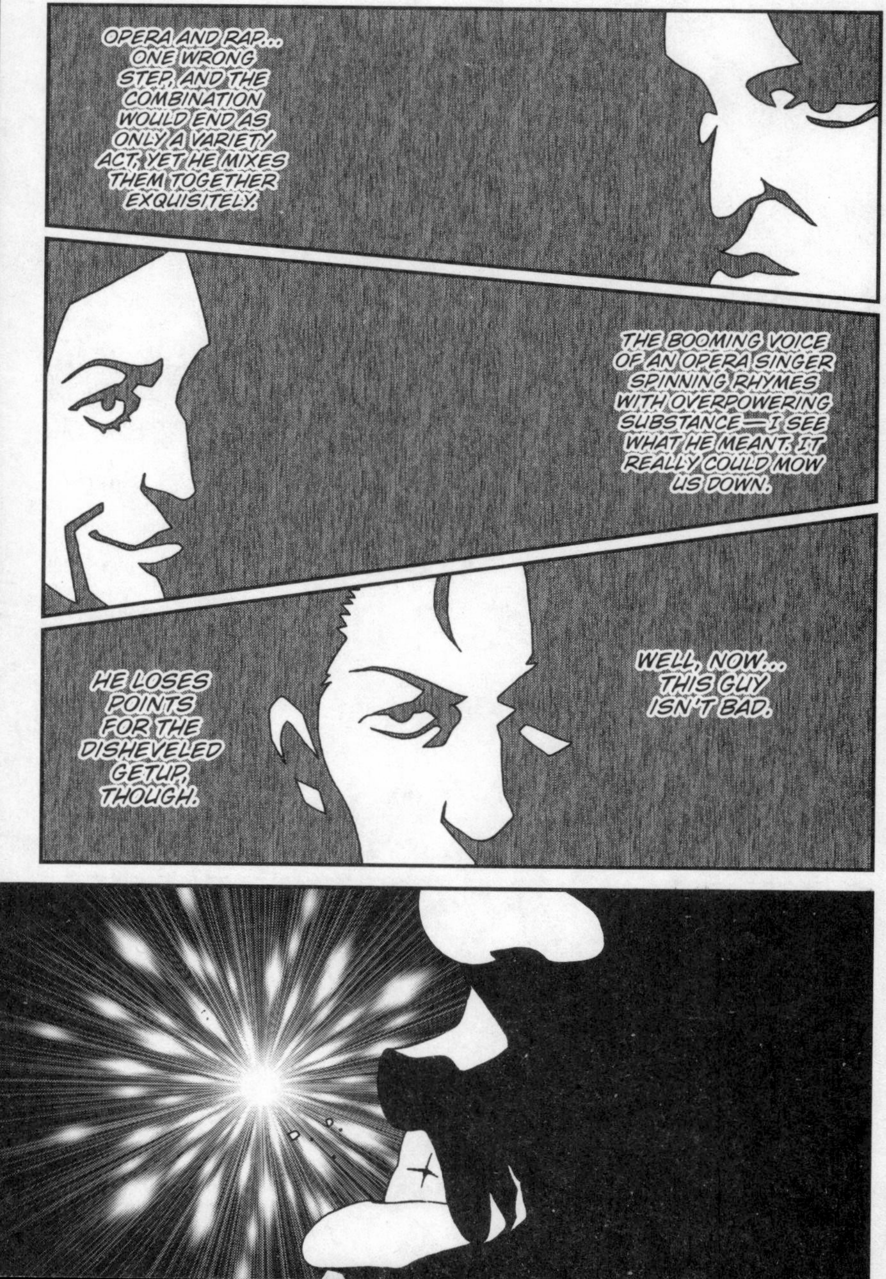
OPERA AND RAP... ONE WRONG STEP, AND THE COMBINATION WOULD END AS ONLY A VARIETY ACT, YET HE MIXES THEM TOGETHER EXQUISITELY.
THE BOOMING VOICE OF AN OPERA SINGER SPINNING RHYMES WITH OVERPOWERING SUBSTANCE—I SEE WHAT HE MEANT. IT REALLY COULD MOW US DOWN.
WELL, NOW... THIS GUY ISN'T BAD.
HE LOSES POINTS FOR THE DISHEVELED GETUP, THOUGH.

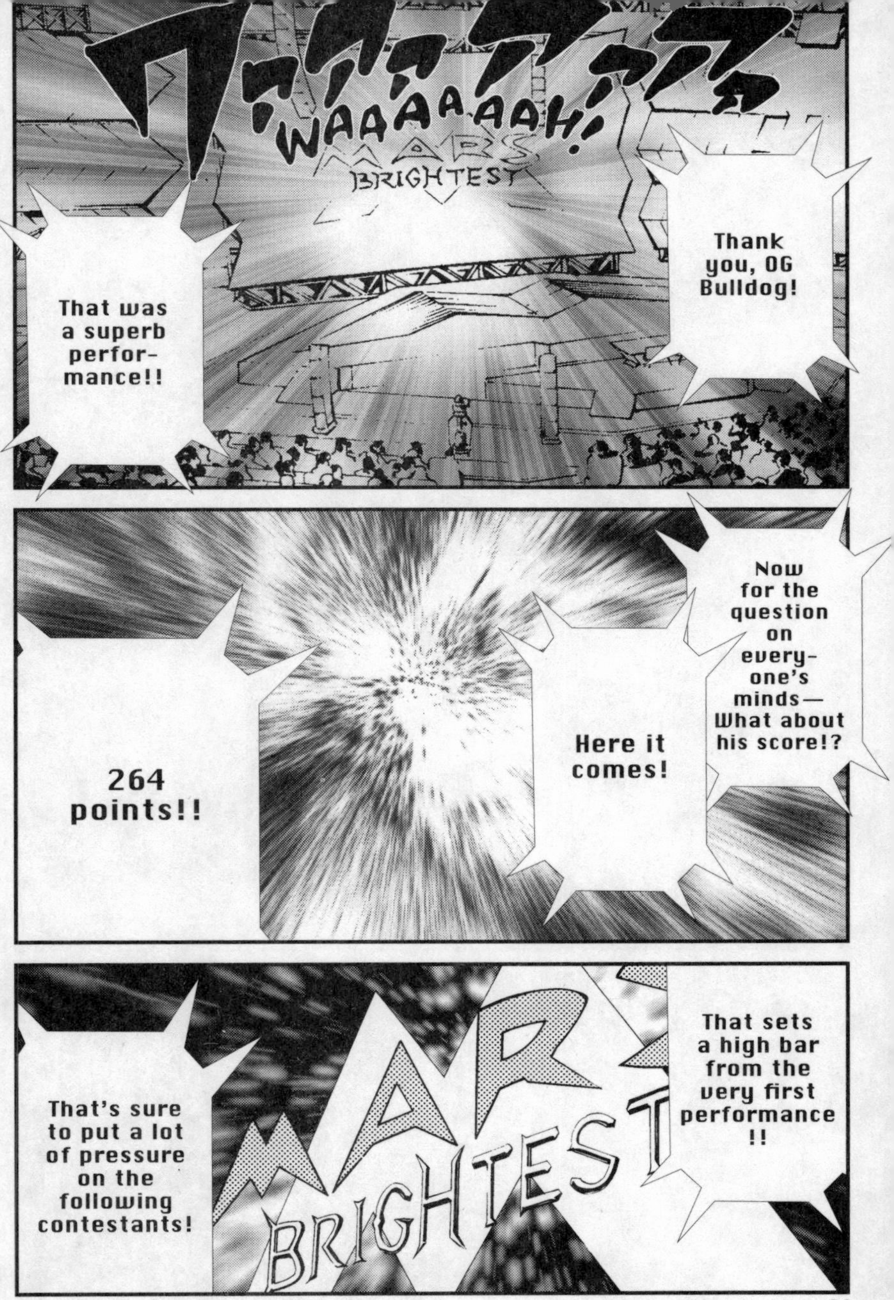
WAAAAAAH!
MARS BRIGHTEST
Thank you, OG Bulldog!
That was a superb performance!!
Now for the question on everyone's minds—What about his score!?
Here it comes!
264 points!!
That sets a high bar from the very first performance!!
MARS BRIGHTEST
That's sure to put a lot of pressure on the following contestants!

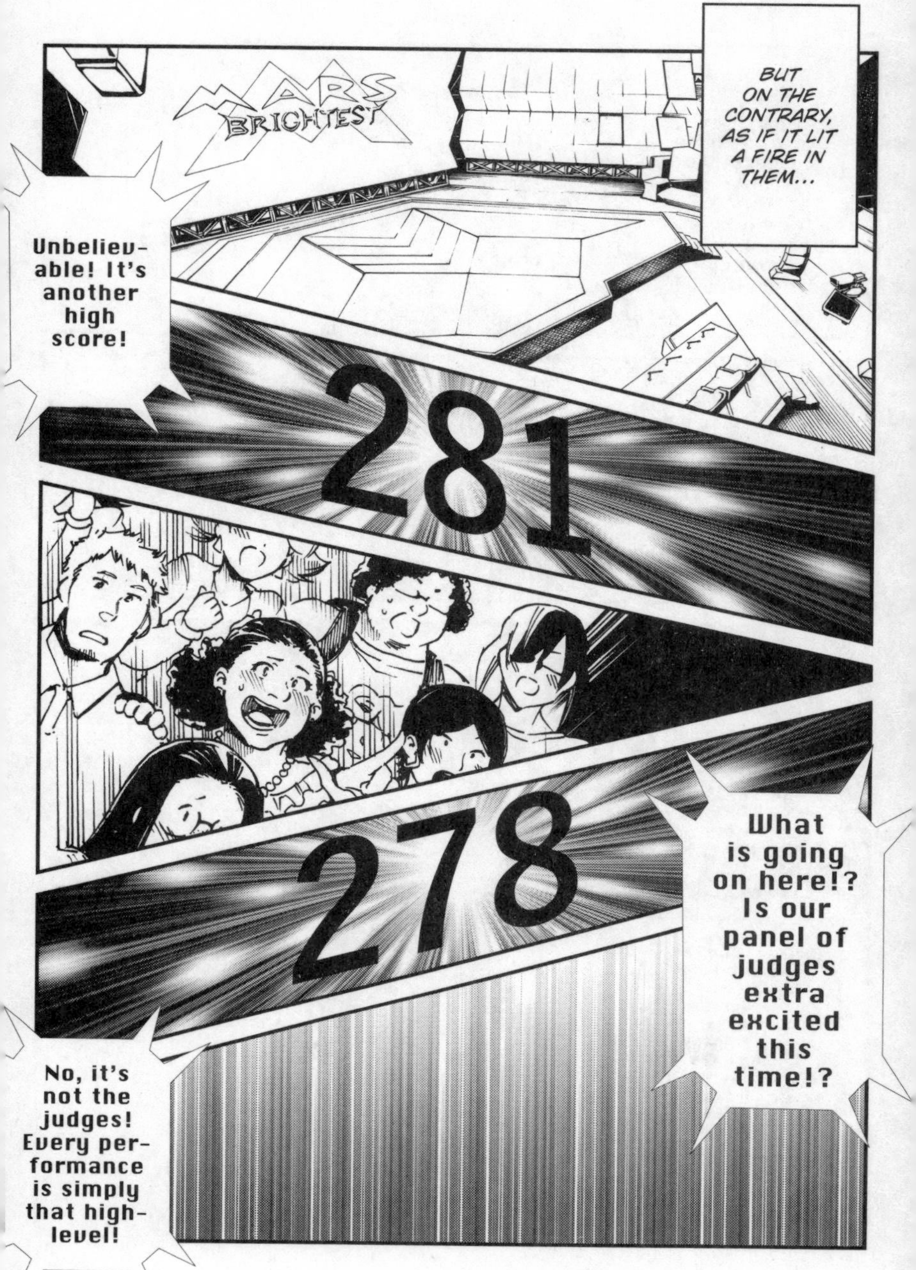
BUT ON THE CONTRARY, AS IF IT LIT A FIRE IN THEM...
MARS BRIGHTEST
Unbelievable! It's another high score!
281
278
What is going on here!? Is our panel of judges extra excited this time!?
No, it's not the judges! Every performance is simply that high-level!

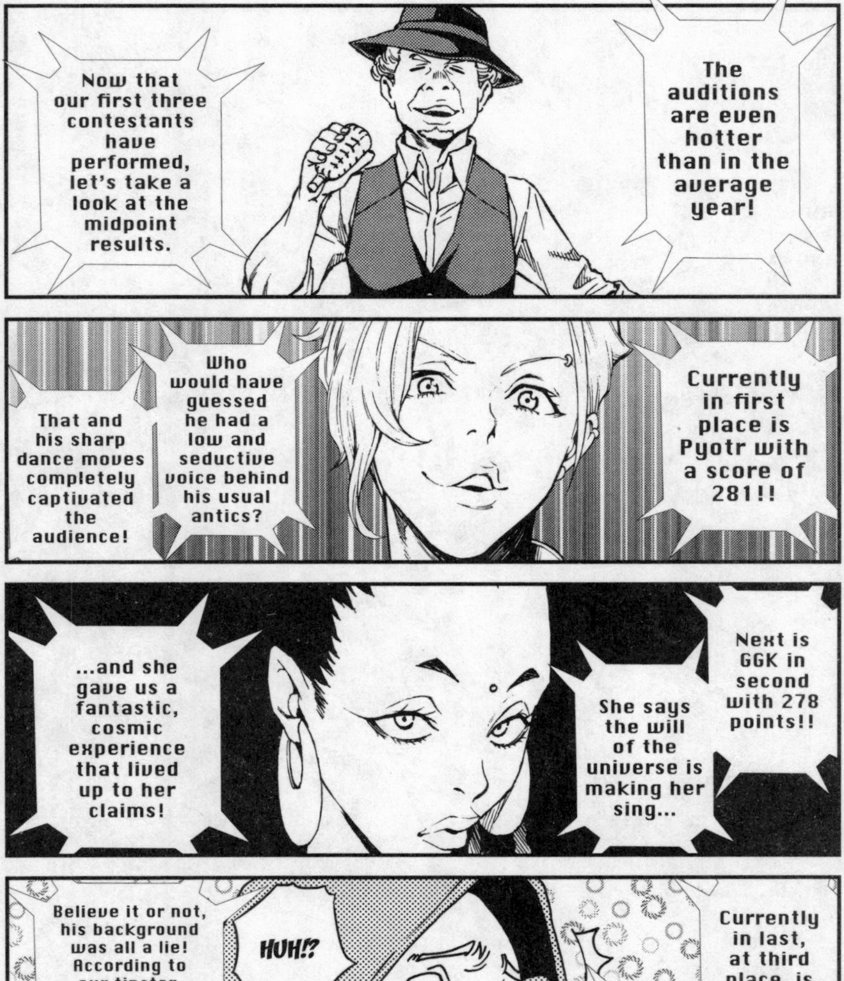
The auditions are even hotter than in the average year!
Now that our first three contestants have performed, let's take a look at the midpoint results.
Currently in first place is Pyotr with a score of 281!!
Who would have guessed he had a low and seductive voice behind his usual antics?
That and his sharp dance moves completely captivated the audience!
Next is GGK in second with 278 points!!
She says the will of the universe is making her sing...
...and she gave us a fantastic, cosmic experience that lived up to her claims!
Currently in last, at third place, is OG Bull-dog with a score of 264!
However! We've received a shocking anonymous tip!
HUH!?
Believe it or not, his background was all a lie! According to our tipster, he's a diligent, kindhearted drugstore worker from the sticks!
You shouldn't worry your mom, y'know!

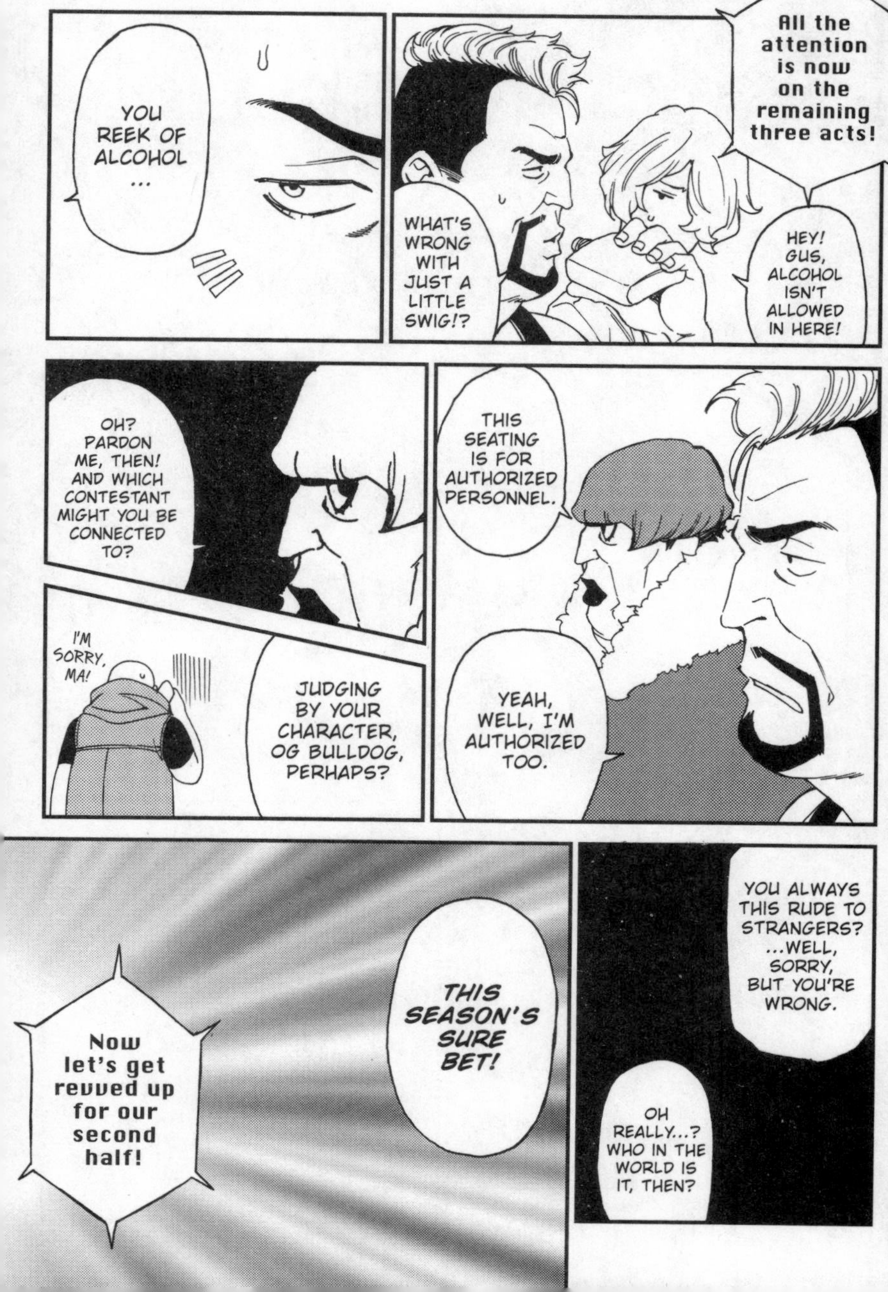
All the attention is now on the remaining three acts!
HEY! GUS, ALCOHOL ISN'T ALLOWED IN HERE!
WHAT'S WRONG WITH JUST A LITTLE SWIG!?
YOU REEK OF ALCOHOL ...
THIS SEATING IS FOR AUTHORIZED PERSONNEL.
YEAH, WELL, I'M AUTHORIZED TOO.
OH? PARDON ME, THEN! AND WHICH CONTESTANT MIGHT YOU BE CONNECTED TO?
JUDGING BY YOUR CHARACTER, OG BULLDOG, PERHAPS?
I'M SORRY, MA!
YOU ALWAYS THIS RUDE TO STRANGERS? ...WELL, SORRY, BUT YOU'RE WRONG.
OH REALLY...? WHO IN THE WORLD IS IT, THEN?
THIS SEASON'S SURE BET!
Now let's get revved up for our second half!

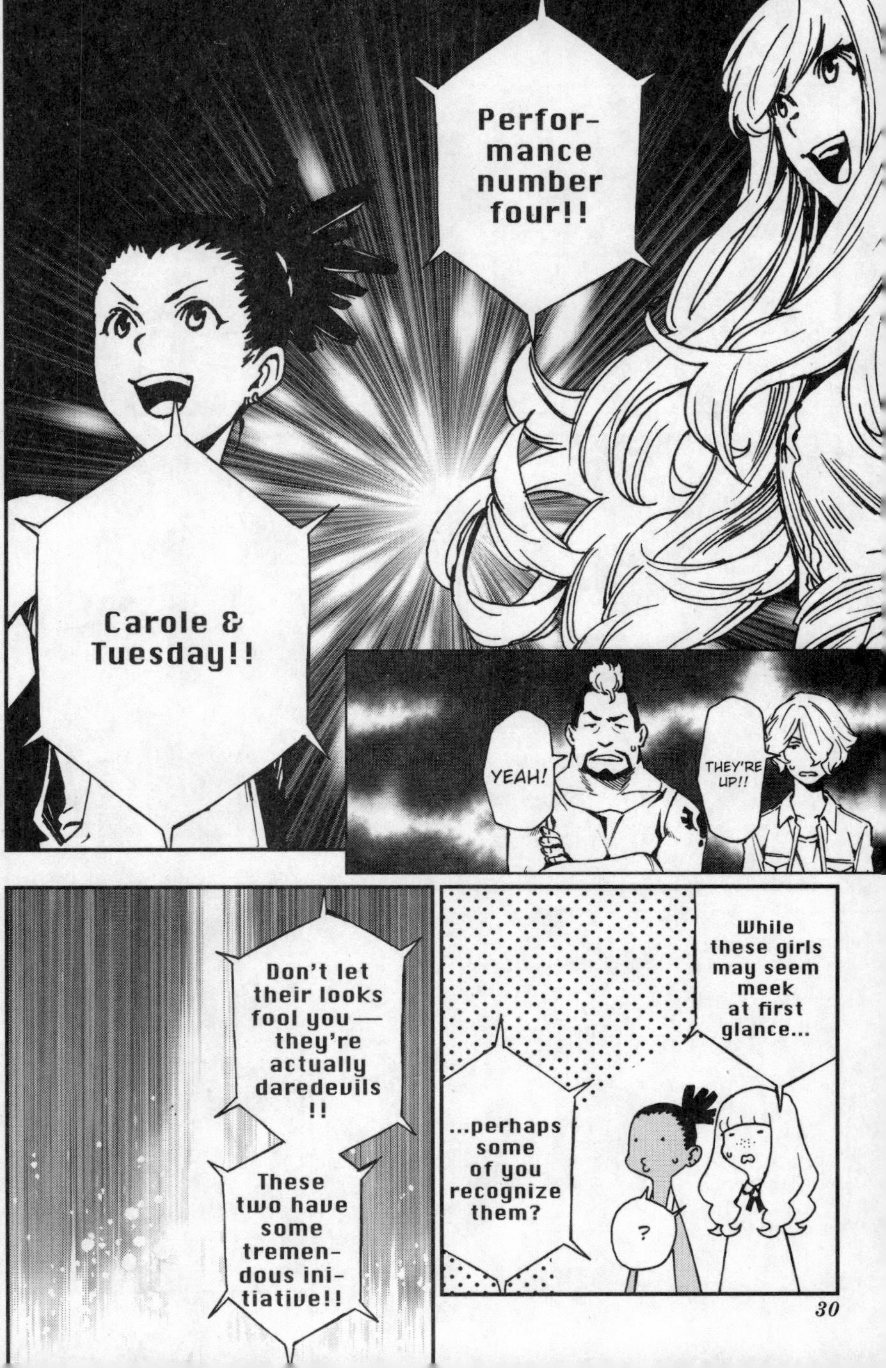
Perfor-
mance
number
four!!
Carole &
Tuesday!!
THEY'RE UP!!
YEAH!
While these girls may seem meek at first glance...
...perhaps some of you recognize them?
?
Don't let their looks fool you— they're actually daredevils!!
These two have some tremendous initiative!!

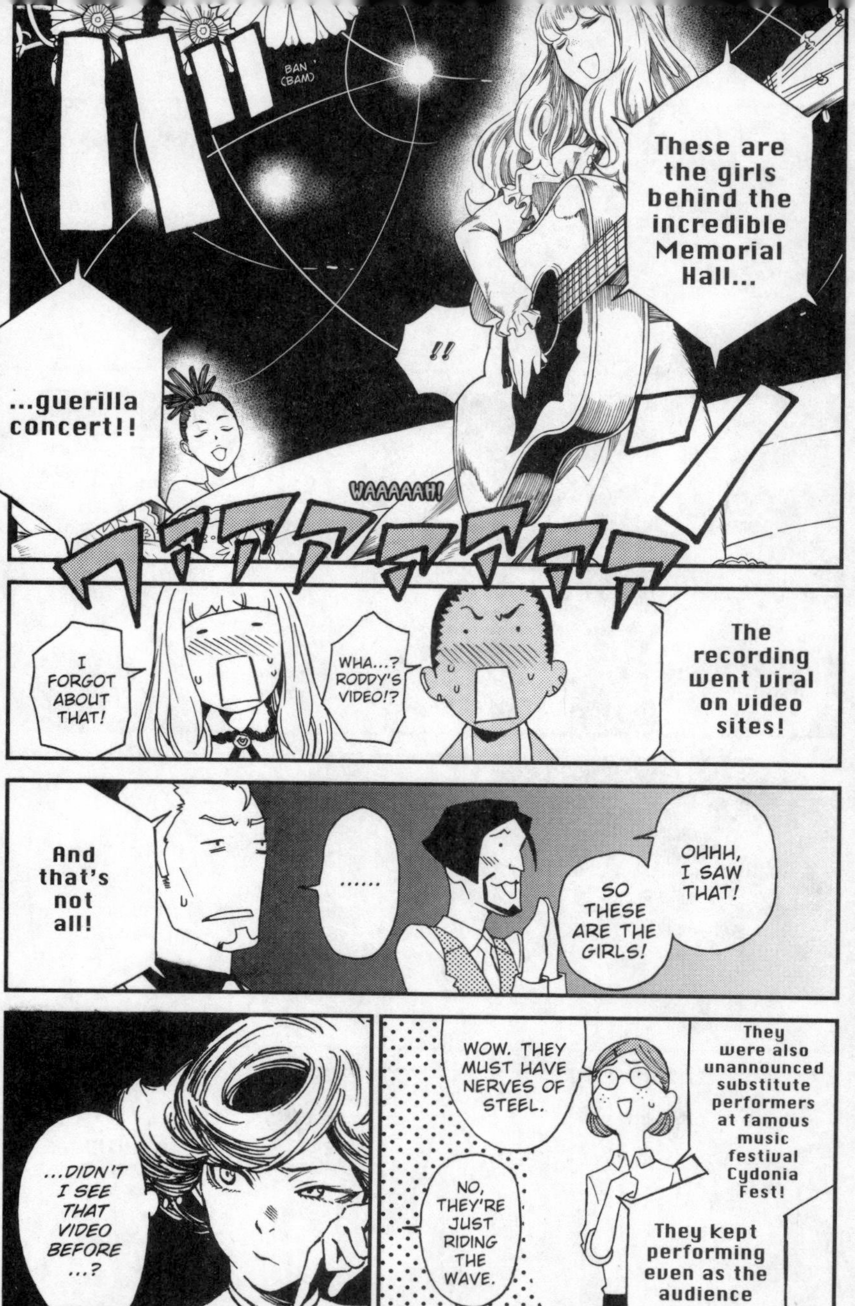
These are the girls behind the incredible Memorial Hall...
BAN (BAM)
!!
...guerilla concert!!
WAAAAAH!
The recording went viral on video sites!
WHA...? RODDY'S VIDEO!?
I FORGOT ABOUT THAT!
OHHH, I SAW THAT!
SO THESE ARE THE GIRLS!
......
And that's not all!
They were also unannounced substitute performers at famous music festival Cydonia Fest!
WOW. THEY MUST HAVE NERVES OF STEEL.
NO, THEY'RE JUST RIDING THE WAVE.
They kept performing even as the audience booed!
...DIDN'T I SEE THAT VIDEO BEFORE ...?

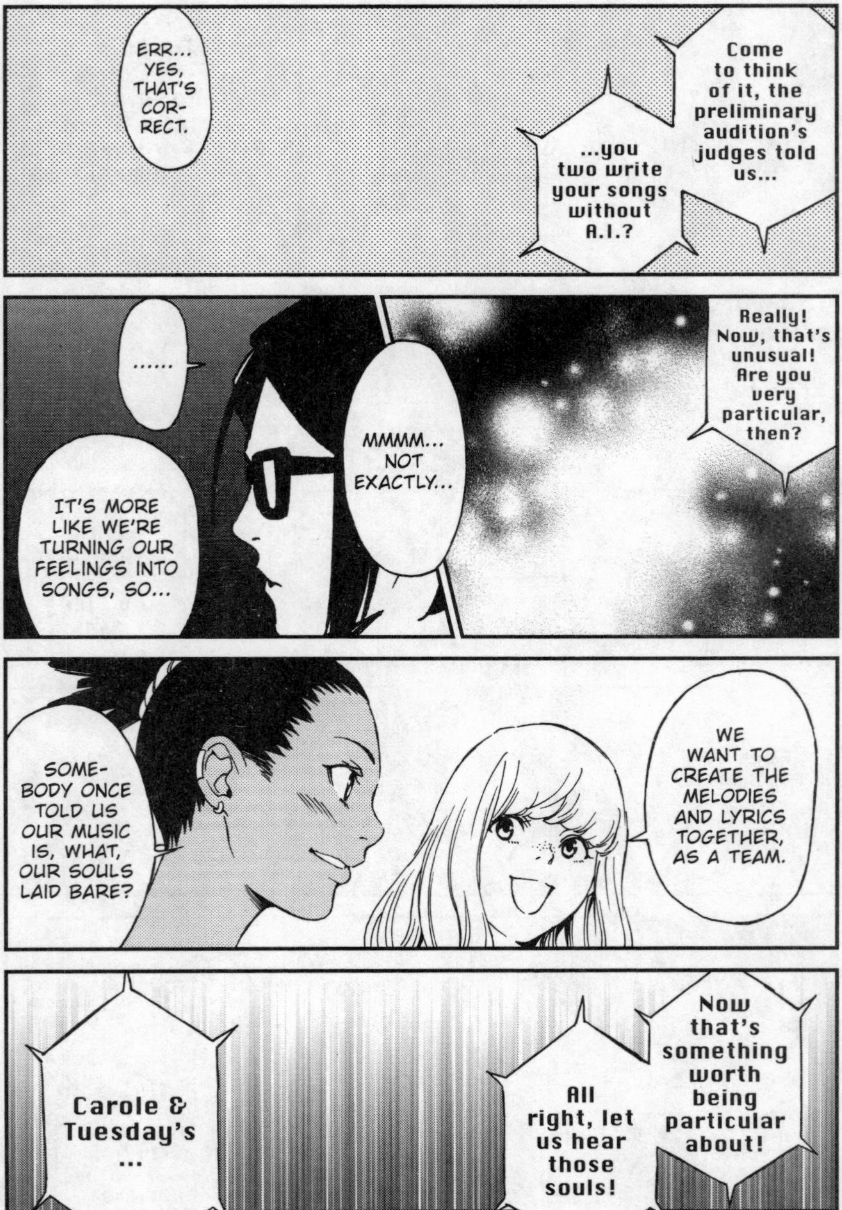
Come to think of it, the preliminary audition's judges told us...
...you two write your songs without A.I.?
ERR... YES, THAT'S COR-RECT.
Really! Now, that's unusual! Are you very particular, then?
MMMM... NOT EXACTLY...
......
IT'S MORE LIKE WE'RE TURNING OUR FEELINGS INTO SONGS, SO...
WE WANT TO CREATE THE MELODIES AND LYRICS TOGETHER, AS A TEAM.
SOME-BODY ONCE TOLD US OUR MUSIC IS, WHAT, OUR SOULS LAID BARE?
Now that's something worth being particular about!
All right, let us hear those souls!
Carole & Tuesday's ...

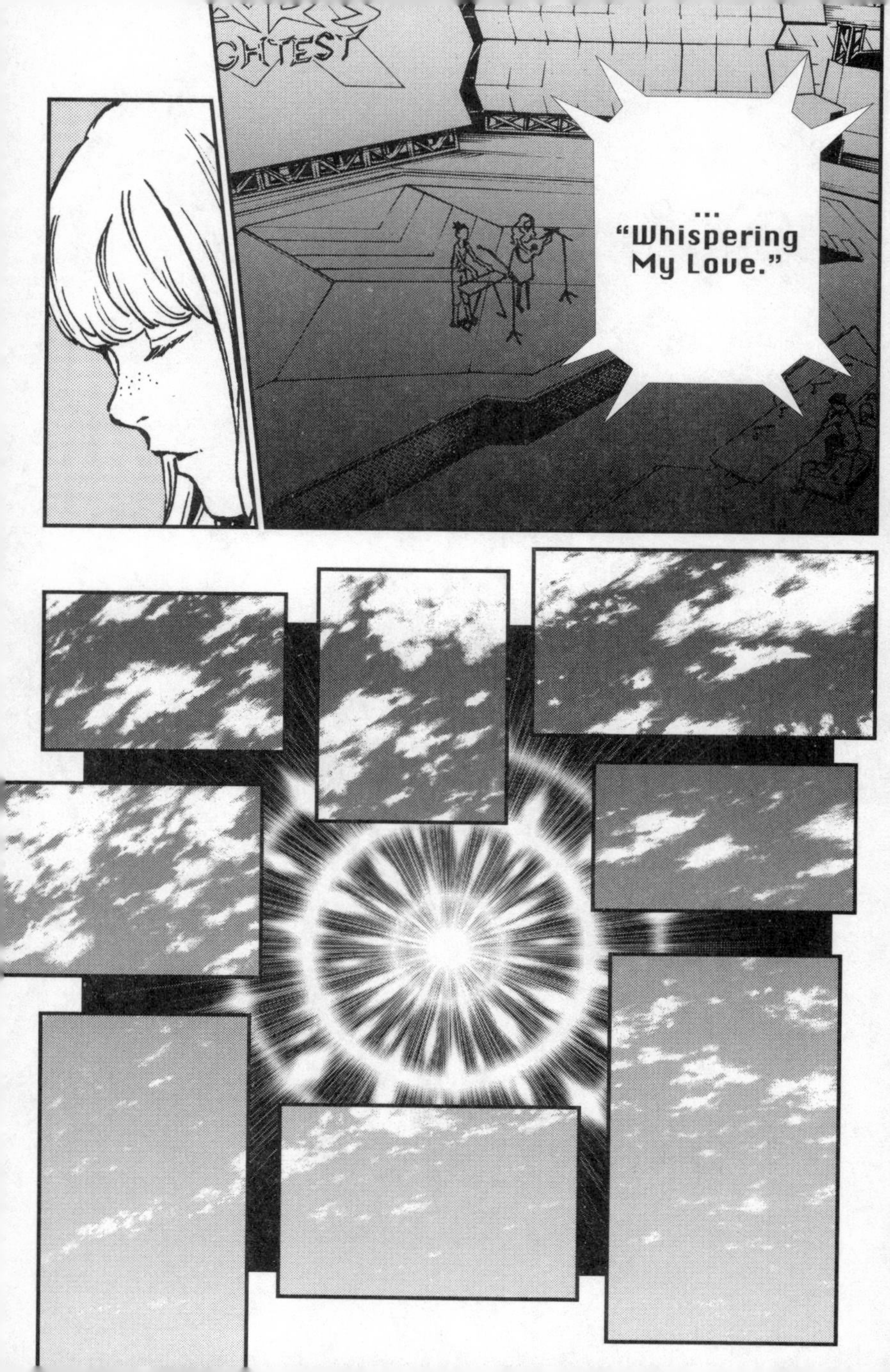
GHTEST
... "Whispering My Love."

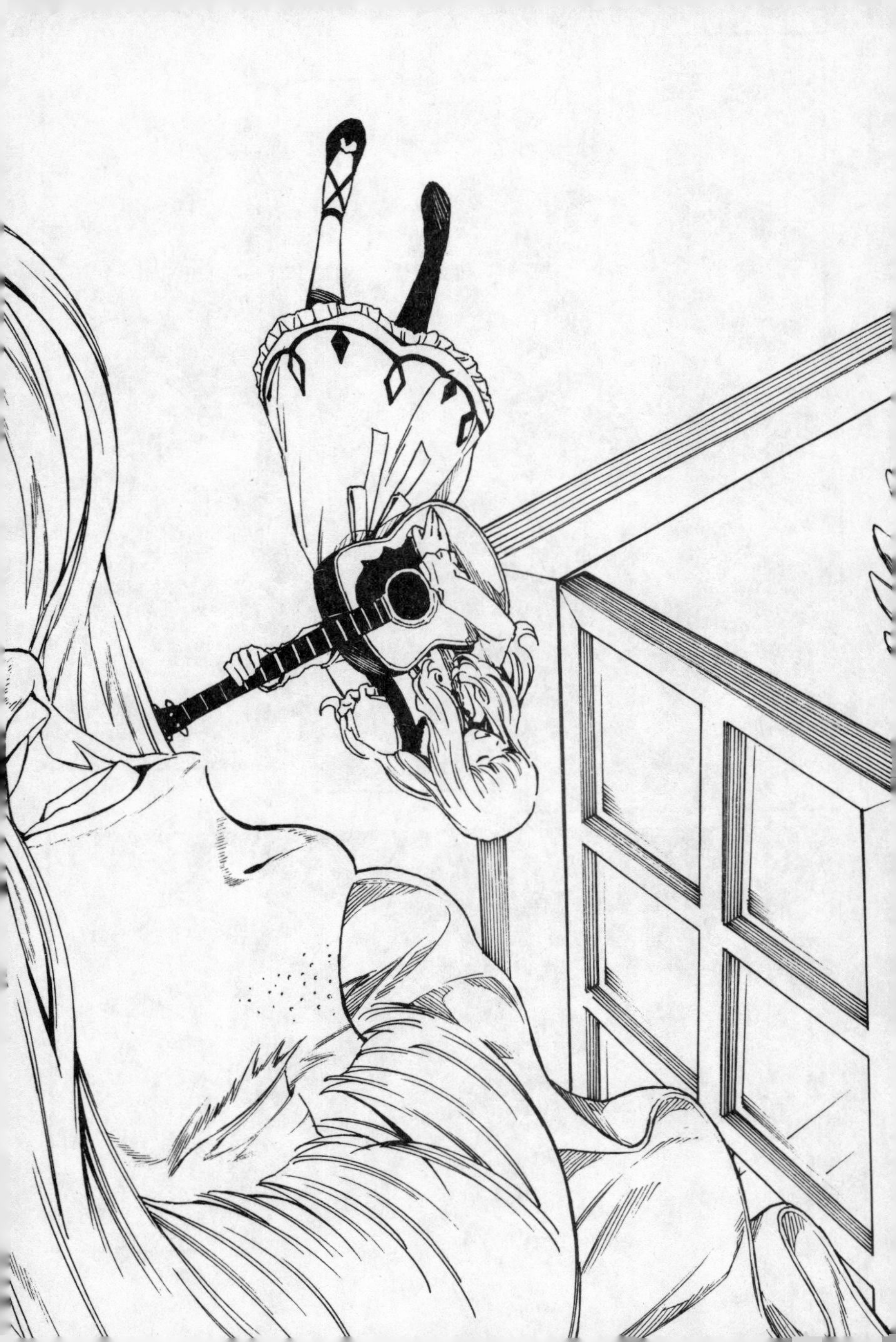

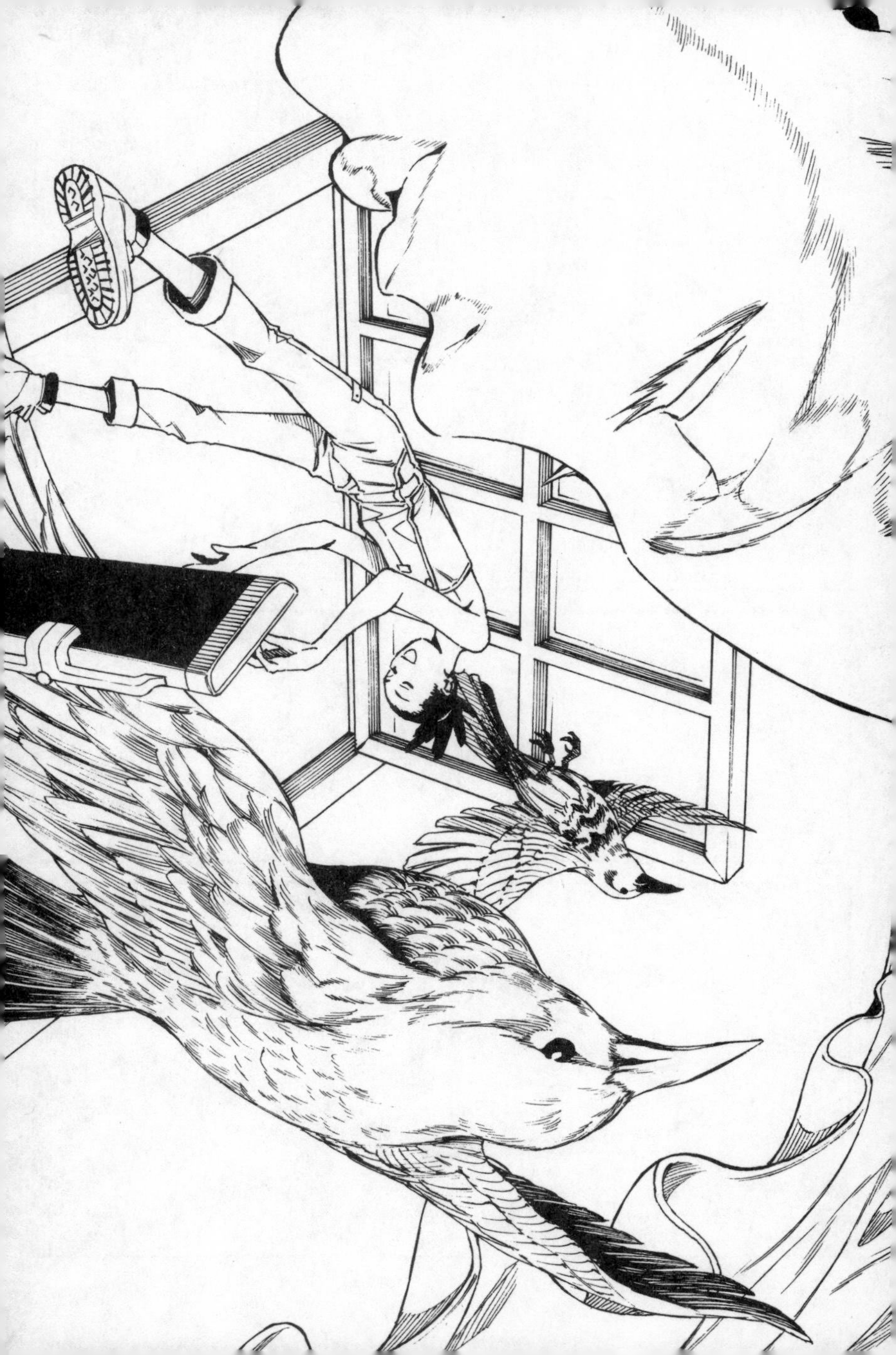

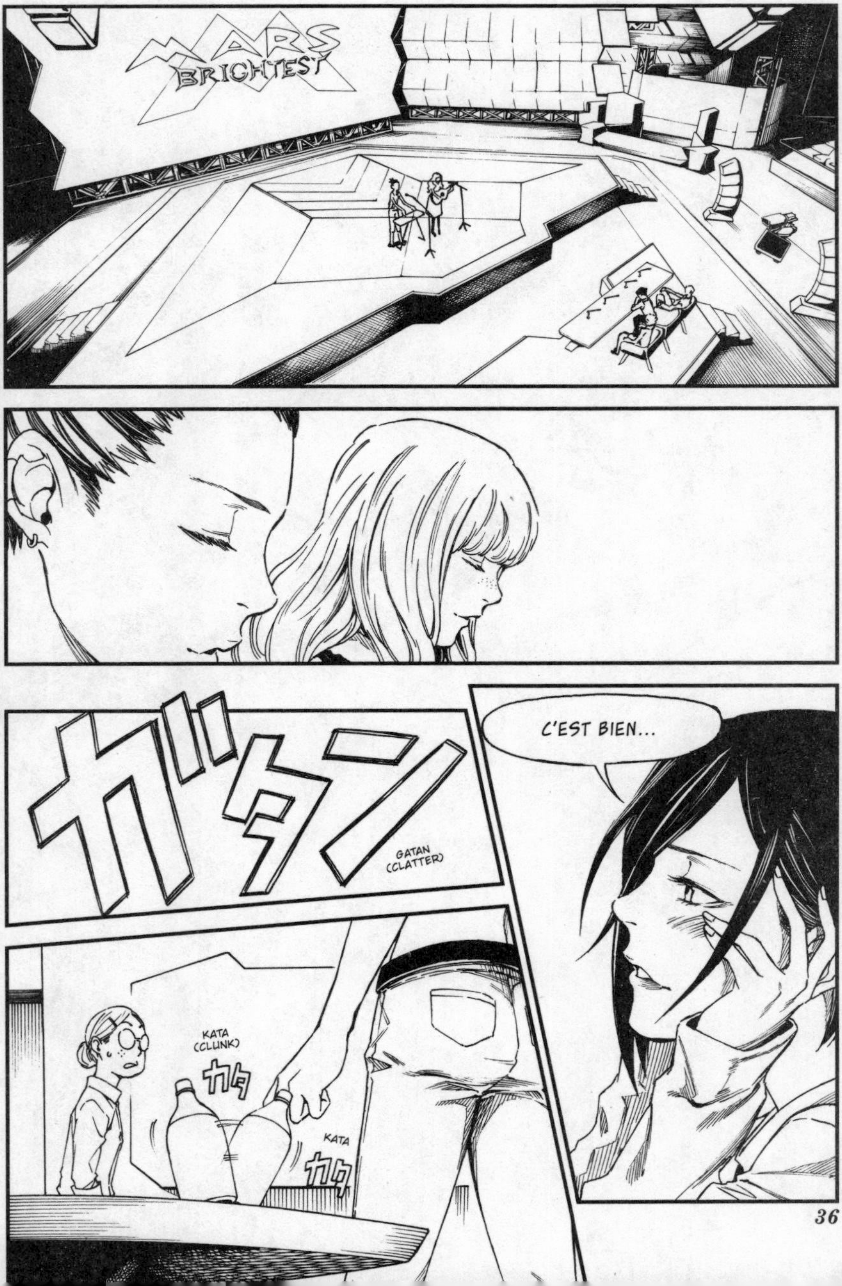
MARS
BRIGHTEST
C'EST BIEN...
ガタン
GATAN
(CLATTER)
KATA
(CLUNK)
カタ
KATA
カタ

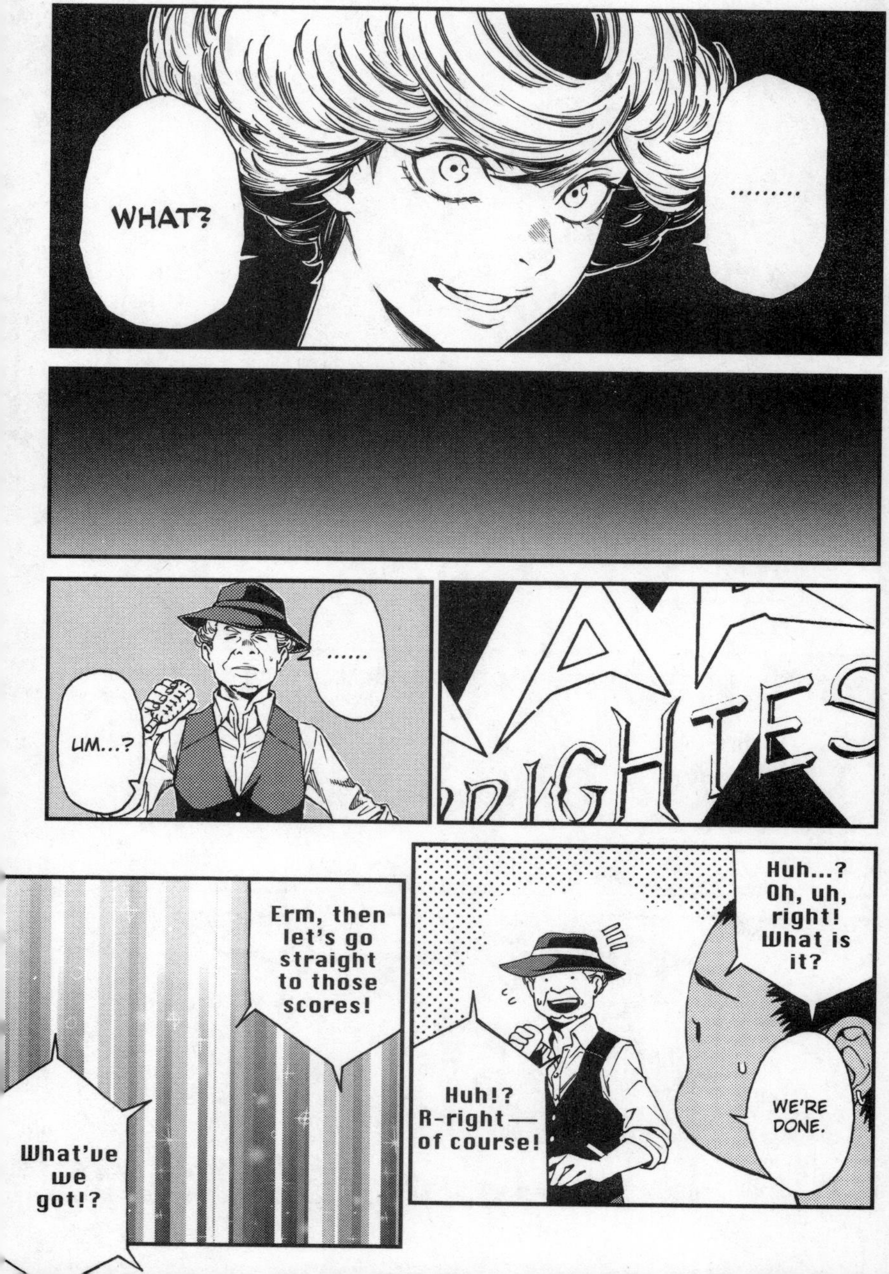
....
WHAT?
......
UM...?
Huh...? Oh, uh, right! What is it?
WE'RE DONE.
Huh!? R-right— of course!
Erm, then let's go straight to those scores!
What've we got!?

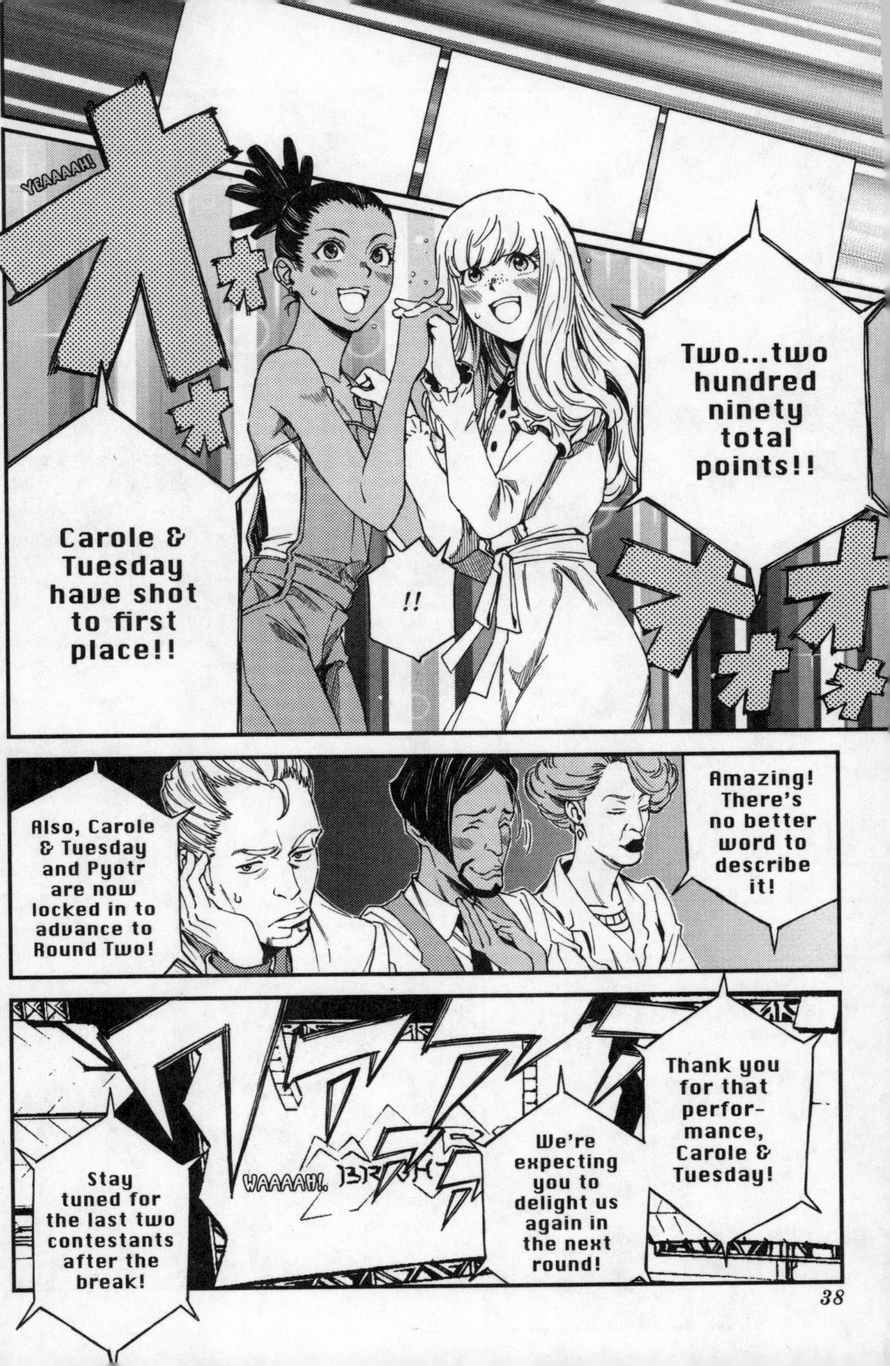

YEAAAAH!
Two...two hundred ninety total points!!
!!
Carole & Tuesday have shot to first place!!
Amazing! There's no better word to describe it!
Also, Carole & Tuesday and Pyotr are now locked in to advance to Round Two!
Thank you for that perfor-mance, Carole & Tuesday!
We're expecting you to delight us again in the next round!
WAAAAH!, BRRRH
Stay tuned for the last two contestants after the break!

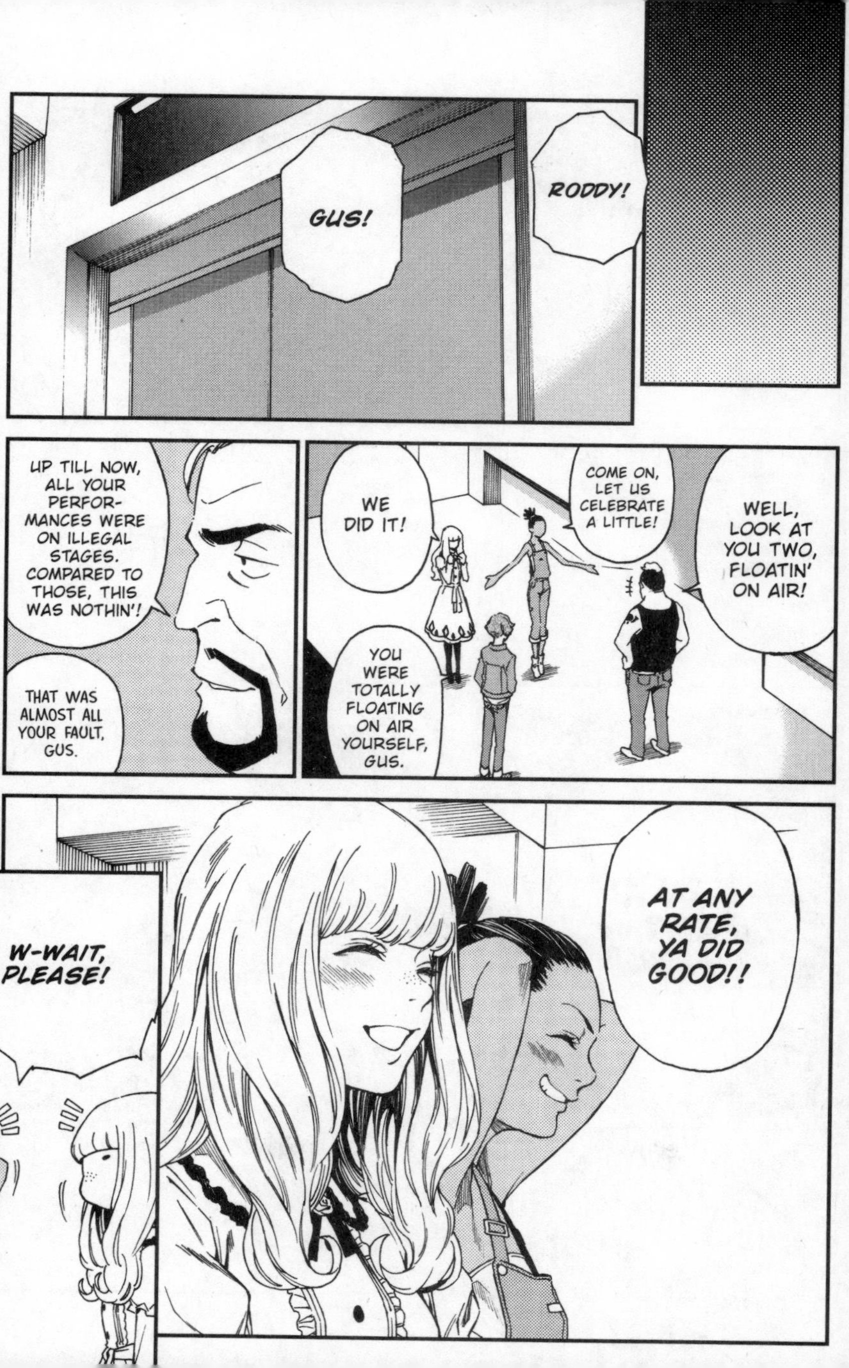
RODDY!
GUS!
WELL, LOOK AT YOU TWO, FLOATIN' ON AIR!
COME ON, LET US CELEBRATE A LITTLE!
WE DID IT!
YOU WERE TOTALLY FLOATING ON AIR YOURSELF, GUS.
UP TILL NOW, ALL YOUR PERFORMANCES WERE ON ILLEGAL STAGES. COMPARED TO THOSE, THIS WAS NOTHIN'!
THAT WAS ALMOST ALL YOUR FAULT, GUS.
AT ANY RATE, YA DID GOOD!!
W-WAIT, PLEASE!

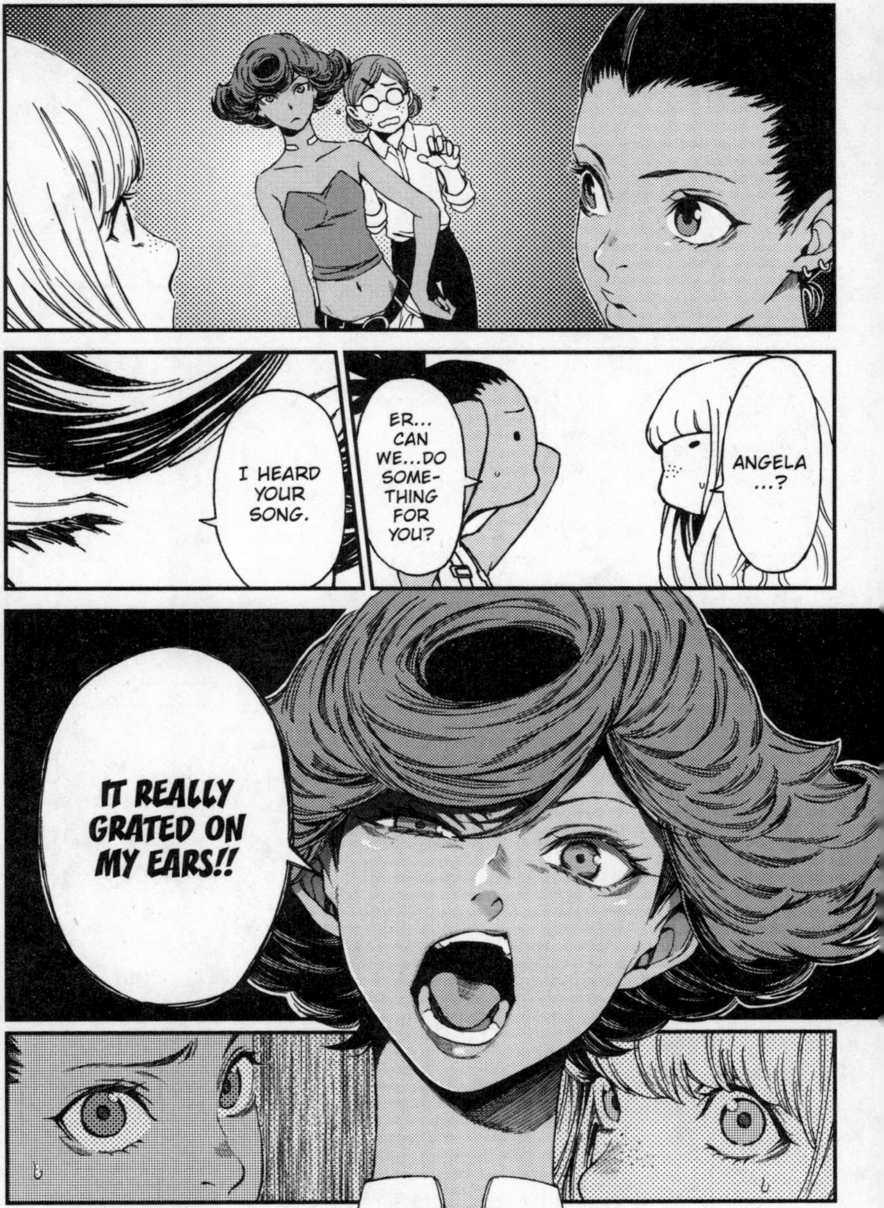
ANGELA ...?
ER... CAN WE...DO SOME-THING FOR YOU?
I HEARD YOUR SONG.
IT REALLY GRATED ON MY EARS!!

END

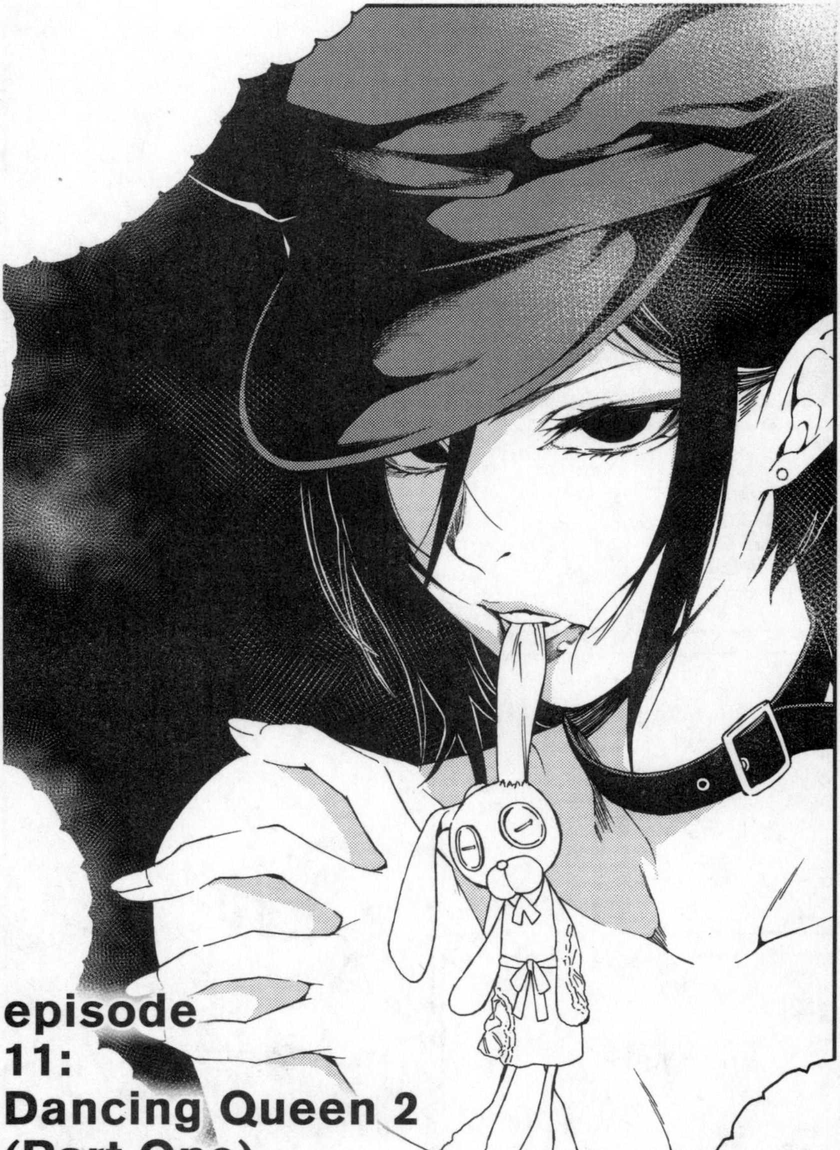
episode
11:
Dancing Queen 2
(Part One)

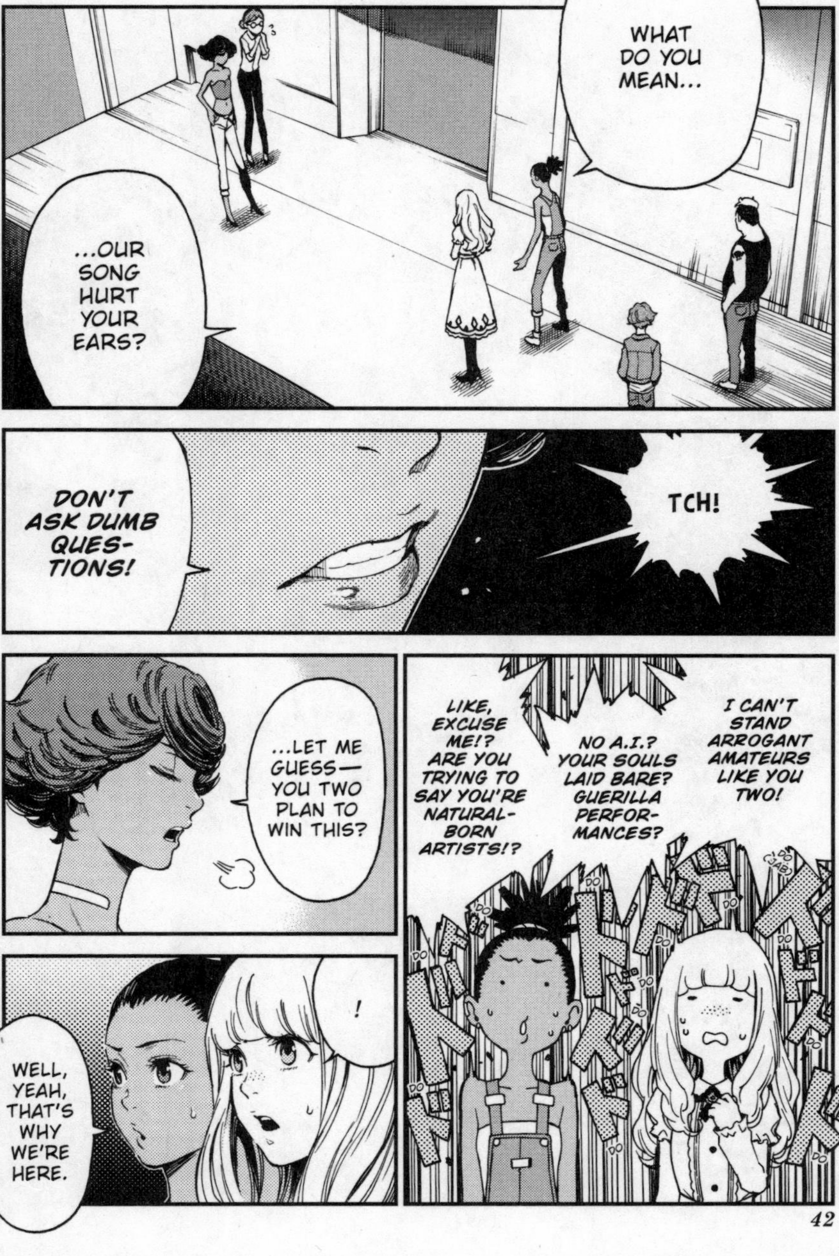
WHAT DO YOU MEAN...
...OUR SONG HURT YOUR EARS?
TCH!
DON'T ASK DUMB QUES-TIONS!
I CAN'T STAND ARROGANT AMATEURS LIKE YOU TWO!
NO A.I.? YOUR SOULS LAID BARE? GUERILLA PERFOR-MANCES?
LIKE, EXCUSE ME!? ARE YOU TRYING TO SAY YOU'RE NATURAL-BORN ARTISTS!?
DO (JAB)
DO
DO
DO
DO
DO
DO
DO
DO
...LET ME GUESS—YOU TWO PLAN TO WIN THIS?
!
WELL, YEAH, THAT'S WHY WE'RE HERE.

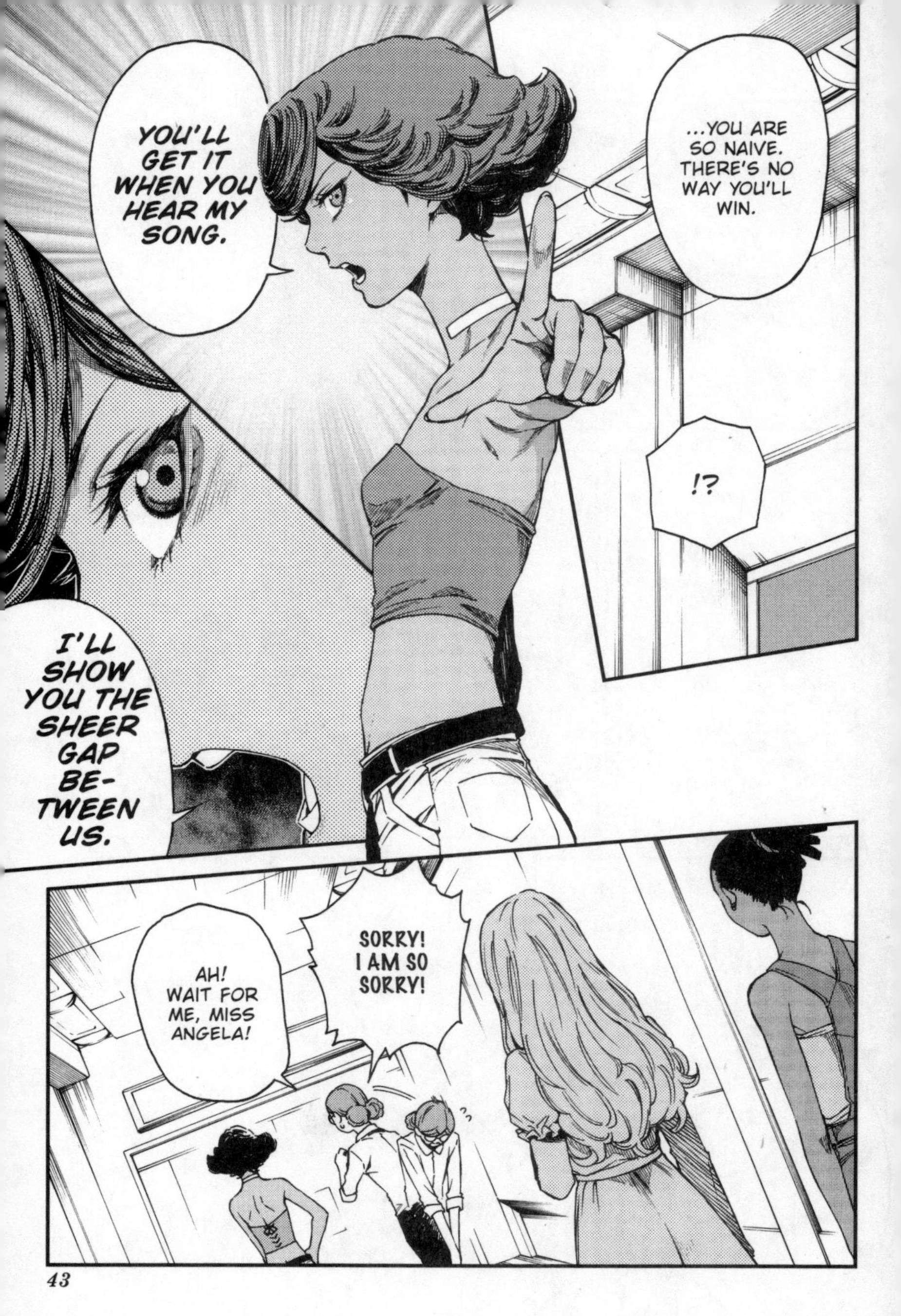
...YOU ARE SO NAIVE. THERE'S NO WAY YOU'LL WIN.
YOU'LL GET IT WHEN YOU HEAR MY SONG.
!?
I'LL SHOW YOU THE SHEER GAP BE- TWEEN US.
SORRY! I AM SO SORRY!
AH! WAIT FOR ME, MISS ANGELA!

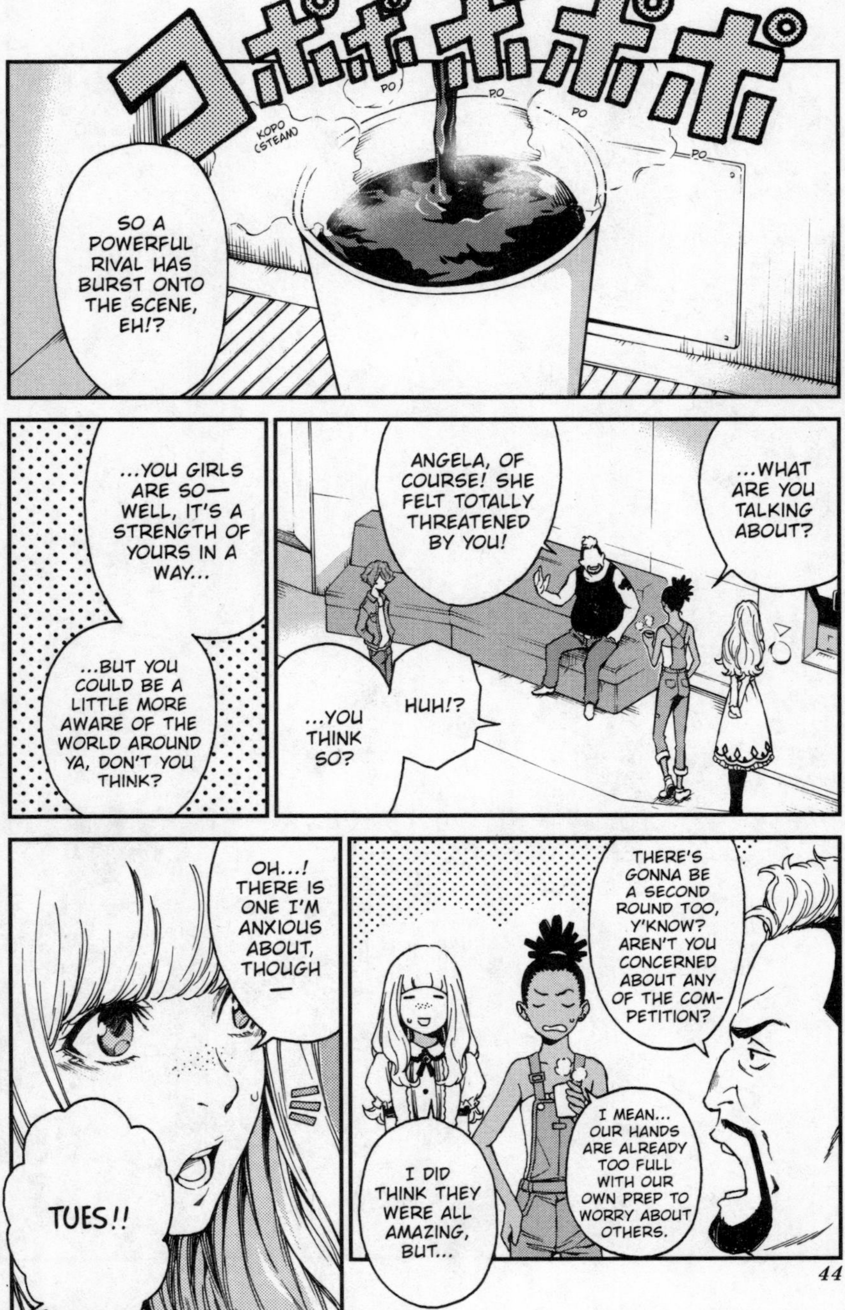
KOPO (STEAM)
PO
PO
PO
PO
SO A POWERFUL RIVAL HAS BURST ONTO THE SCENE, EH!?
...WHAT ARE YOU TALKING ABOUT?
ANGELA, OF COURSE! SHE FELT TOTALLY THREATENED BY YOU!
HUH!?
...YOU THINK SO?
...YOU GIRLS ARE SO— WELL, IT'S A STRENGTH OF YOURS IN A WAY...
...BUT YOU COULD BE A LITTLE MORE AWARE OF THE WORLD AROUND YA, DON'T YOU THINK?
THERE'S GONNA BE A SECOND ROUND TOO, Y'KNOW? AREN'T YOU CONCERNED ABOUT ANY OF THE COM-PETITION?
I MEAN... OUR HANDS ARE ALREADY TOO FULL WITH OUR OWN PREP TO WORRY ABOUT OTHERS.
I DID THINK THEY WERE ALL AMAZING, BUT...
OH...! THERE IS ONE I'M ANXIOUS ABOUT, THOUGH—
TUES!!

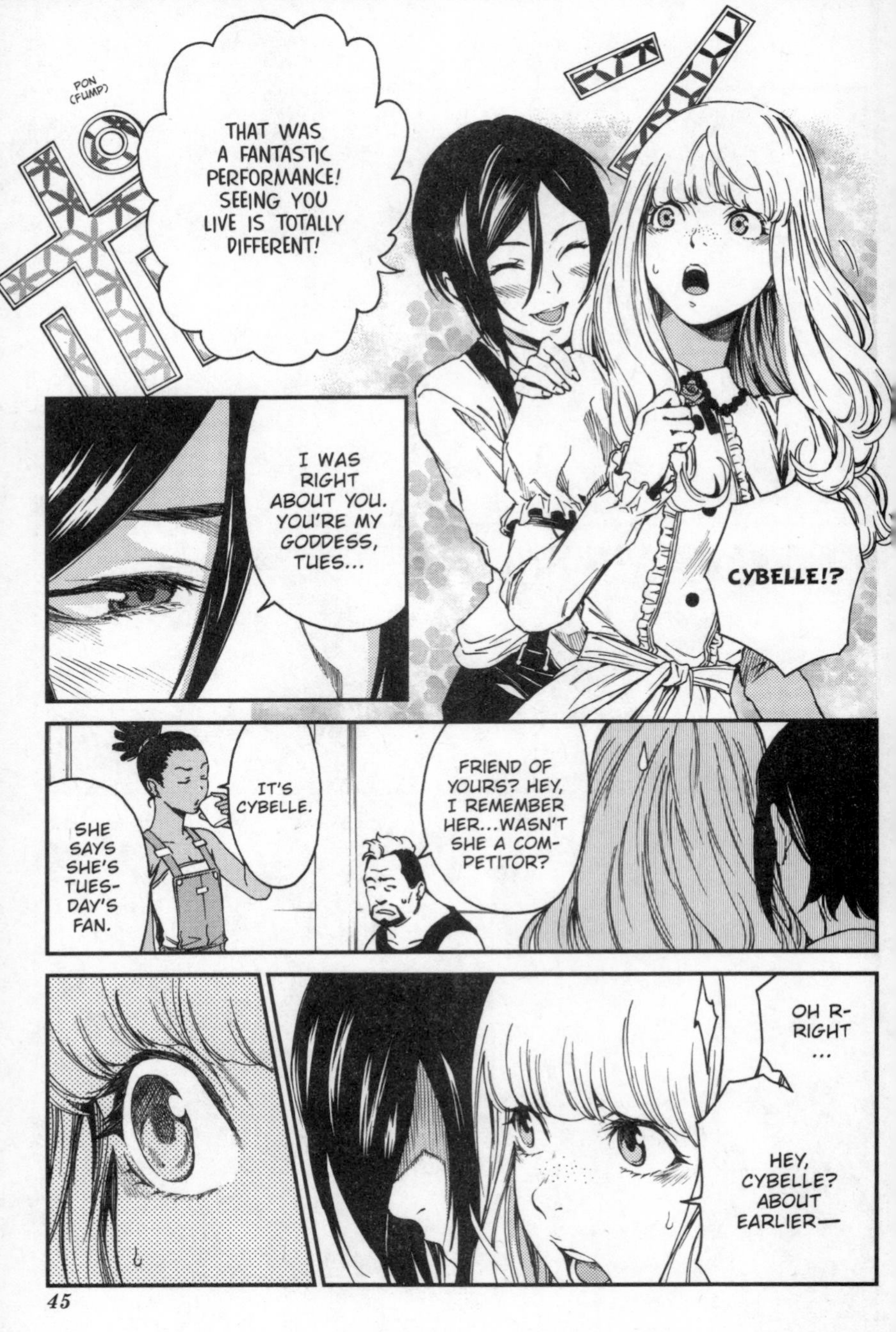
PON (FUMP)
THAT WAS A FANTASTIC PERFORMANCE! SEEING YOU LIVE IS TOTALLY DIFFERENT!
CYBELLE!?
I WAS RIGHT ABOUT YOU. YOU'RE MY GODDESS, TUES...
FRIEND OF YOURS? HEY, I REMEMBER HER...WASN'T SHE A COM-PETITOR?
IT'S CYBELLE.
SHE SAYS SHE'S TUES-DAY'S FAN.
OH R-RIGHT ...
HEY, CYBELLE? ABOUT EARLIER—

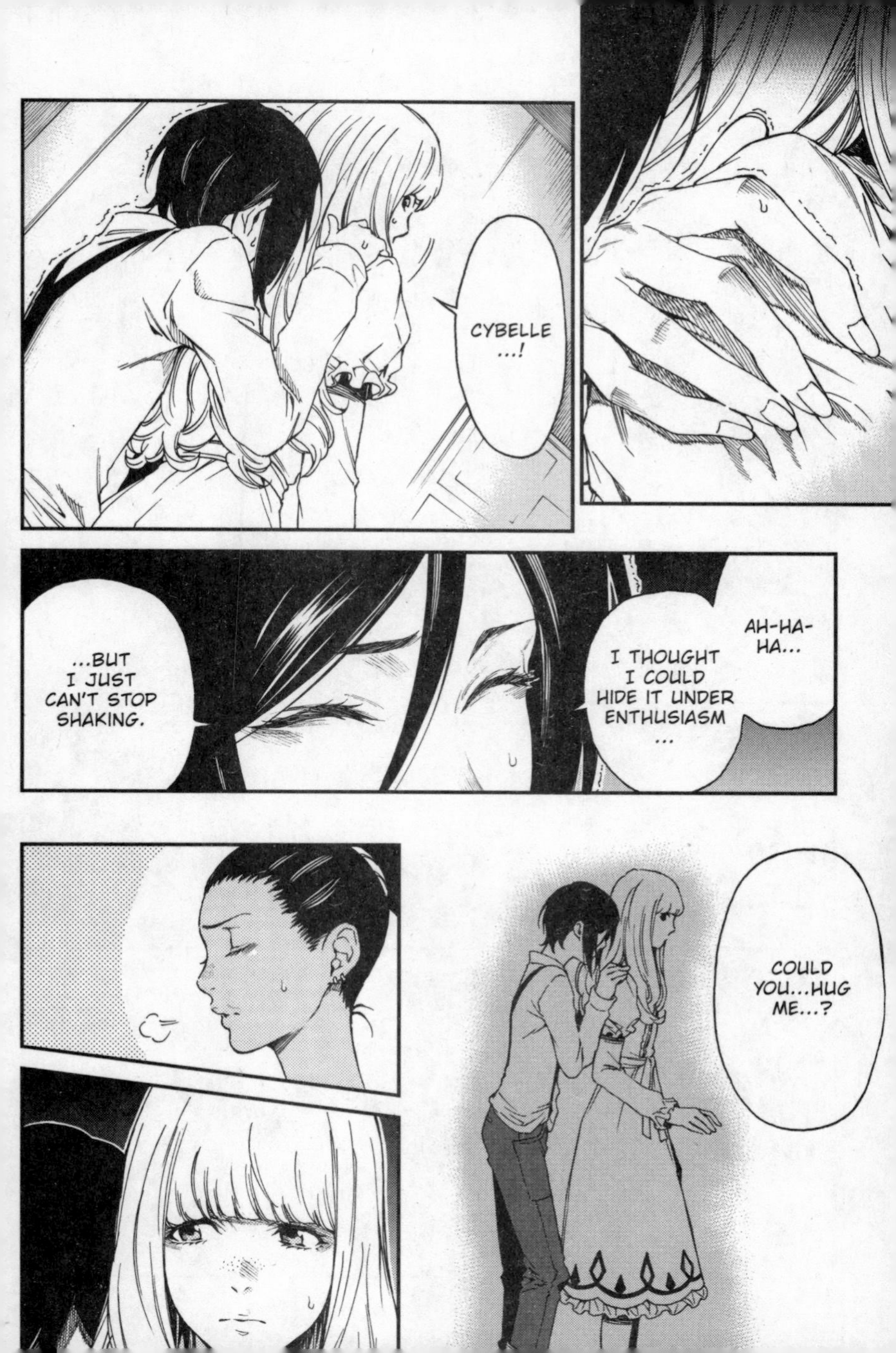
CYBELLE ...!
AH-HA-HA...
I THOUGHT I COULD HIDE IT UNDER ENTHUSIASM ...
...BUT I JUST CAN'T STOP SHAKING.
COULD YOU...HUG ME...?

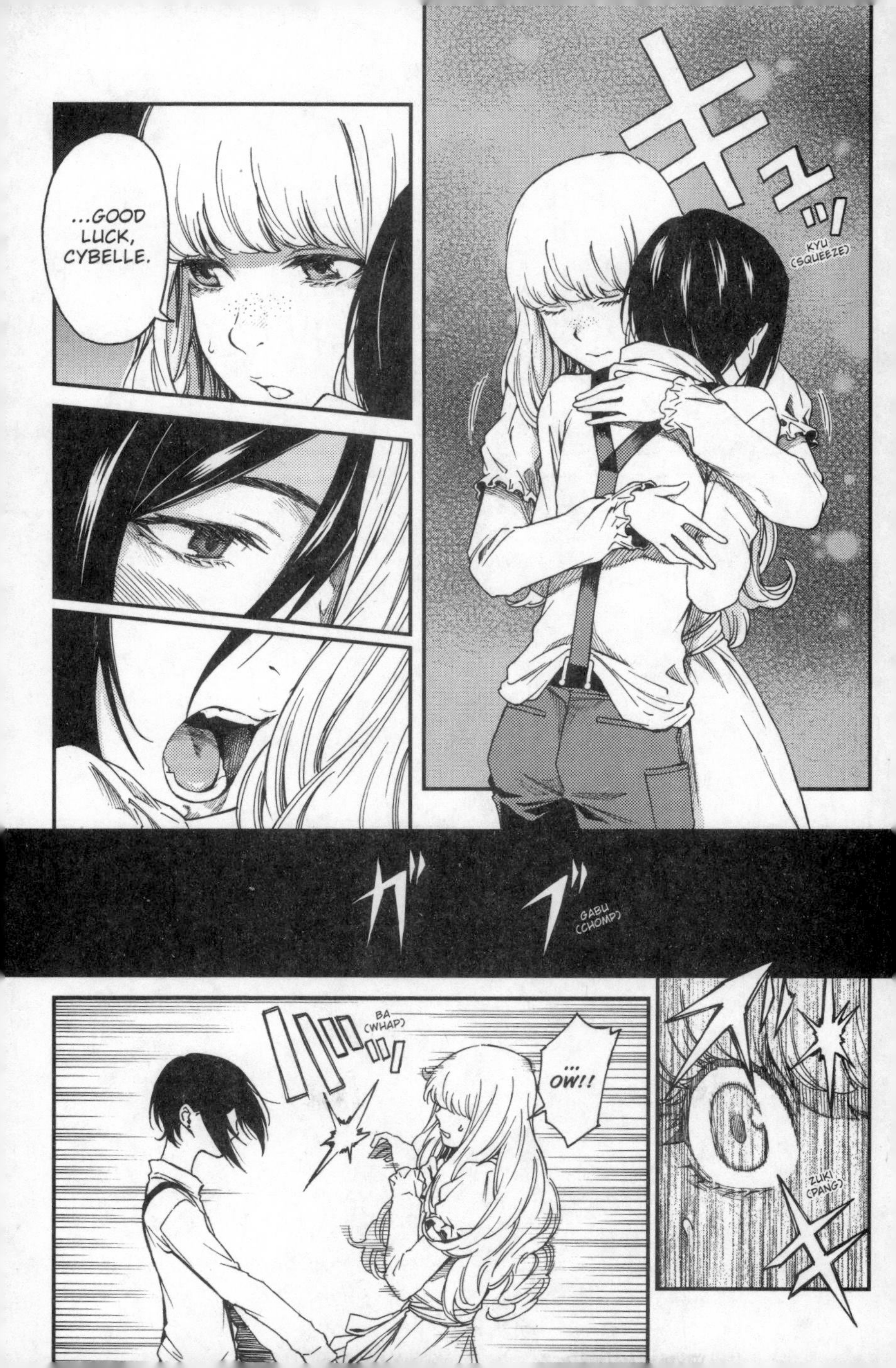
KYU (SQUEEZE)
...GOOD LUCK, CYBELLE.
GABU (CHOMP)
ZUKI (PANG)
BA (WHAP)
...OW!!

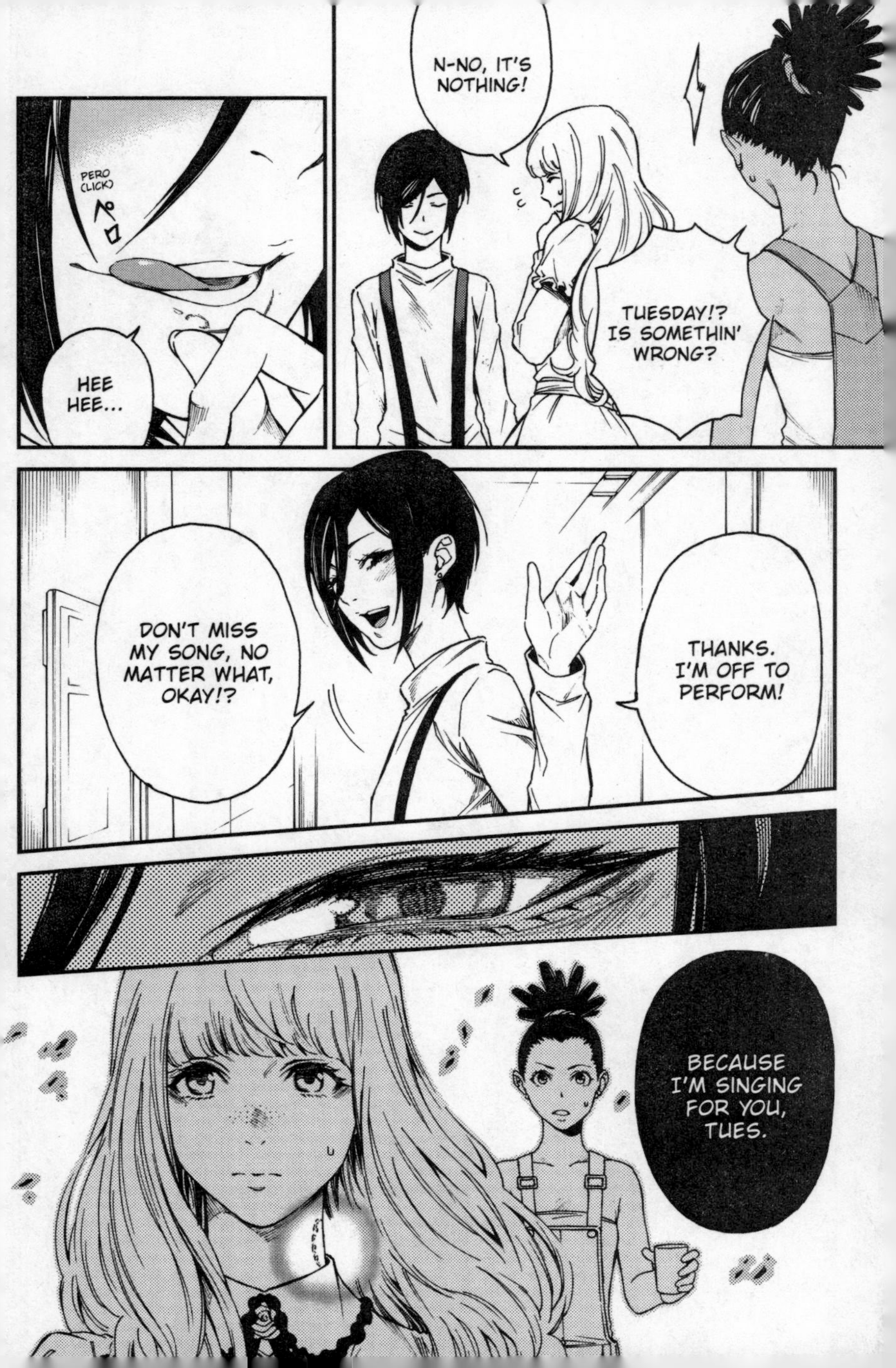
TUESDAY!? IS SOMETHIN' WRONG?
N-NO, IT'S NOTHING!
PERO (LICK)
HEE HEE...
THANKS. I'M OFF TO PERFORM!
DON'T MISS MY SONG, NO MATTER WHAT, OKAY!?
BECAUSE I'M SINGING FOR YOU, TUES.

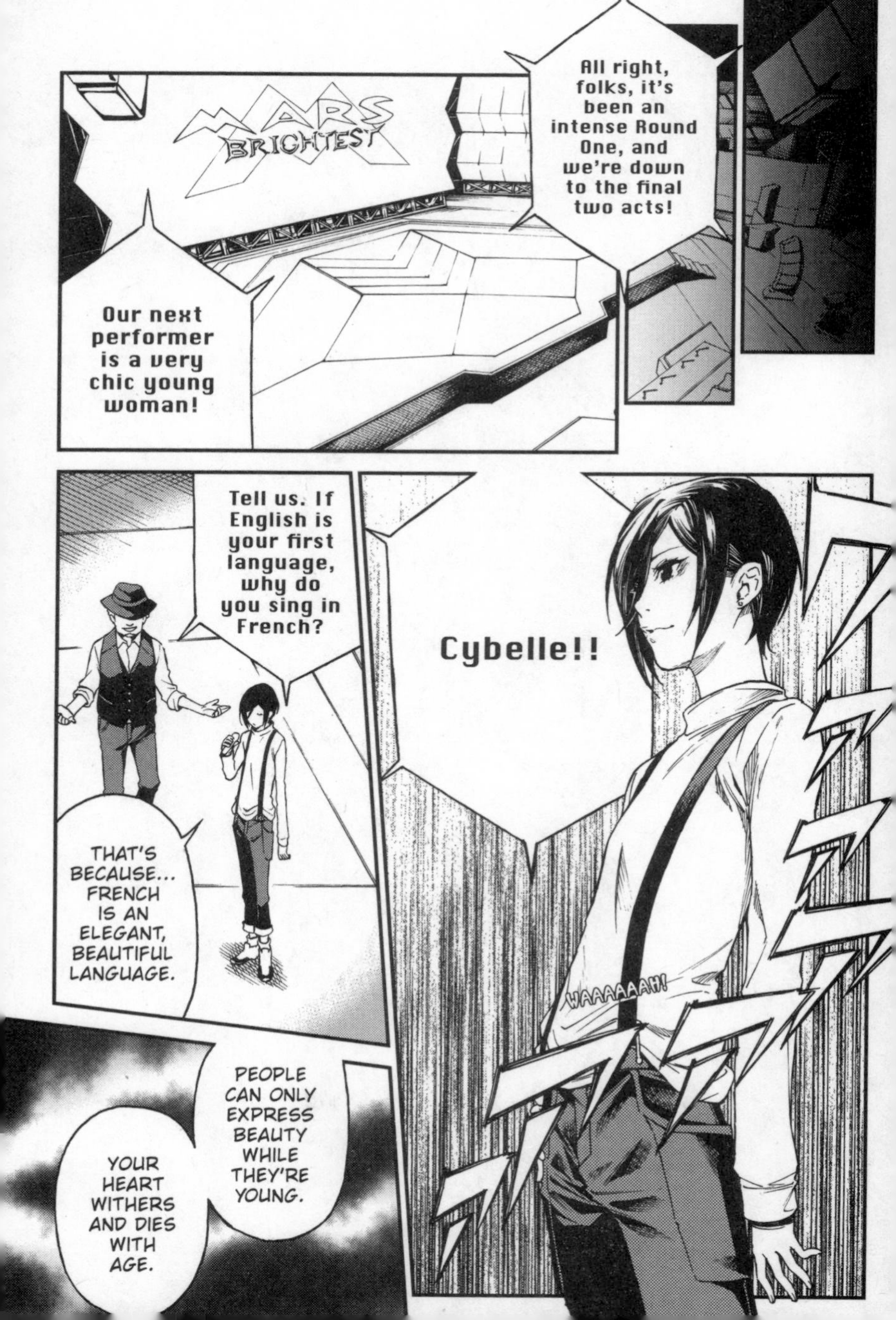
All right, folks, it's been an intense Round One, and we're down to the final two acts!
MARS BRIGHTEST
Our next performer is a very chic young woman!
Cybelle!!
WAAAAAAH!
Tell us. If English is your first language, why do you sing in French?
THAT'S BECAUSE... FRENCH IS AN ELEGANT, BEAUTIFUL LANGUAGE.
PEOPLE CAN ONLY EXPRESS BEAUTY WHILE THEY'RE YOUNG.
YOUR HEART WITHERS AND DIES WITH AGE.

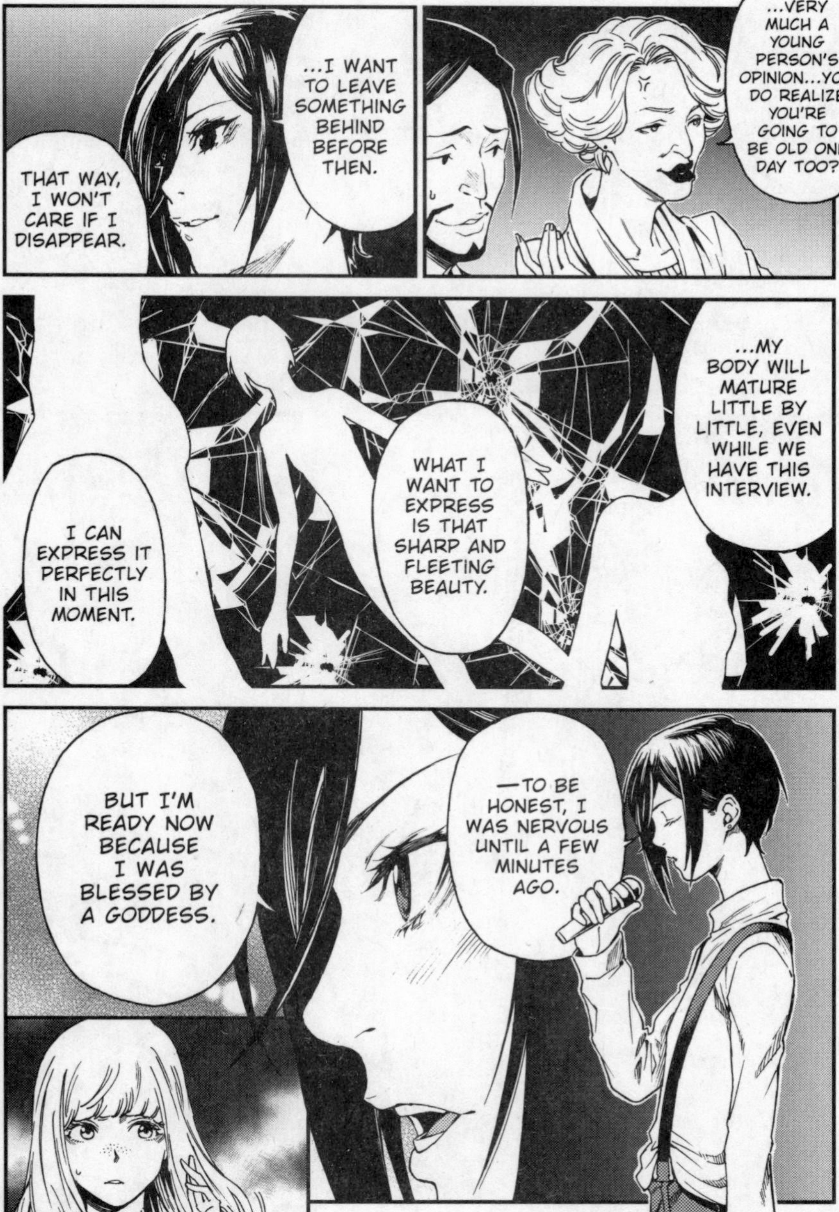
...VERY MUCH A YOUNG PERSON'S OPINION...YOU DO REALIZE YOU'RE GOING TO BE OLD ONE DAY TOO?
...I WANT TO LEAVE SOMETHING BEHIND BEFORE THEN.
THAT WAY, I WON'T CARE IF I DISAPPEAR.
...MY BODY WILL MATURE LITTLE BY LITTLE, EVEN WHILE WE HAVE THIS INTERVIEW.
WHAT I WANT TO EXPRESS IS THAT SHARP AND FLEETING BEAUTY.
I CAN EXPRESS IT PERFECTLY IN THIS MOMENT.
—TO BE HONEST, I WAS NERVOUS UNTIL A FEW MINUTES AGO.
BUT I'M READY NOW BECAUSE I WAS BLESSED BY A GODDESS.

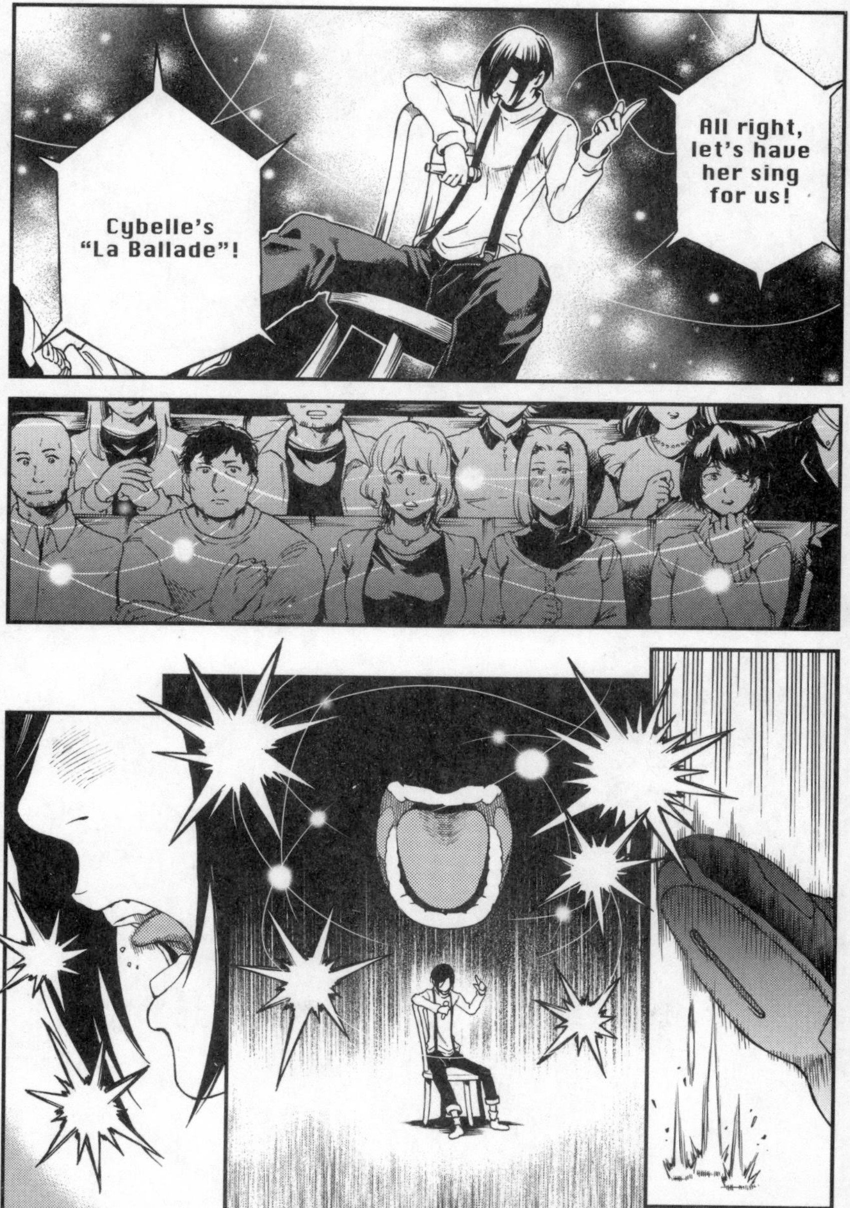
All right, let's have her sing for us!
Cybelle's "La Ballade"!

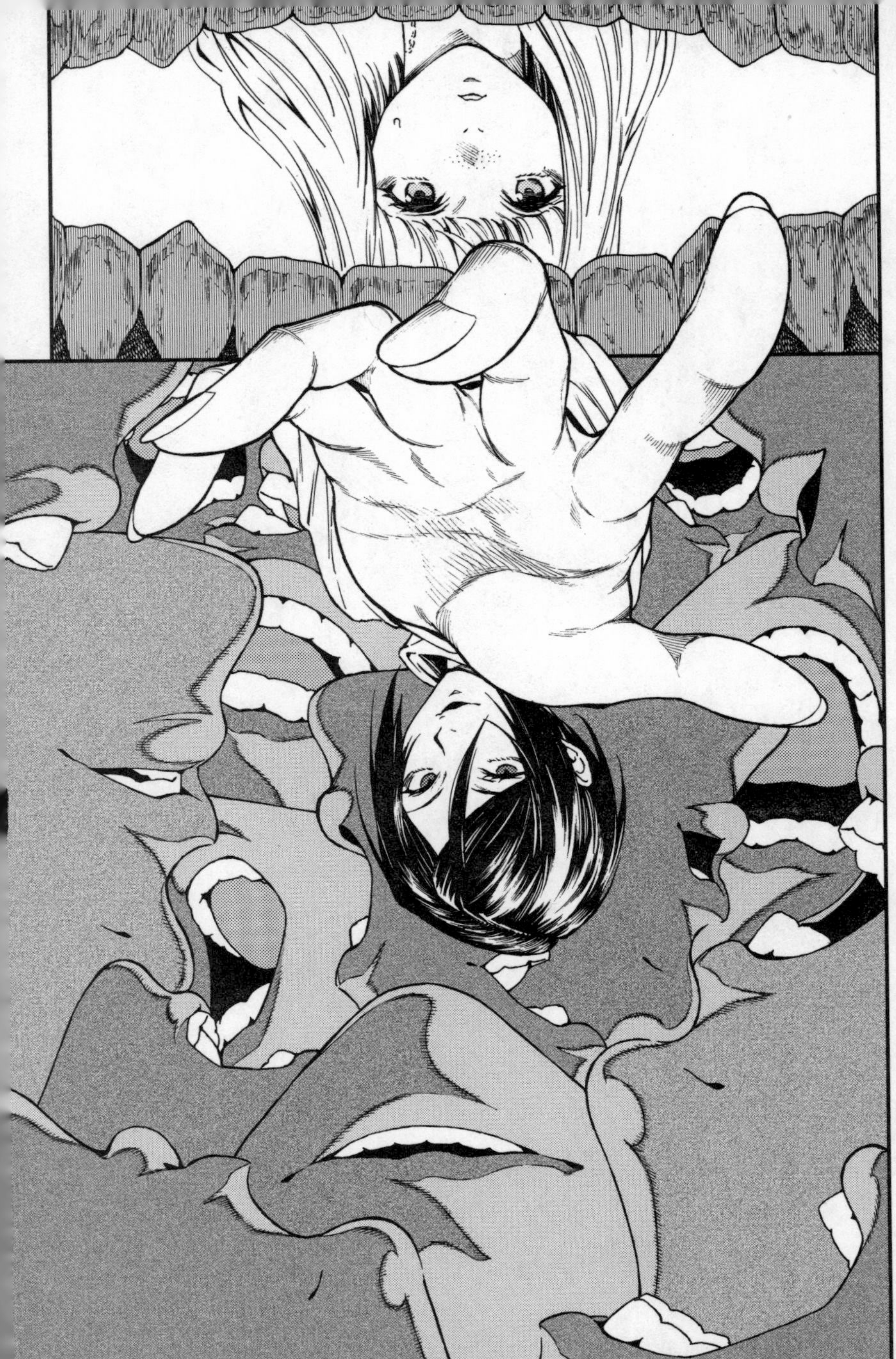

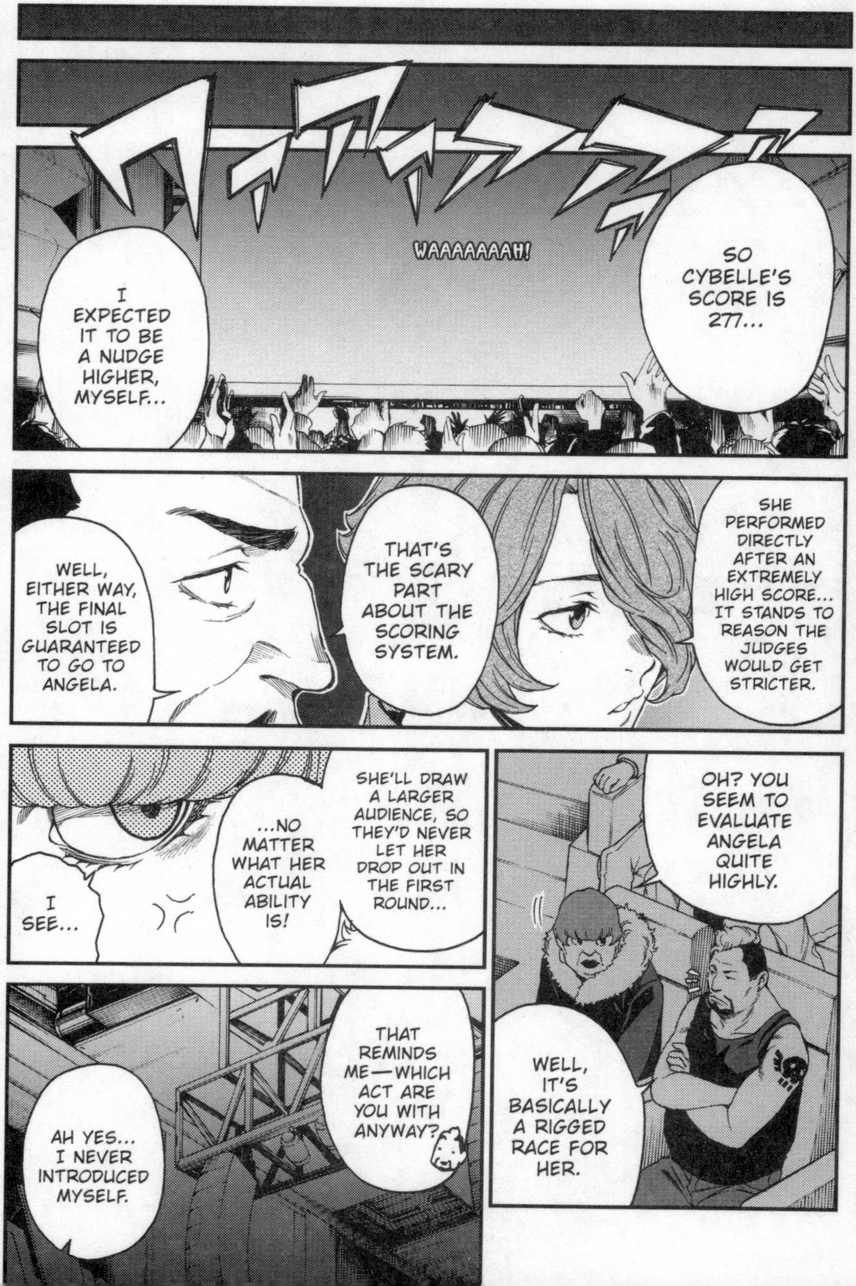
SO CYBELLE'S SCORE IS 277...
WAAAAAAAH!
I EXPECTED IT TO BE A NUDGE HIGHER, MYSELF...
SHE PERFORMED DIRECTLY AFTER AN EXTREMELY HIGH SCORE... IT STANDS TO REASON THE JUDGES WOULD GET STRICTER.
THAT'S THE SCARY PART ABOUT THE SCORING SYSTEM.
WELL, EITHER WAY, THE FINAL SLOT IS GUARANTEED TO GO TO ANGELA.
OH? YOU SEEM TO EVALUATE ANGELA QUITE HIGHLY.
WELL, IT'S BASICALLY A RIGGED RACE FOR HER.
SHE'LL DRAW A LARGER AUDIENCE, SO THEY'D NEVER LET HER DROP OUT IN THE FIRST ROUND...
...NO MATTER WHAT HER ACTUAL ABILITY IS!
I SEE...
THAT REMINDS ME—WHICH ACT ARE YOU WITH ANYWAY?
AH YES... I NEVER INTRODUCED MYSELF.

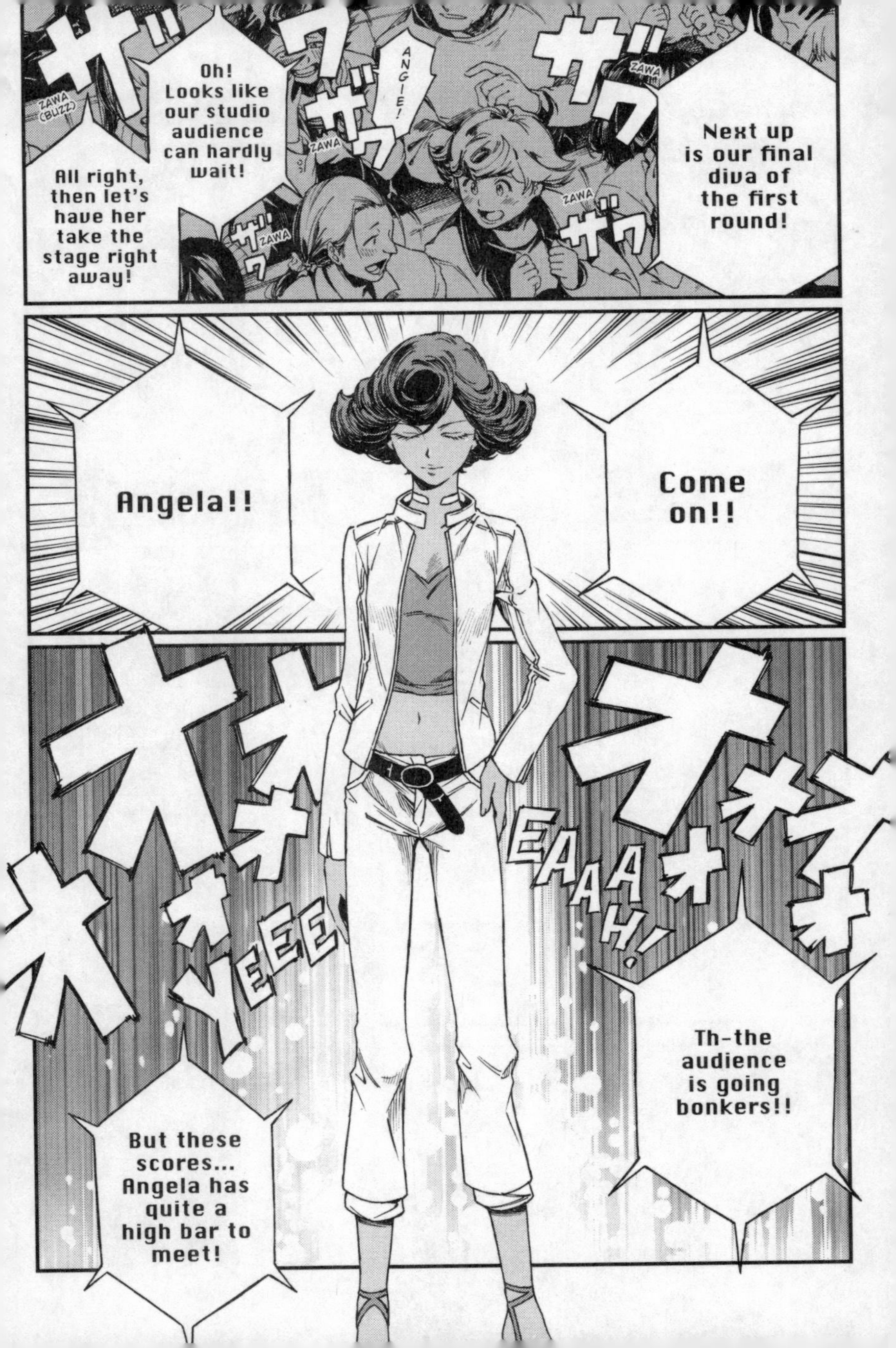
Next up is our final diva of the first round!
ZAWA
ZAWA
ANGIE!
ZAWA
Oh! Looks like our studio audience can hardly wait!
ZAWA
ZAWA (BUZZ)
All right, then let's have her take the stage right away!
Come on!!
Angela!!
EAAAAH!
YEEE
Th-the audience is going bonkers!!
But these scores... Angela has quite a high bar to meet!

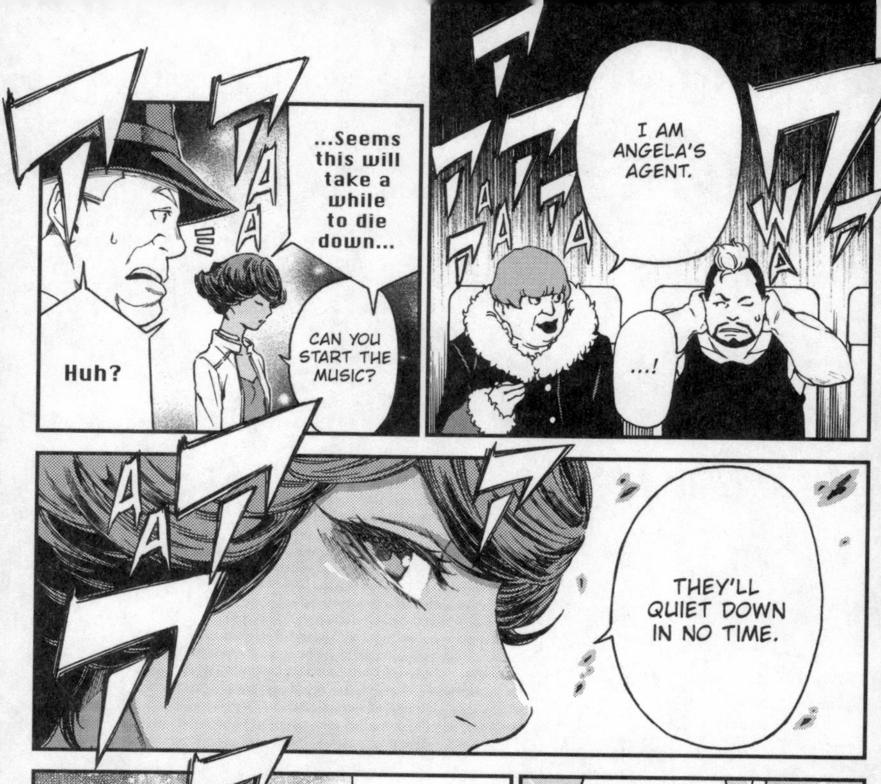
I AM ANGELA'S AGENT.
...!
...Seems this will take a while to die down...
CAN YOU START THE MUSIC?
Huh?
THEY'LL QUIET DOWN IN NO TIME.
? HER VIBE HAS...
PIRI (CRACKLE)
...COM-PLETELY CHANGED FROM JUST A MOMENT AGO...
O-okay! Let's have that song!
"Move Mountains."
AAAH!

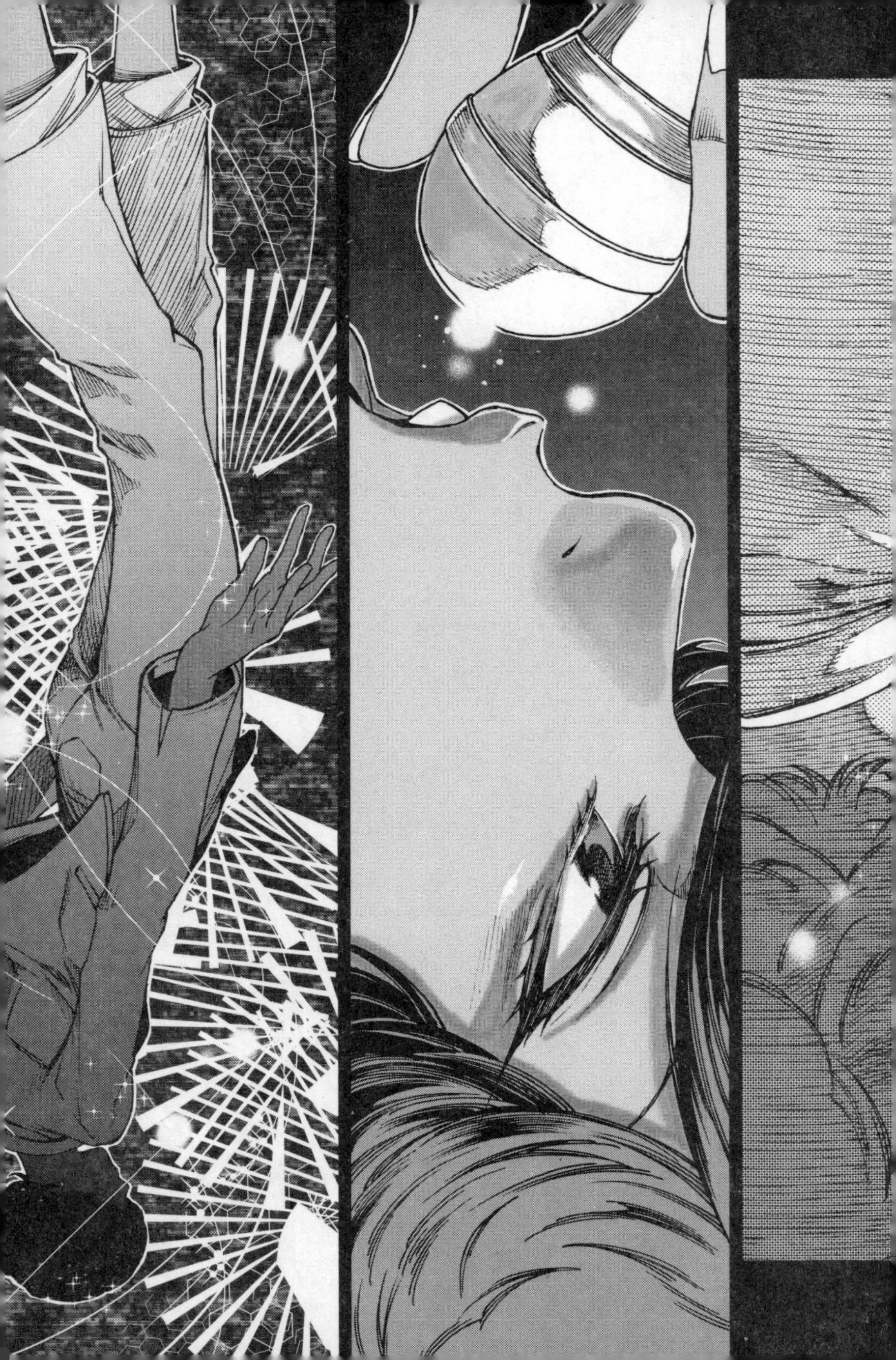

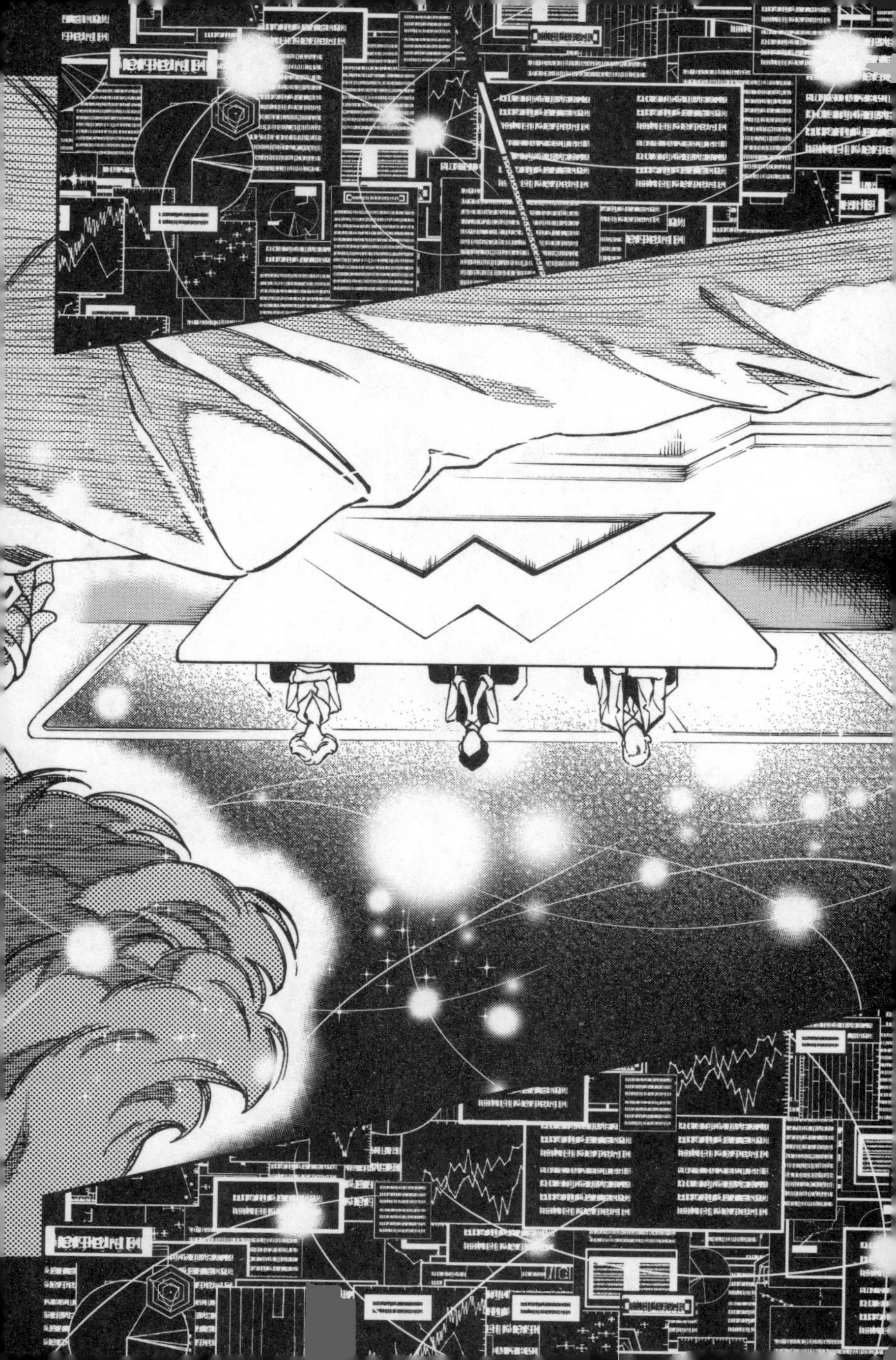

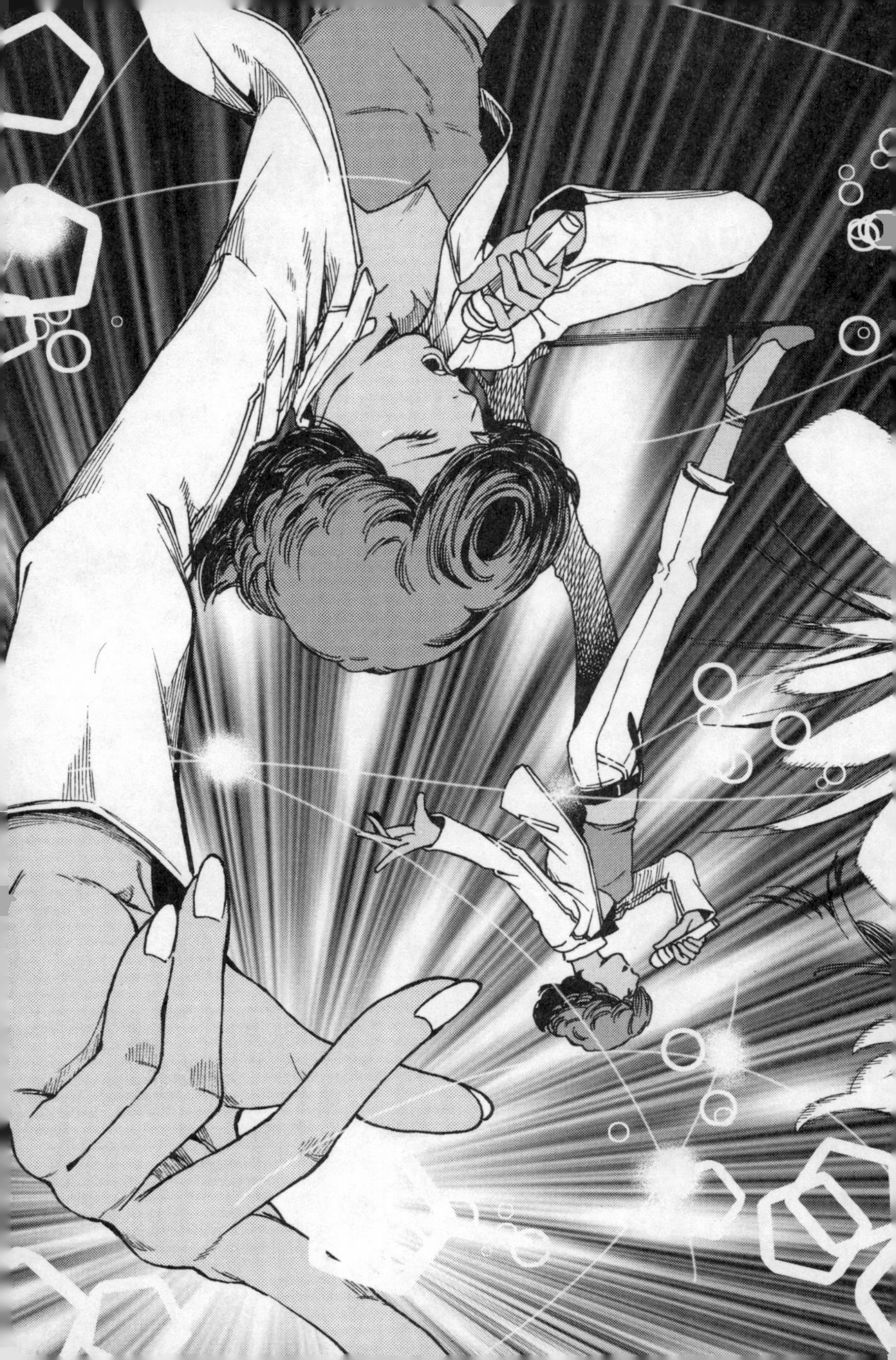

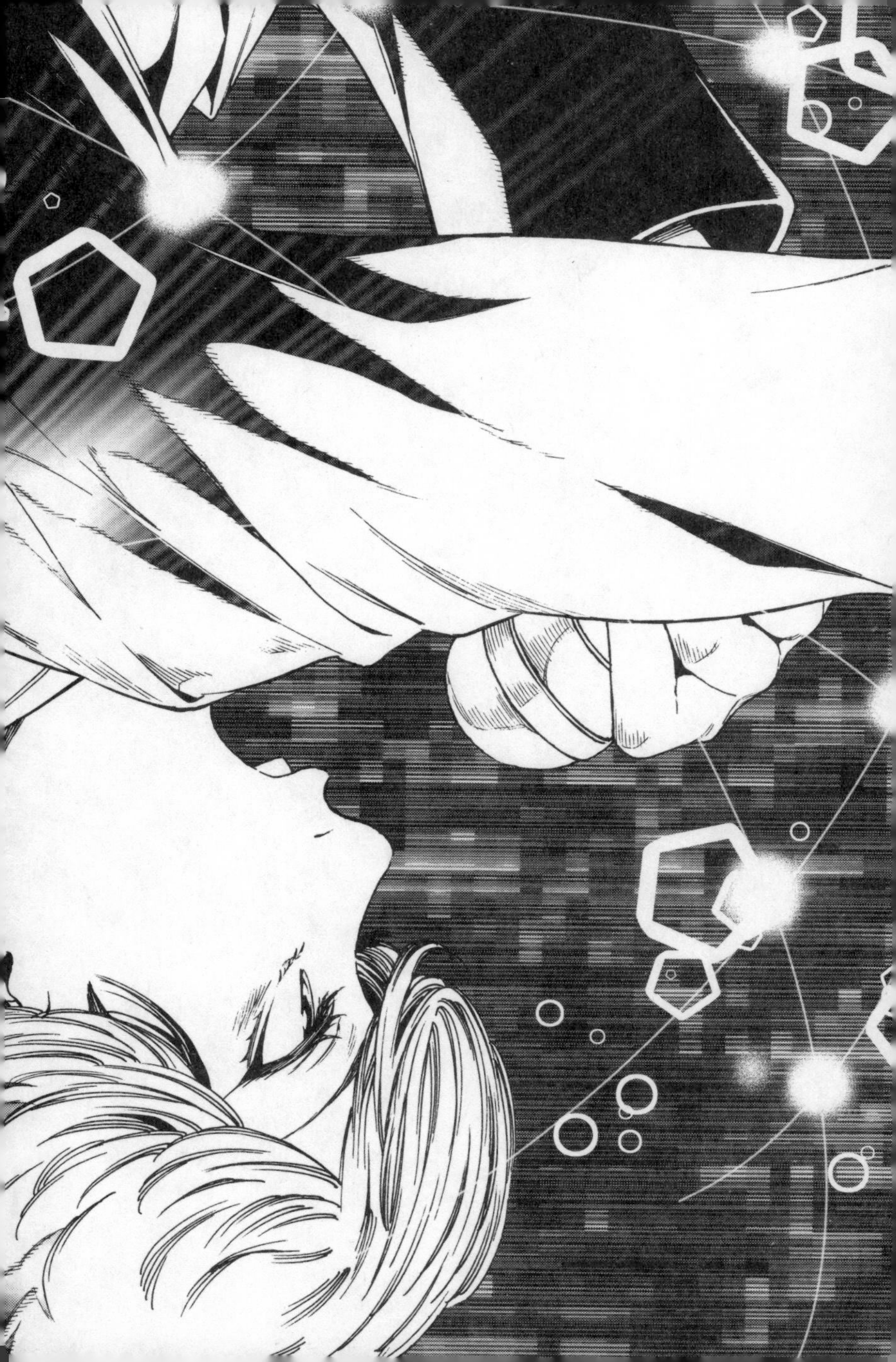

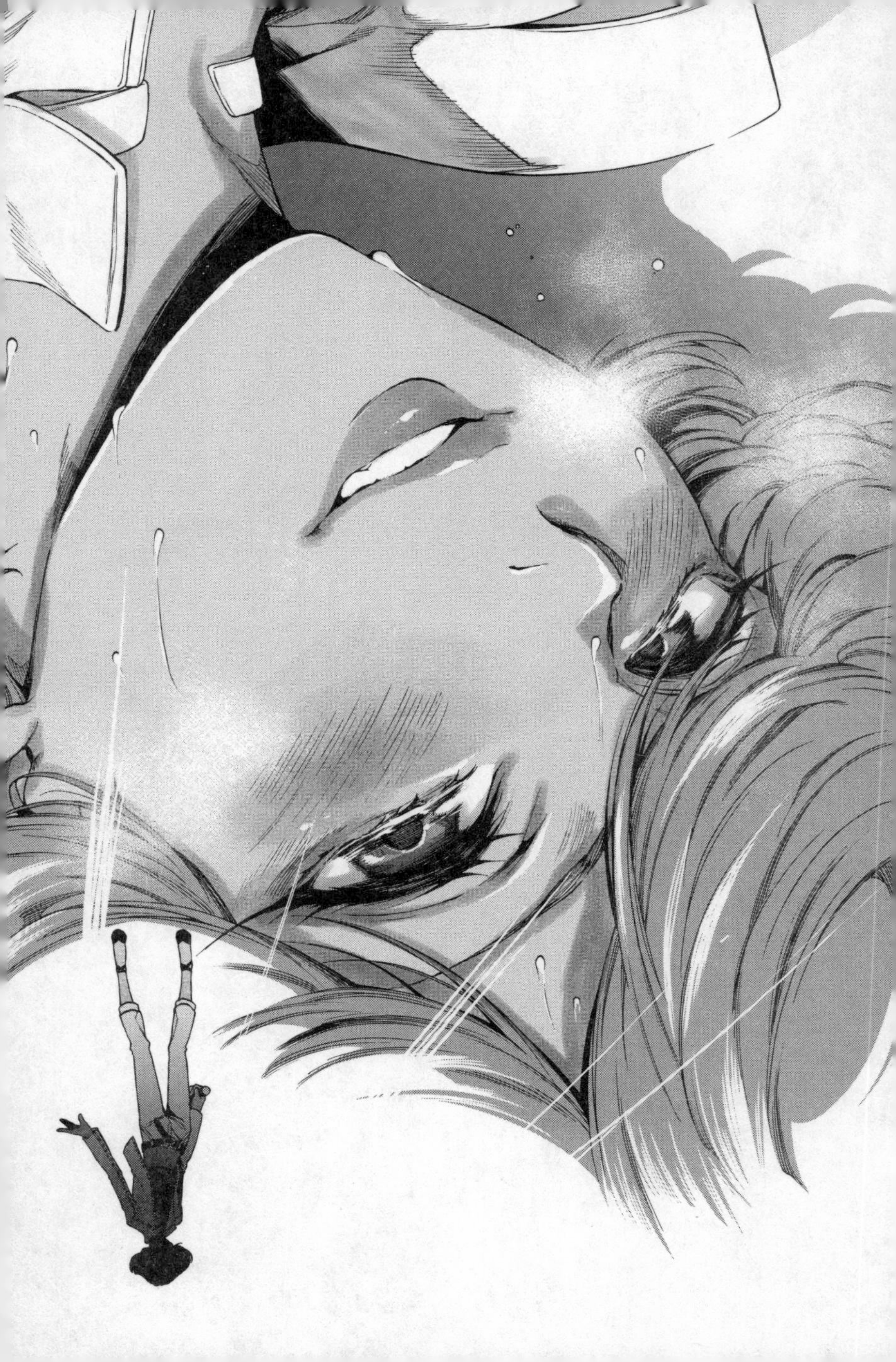

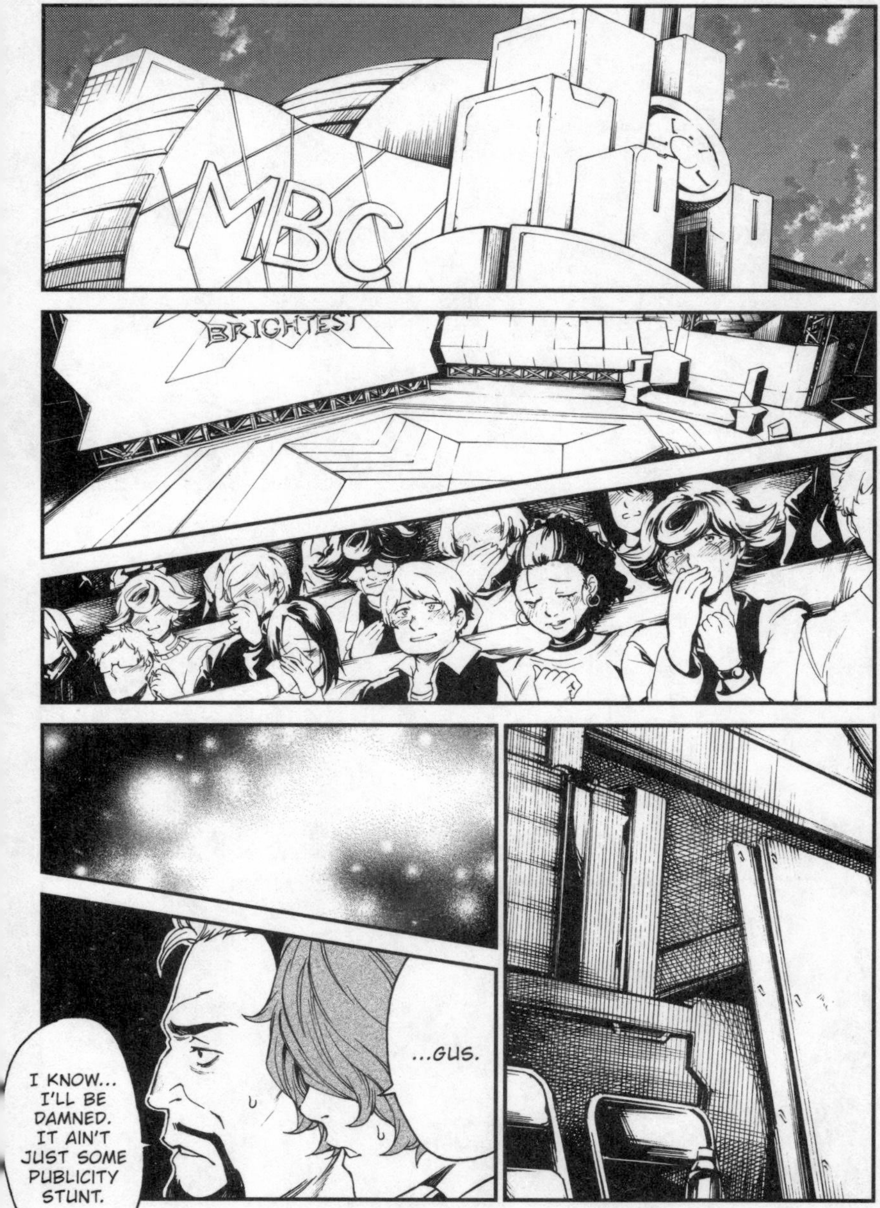
MBC
BRIGHTEST
...GUS.
I KNOW... I'LL BE DAMNED. IT AIN'T JUST SOME PUBLICITY STUNT.

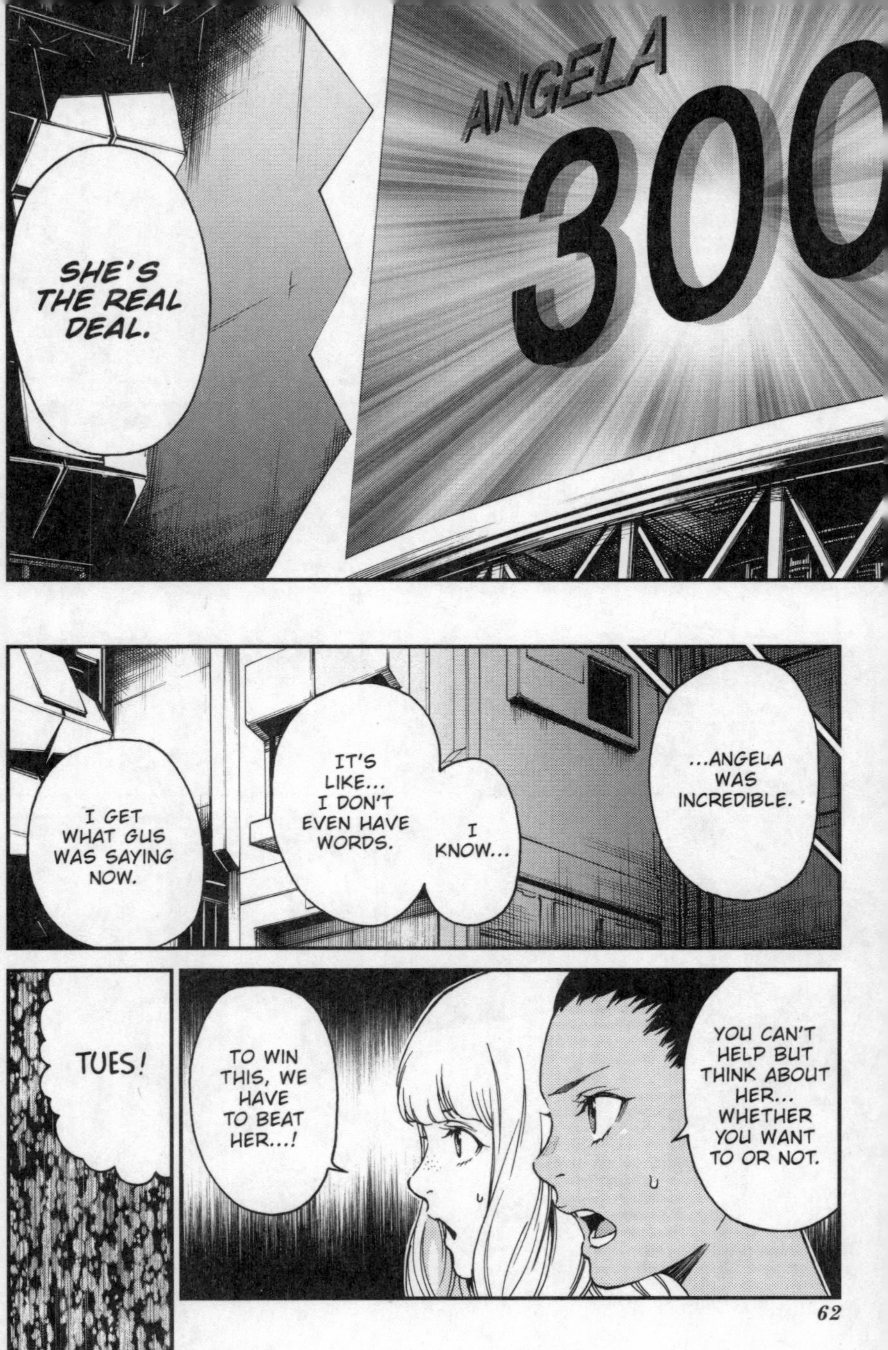
ANGELA
300
SHE'S THE REAL DEAL.
...ANGELA WAS INCREDIBLE.
I KNOW...
IT'S LIKE... I DON'T EVEN HAVE WORDS.
I GET WHAT GUS WAS SAYING NOW.
YOU CAN'T HELP BUT THINK ABOUT HER... WHETHER YOU WANT TO OR NOT.
TO WIN THIS, WE HAVE TO BEAT HER...!
TUES!

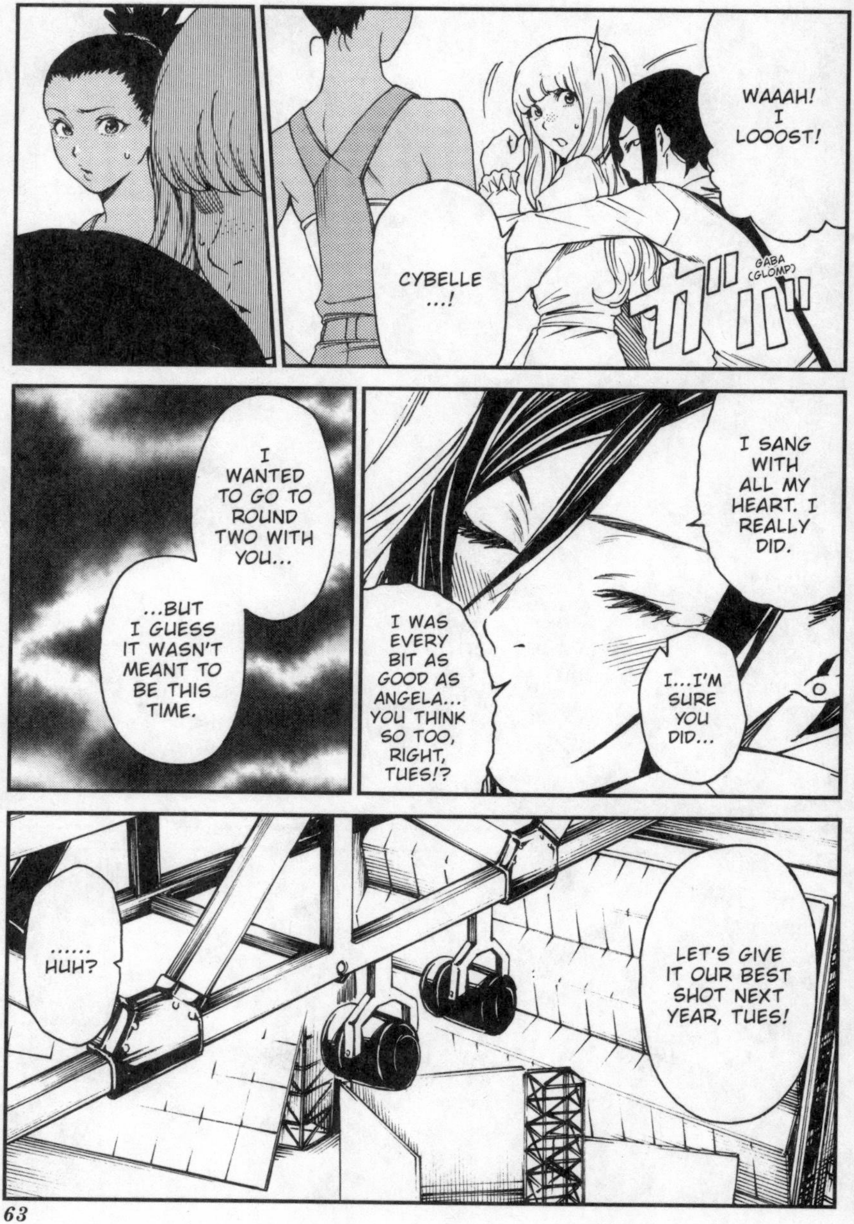
WAAAH! I LOOOST!
GABA (GLOMP)
CYBELLE ...!
I SANG WITH ALL MY HEART. I REALLY DID.
I WAS EVERY BIT AS GOOD AS ANGELA... YOU THINK SO TOO, RIGHT, TUES!?
I...I'M SURE YOU DID...
I WANTED TO GO TO ROUND TWO WITH YOU...
...BUT I GUESS IT WASN'T MEANT TO BE THIS TIME.
LET'S GIVE IT OUR BEST SHOT NEXT YEAR, TUES!
...... HUH?

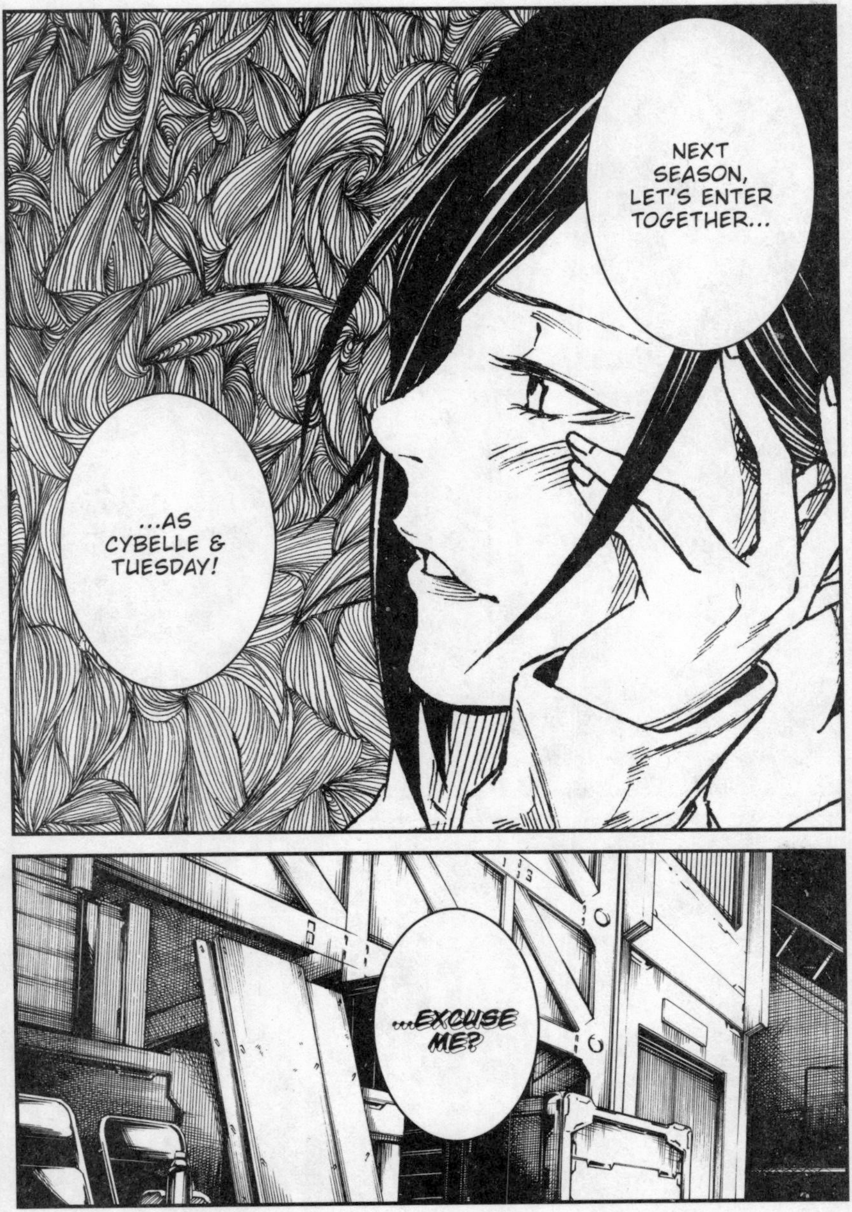
NEXT SEASON, LET'S ENTER TOGETHER...
...AS CYBELLE & TUESDAY!
...EXCUSE ME?

END

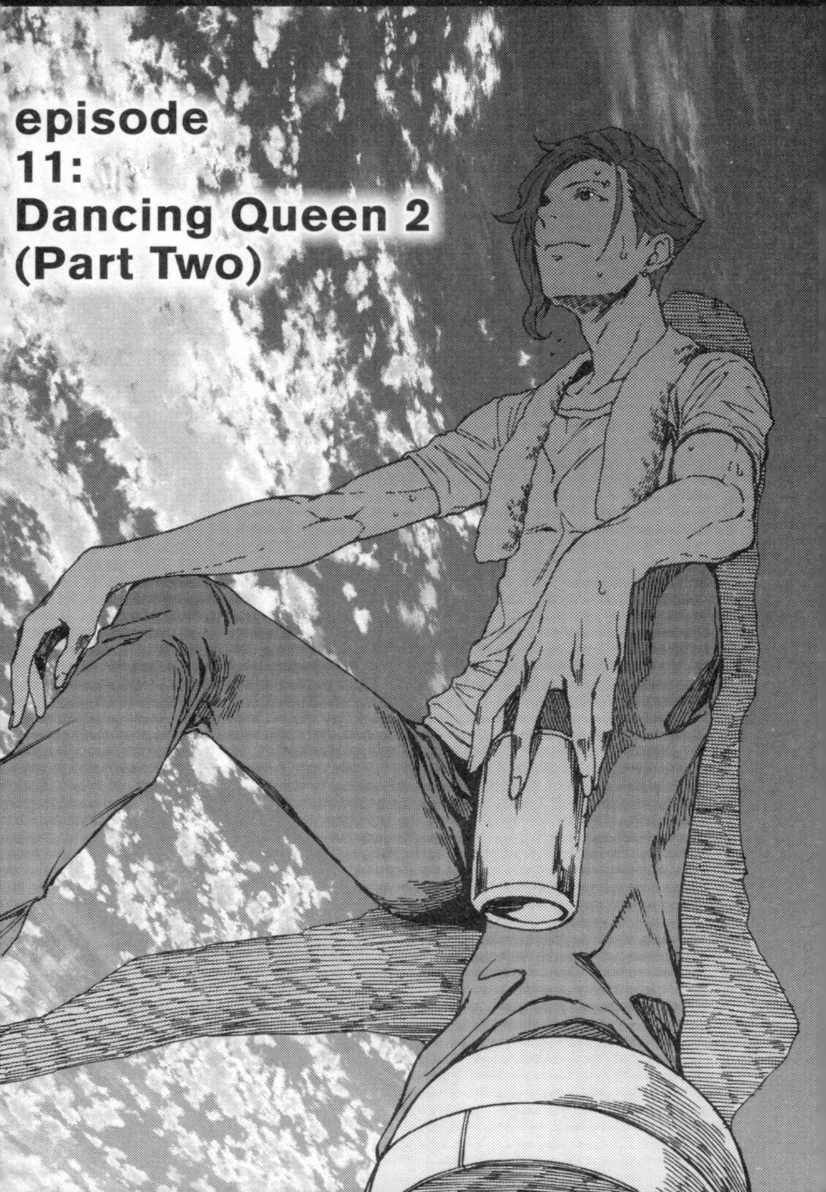
episode
11:
Dancing Queen 2
(Part Two)

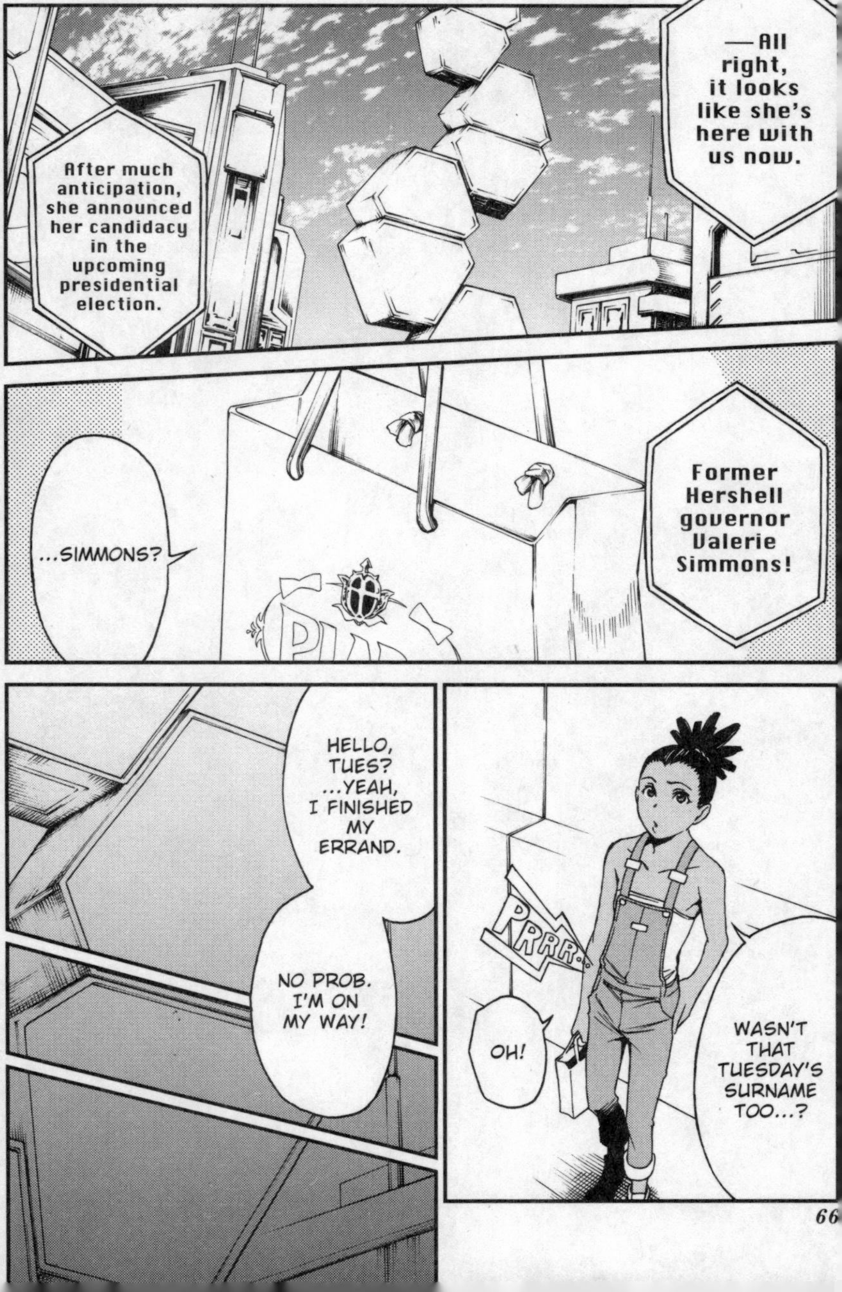
—All right, it looks like she's here with us now.
After much anticipation, she announced her candidacy in the upcoming presidential election.
Former Hershell governor Valerie Simmons!
...SIMMONS?
WASN'T THAT TUESDAY'S SURNAME TOO...?
OH!
PRRR..
HELLO, TUES? ...YEAH, I FINISHED MY ERRAND.
NO PROB. I'M ON MY WAY!

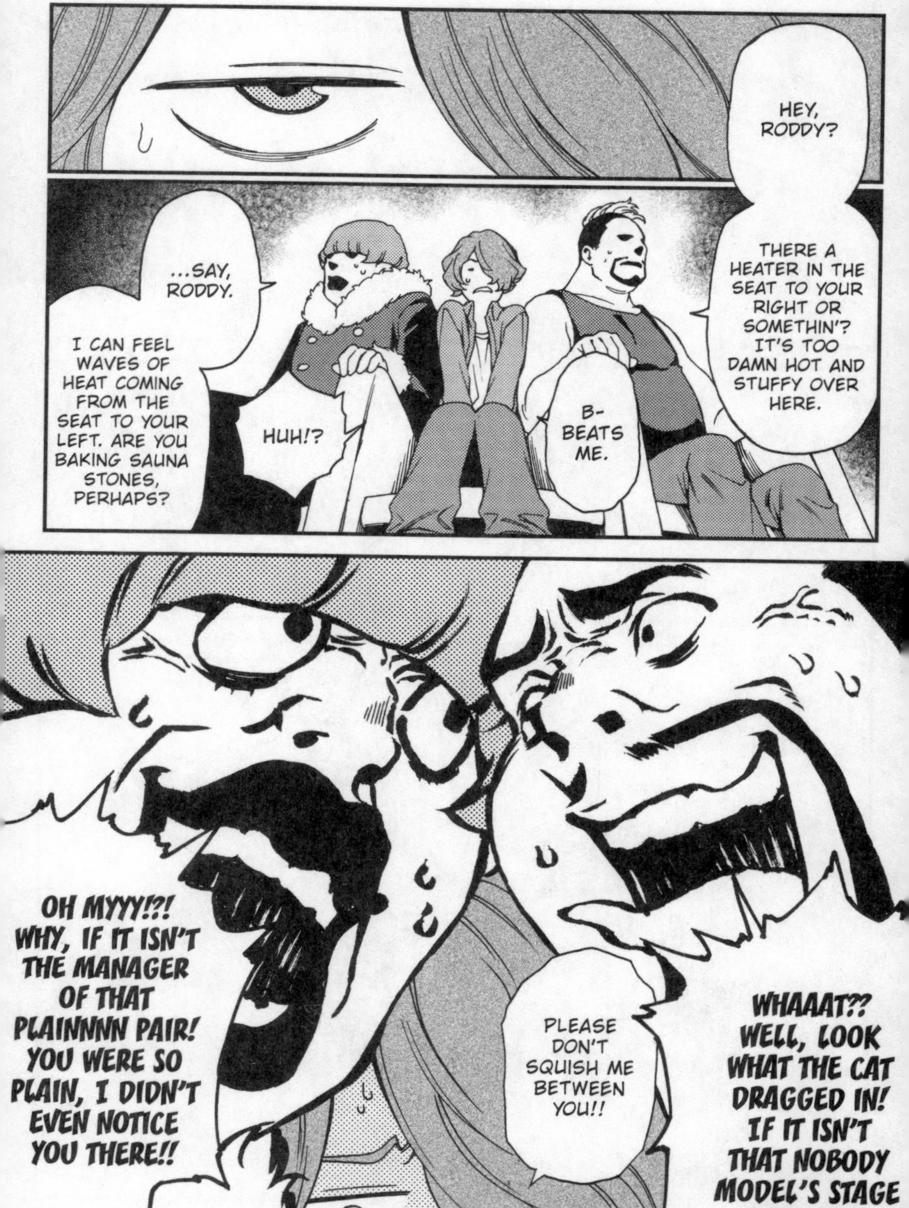
HEY, RODDY?
THERE A HEATER IN THE SEAT TO YOUR RIGHT OR SOMETHIN'? IT'S TOO DAMN HOT AND STUFFY OVER HERE.
B-BEATS ME.
HUH!?
...SAY, RODDY.
I CAN FEEL WAVES OF HEAT COMING FROM THE SEAT TO YOUR LEFT. ARE YOU BAKING SAUNA STONES, PERHAPS?
WHAAAT?? WELL, LOOK WHAT THE CAT DRAGGED IN! IF IT ISN'T THAT NOBODY MODEL'S STAGE MOTHER!
PLEASE DON'T SQUISH ME BETWEEN YOU!!
OH MYYY!?! WHY, IF IT ISN'T THE MANAGER OF THAT PLAINNNN PAIR! YOU WERE SO PLAIN, I DIDN'T EVEN NOTICE YOU THERE!!

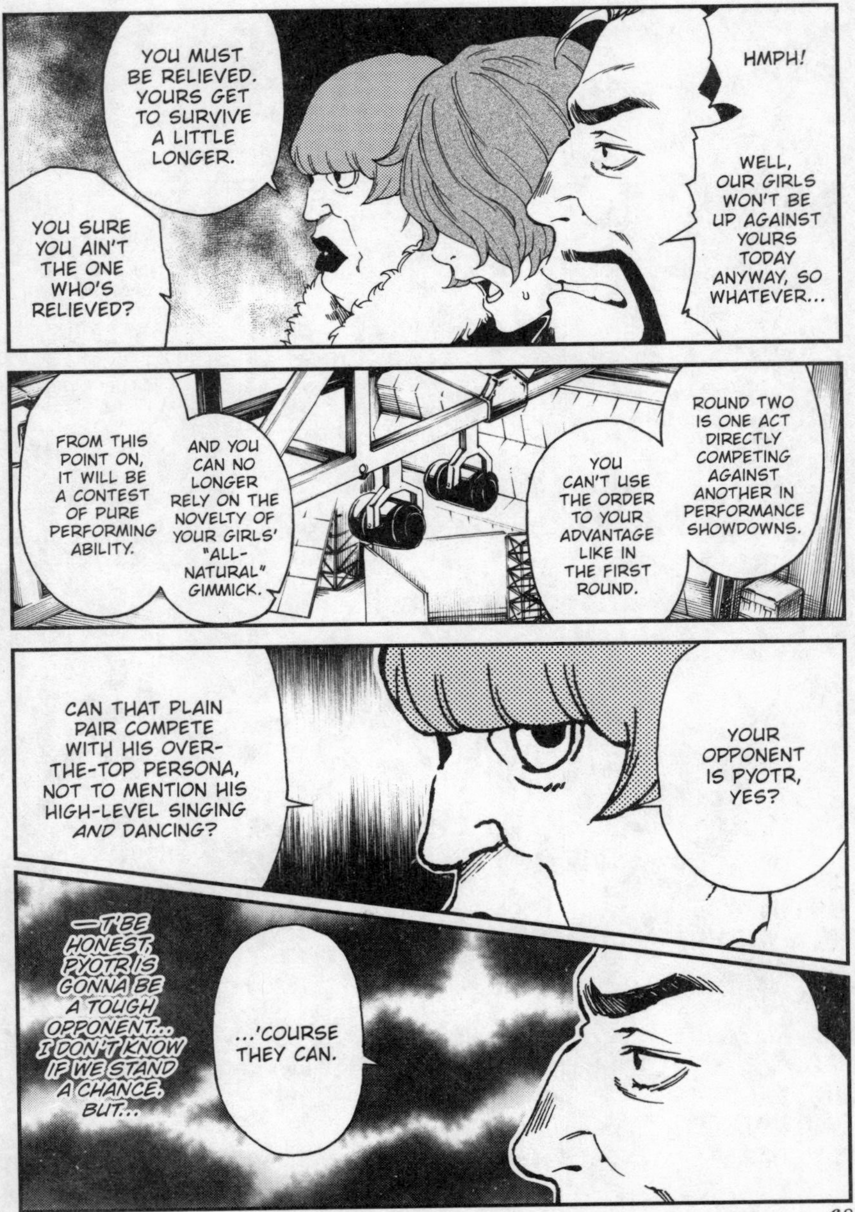
HMPH!
WELL, OUR GIRLS WON'T BE UP AGAINST YOURS TODAY ANYWAY, SO WHATEVER...
YOU MUST BE RELIEVED. YOURS GET TO SURVIVE A LITTLE LONGER.
YOU SURE YOU AIN'T THE ONE WHO'S RELIEVED?
ROUND TWO IS ONE ACT DIRECTLY COMPETING AGAINST ANOTHER IN PERFORMANCE SHOWDOWNS.
YOU CAN'T USE THE ORDER TO YOUR ADVANTAGE LIKE IN THE FIRST ROUND.
AND YOU CAN NO LONGER RELY ON THE NOVELTY OF YOUR GIRLS' "ALL-NATURAL" GIMMICK.
FROM THIS POINT ON, IT WILL BE A CONTEST OF PURE PERFORMING ABILITY.
YOUR OPPONENT IS PYOTR, YES?
CAN THAT PLAIN PAIR COMPETE WITH HIS OVER-THE-TOP PERSONA, NOT TO MENTION HIS HIGH-LEVEL SINGING AND DANCING?
...'COURSE THEY CAN.
—T'BE HONEST, PYOTR IS GONNA BE A TOUGH OPPONENT... I DON'T KNOW IF WE STAND A CHANCE. BUT...

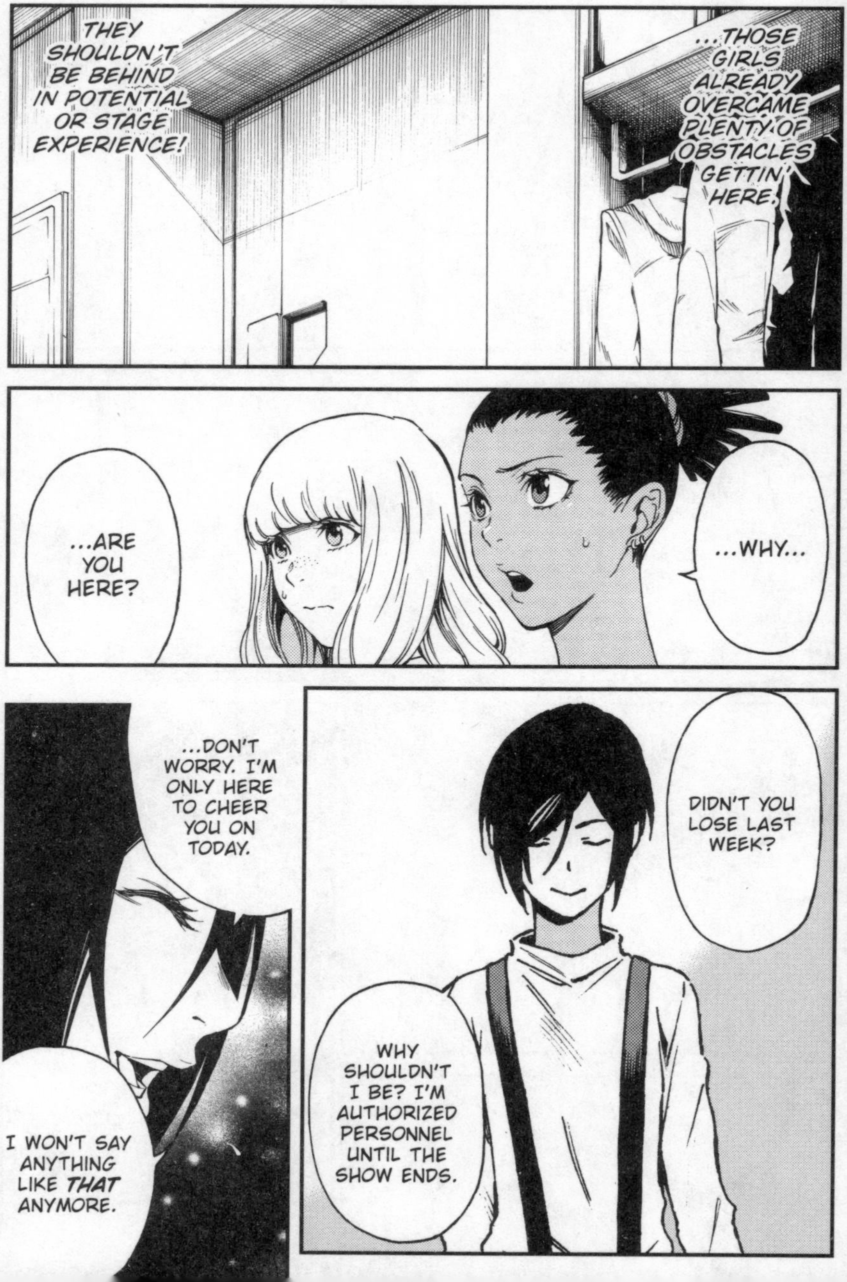
...THOSE GIRLS ALREADY OVERCAME PLENTY OF OBSTACLES GETTIN' HERE.
THEY SHOULDN'T BE BEHIND IN POTENTIAL OR STAGE EXPERIENCE!
...WHY...
...ARE YOU HERE?
DIDN'T YOU LOSE LAST WEEK?
WHY SHOULDN'T I BE? I'M AUTHORIZED PERSONNEL UNTIL THE SHOW ENDS.
...DON'T WORRY. I'M ONLY HERE TO CHEER YOU ON TODAY.
I WON'T SAY ANYTHING LIKE *THAT* ANYMORE.

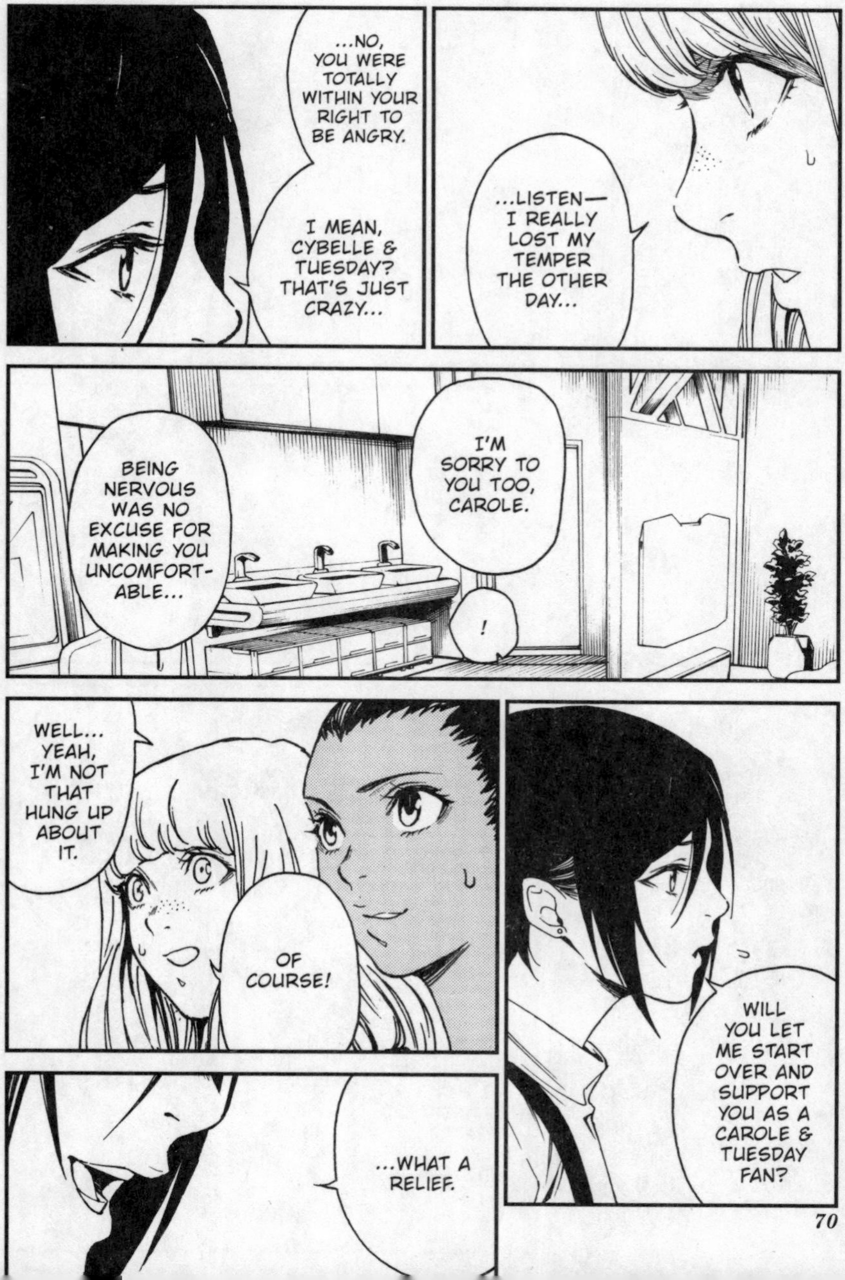
...LISTEN— I REALLY LOST MY TEMPER THE OTHER DAY...
...NO, YOU WERE TOTALLY WITHIN YOUR RIGHT TO BE ANGRY.
I MEAN, CYBELLE & TUESDAY? THAT'S JUST CRAZY...
I'M SORRY TO YOU TOO, CAROLE.
!
BEING NERVOUS WAS NO EXCUSE FOR MAKING YOU UNCOMFORT-ABLE...
WILL YOU LET ME START OVER AND SUPPORT YOU AS A CAROLE & TUESDAY FAN?
OF COURSE!
WELL... YEAH, I'M NOT THAT HUNG UP ABOUT IT.
...WHAT A RELIEF.

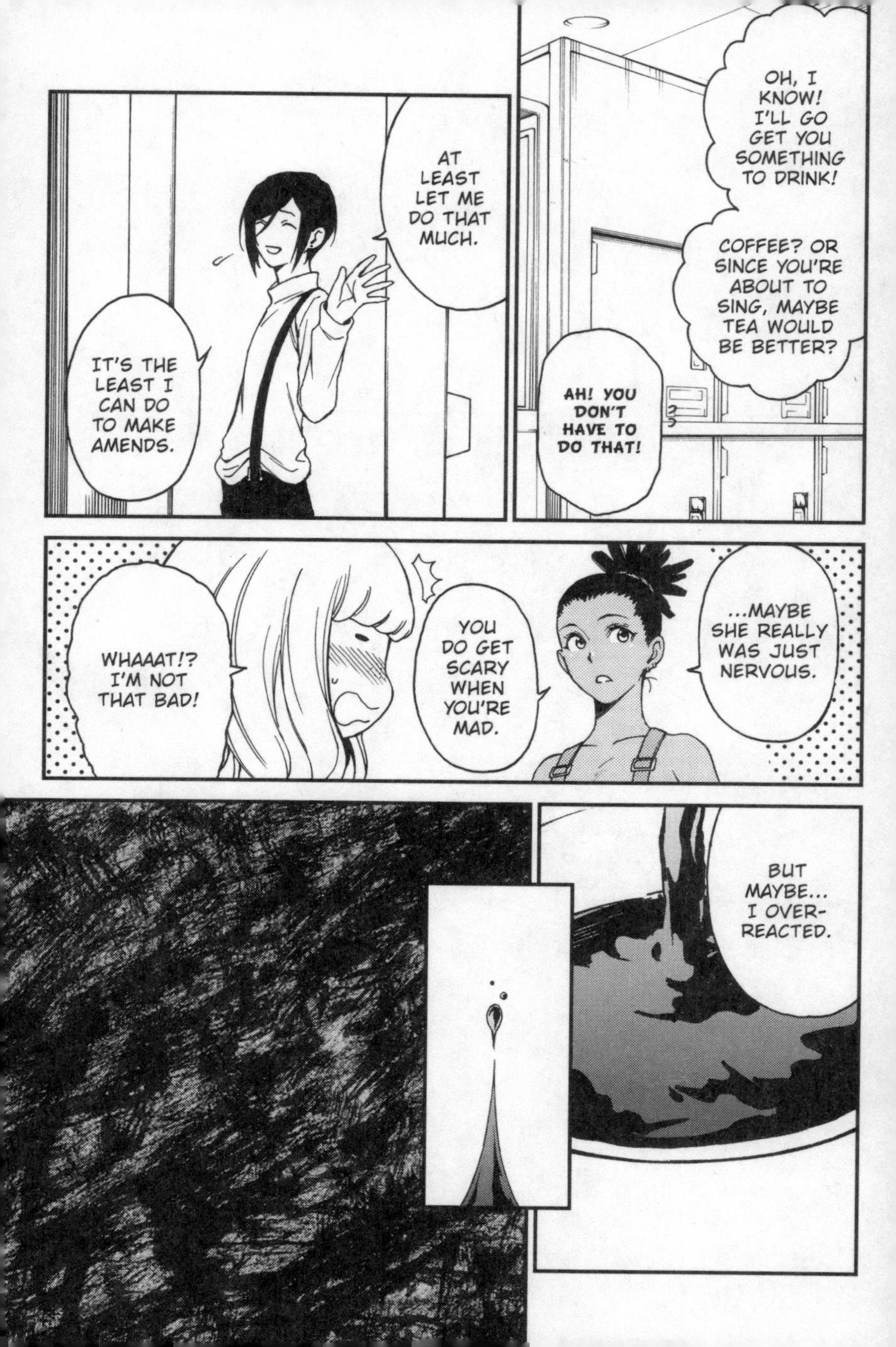
OH, I KNOW! I'LL GO GET YOU SOMETHING TO DRINK!
COFFEE? OR SINCE YOU'RE ABOUT TO SING, MAYBE TEA WOULD BE BETTER?
AH! YOU DON'T HAVE TO DO THAT!
AT LEAST LET ME DO THAT MUCH.
IT'S THE LEAST I CAN DO TO MAKE AMENDS.
...MAYBE SHE REALLY WAS JUST NERVOUS.
YOU DO GET SCARY WHEN YOU'RE MAD.
WHAAAT!? I'M NOT THAT BAD!
BUT MAYBE... I OVER-REACTED.

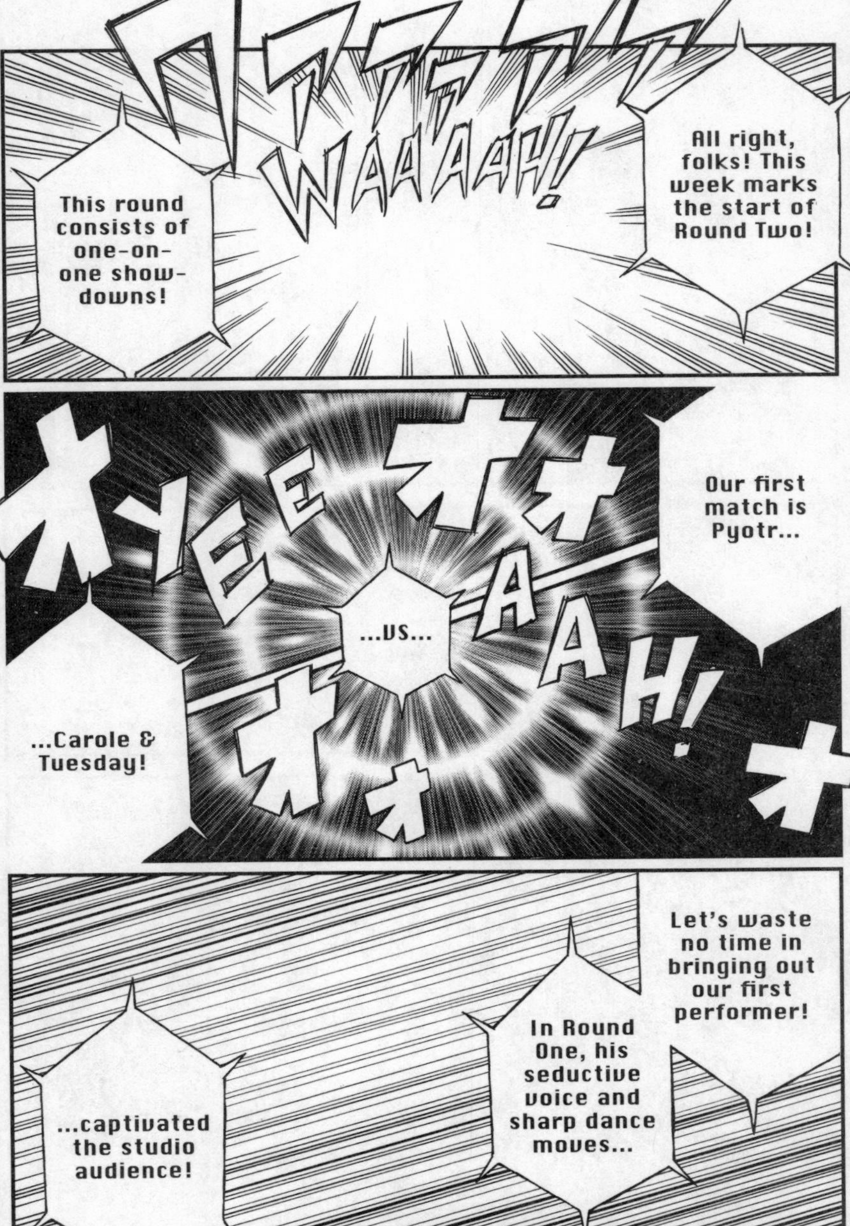
All right, folks! This week marks the start of Round Two!
WAAAAH!
This round consists of one-on-one show-downs!
Our first match is Pyotr...
YEEAAH!
...vs...
...Carole & Tuesday!
Let's waste no time in bringing out our first performer!
In Round One, his seductive voice and sharp dance moves...
...captivated the studio audience!

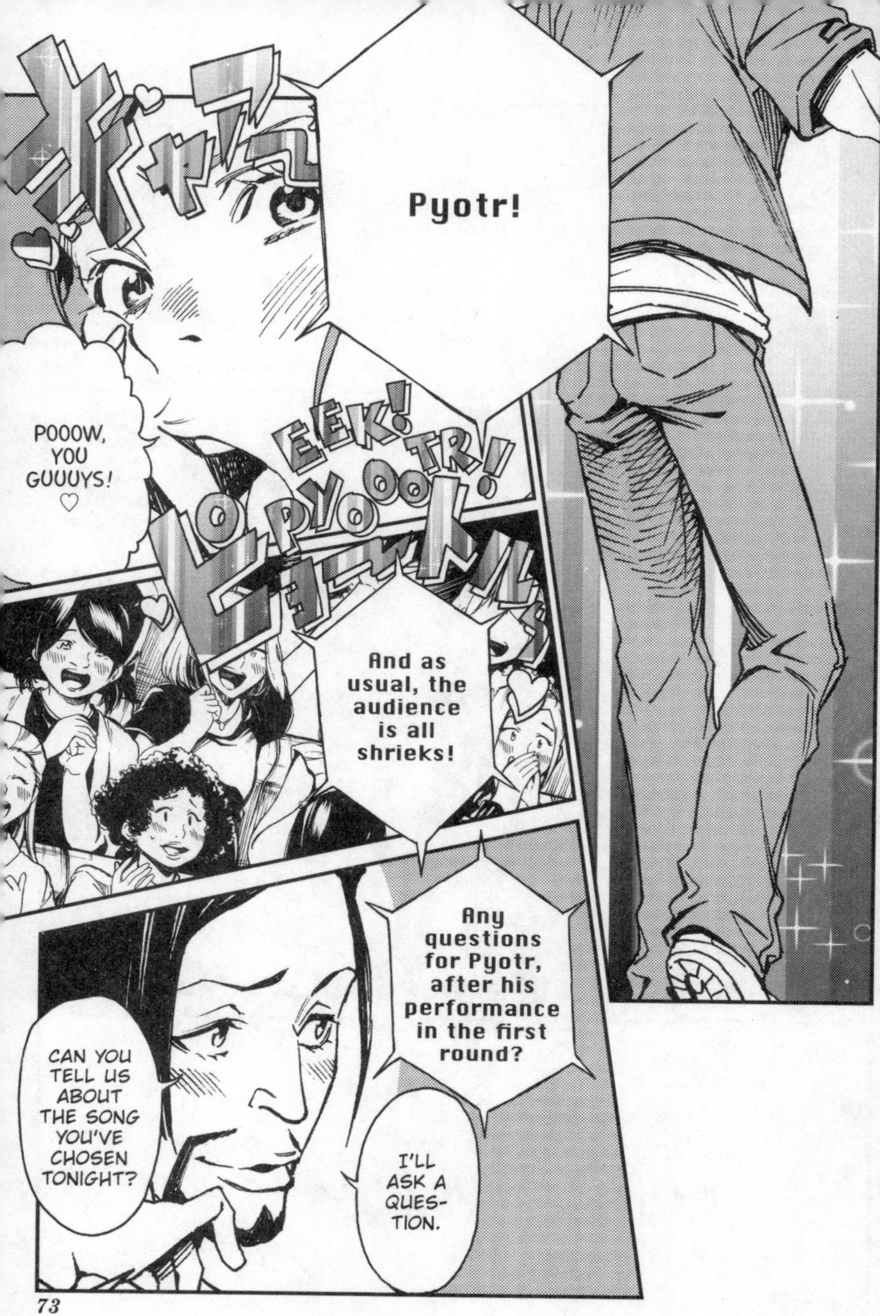
Pyotr!
POOOW, YOU GUUUYS! ♡
EEK! PYOOOTR!
And as usual, the audience is all shrieks!
Any questions for Pyotr, after his performance in the first round?
I'LL ASK A QUES-TION.
CAN YOU TELL US ABOUT THE SONG YOU'VE CHOSEN TONIGHT?

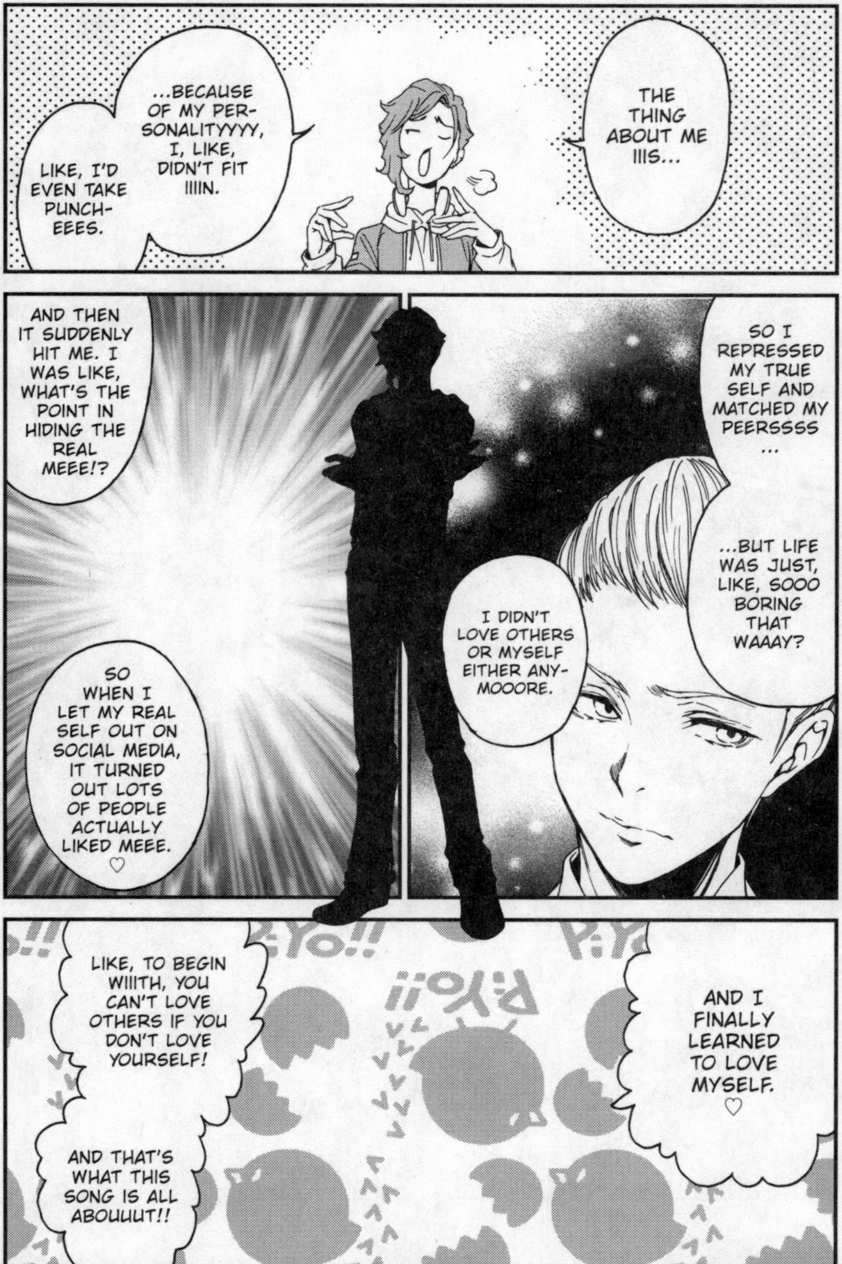
THE THING ABOUT ME IIIS...
...BECAUSE OF MY PER-SONALITYYYY, I, LIKE, DIDN'T FIT IIIIN.
LIKE, I'D EVEN TAKE PUNCH-EEES.
SO I REPRESSED MY TRUE SELF AND MATCHED MY PEERSSSS ...
...BUT LIFE WAS JUST, LIKE, SOOO BORING THAT WAAAY?
I DIDN'T LOVE OTHERS OR MYSELF EITHER ANY-MOOORE.
AND THEN IT SUDDENLY HIT ME. I WAS LIKE, WHAT'S THE POINT IN HIDING THE REAL MEEE!?
SO WHEN I LET MY REAL SELF OUT ON SOCIAL MEDIA, IT TURNED OUT LOTS OF PEOPLE ACTUALLY LIKED MEEE. ♡
AND I FINALLY LEARNED TO LOVE MYSELF. ♡
LIKE, TO BEGIN WIIITH, YOU CAN'T LOVE OTHERS IF YOU DON'T LOVE YOURSELF!
AND THAT'S WHAT THIS SONG IS ALL ABOUUUT!!

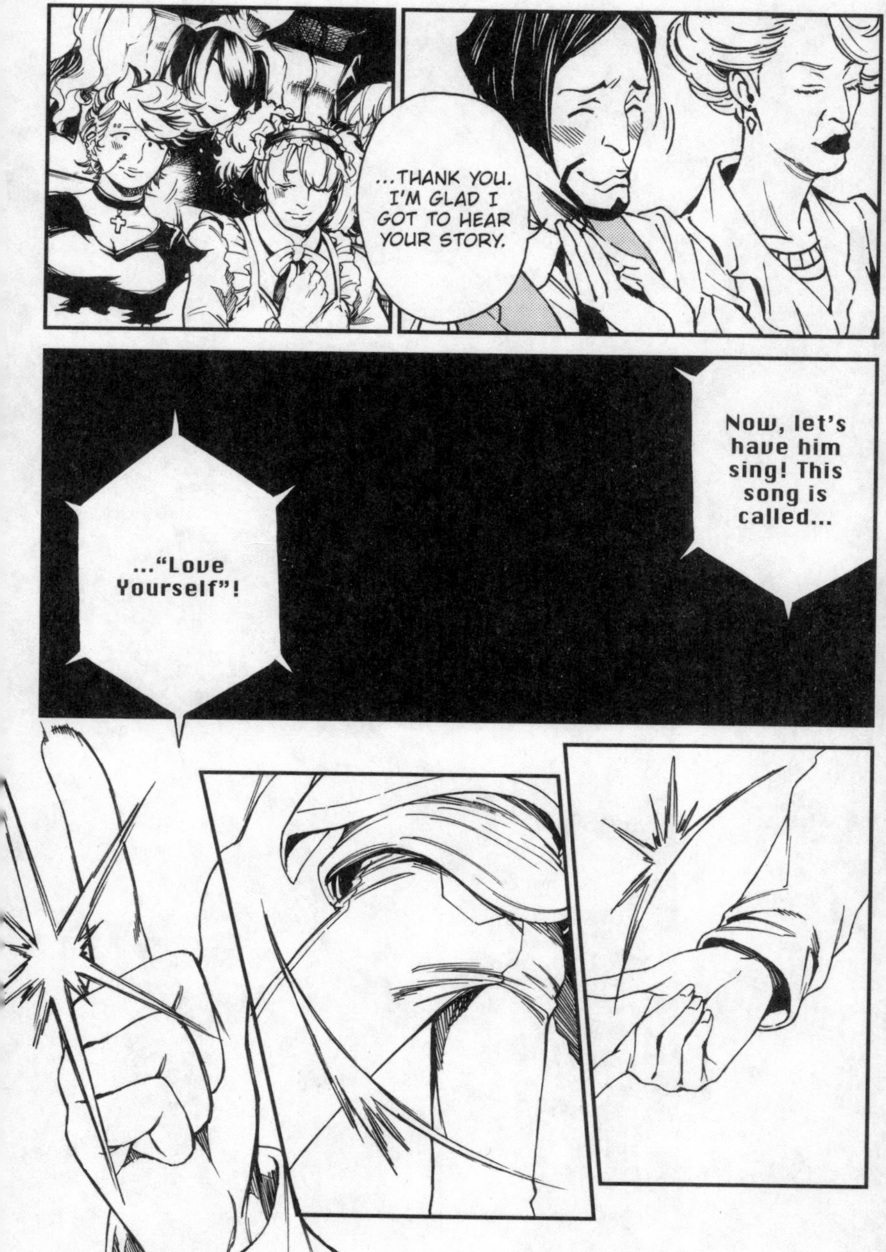
...THANK YOU. I'M GLAD I GOT TO HEAR YOUR STORY.
Now, let's have him sing! This song is called...
..."Love Yourself"!

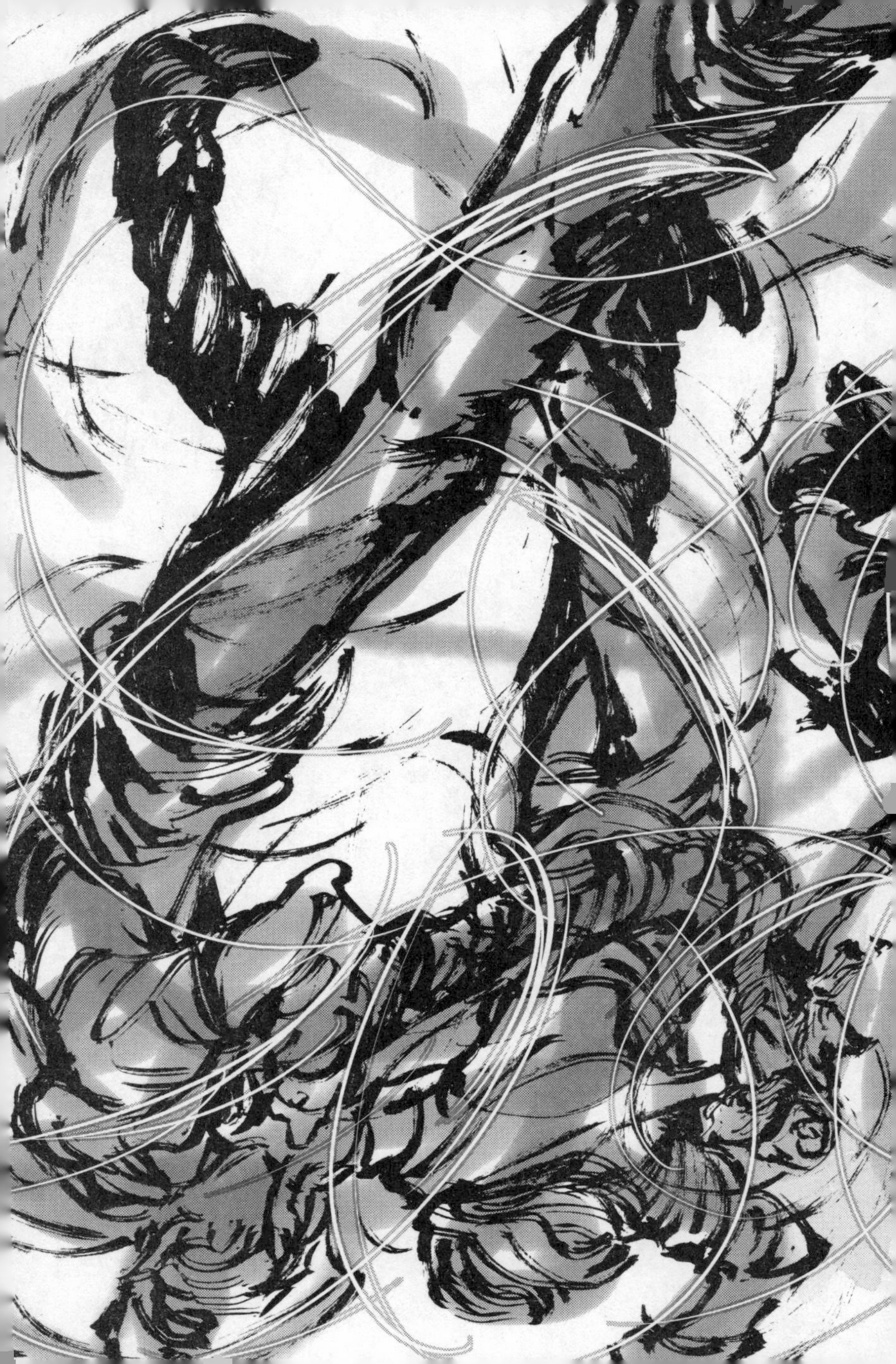

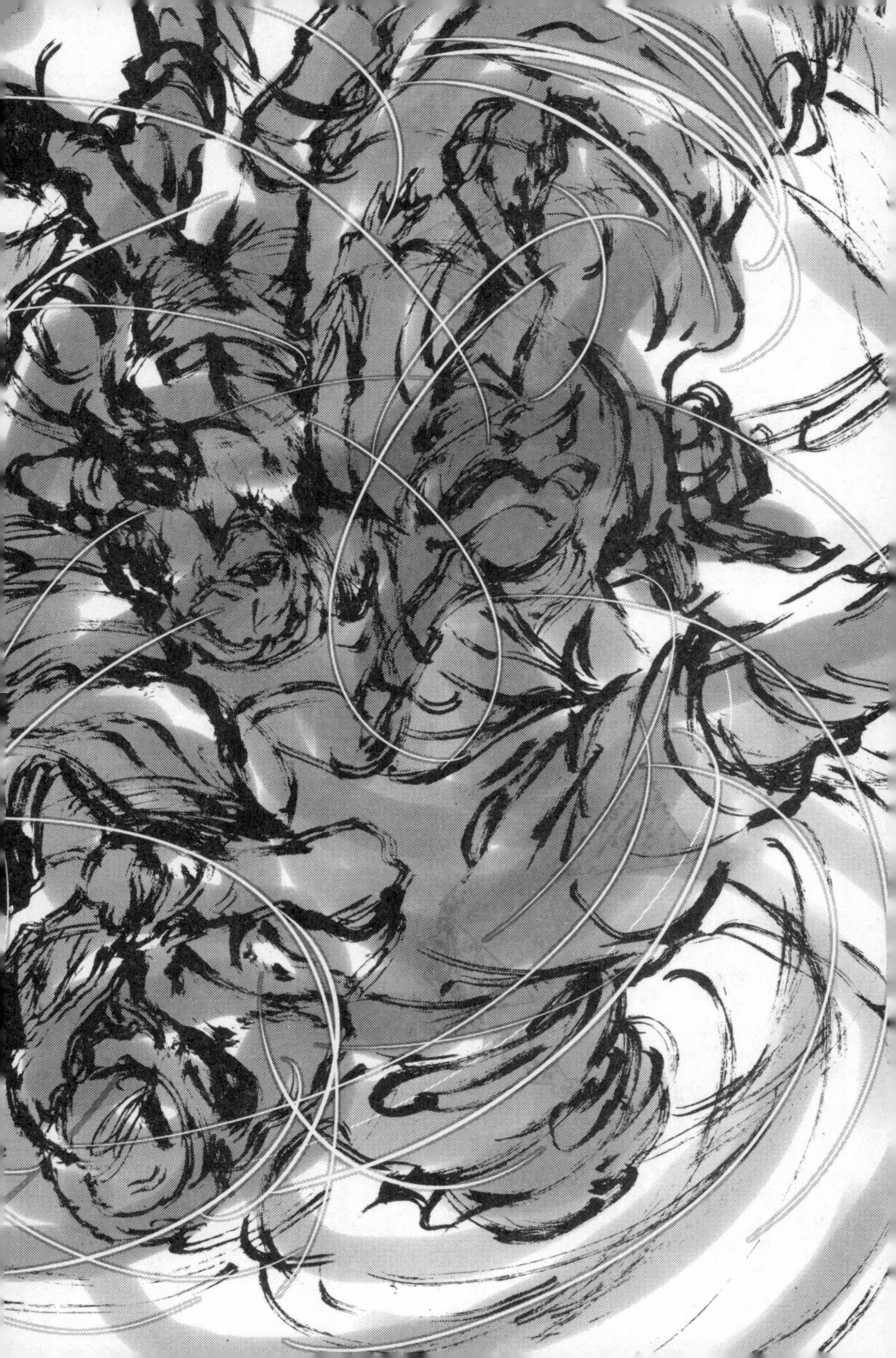

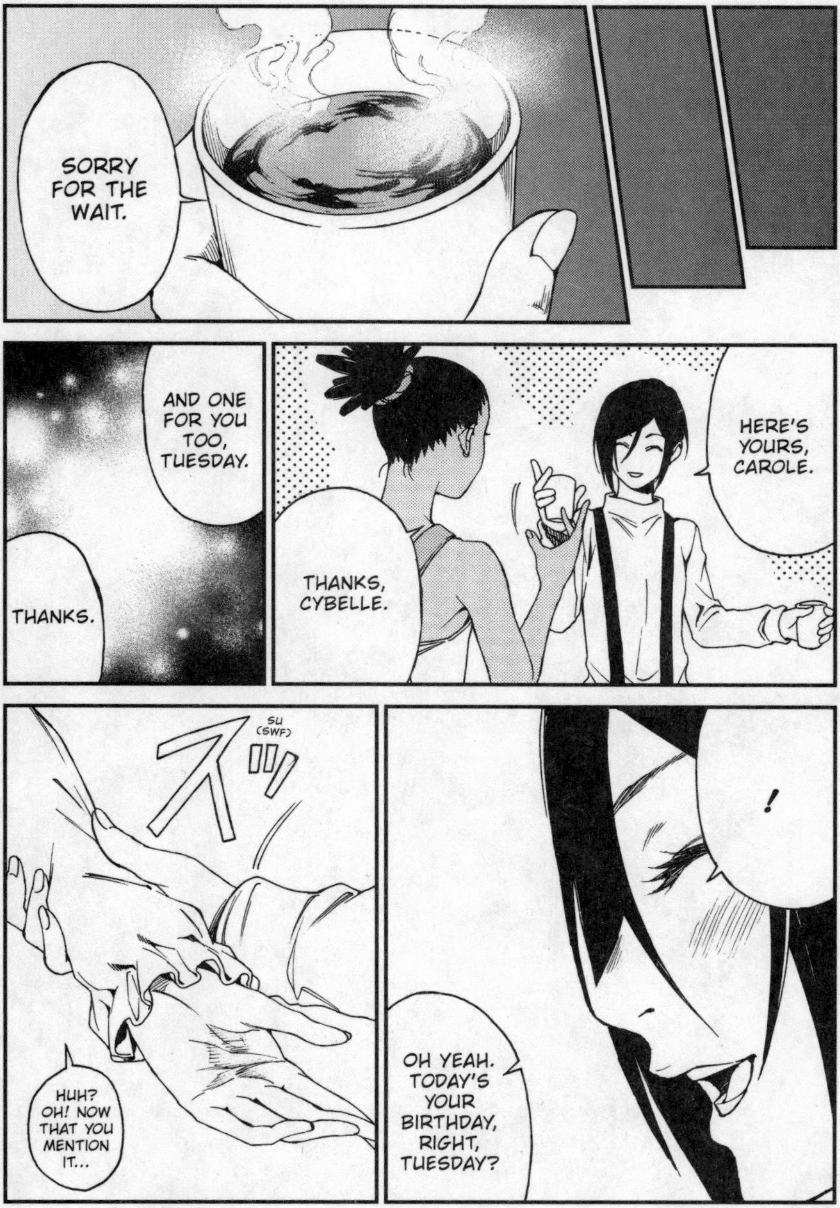
SORRY FOR THE WAIT.
HERE'S YOURS, CAROLE.
THANKS, CYBELLE.
AND ONE FOR YOU TOO, TUESDAY.
THANKS.
!
OH YEAH. TODAY'S YOUR BIRTHDAY, RIGHT, TUESDAY?
SU (SWF)
HUH? OH! NOW THAT YOU MENTION IT...

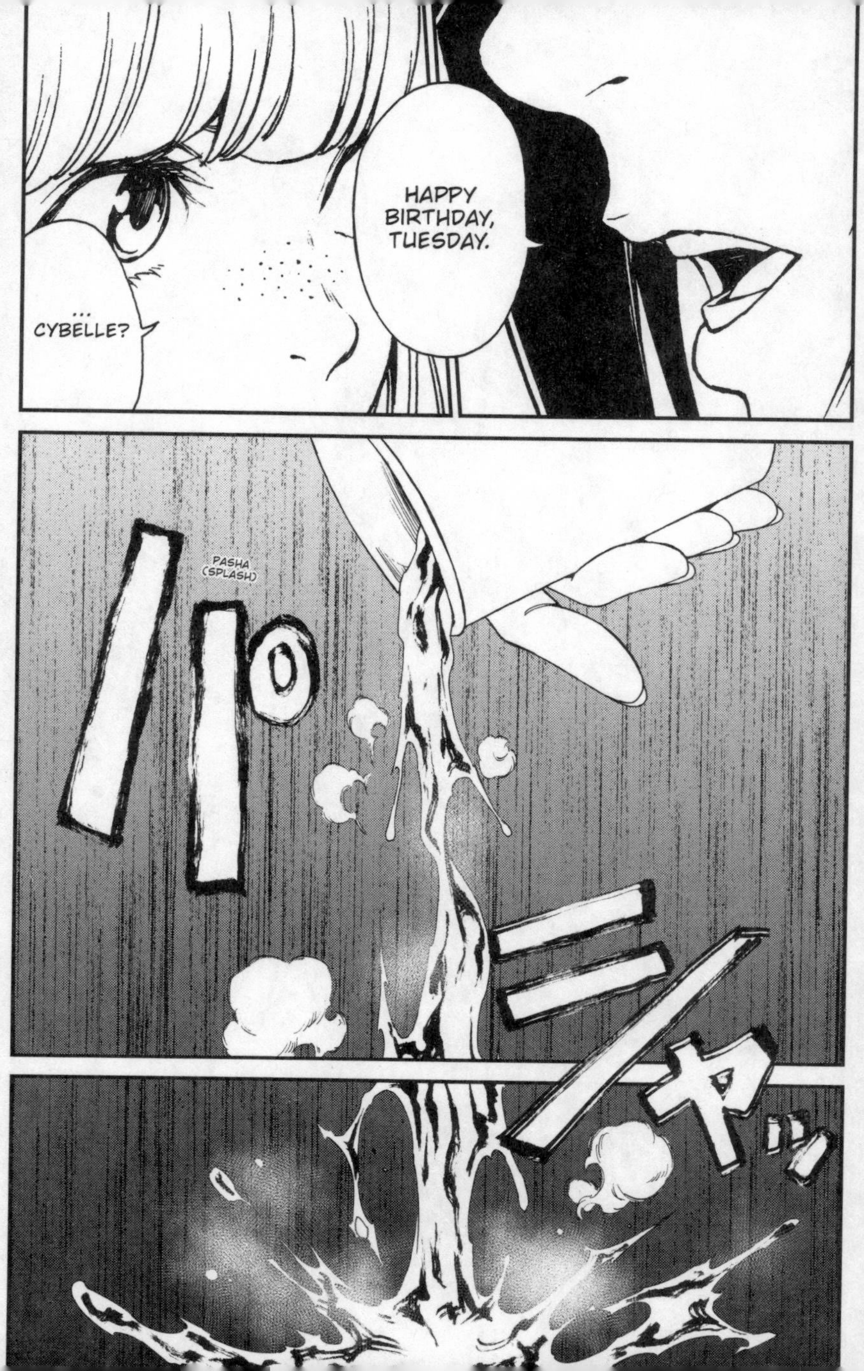
HAPPY BIRTHDAY, TUESDAY.
... CYBELLE?
PASHA (SPLASH)

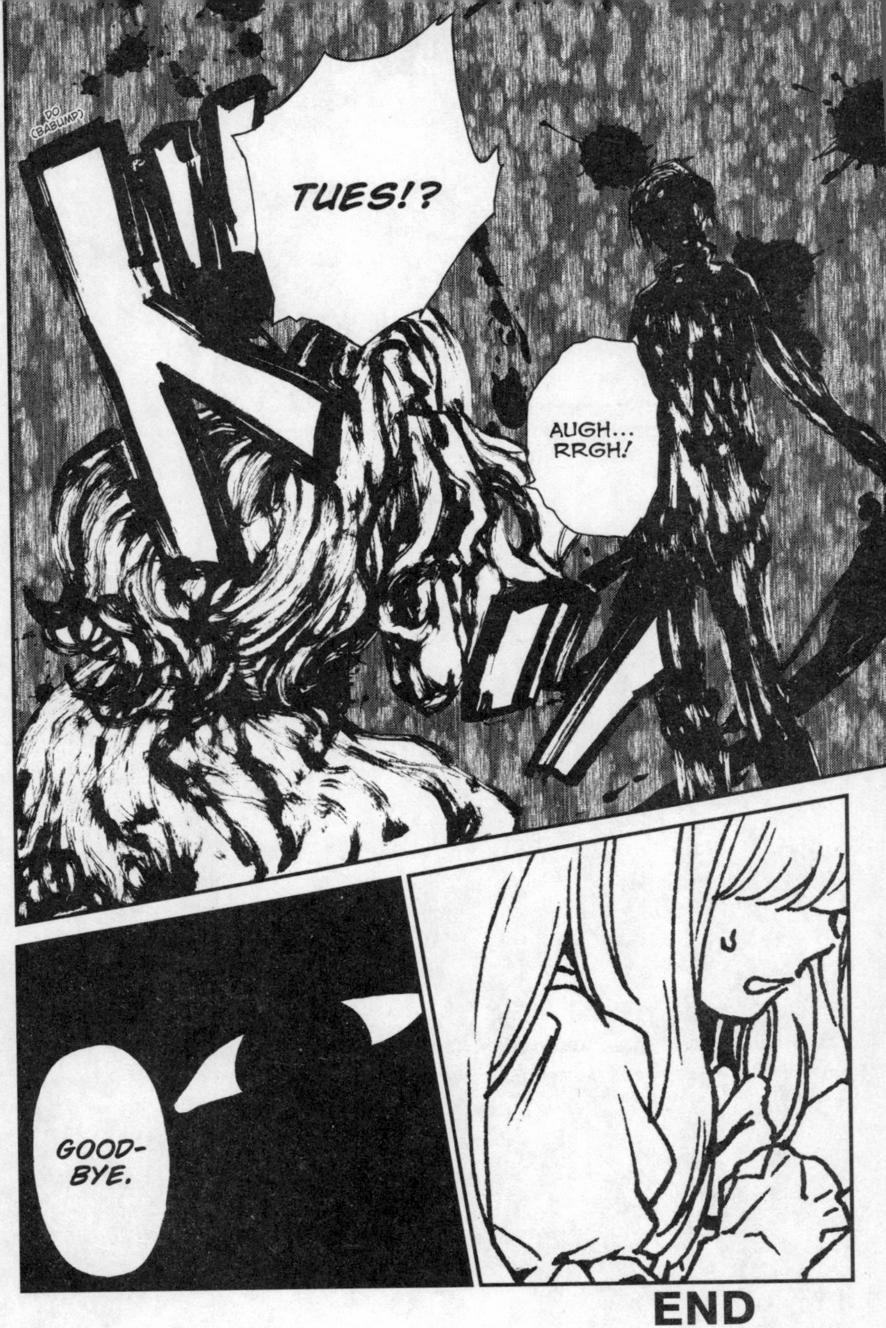
TUES!?
DO (BABUMP)
AUGH... RRGH!
GOOD-BYE.

END

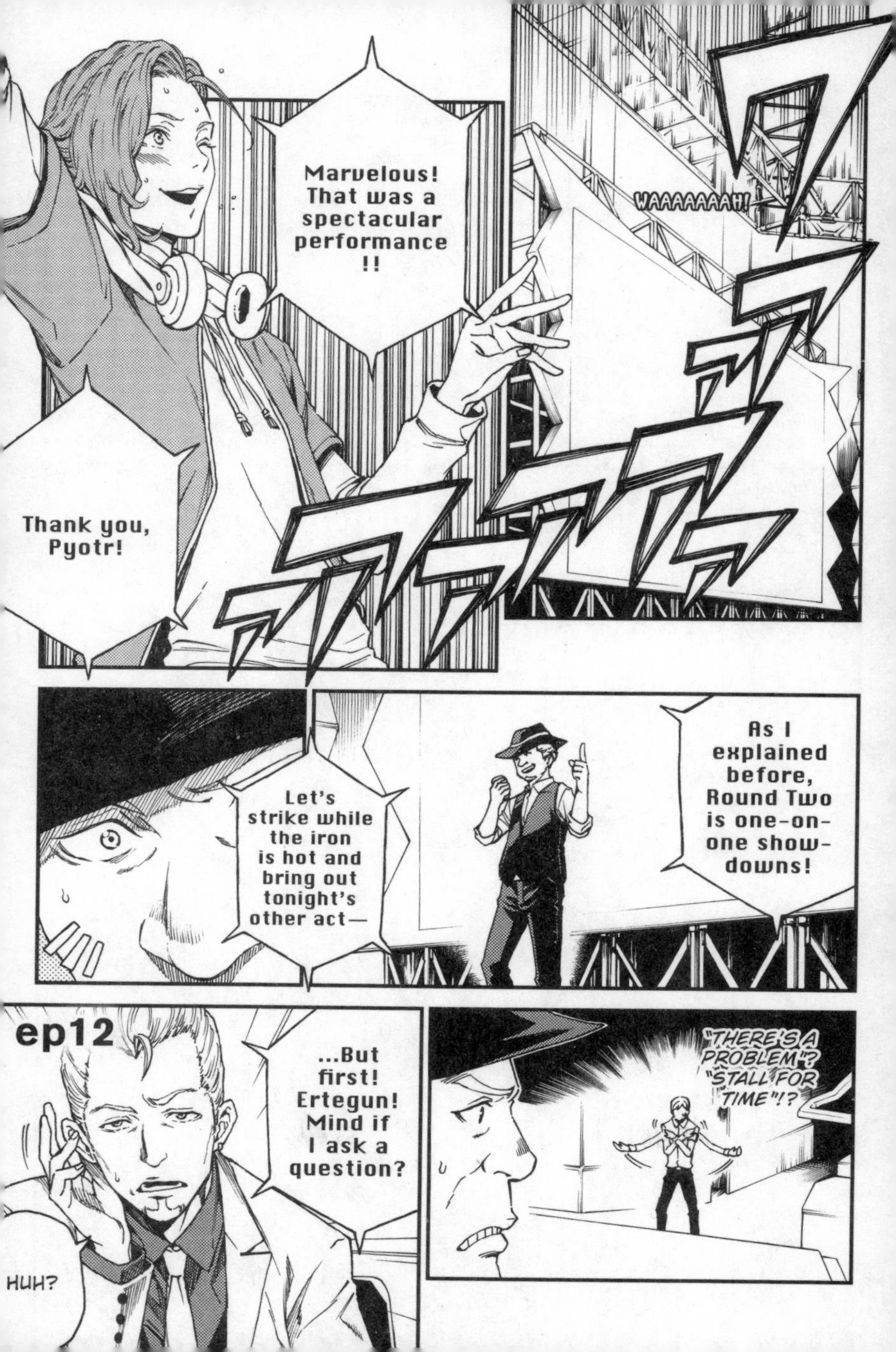
WAAAAAAAH!
Marvelous! That was a spectacular performance !!
Thank you, Pyotr!
As I explained before, Round Two is one-on-one show-downs!
Let's strike while the iron is hot and bring out tonight's other act—
"THERE'S A PROBLEM"? "STALL FOR TIME"!?
ep12
...But first! Ertegun! Mind if I ask a question?
HUH?

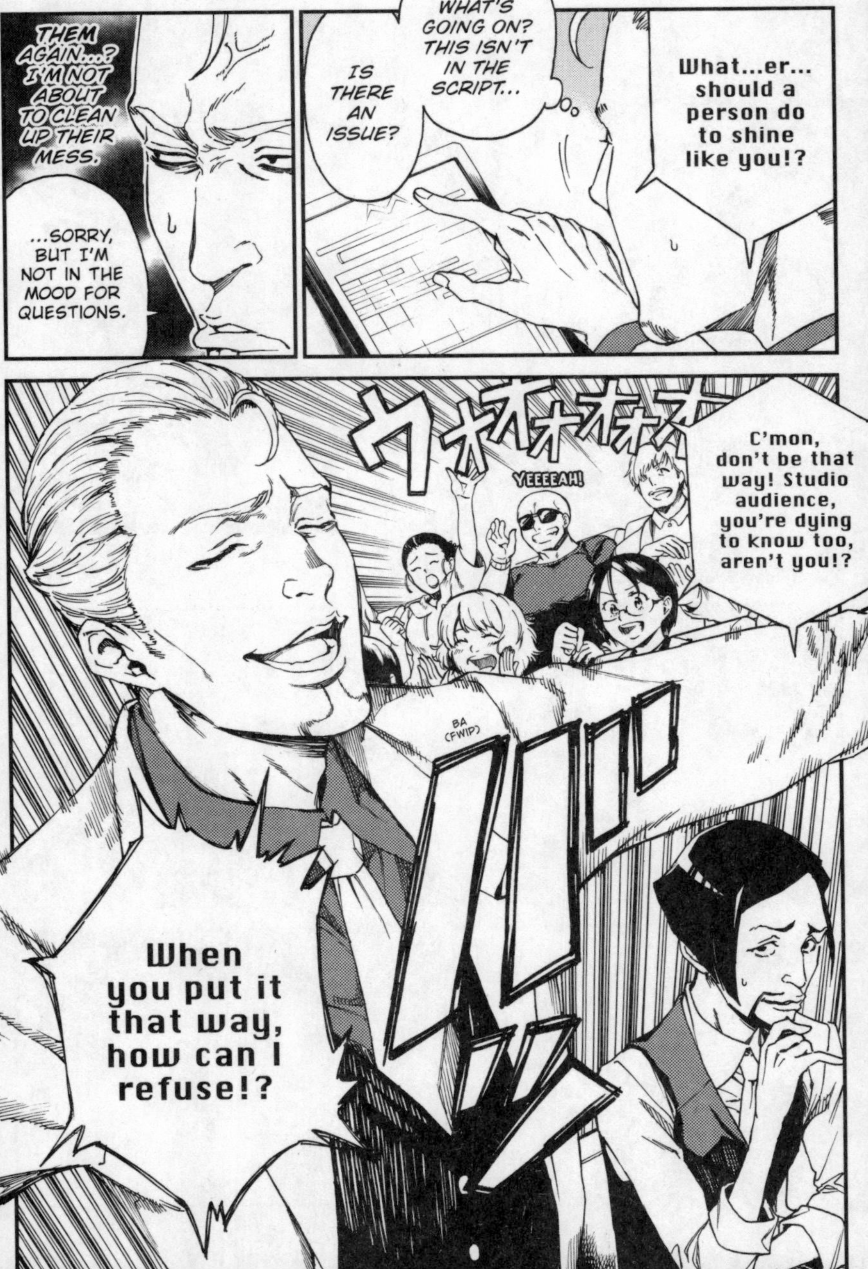
What...er... should a person do to shine like you!?
WHAT'S GOING ON? THIS ISN'T IN THE SCRIPT...
IS THERE AN ISSUE?
THEM AGAIN...? I'M NOT ABOUT TO CLEAN UP THEIR MESS.
...SORRY, BUT I'M NOT IN THE MOOD FOR QUESTIONS.
C'mon, don't be that way! Studio audience, you're dying to know too, aren't you!?
YEEEEAH!
BA (FWIP)
When you put it that way, how can I refuse!?

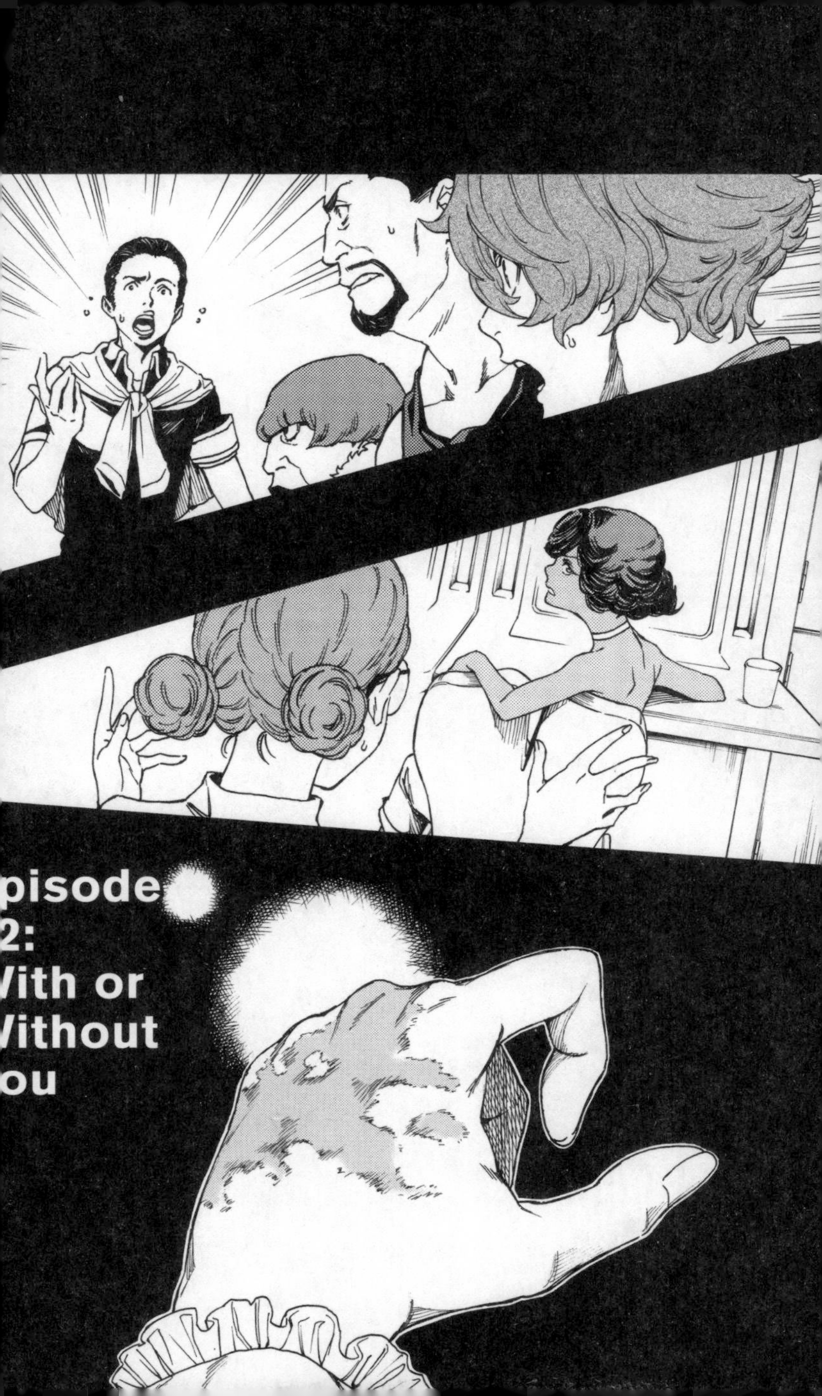
pisode
2:
/ith or
/ithout
ou

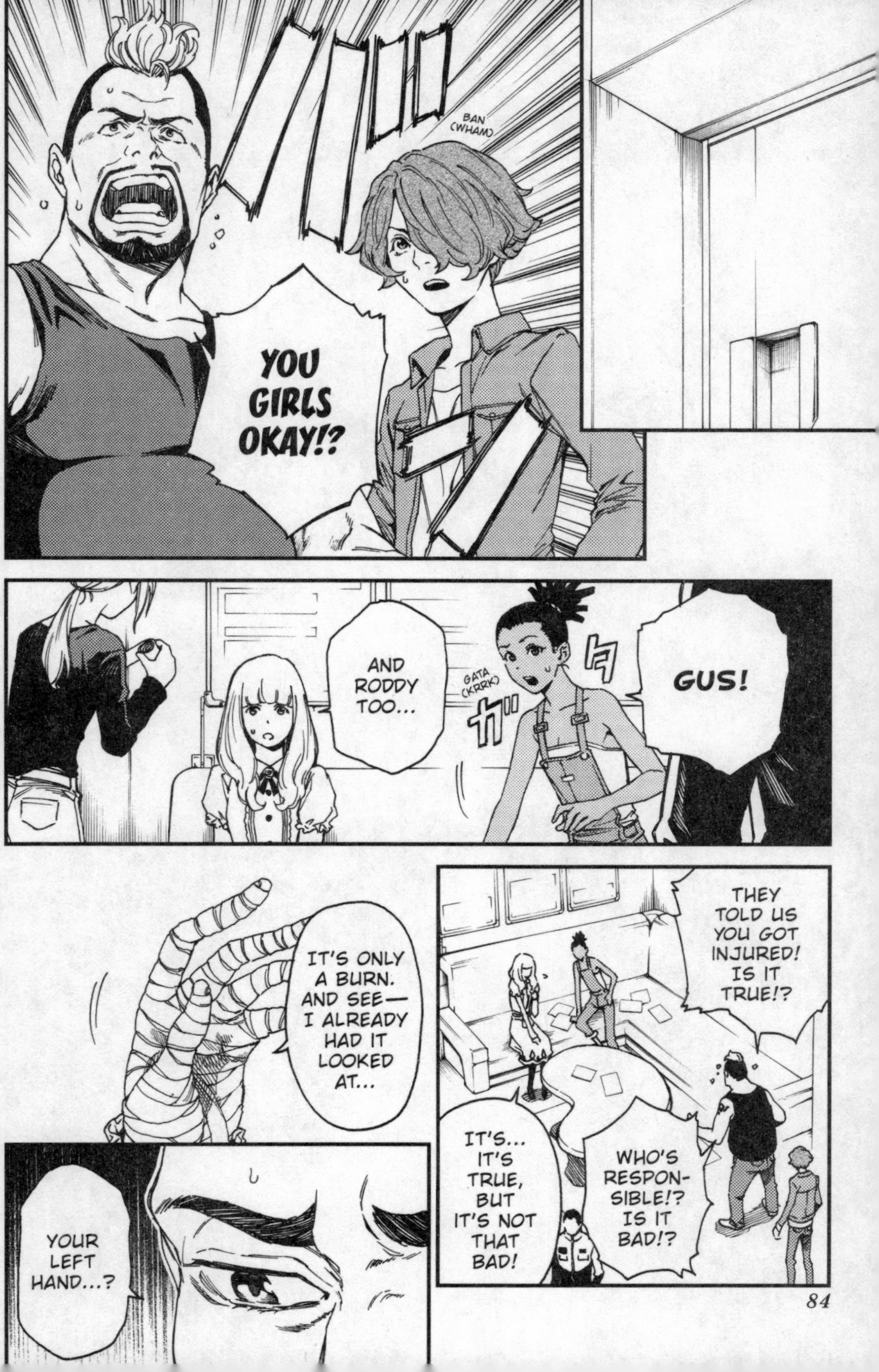
BAN (WHAM)
YOU GIRLS OKAY!?
GUS!
GATA (KRRK)
AND RODDY TOO...
THEY TOLD US YOU GOT INJURED! IS IT TRUE!?
WHO'S RESPON-SIBLE!? IS IT BAD!?
IT'S... IT'S TRUE, BUT IT'S NOT THAT BAD!
IT'S ONLY A BURN. AND SEE—I ALREADY HAD IT LOOKED AT...
YOUR LEFT HAND...?

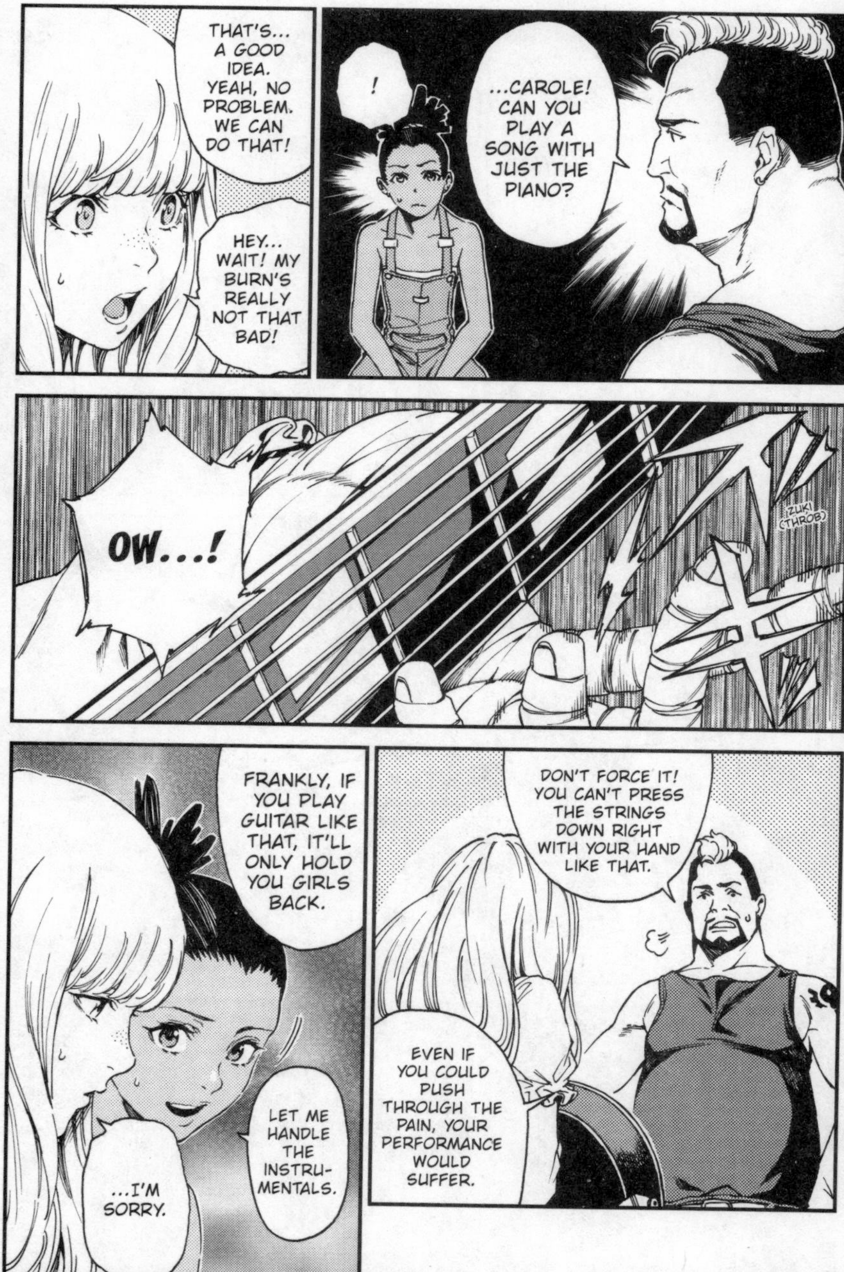
...CAROLE! CAN YOU PLAY A SONG WITH JUST THE PIANO?
!
THAT'S... A GOOD IDEA. YEAH, NO PROBLEM. WE CAN DO THAT!
HEY... WAIT! MY BURN'S REALLY NOT THAT BAD!
ZUKI (THROB)
OW...!
DON'T FORCE IT! YOU CAN'T PRESS THE STRINGS DOWN RIGHT WITH YOUR HAND LIKE THAT.
EVEN IF YOU COULD PUSH THROUGH THE PAIN, YOUR PERFORMANCE WOULD SUFFER.
FRANKLY, IF YOU PLAY GUITAR LIKE THAT, IT'LL ONLY HOLD YOU GIRLS BACK.
LET ME HANDLE THE INSTRU-MENTALS.
...I'M SORRY.

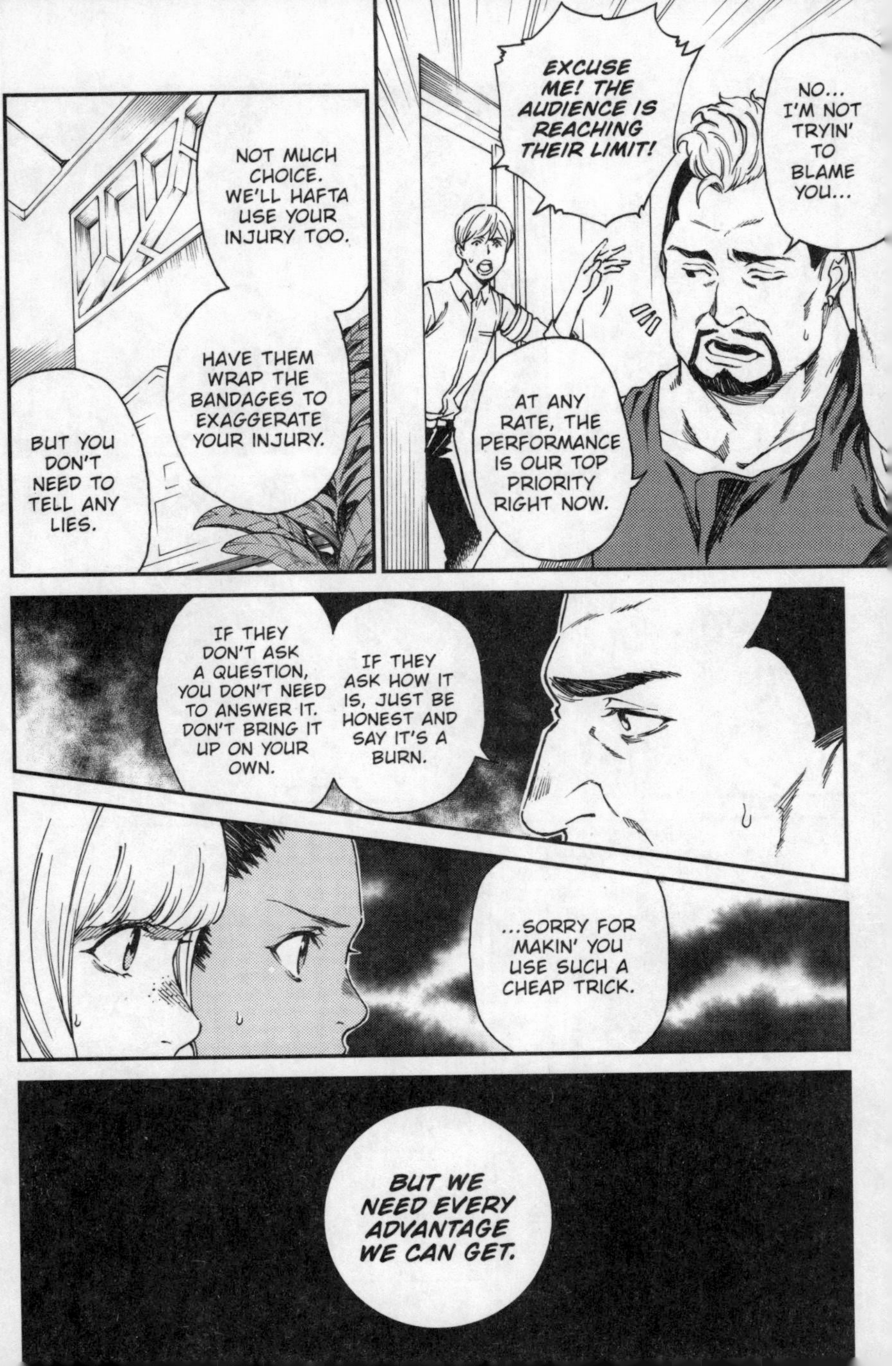
NO… I'M NOT TRYIN' TO BLAME YOU…
EXCUSE ME! THE AUDIENCE IS REACHING THEIR LIMIT!
AT ANY RATE, THE PERFORMANCE IS OUR TOP PRIORITY RIGHT NOW.
NOT MUCH CHOICE. WE'LL HAFTA USE YOUR INJURY TOO.
HAVE THEM WRAP THE BANDAGES TO EXAGGERATE YOUR INJURY.
BUT YOU DON'T NEED TO TELL ANY LIES.
IF THEY ASK HOW IT IS, JUST BE HONEST AND SAY IT'S A BURN.
IF THEY DON'T ASK A QUESTION, YOU DON'T NEED TO ANSWER IT. DON'T BRING IT UP ON YOUR OWN.
…SORRY FOR MAKIN' YOU USE SUCH A CHEAP TRICK.
BUT WE NEED EVERY ADVANTAGE WE CAN GET.

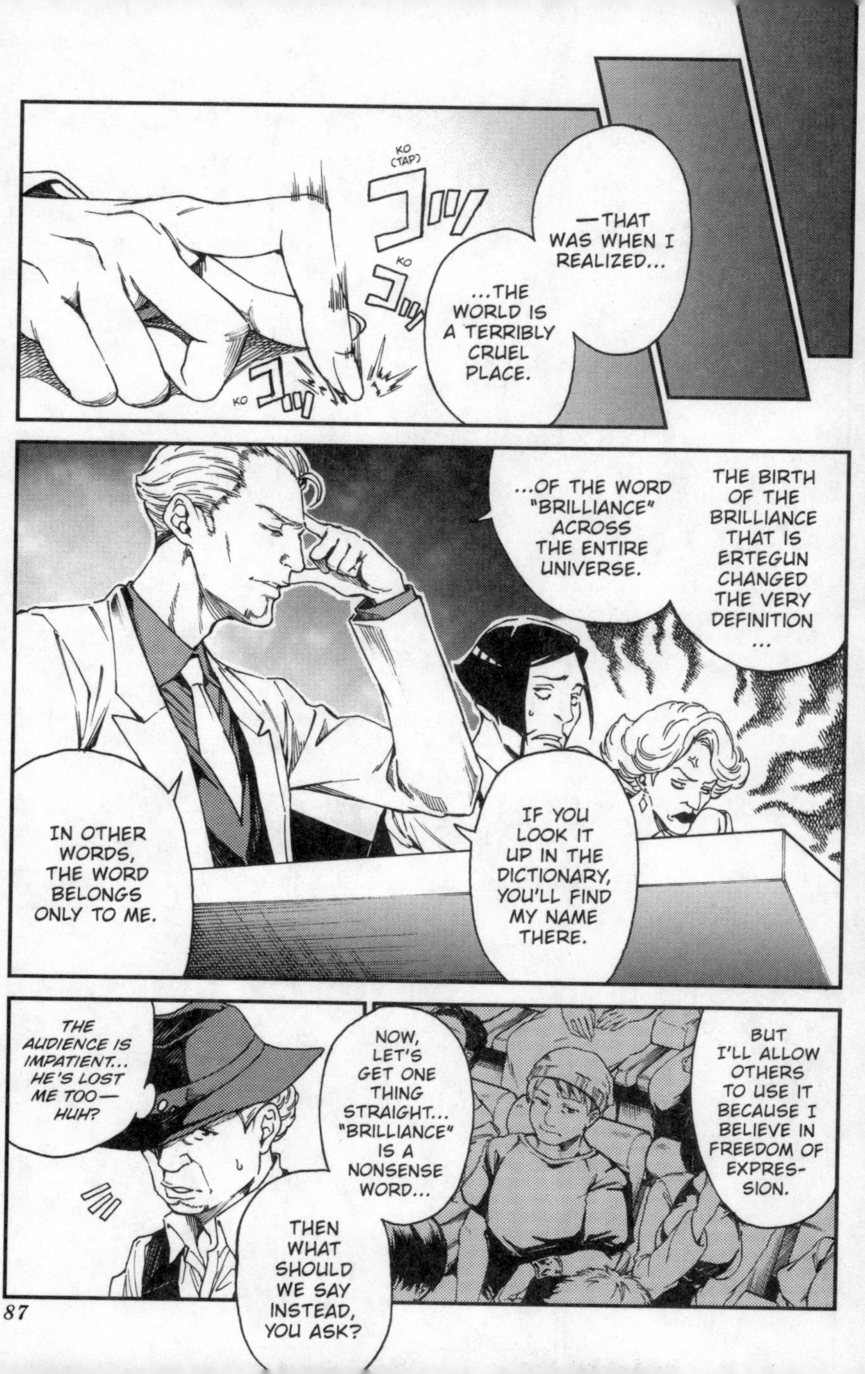
—THAT WAS WHEN I REALIZED...
...THE WORLD IS A TERRIBLY CRUEL PLACE.
KO (TAP)
KO
KO
THE BIRTH OF THE BRILLIANCE THAT IS ERTEGUN CHANGED THE VERY DEFINITION ...
...OF THE WORD "BRILLIANCE" ACROSS THE ENTIRE UNIVERSE.
IF YOU LOOK IT UP IN THE DICTIONARY, YOU'LL FIND MY NAME THERE.
IN OTHER WORDS, THE WORD BELONGS ONLY TO ME.
BUT I'LL ALLOW OTHERS TO USE IT BECAUSE I BELIEVE IN FREEDOM OF EXPRES-SION.
NOW, LET'S GET ONE THING STRAIGHT... "BRILLIANCE" IS A NONSENSE WORD...
THEN WHAT SHOULD WE SAY INSTEAD, YOU ASK?
THE AUDIENCE IS IMPATIENT... HE'S LOST ME TOO—HUH?

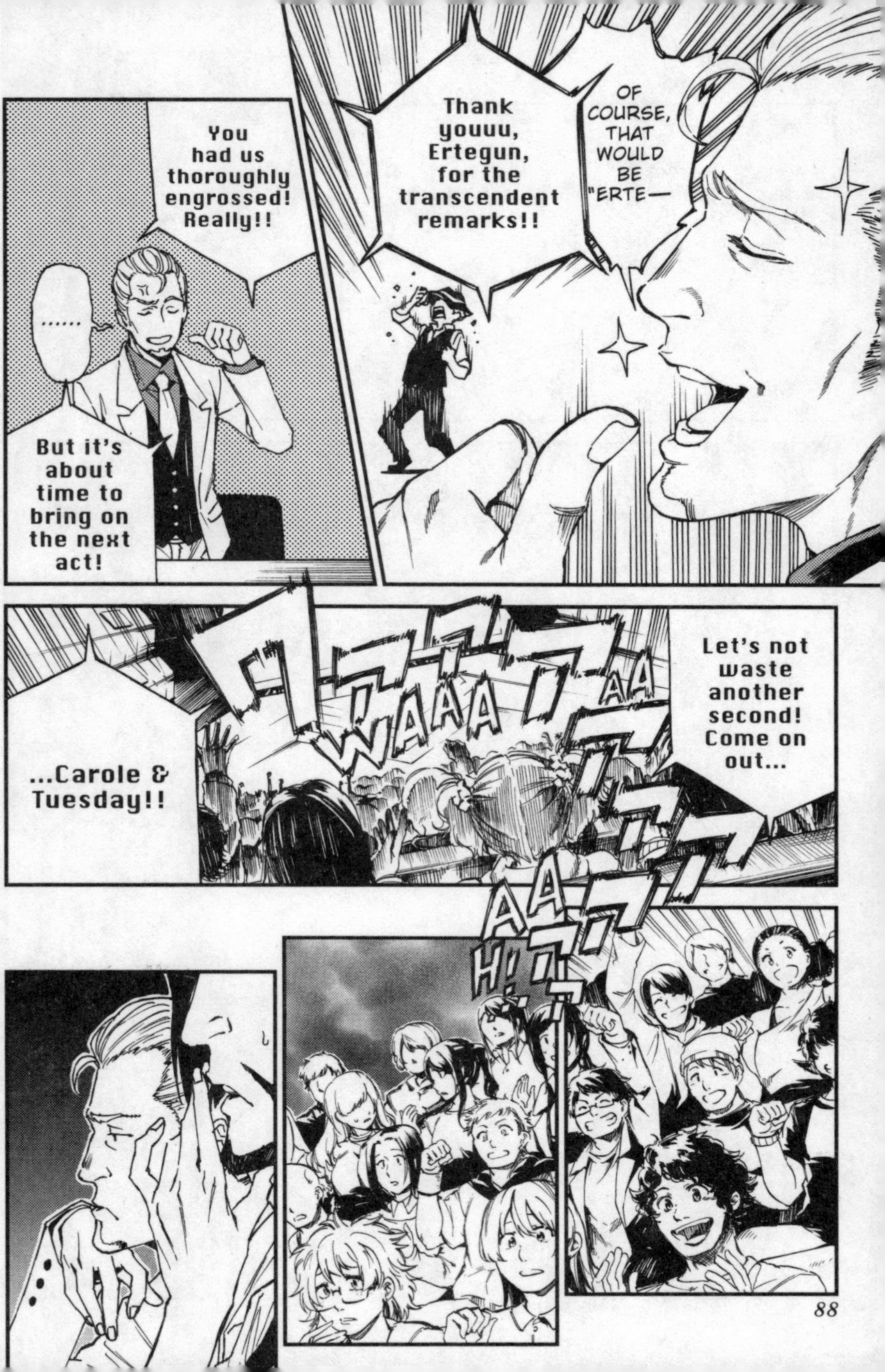
OF COURSE, THAT WOULD BE "ERTE—
Thank youuu, Ertegun, for the transcendent remarks!!
You had us thoroughly engrossed! Really!!
......
But it's about time to bring on the next act!
Let's not waste another second! Come on out...
WAAA
AA
...Carole & Tuesday!!
AAH!

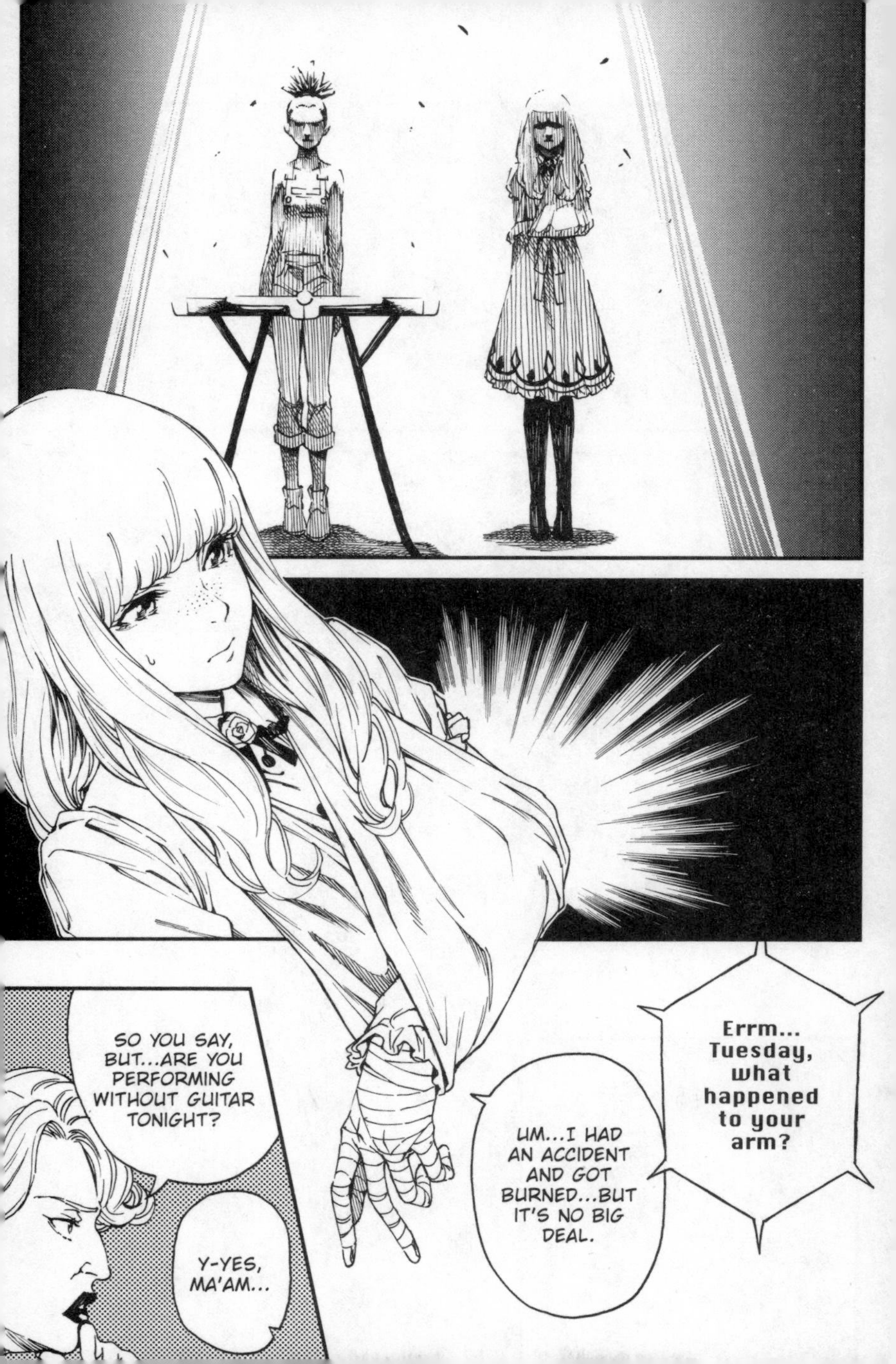
Errm... Tuesday, what happened to your arm?
UM...I HAD AN ACCIDENT AND GOT BURNED...BUT IT'S NO BIG DEAL.
SO YOU SAY, BUT...ARE YOU PERFORMING WITHOUT GUITAR TONIGHT?
Y-YES, MA'AM...

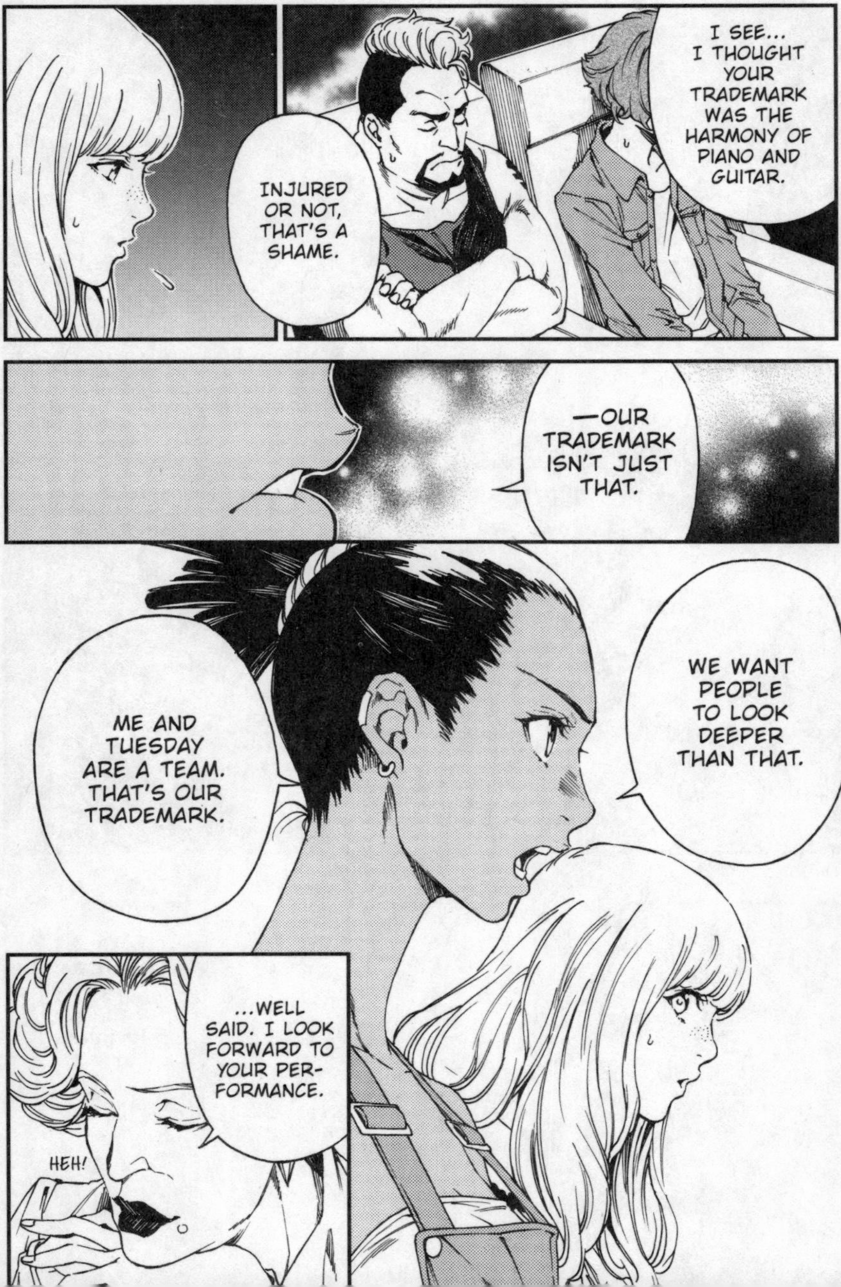
I SEE... I THOUGHT YOUR TRADEMARK WAS THE HARMONY OF PIANO AND GUITAR.
INJURED OR NOT, THAT'S A SHAME.
—OUR TRADEMARK ISN'T JUST THAT.
WE WANT PEOPLE TO LOOK DEEPER THAN THAT.
ME AND TUESDAY ARE A TEAM. THAT'S OUR TRADEMARK.
...WELL SAID. I LOOK FORWARD TO YOUR PER-FORMANCE.
HEH!

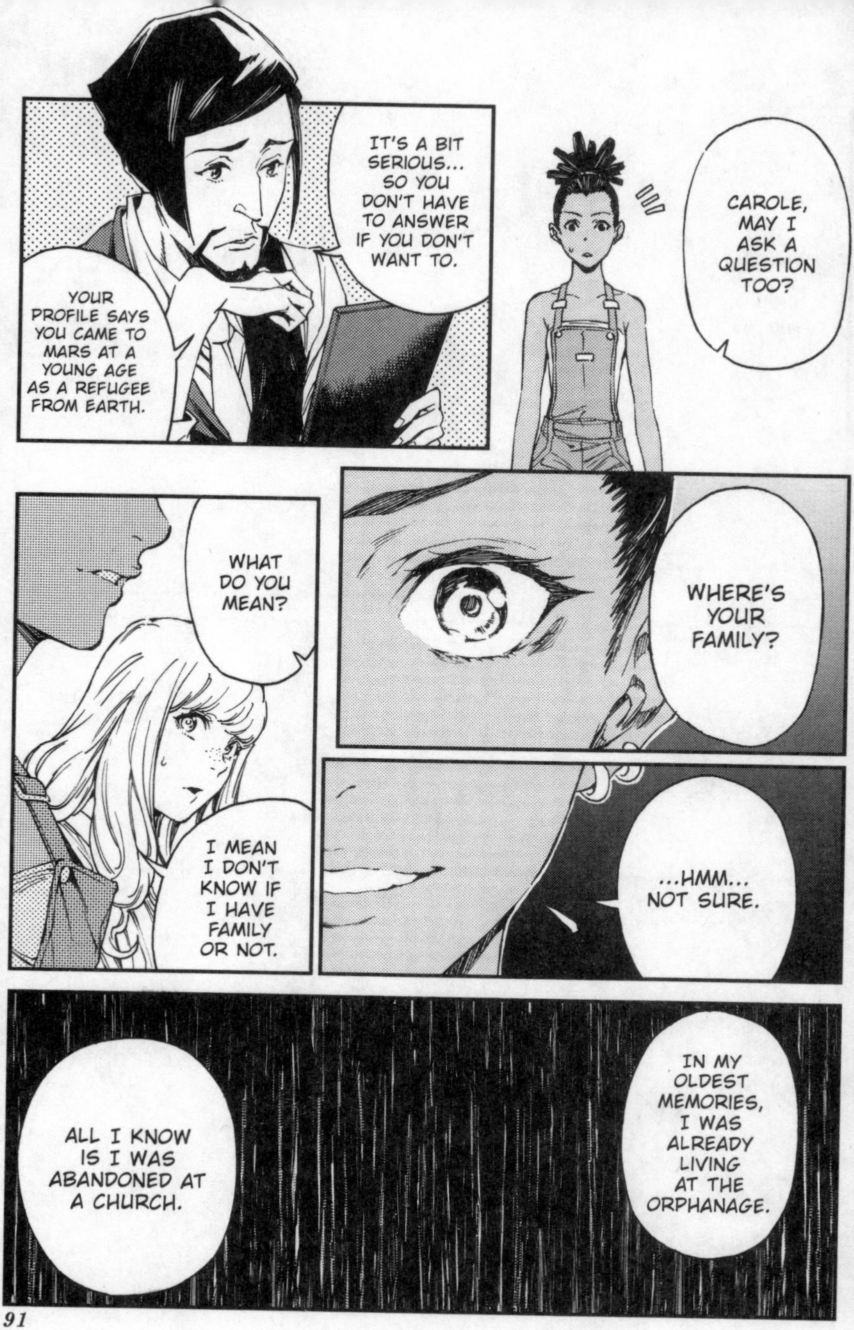
IT'S A BIT SERIOUS... SO YOU DON'T HAVE TO ANSWER IF YOU DON'T WANT TO.
YOUR PROFILE SAYS YOU CAME TO MARS AT A YOUNG AGE AS A REFUGEE FROM EARTH.
CAROLE, MAY I ASK A QUESTION TOO?
WHERE'S YOUR FAMILY?
...HMM... NOT SURE.
WHAT DO YOU MEAN?
I MEAN I DON'T KNOW IF I HAVE FAMILY OR NOT.
IN MY OLDEST MEMORIES, I WAS ALREADY LIVING AT THE ORPHANAGE.
ALL I KNOW IS I WAS ABANDONED AT A CHURCH.

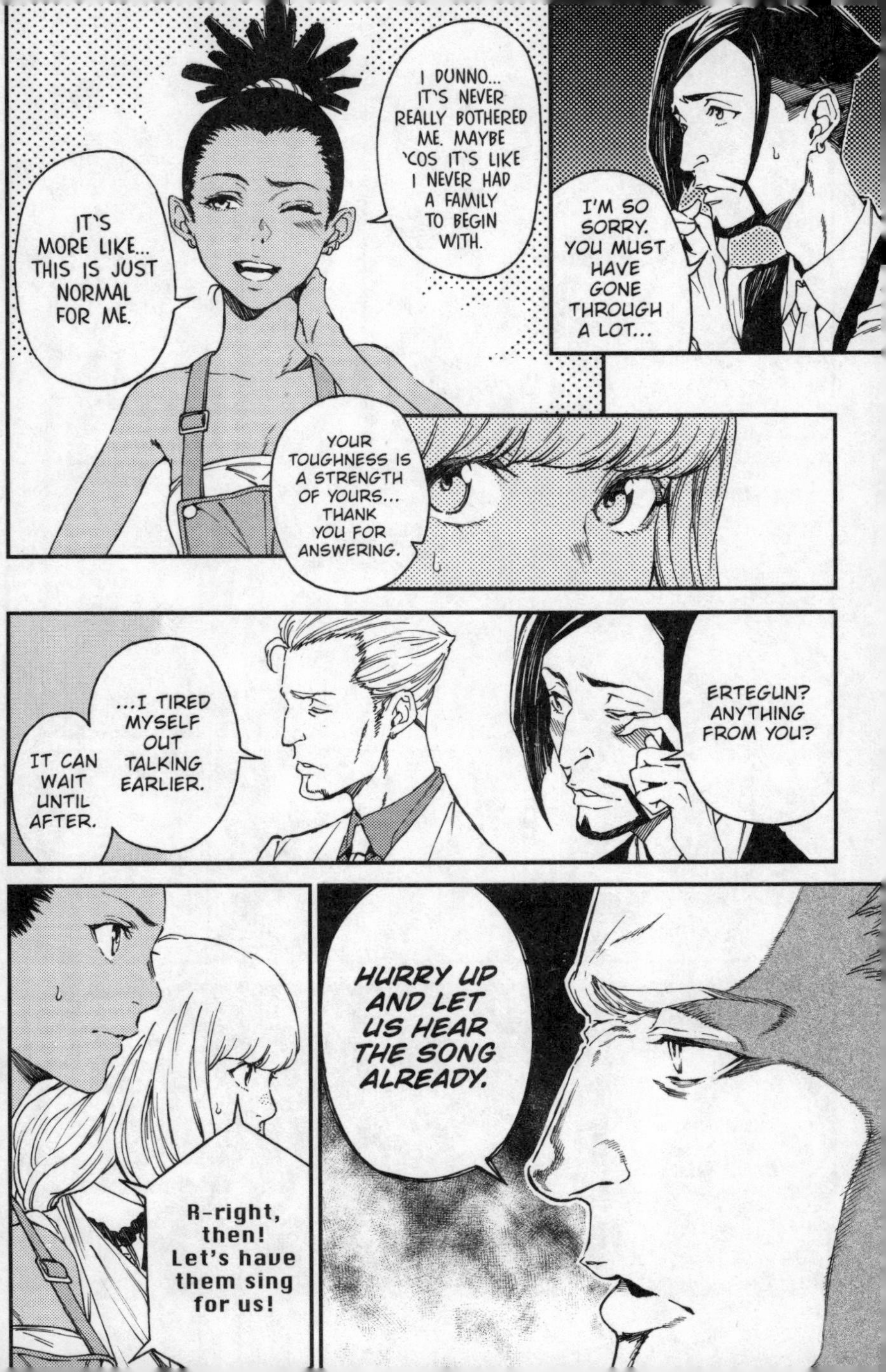
I'M SO SORRY. YOU MUST HAVE GONE THROUGH A LOT...
I DUNNO... IT'S NEVER REALLY BOTHERED ME. MAYBE 'COS IT'S LIKE I NEVER HAD A FAMILY TO BEGIN WITH.
IT'S MORE LIKE... THIS IS JUST NORMAL FOR ME.
YOUR TOUGHNESS IS A STRENGTH OF YOURS... THANK YOU FOR ANSWERING.
ERTEGUN? ANYTHING FROM YOU?
...I TIRED MYSELF OUT TALKING EARLIER.
IT CAN WAIT UNTIL AFTER.
HURRY UP AND LET US HEAR THE SONG ALREADY.
R-right, then! Let's have them sing for us!

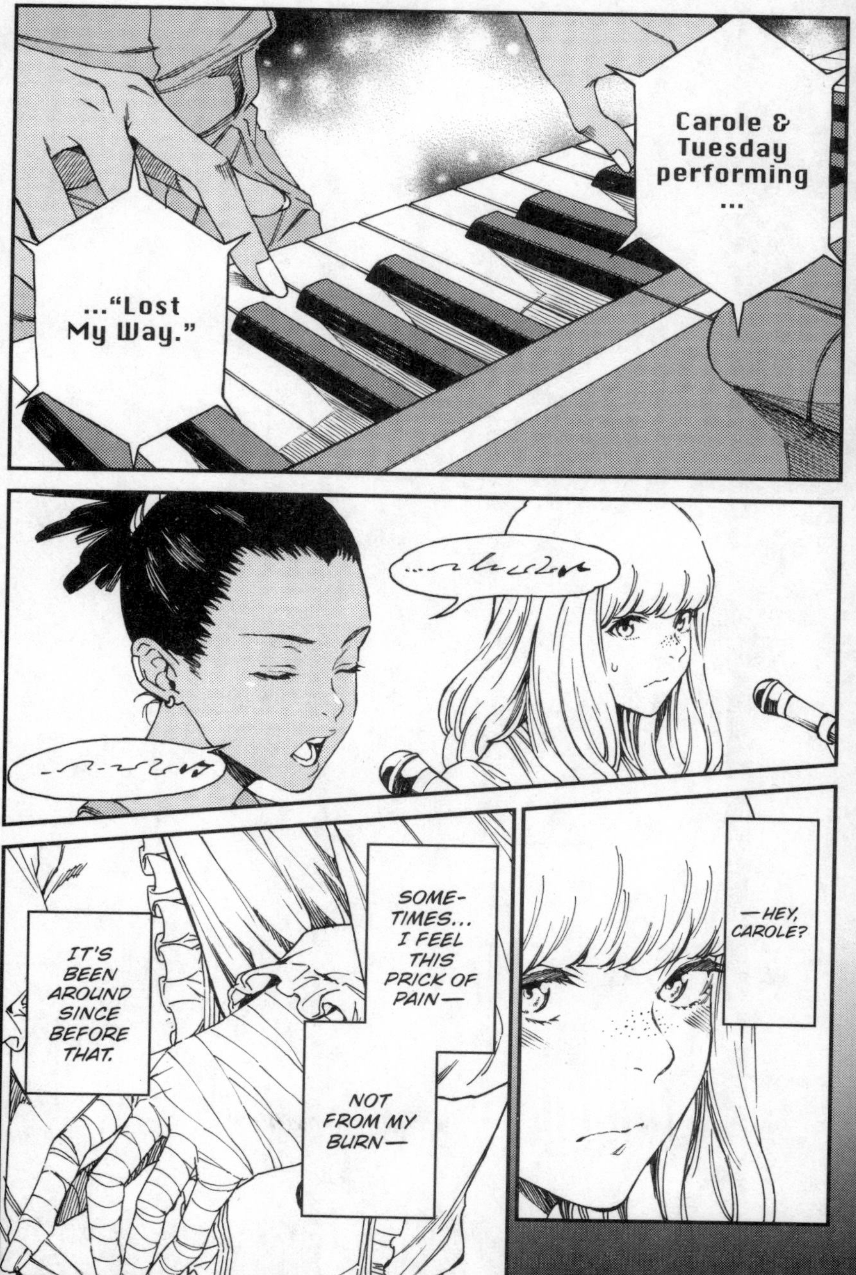
Carole & Tuesday performing ...
..."Lost My Way."
—HEY, CAROLE?
SOME-TIMES... I FEEL THIS PRICK OF PAIN—
NOT FROM MY BURN—
IT'S BEEN AROUND SINCE BEFORE THAT.

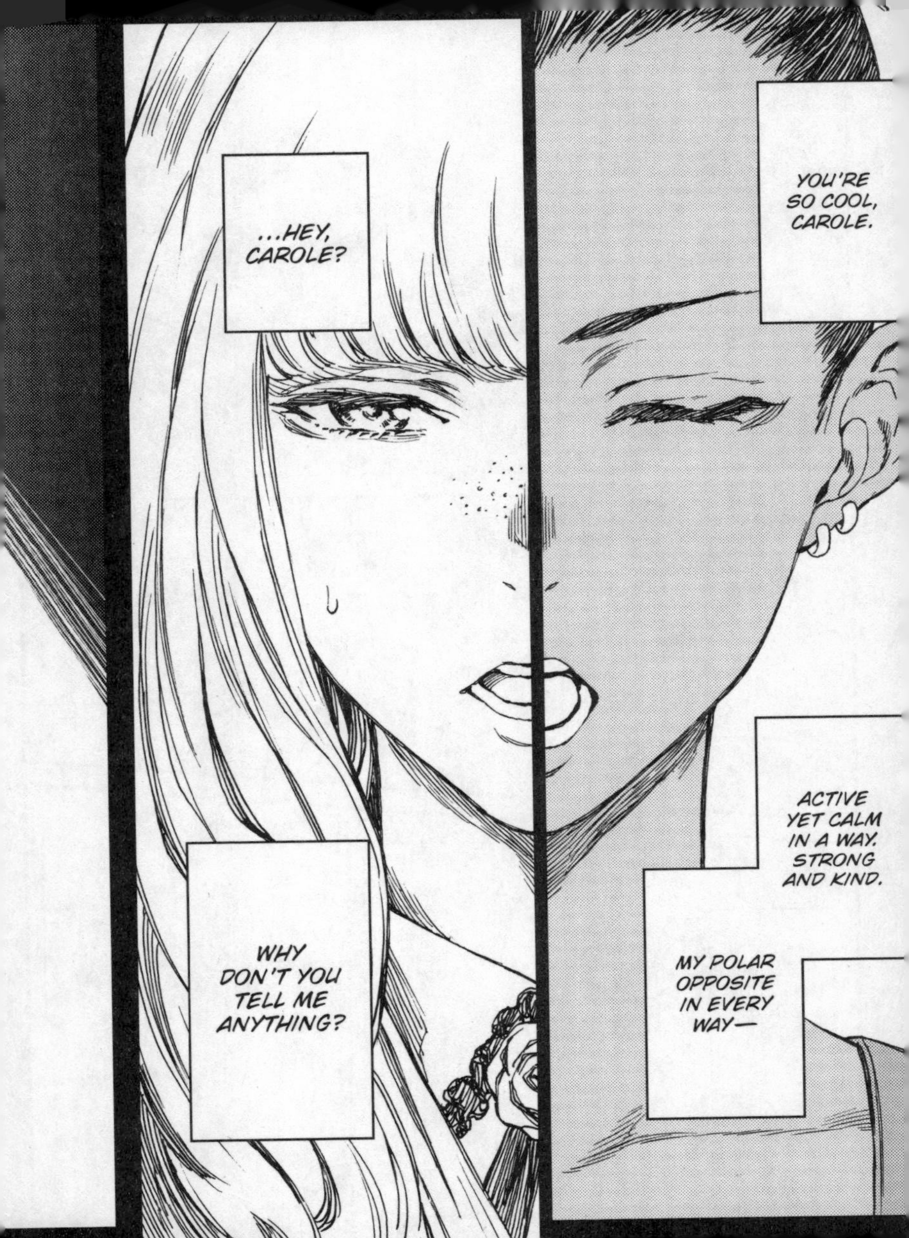
YOU'RE SO COOL, CAROLE.
ACTIVE YET CALM IN A WAY. STRONG AND KIND.
MY POLAR OPPOSITE IN EVERY WAY—
...HEY, CAROLE?
WHY DON'T YOU TELL ME ANYTHING?

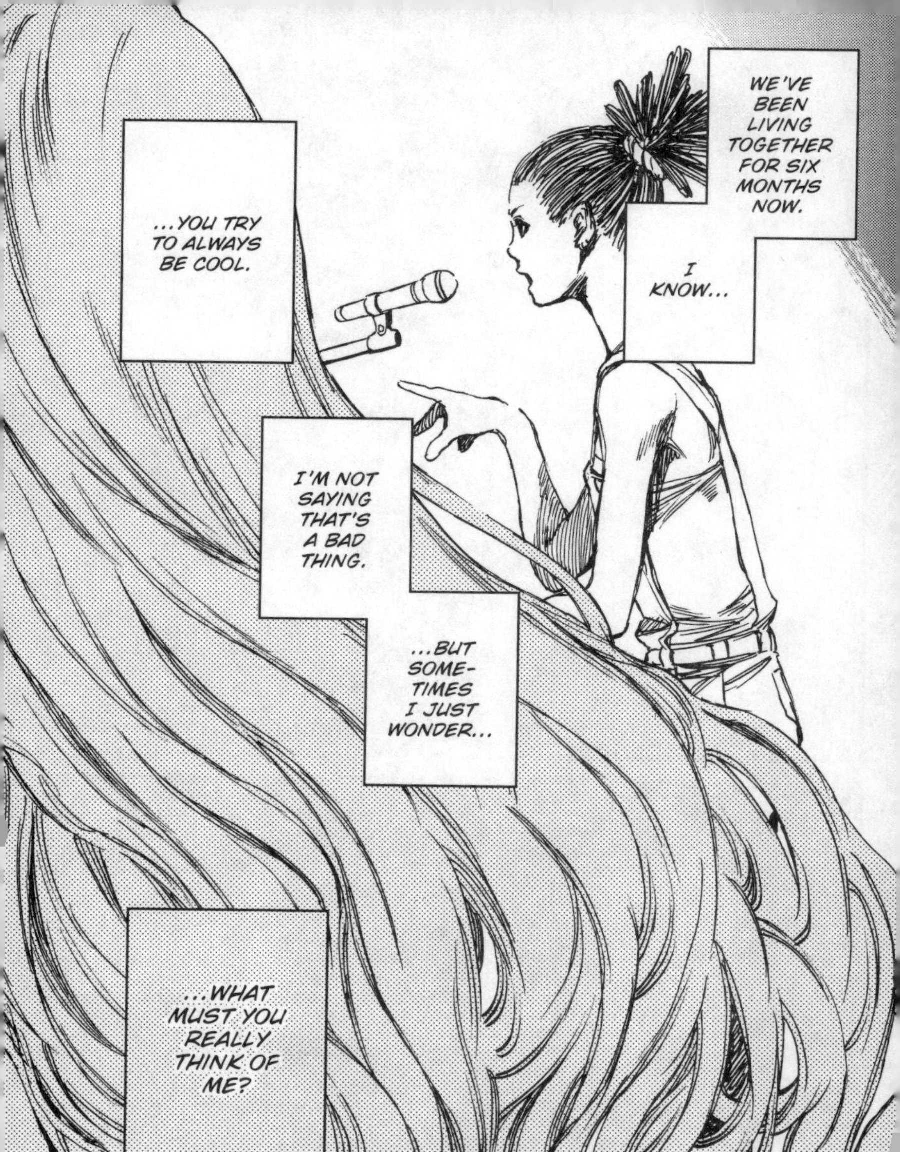
WE'VE BEEN LIVING TOGETHER FOR SIX MONTHS NOW.
I KNOW...
...YOU TRY TO ALWAYS BE COOL.
I'M NOT SAYING THAT'S A BAD THING.
...BUT SOME-TIMES I JUST WONDER...
...WHAT MUST YOU REALLY THINK OF ME?

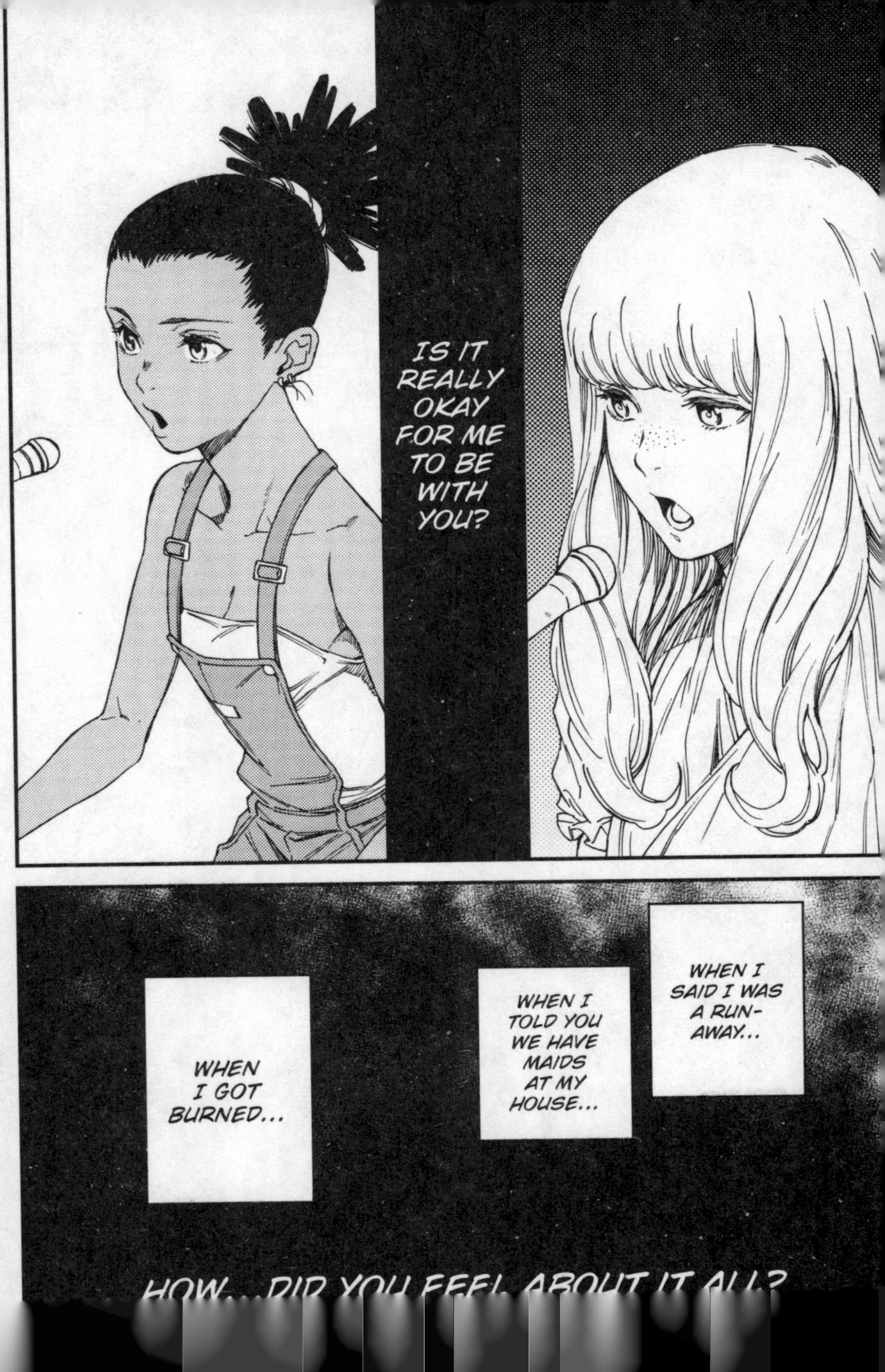
IS IT REALLY OKAY FOR ME TO BE WITH YOU?
WHEN I SAID I WAS A RUN-AWAY...
WHEN I TOLD YOU WE HAVE MAIDS AT MY HOUSE...
WHEN I GOT BURNED...
HOW...DID YOU FEEL ABOUT IT ALL?

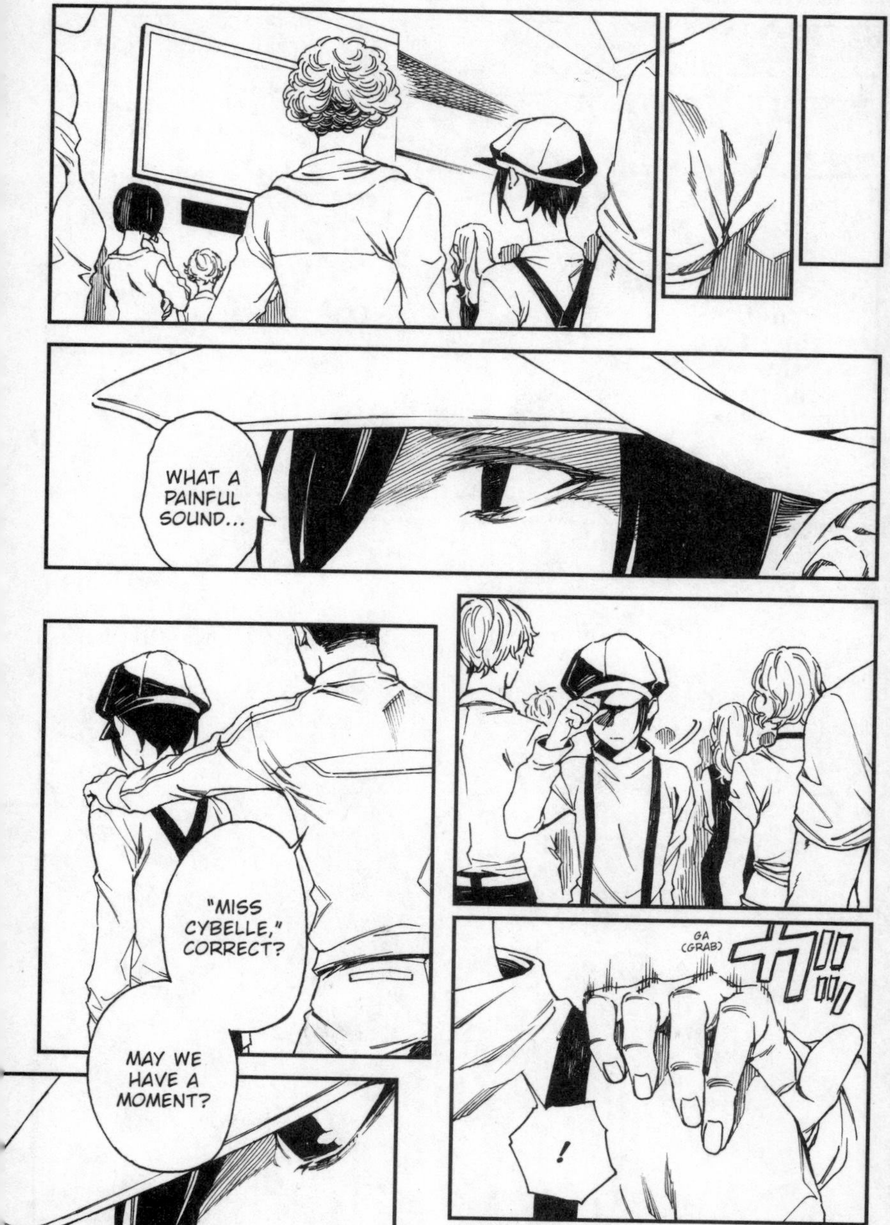
WHAT A PAINFUL SOUND...
GA (GRAB)
!
"MISS CYBELLE," CORRECT?
MAY WE HAVE A MOMENT?

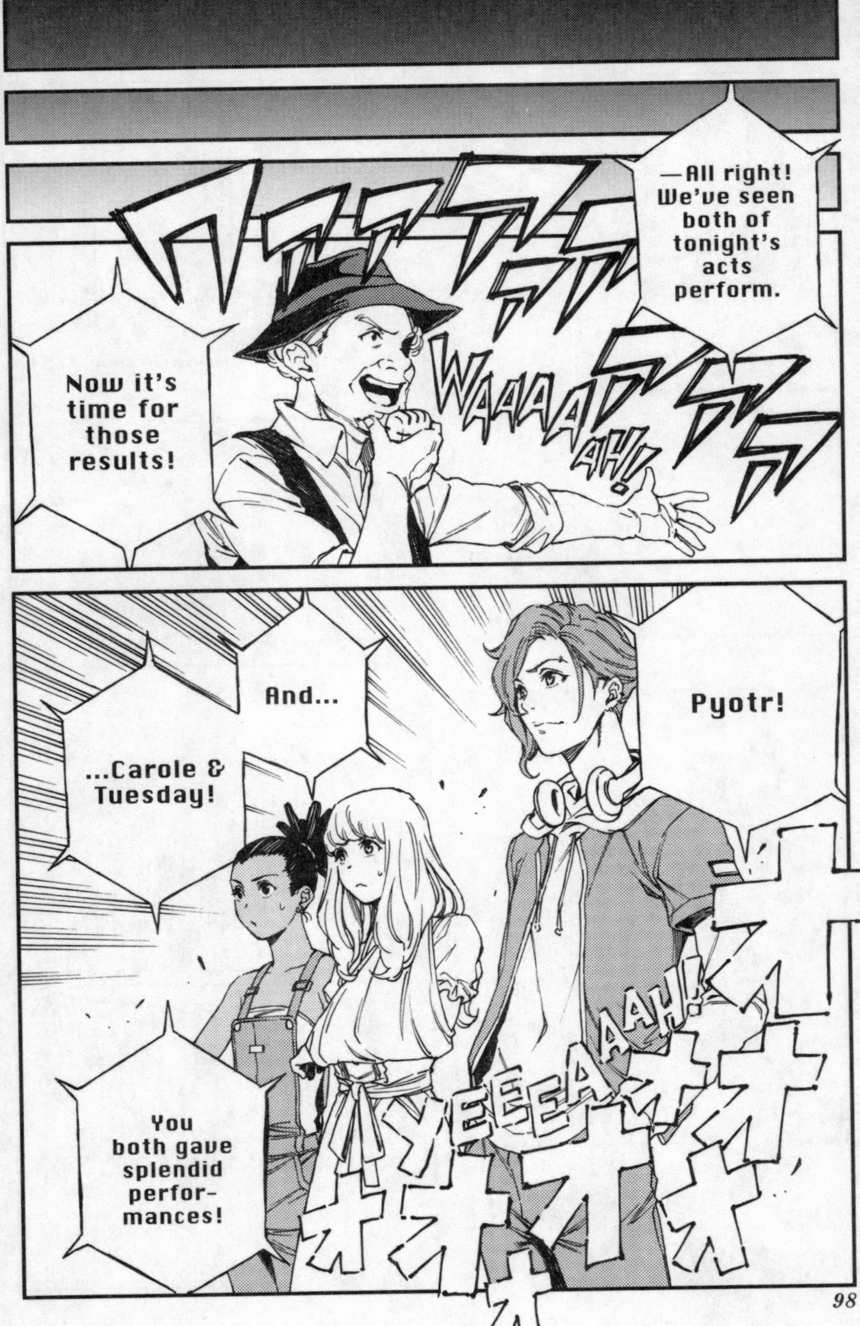
—All right! We've seen both of tonight's acts perform.
WAAAAAAH!
Now it's time for those results!
Pyotr!
And...
...Carole & Tuesday!
YEEEAAAH!
You both gave splendid perfor-mances!

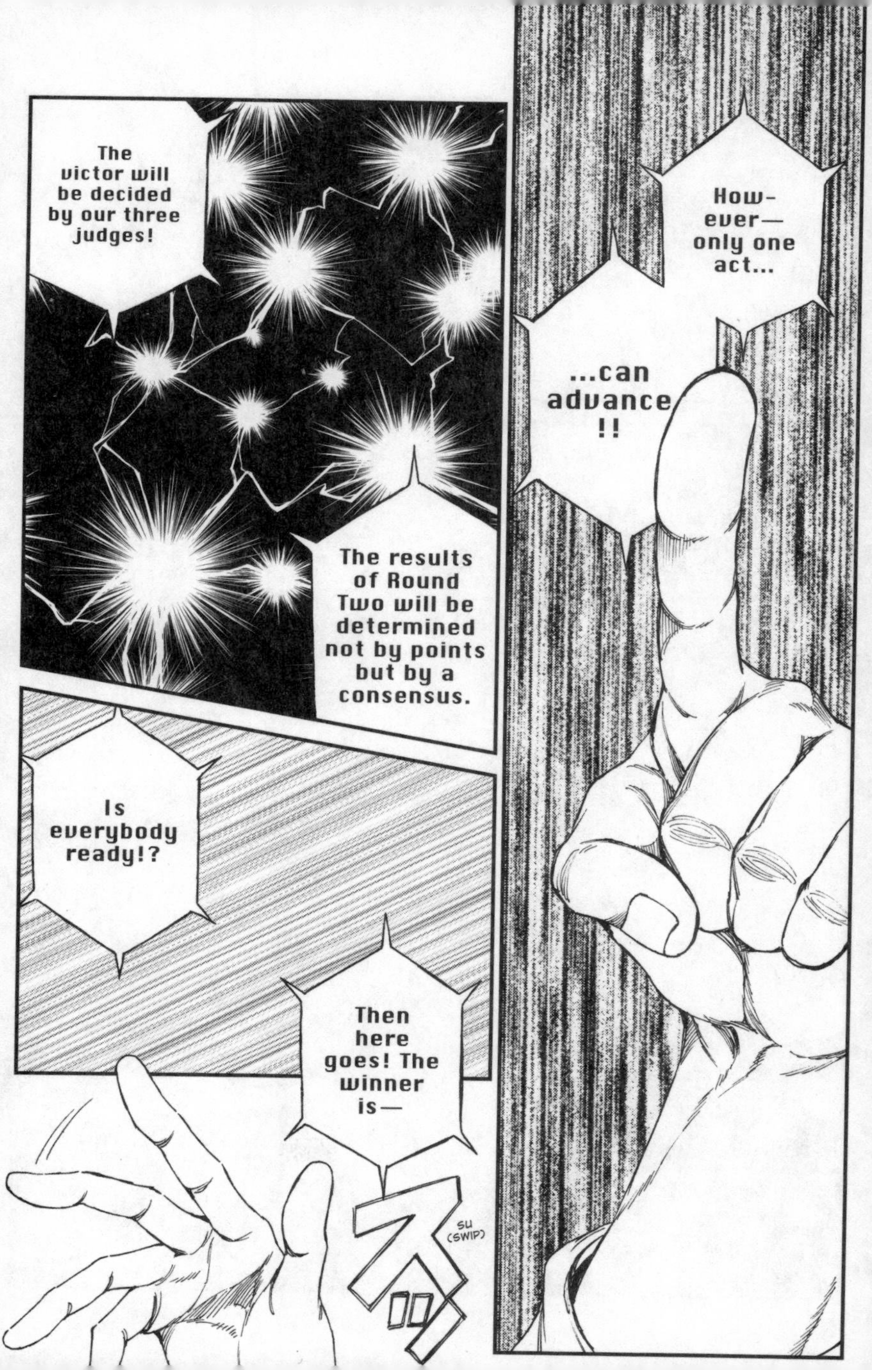
How-ever—only one act...
...can advance!!
The results of Round Two will be determined not by points but by a consensus.
The victor will be decided by our three judges!
Is everybody ready!?
Then here goes! The winner is—
SU (SWIP)

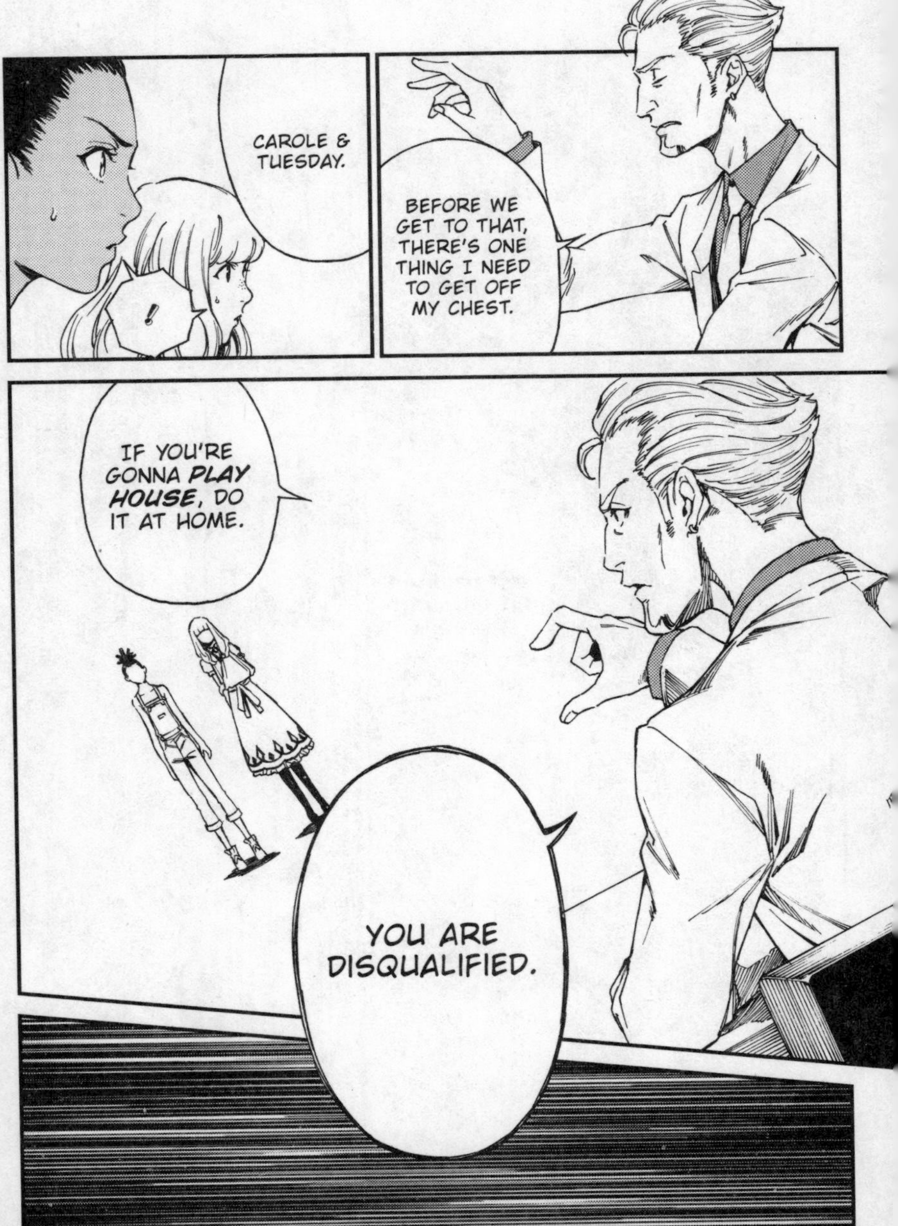
BEFORE WE GET TO THAT, THERE'S ONE THING I NEED TO GET OFF MY CHEST.
CAROLE & TUESDAY.
!
IF YOU'RE GONNA *PLAY HOUSE*, DO IT AT HOME.
YOU ARE DISQUALIFIED.

END

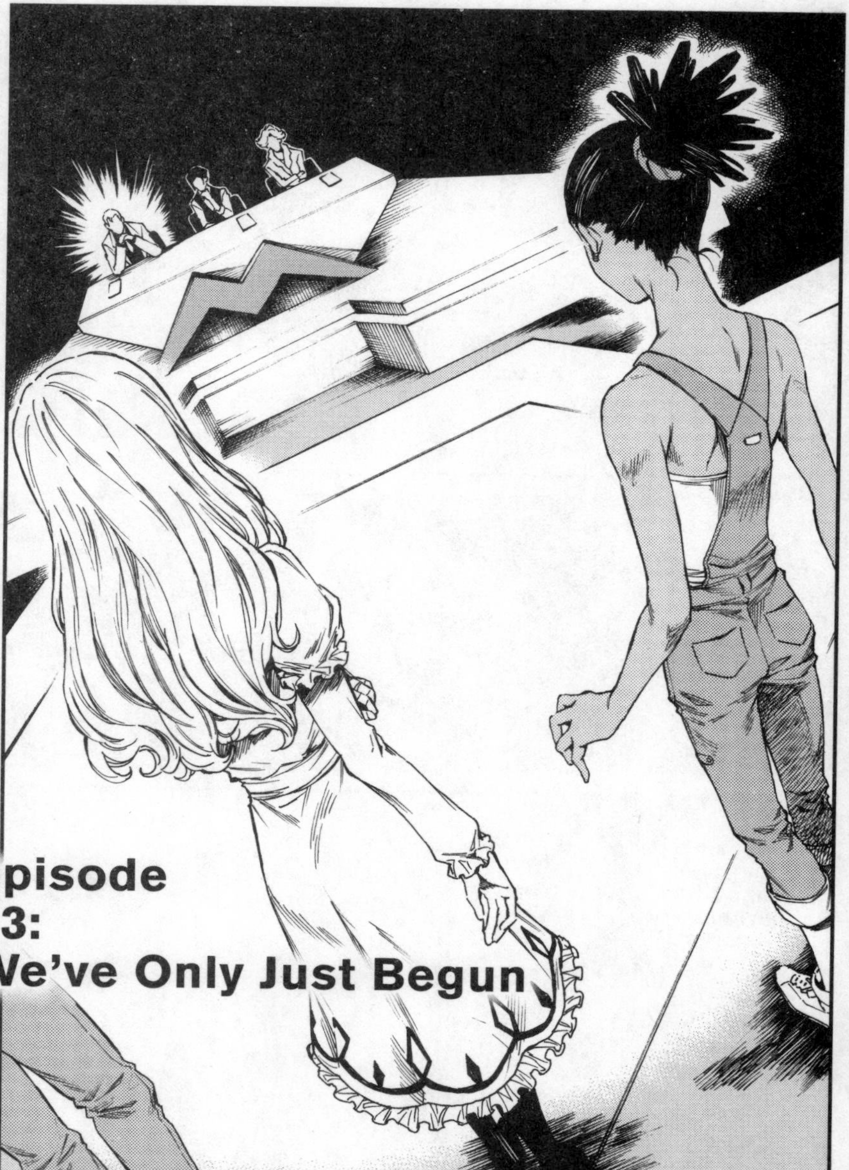
episode
13:
We’ve Only Just Begun

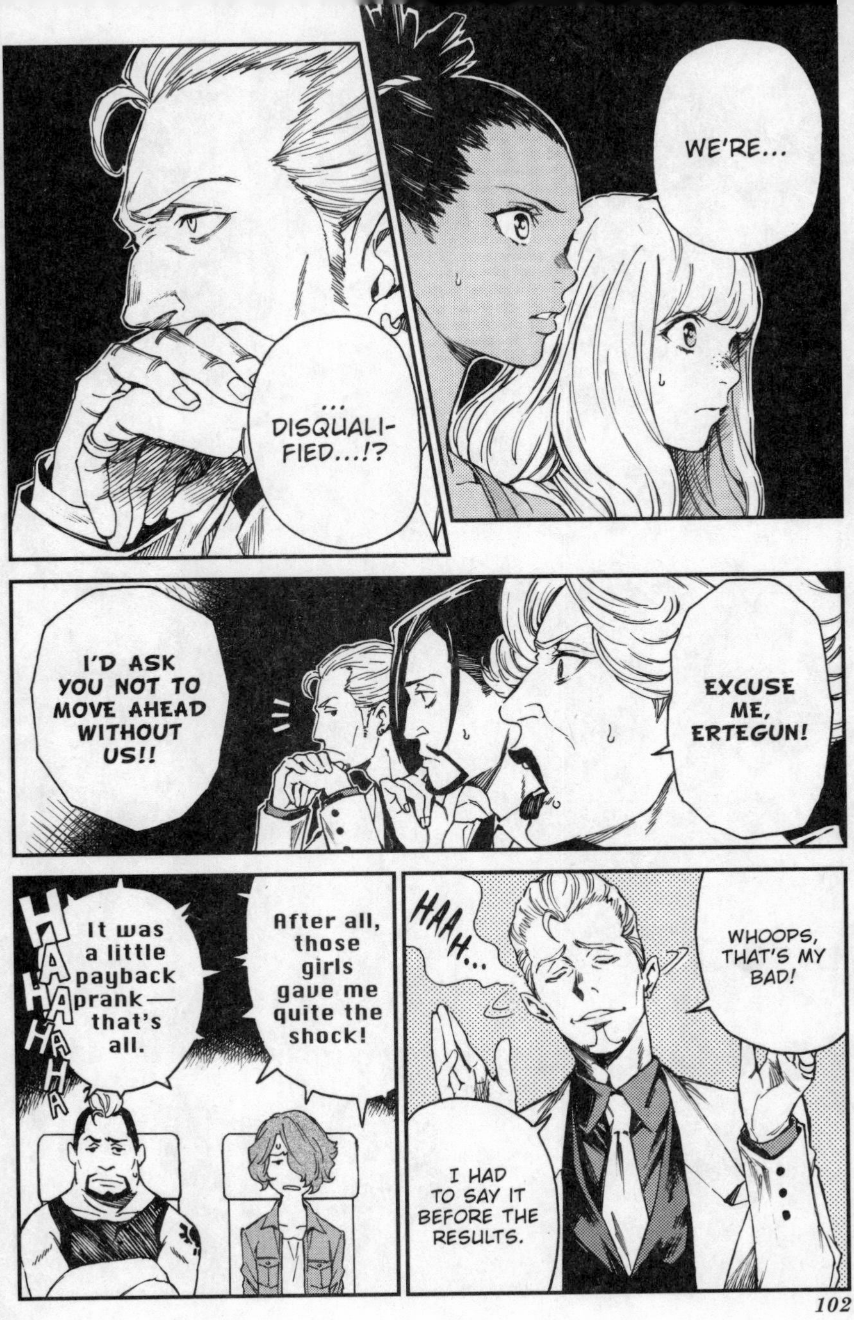
WE'RE...
...DISQUALIFIED...!?
EXCUSE ME, ERTEGUN!
I'D ASK YOU NOT TO MOVE AHEAD WITHOUT US!!
WHOOPS, THAT'S MY BAD!
HAAH...
I HAD TO SAY IT BEFORE THE RESULTS.
After all, those girls gave me quite the shock!
It was a little payback prank—that's all.
HAHAHAHAHA

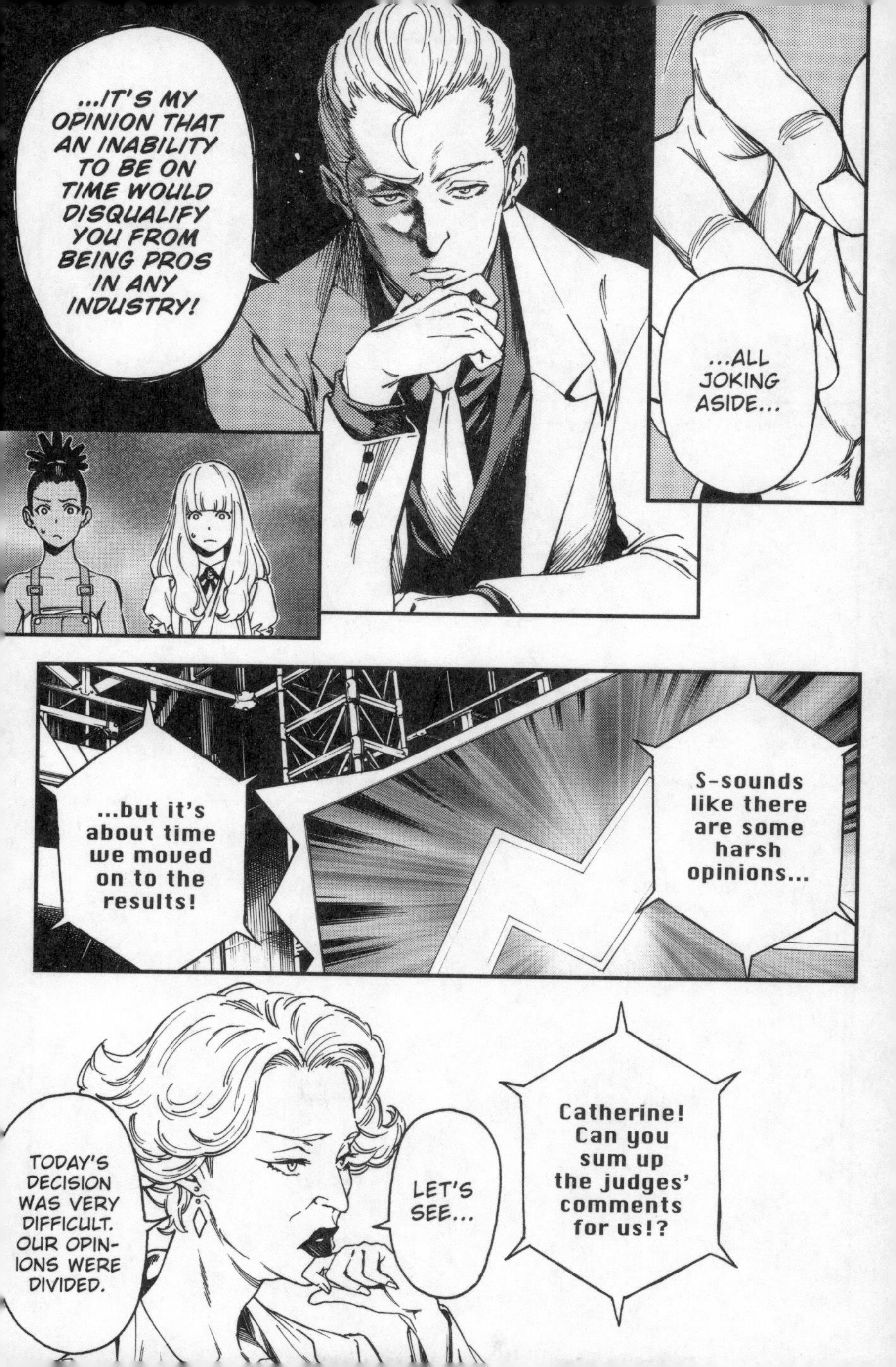
...ALL JOKING ASIDE...
...IT'S MY OPINION THAT AN INABILITY TO BE ON TIME WOULD DISQUALIFY YOU FROM BEING PROS IN ANY INDUSTRY!
S-sounds like there are some harsh opinions...
...but it's about time we moved on to the results!
Catherine! Can you sum up the judges' comments for us!?
LET'S SEE...
TODAY'S DECISION WAS VERY DIFFICULT. OUR OPIN-IONS WERE DIVIDED.

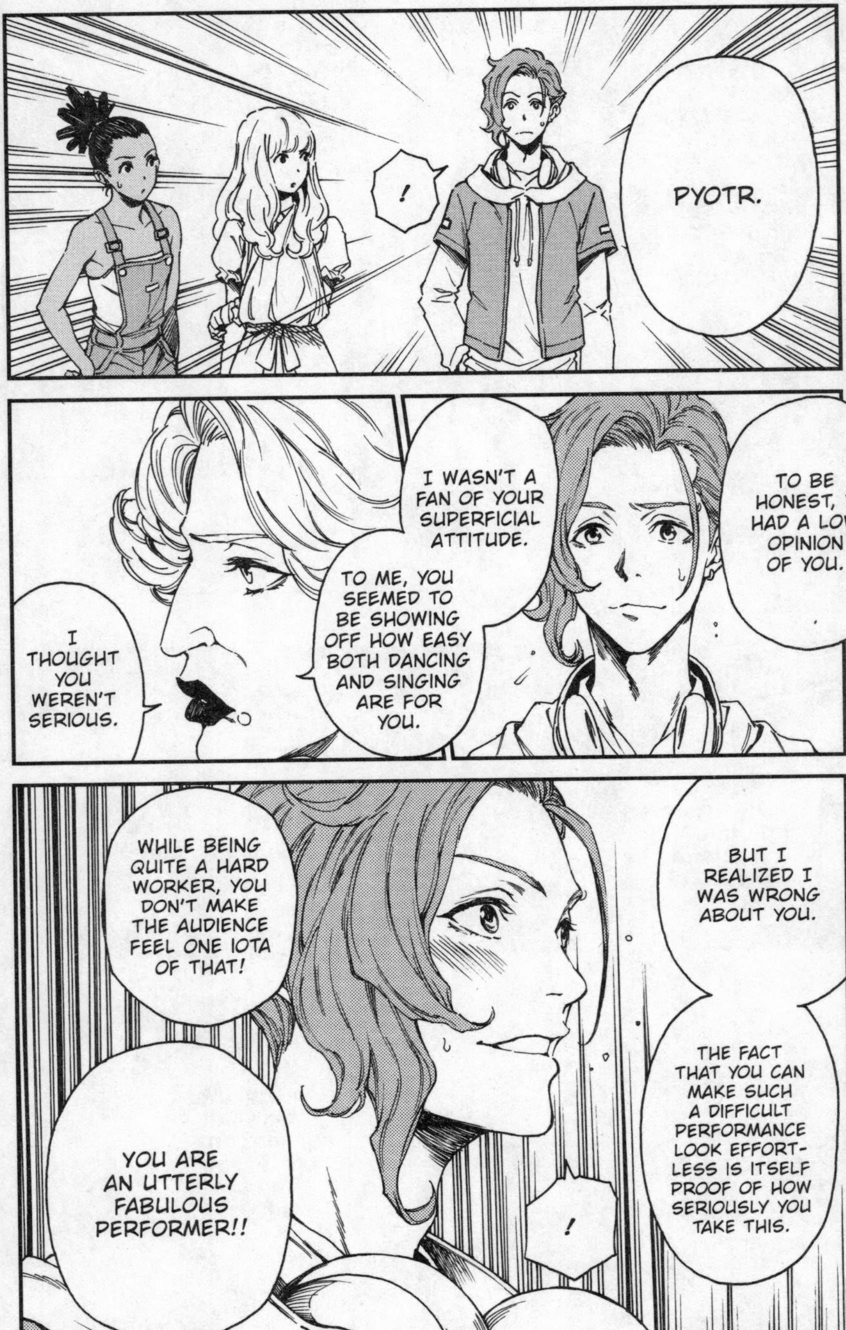
PYOTR.
!
TO BE HONEST, I HAD A LOW OPINION OF YOU.
I WASN'T A FAN OF YOUR SUPERFICIAL ATTITUDE.
TO ME, YOU SEEMED TO BE SHOWING OFF HOW EASY BOTH DANCING AND SINGING ARE FOR YOU.
I THOUGHT YOU WEREN'T SERIOUS.
BUT I REALIZED I WAS WRONG ABOUT YOU.
THE FACT THAT YOU CAN MAKE SUCH A DIFFICULT PERFORMANCE LOOK EFFORT-LESS IS ITSELF PROOF OF HOW SERIOUSLY YOU TAKE THIS.
!
WHILE BEING QUITE A HARD WORKER, YOU DON'T MAKE THE AUDIENCE FEEL ONE IOTA OF THAT!
YOU ARE AN UTTERLY FABULOUS PERFORMER!!

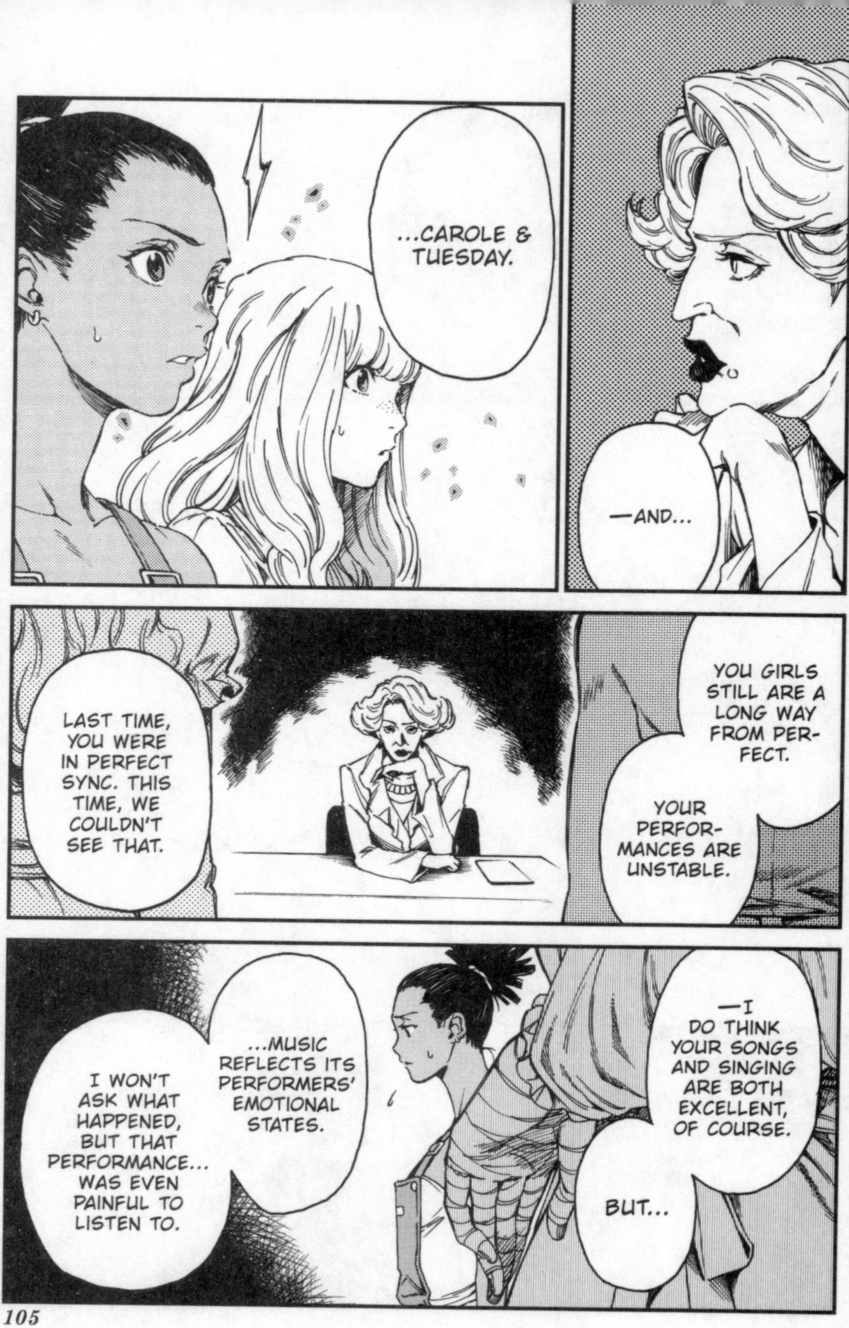
—AND...
...CAROLE & TUESDAY.
YOU GIRLS STILL ARE A LONG WAY FROM PER-FECT.
YOUR PERFOR-MANCES ARE UNSTABLE.
LAST TIME, YOU WERE IN PERFECT SYNC. THIS TIME, WE COULDN'T SEE THAT.
—I DO THINK YOUR SONGS AND SINGING ARE BOTH EXCELLENT, OF COURSE.
BUT...
...MUSIC REFLECTS ITS PERFORMERS' EMOTIONAL STATES.
I WON'T ASK WHAT HAPPENED, BUT THAT PERFORMANCE... WAS EVEN PAINFUL TO LISTEN TO.

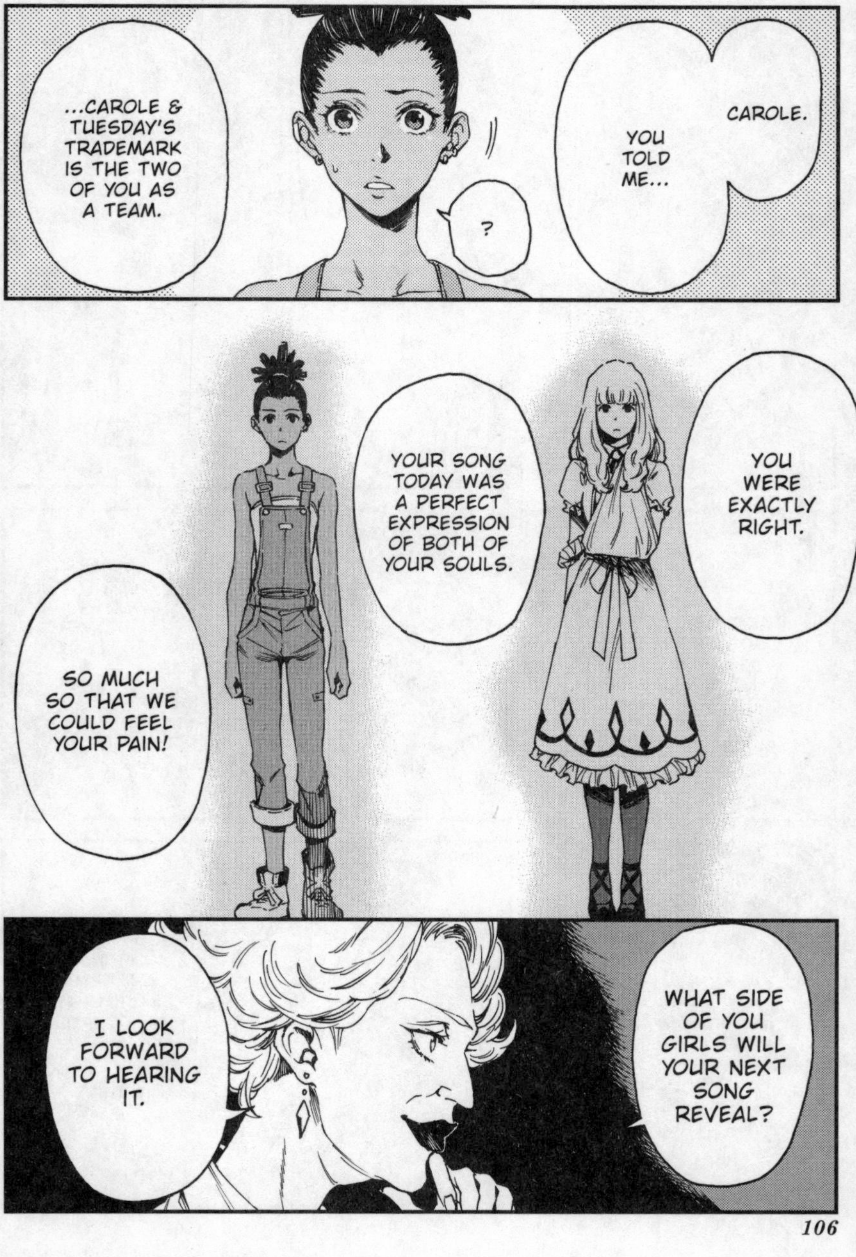
CAROLE.
YOU TOLD ME...
?
...CAROLE & TUESDAY'S TRADEMARK IS THE TWO OF YOU AS A TEAM.
YOU WERE EXACTLY RIGHT.
YOUR SONG TODAY WAS A PERFECT EXPRESSION OF BOTH OF YOUR SOULS.
SO MUCH SO THAT WE COULD FEEL YOUR PAIN!
WHAT SIDE OF YOU GIRLS WILL YOUR NEXT SONG REVEAL?
I LOOK FORWARD TO HEARING IT.

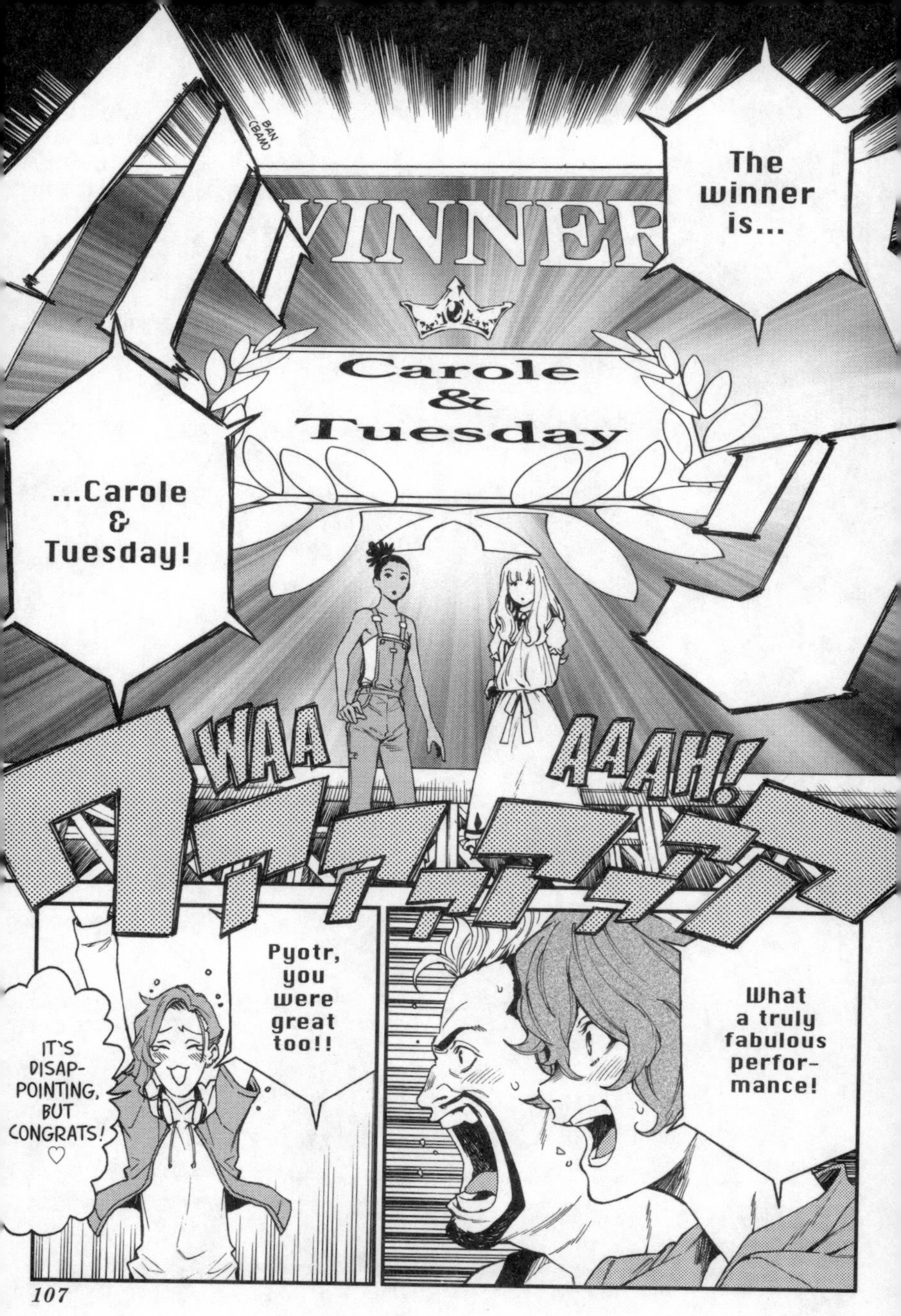
The winner is...
BAN (BAM)
WINNER
Carole & Tuesday
...Carole & Tuesday!
WAA AAAH!
What a truly fabulous perfor-mance!
Pyotr, you were great too!!
IT'S DISAP-POINTING, BUT CONGRATS! ♡

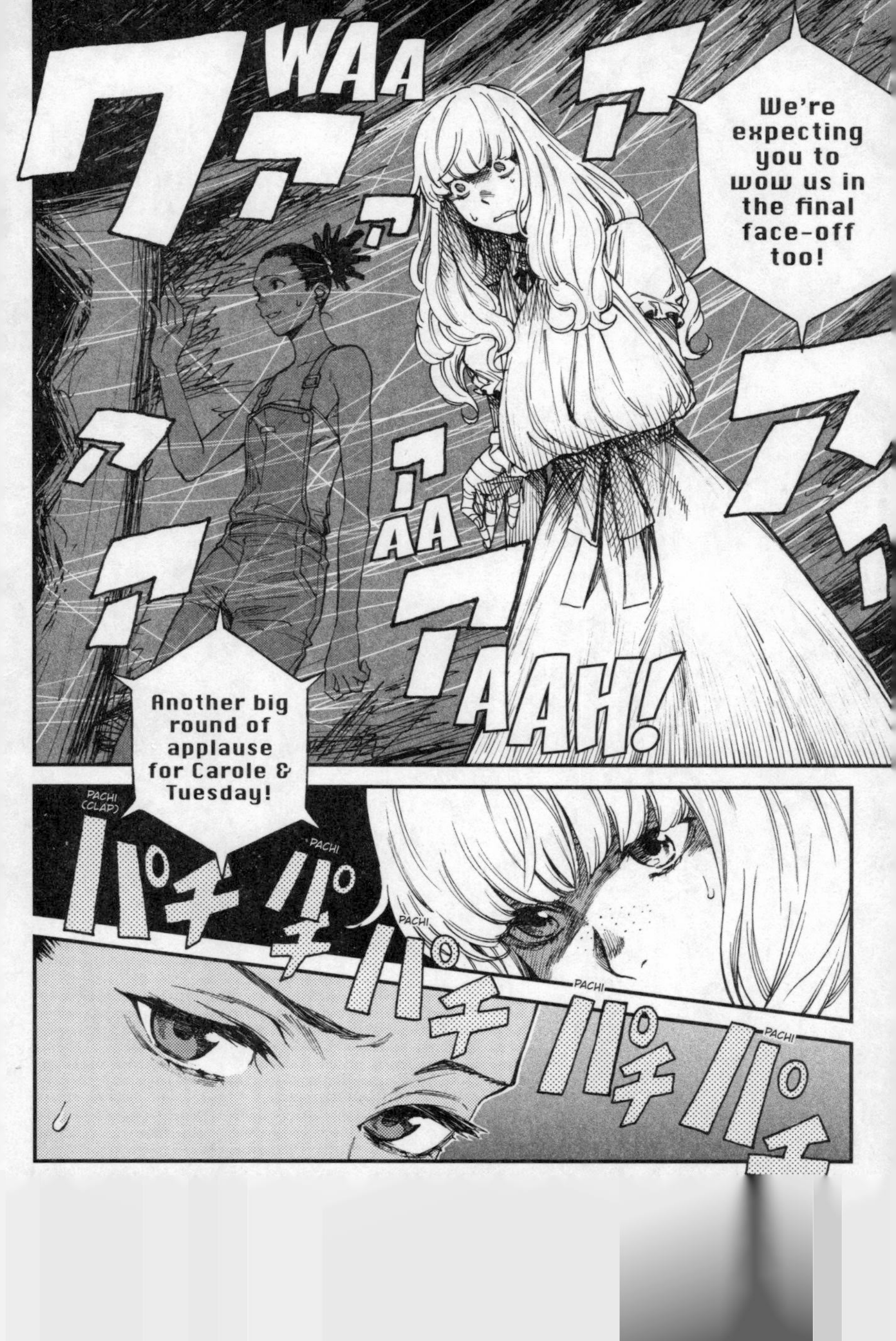
We're expecting you to wow us in the final face-off too!
WAA
AA
AAH!
Another big round of applause for Carole & Tuesday!
PACHI (CLAP)
PACHI
PACHI
PACHI
PACHI

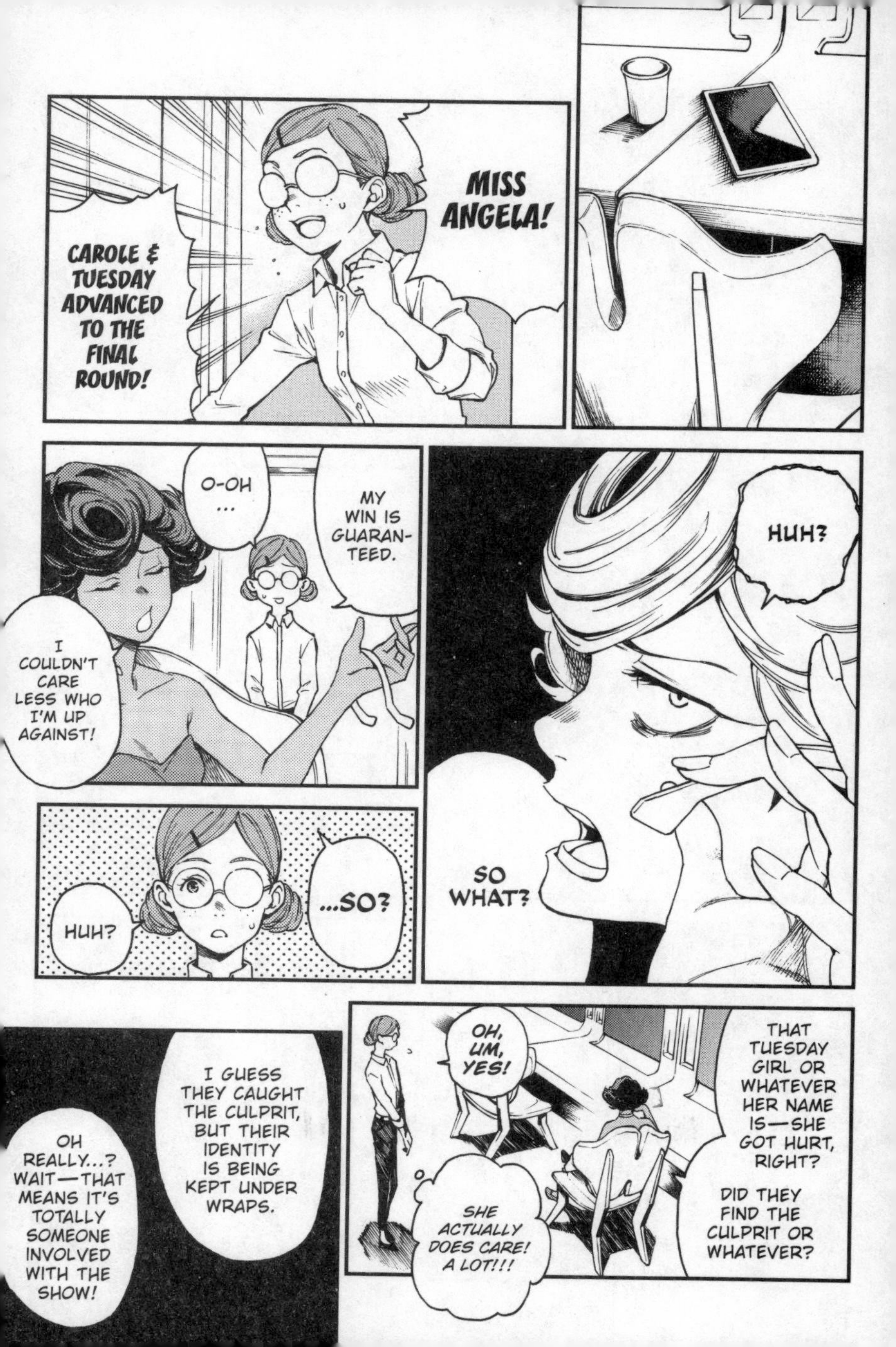
MISS ANGELA!
CAROLE & TUESDAY ADVANCED TO THE FINAL ROUND!
HUH?
SO WHAT?
MY WIN IS GUARAN-TEED.
O-OH ...
I COULDN'T CARE LESS WHO I'M UP AGAINST!
...SO?
HUH?
THAT TUESDAY GIRL OR WHATEVER HER NAME IS—SHE GOT HURT, RIGHT?
DID THEY FIND THE CULPRIT OR WHATEVER?
OH, UM, YES!
SHE ACTUALLY DOES CARE! A LOT!!!
I GUESS THEY CAUGHT THE CULPRIT, BUT THEIR IDENTITY IS BEING KEPT UNDER WRAPS.
OH REALLY...? WAIT—THAT MEANS IT'S TOTALLY SOMEONE INVOLVED WITH THE SHOW!

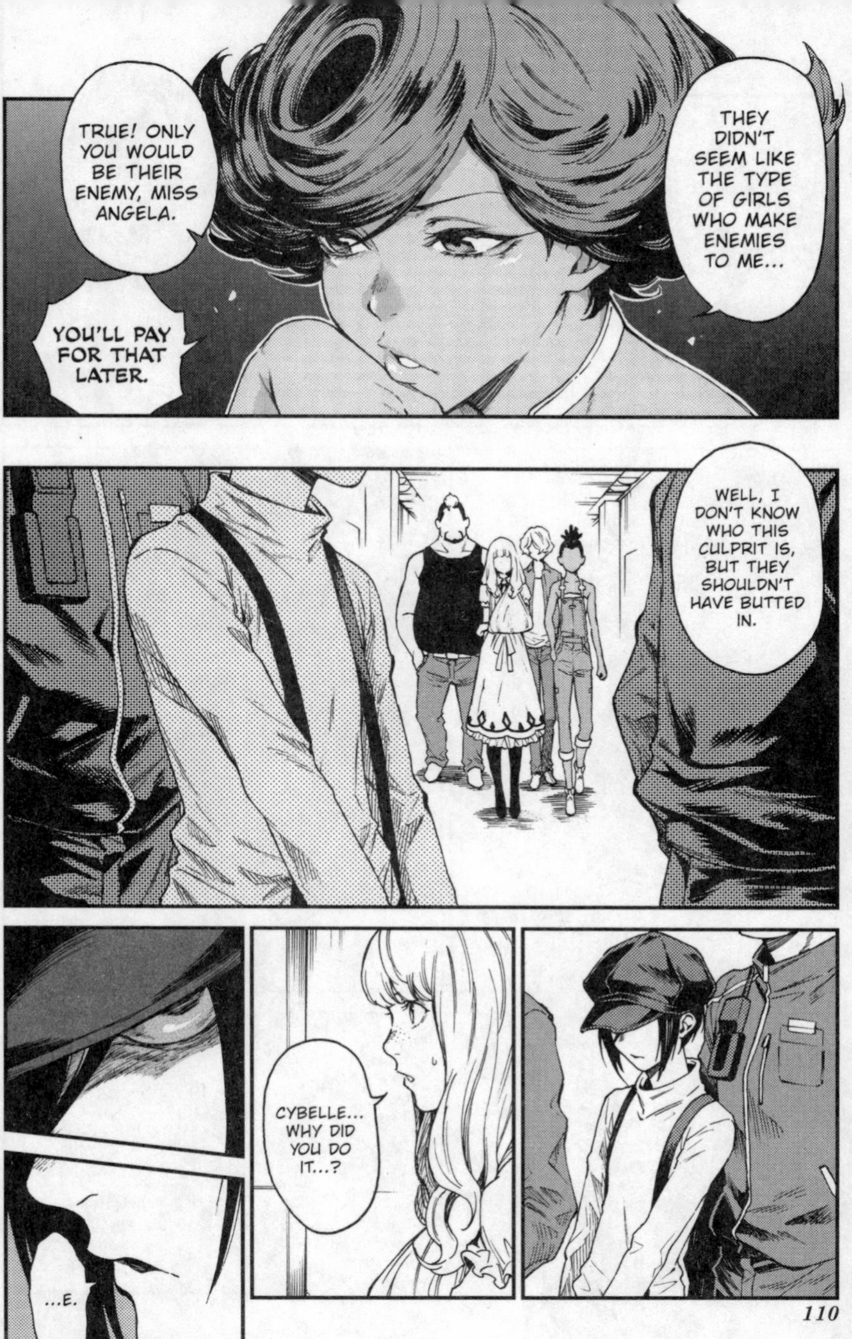
THEY DIDN'T SEEM LIKE THE TYPE OF GIRLS WHO MAKE ENEMIES TO ME...
TRUE! ONLY YOU WOULD BE THEIR ENEMY, MISS ANGELA.
YOU'LL PAY FOR THAT LATER.
WELL, I DON'T KNOW WHO THIS CULPRIT IS, BUT THEY SHOULDN'T HAVE BUTTED IN.
CYBELLE... WHY DID YOU DO IT...?
...E.

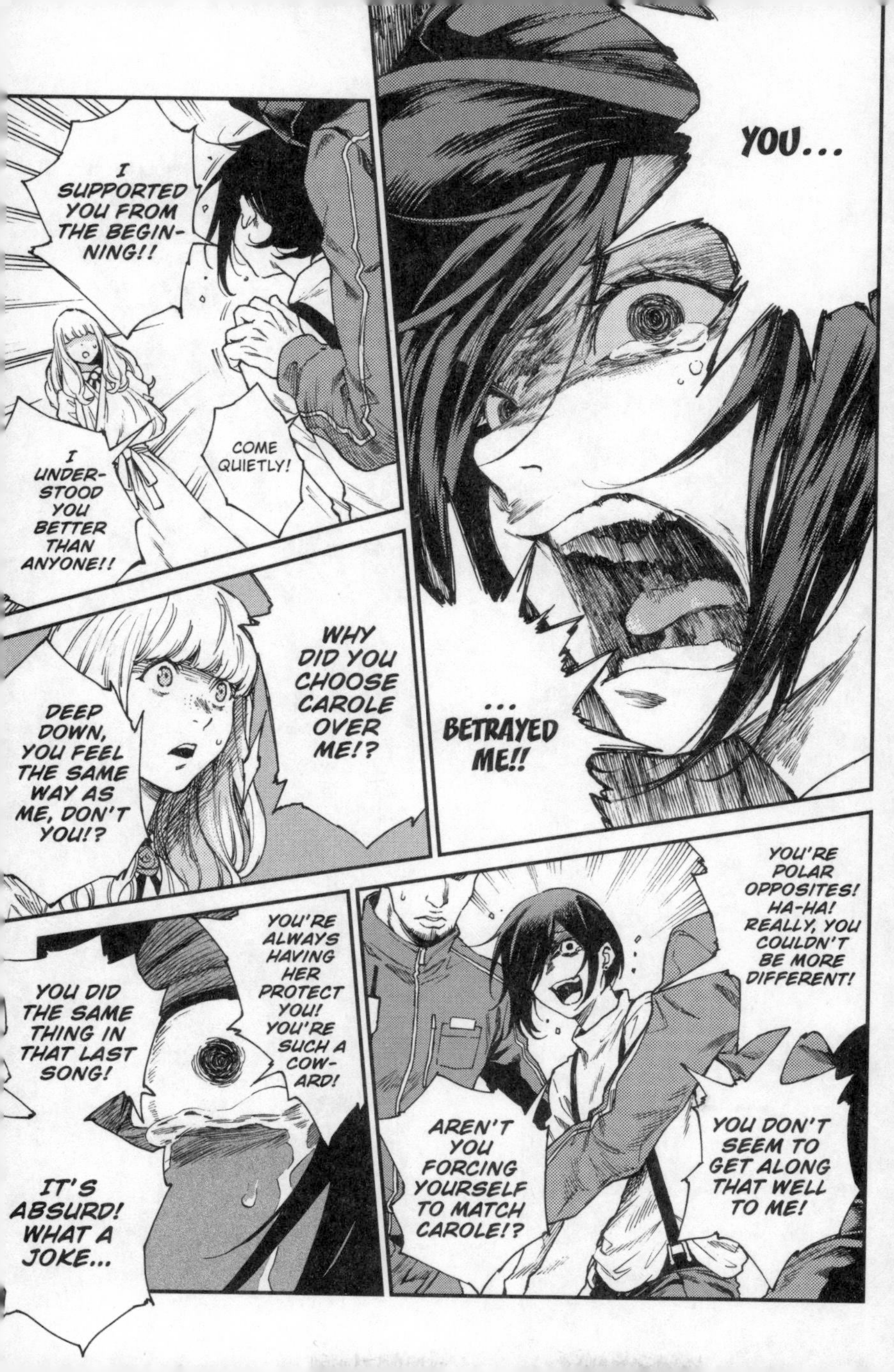
YOU...
... BETRAYED ME!!
I SUPPORTED YOU FROM THE BEGINNING!!
COME QUIETLY!
I UNDERSTOOD YOU BETTER THAN ANYONE!!
WHY DID YOU CHOOSE CAROLE OVER ME!?
DEEP DOWN, YOU FEEL THE SAME WAY AS ME, DON'T YOU!?
YOU'RE POLAR OPPOSITES! HA-HA! REALLY, YOU COULDN'T BE MORE DIFFERENT!
YOU DON'T SEEM TO GET ALONG THAT WELL TO ME!
AREN'T YOU FORCING YOURSELF TO MATCH CAROLE!?
YOU'RE ALWAYS HAVING HER PROTECT YOU! YOU'RE SUCH A COWARD!
YOU DID THE SAME THING IN THAT LAST SONG!
IT'S ABSURD! WHAT A JOKE...

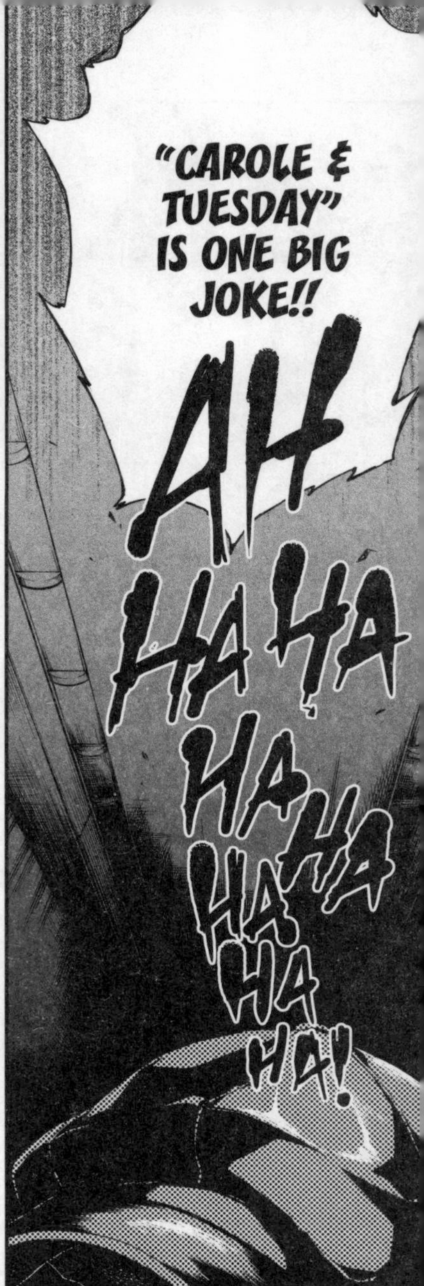
"CAROLE & TUESDAY" IS ONE BIG JOKE!!
AH! HA HA HA HA HA HA HA HA!

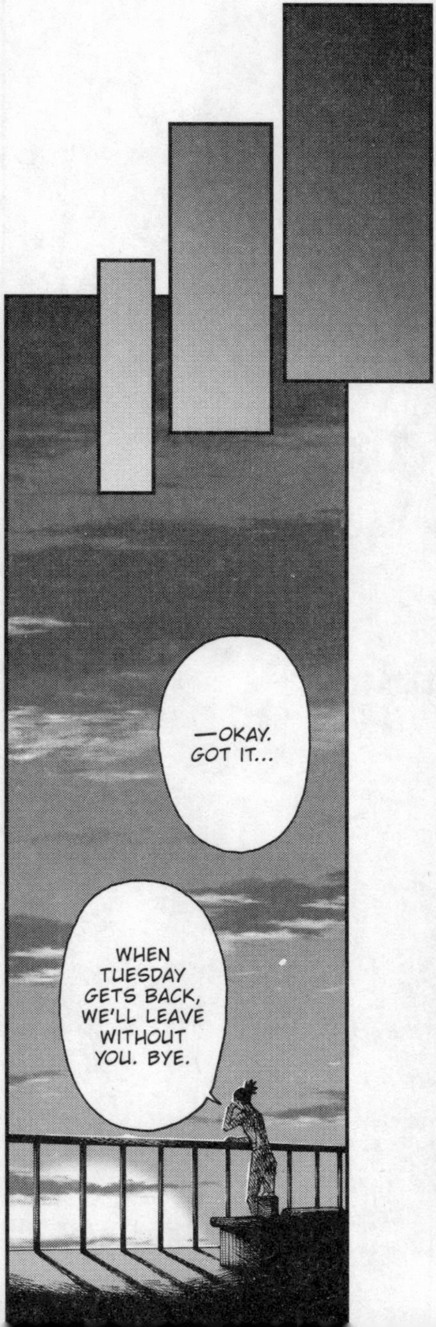
—OKAY. GOT IT...
WHEN TUESDAY GETS BACK, WE'LL LEAVE WITHOUT YOU. BYE.

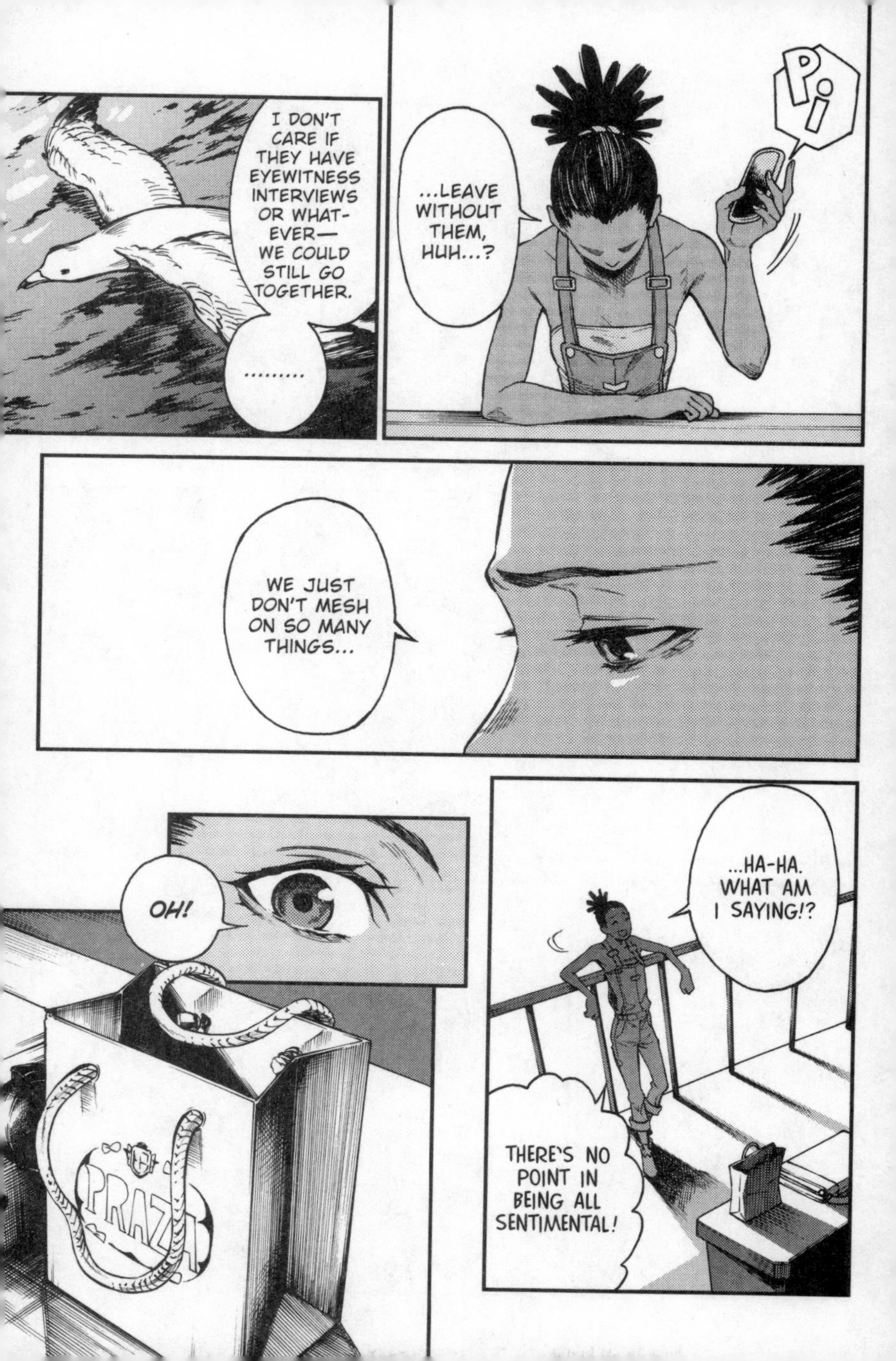
...LEAVE WITHOUT THEM, HUH...?
Pi
I DON'T CARE IF THEY HAVE EYEWITNESS INTERVIEWS OR WHAT-EVER—WE COULD STILL GO TOGETHER.
....
WE JUST DON'T MESH ON SO MANY THINGS...
...HA-HA. WHAT AM I SAYING!?
THERE'S NO POINT IN BEING ALL SENTIMENTAL!
OH!
PRAZA

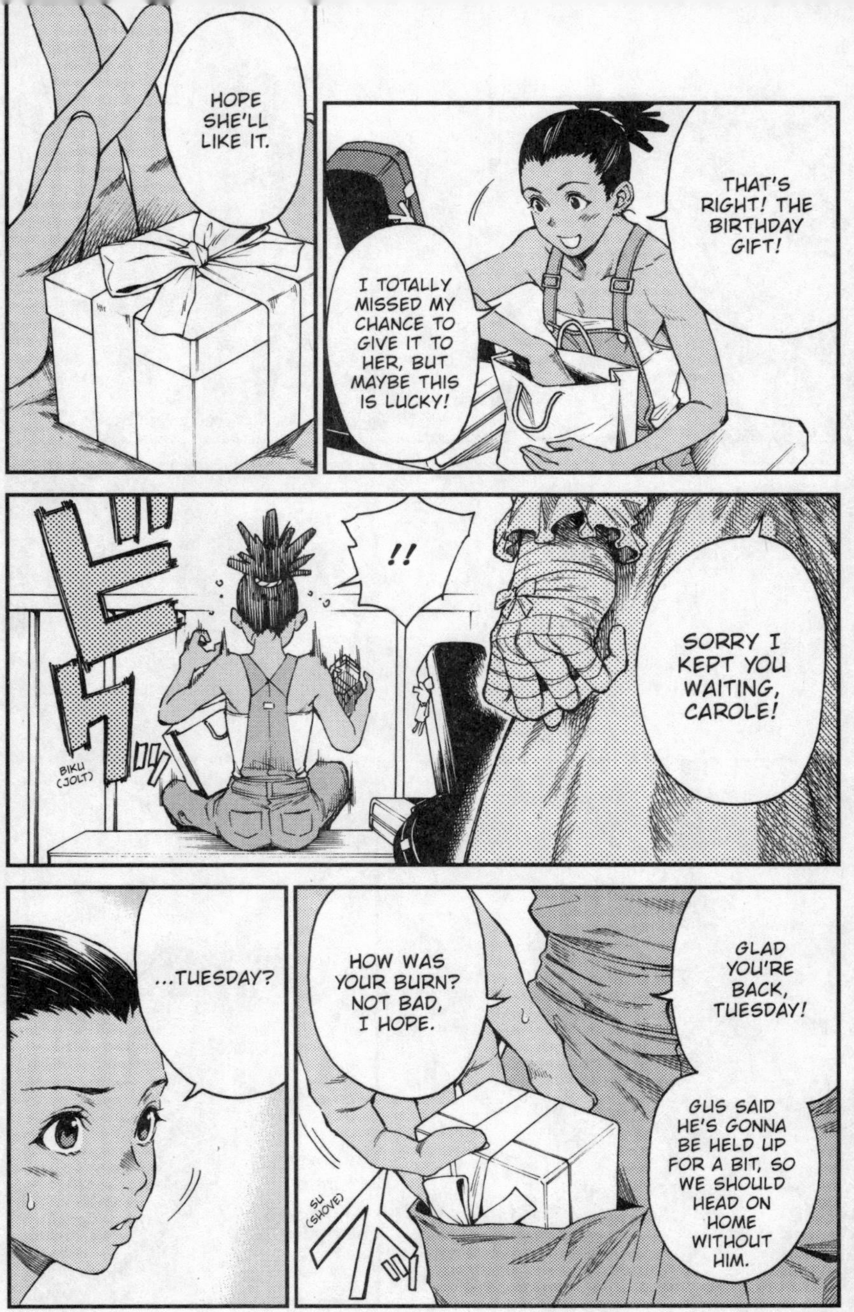
THAT'S RIGHT! THE BIRTHDAY GIFT!
I TOTALLY MISSED MY CHANCE TO GIVE IT TO HER, BUT MAYBE THIS IS LUCKY!
HOPE SHE'LL LIKE IT.
SORRY I KEPT YOU WAITING, CAROLE!
!!
BIKU (JOLT)
GLAD YOU'RE BACK, TUESDAY!
GUS SAID HE'S GONNA BE HELD UP FOR A BIT, SO WE SHOULD HEAD ON HOME WITHOUT HIM.
HOW WAS YOUR BURN? NOT BAD, I HOPE.
SU (SHOVE)
...TUESDAY?

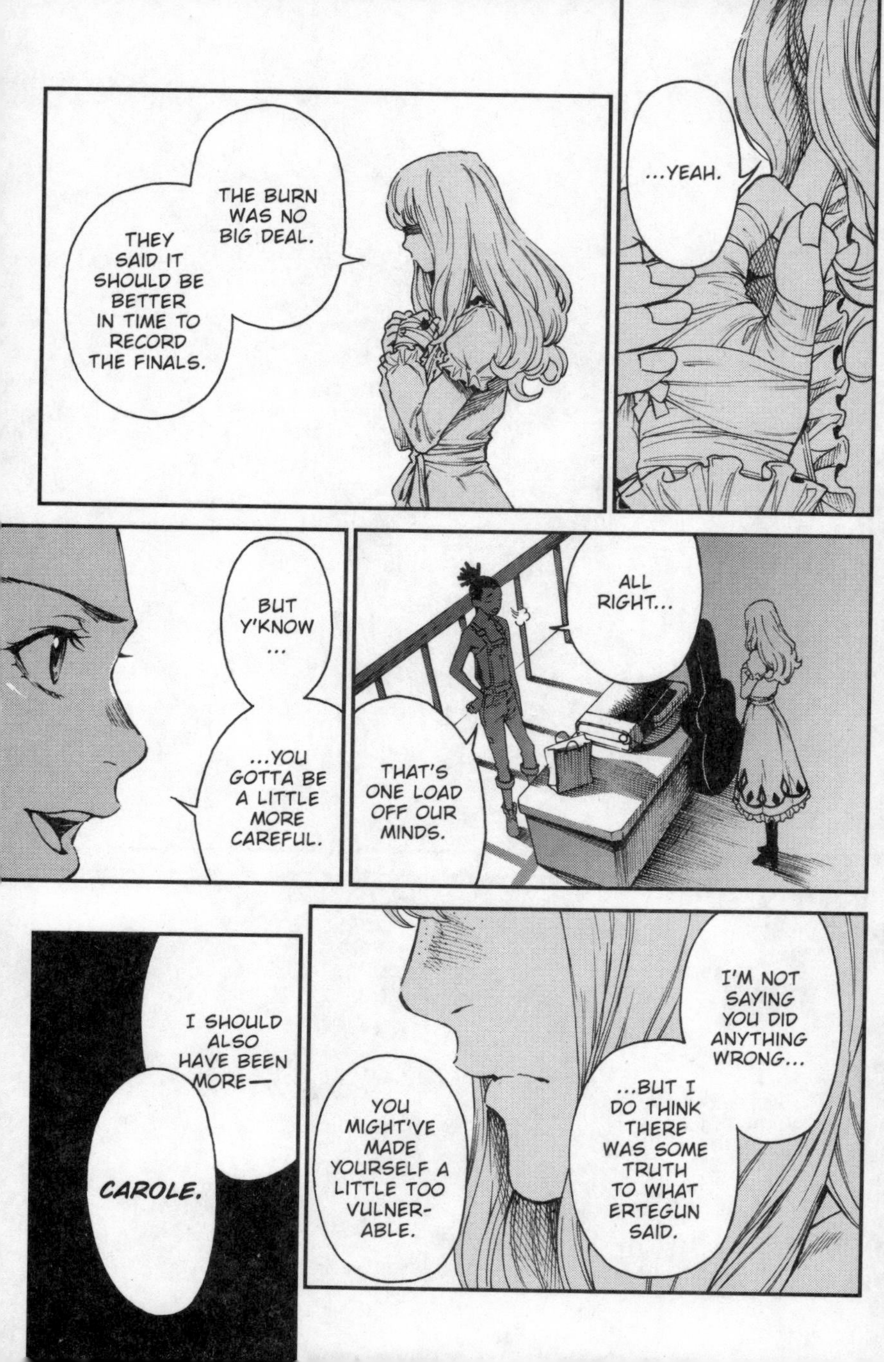
...YEAH.
THE BURN WAS NO BIG DEAL.
THEY SAID IT SHOULD BE BETTER IN TIME TO RECORD THE FINALS.
ALL RIGHT...
THAT'S ONE LOAD OFF OUR MINDS.
BUT Y'KNOW ...
...YOU GOTTA BE A LITTLE MORE CAREFUL.
I'M NOT SAYING YOU DID ANYTHING WRONG...
...BUT I DO THINK THERE WAS SOME TRUTH TO WHAT ERTEGUN SAID.
YOU MIGHT'VE MADE YOURSELF A LITTLE TOO VULNER-ABLE.
I SHOULD ALSO HAVE BEEN MORE—
CAROLE.

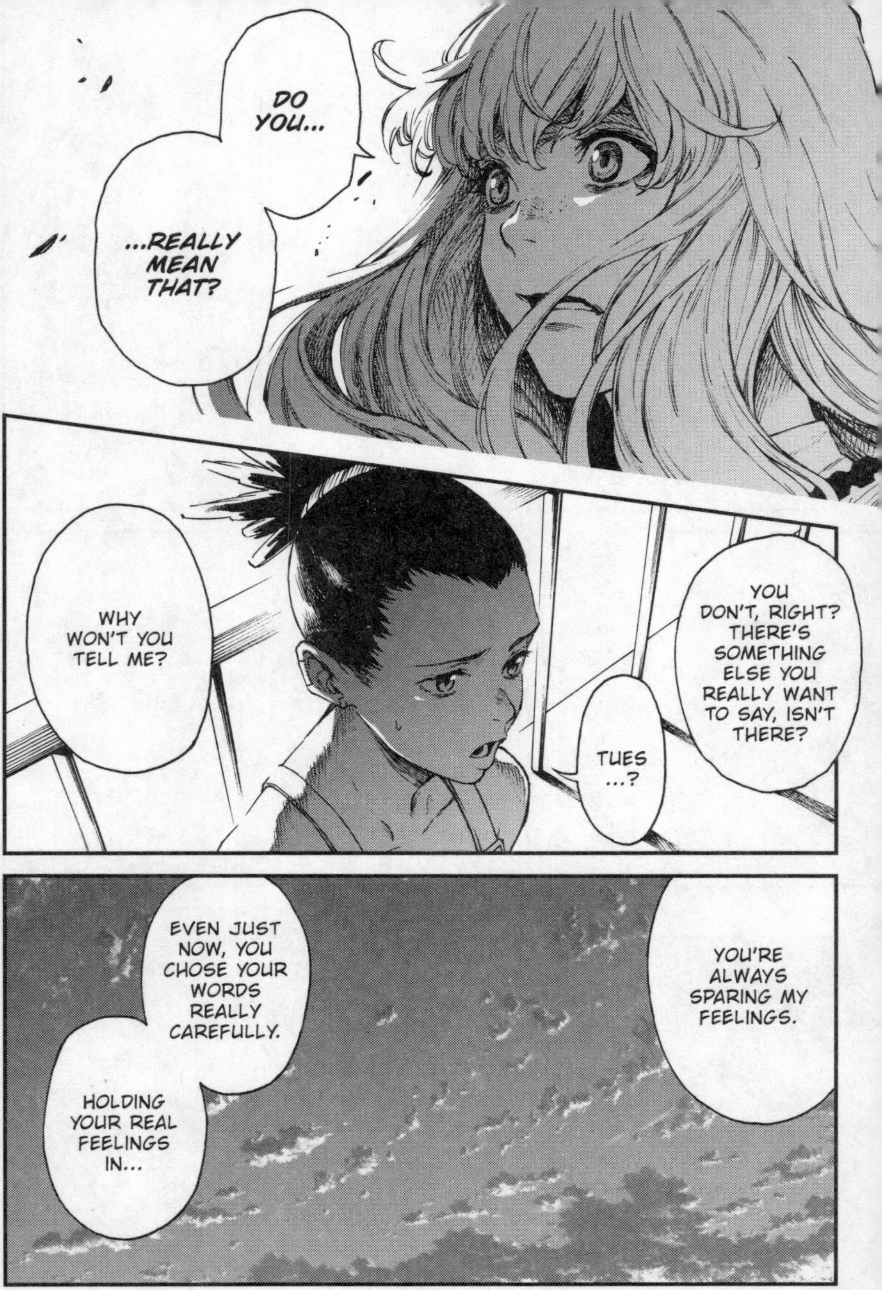
DO YOU...
...REALLY MEAN THAT?
YOU DON'T, RIGHT? THERE'S SOMETHING ELSE YOU REALLY WANT TO SAY, ISN'T THERE?
TUES ...?
WHY WON'T YOU TELL ME?
YOU'RE ALWAYS SPARING MY FEELINGS.
EVEN JUST NOW, YOU CHOSE YOUR WORDS REALLY CAREFULLY.
HOLDING YOUR REAL FEELINGS IN...

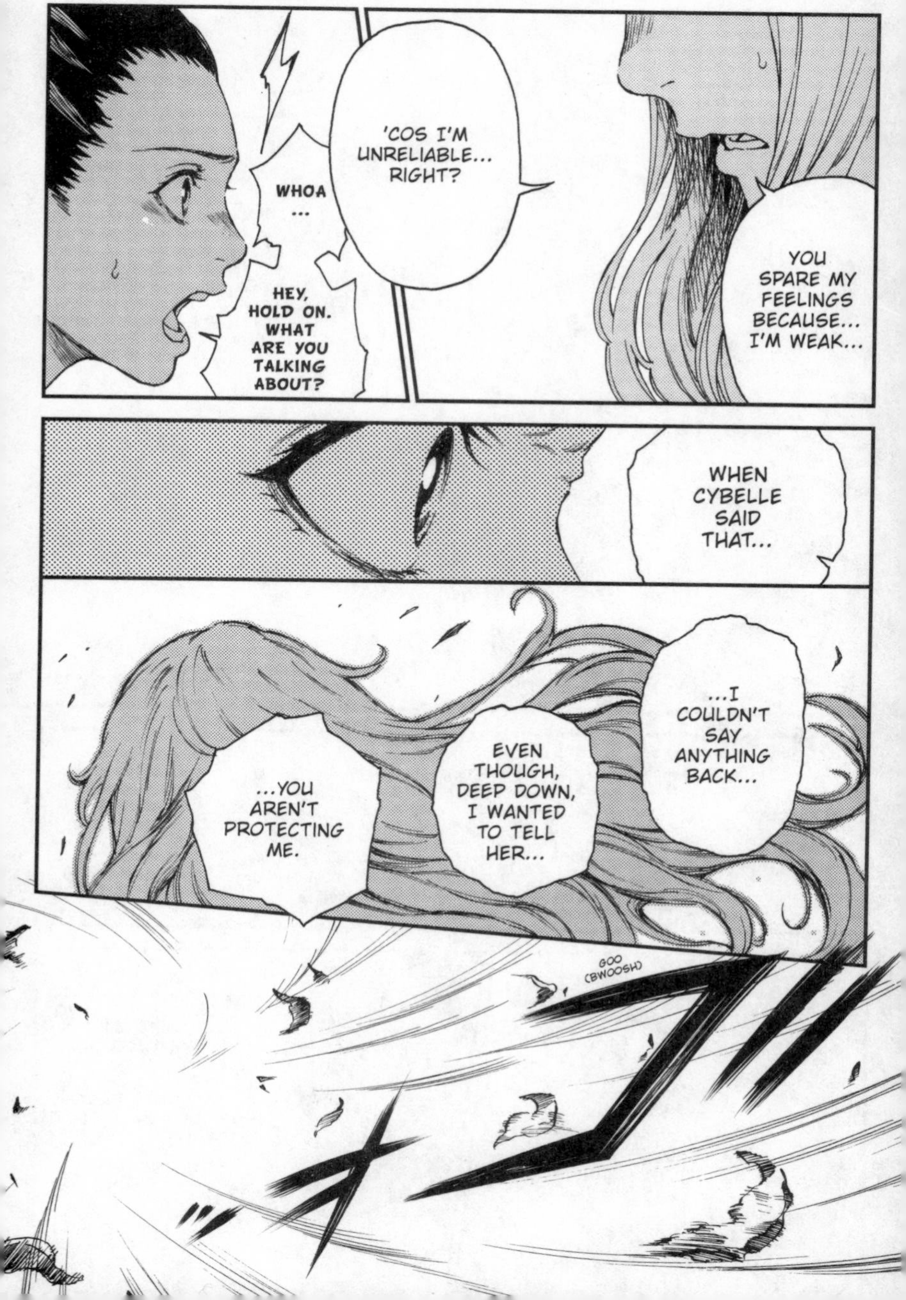
YOU SPARE MY FEELINGS BECAUSE... I'M WEAK...
'COS I'M UNRELIABLE... RIGHT?
WHOA ...
HEY, HOLD ON. WHAT ARE YOU TALKING ABOUT?
WHEN CYBELLE SAID THAT...
...I COULDN'T SAY ANYTHING BACK...
EVEN THOUGH, DEEP DOWN, I WANTED TO TELL HER...
...YOU AREN'T PROTECTING ME.
GOO (BWOOSH)

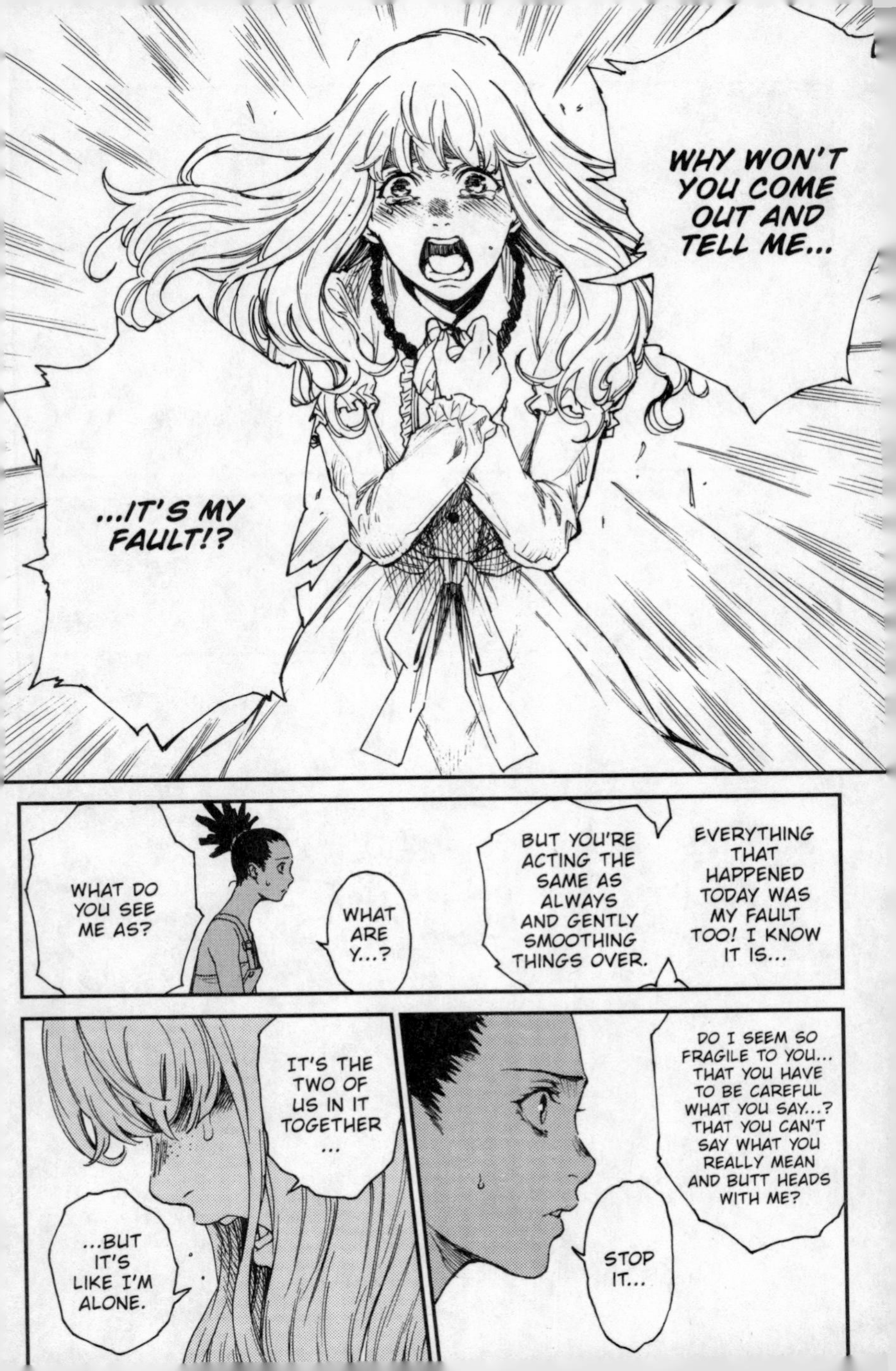
WHY WON'T YOU COME OUT AND TELL ME...
...IT'S MY FAULT!?
EVERYTHING THAT HAPPENED TODAY WAS MY FAULT TOO! I KNOW IT IS...
BUT YOU'RE ACTING THE SAME AS ALWAYS AND GENTLY SMOOTHING THINGS OVER.
WHAT ARE Y...?
WHAT DO YOU SEE ME AS?
DO I SEEM SO FRAGILE TO YOU... THAT YOU HAVE TO BE CAREFUL WHAT YOU SAY...? THAT YOU CAN'T SAY WHAT YOU REALLY MEAN AND BUTT HEADS WITH ME?
STOP IT...
IT'S THE TWO OF US IN IT TOGETHER ...
...BUT IT'S LIKE I'M ALONE.

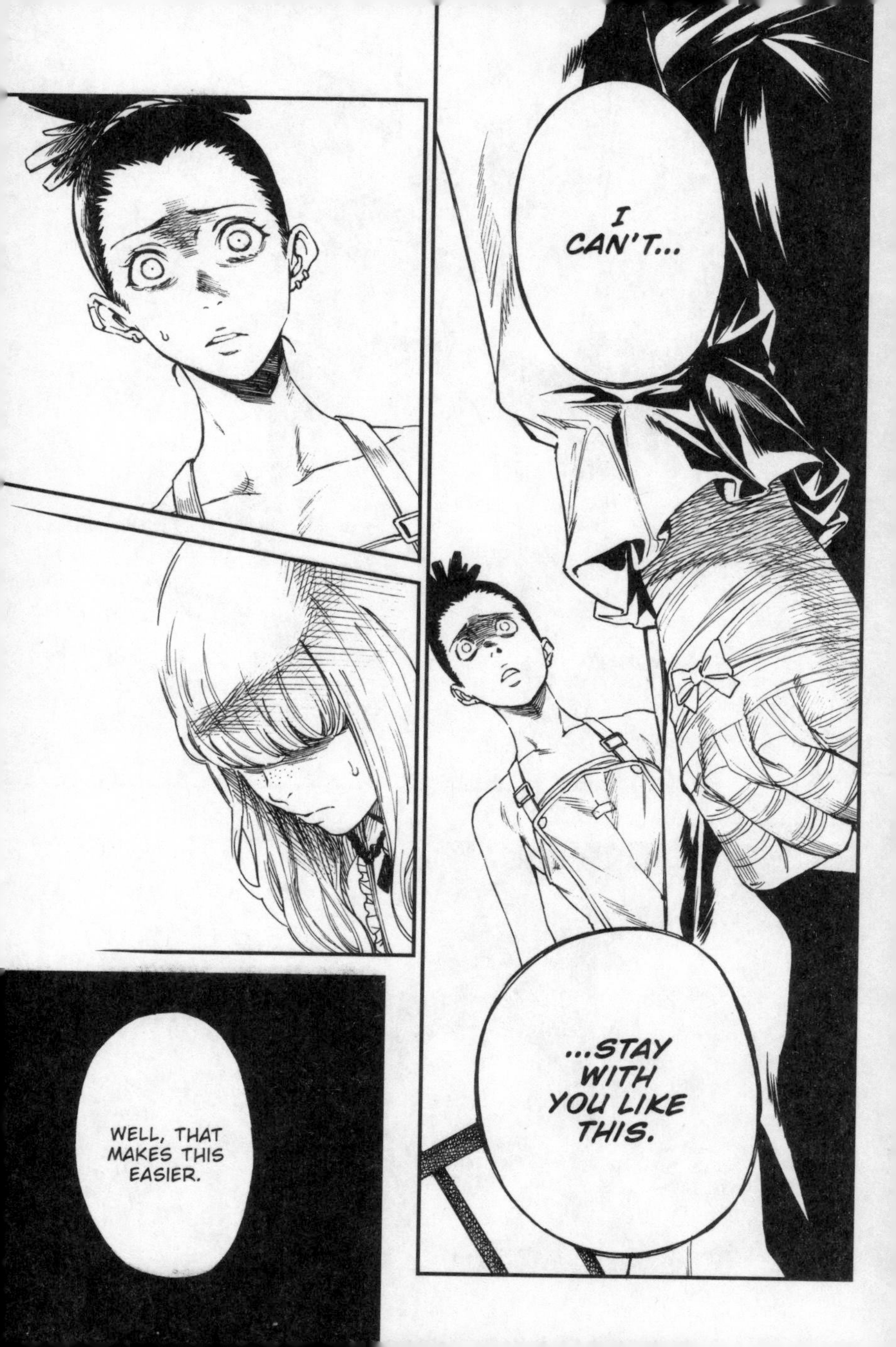
I CAN'T...
...STAY WITH YOU LIKE THIS.
WELL, THAT MAKES THIS EASIER.

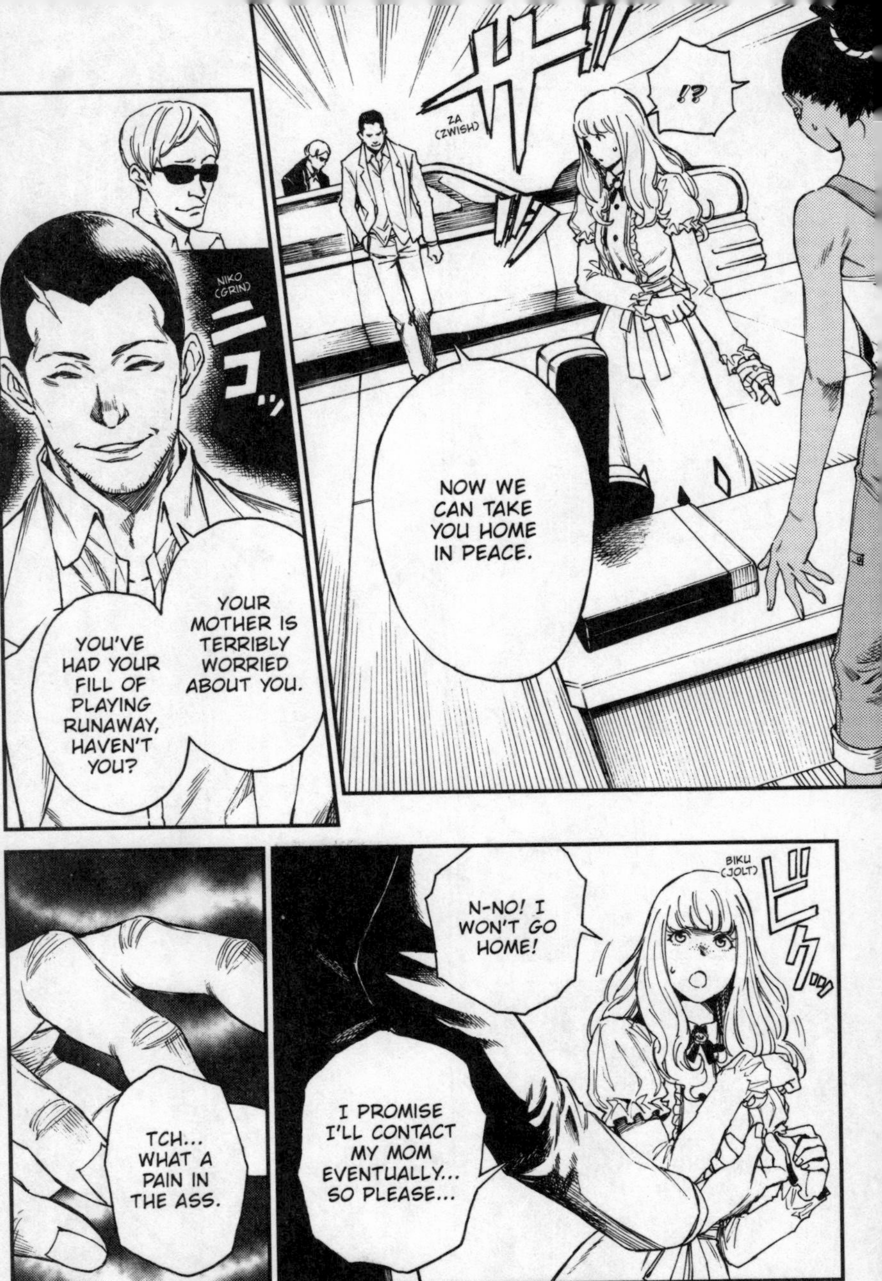
ZA (ZWISH)
!?
NOW WE CAN TAKE YOU HOME IN PEACE.
NIKO (GRIN)
YOUR MOTHER IS TERRIBLY WORRIED ABOUT YOU.
YOU'VE HAD YOUR FILL OF PLAYING RUNAWAY, HAVEN'T YOU?
BIKU (JOLT)
N-NO! I WON'T GO HOME!
I PROMISE I'LL CONTACT MY MOM EVENTUALLY... SO PLEASE...
TCH... WHAT A PAIN IN THE ASS.

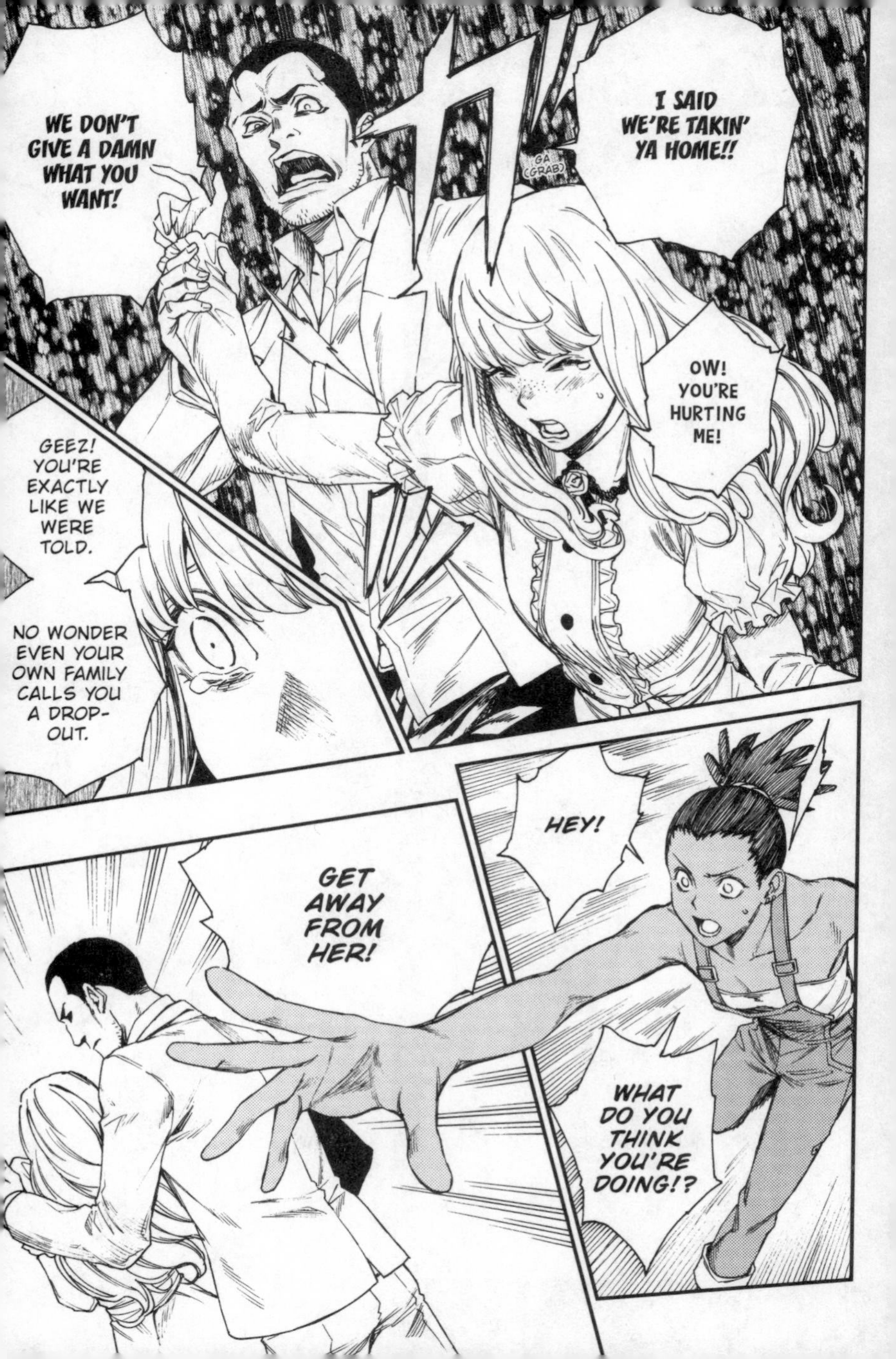
I SAID WE'RE TAKIN' YA HOME!!
GA (GRAB)
WE DON'T GIVE A DAMN WHAT YOU WANT!
OW! YOU'RE HURTING ME!
GEEZ! YOU'RE EXACTLY LIKE WE WERE TOLD.
NO WONDER EVEN YOUR OWN FAMILY CALLS YOU A DROP-OUT.
HEY!
WHAT DO YOU THINK YOU'RE DOING!?
GET AWAY FROM HER!

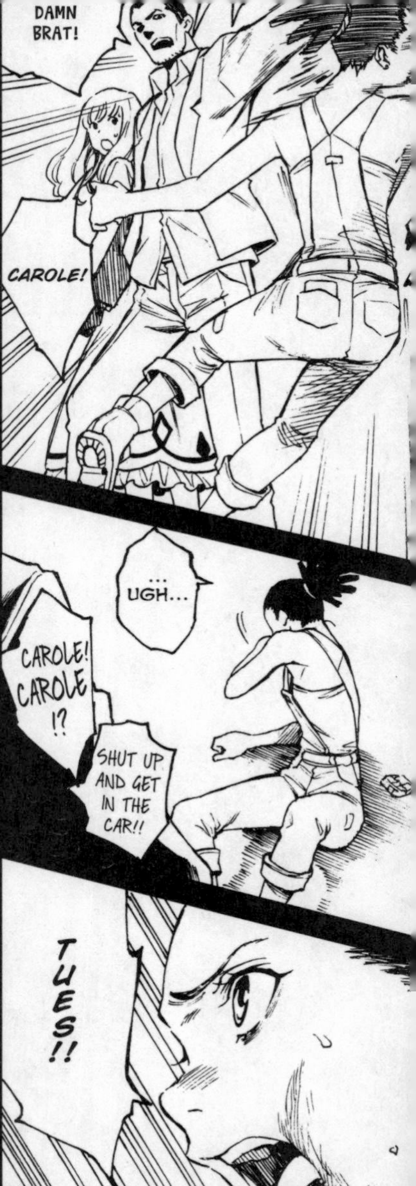
DAMN BRAT!
CAROLE!
...UGH...
CAROLE! CAROLE!?
SHUT UP AND GET IN THE CAR!!
TUES!!
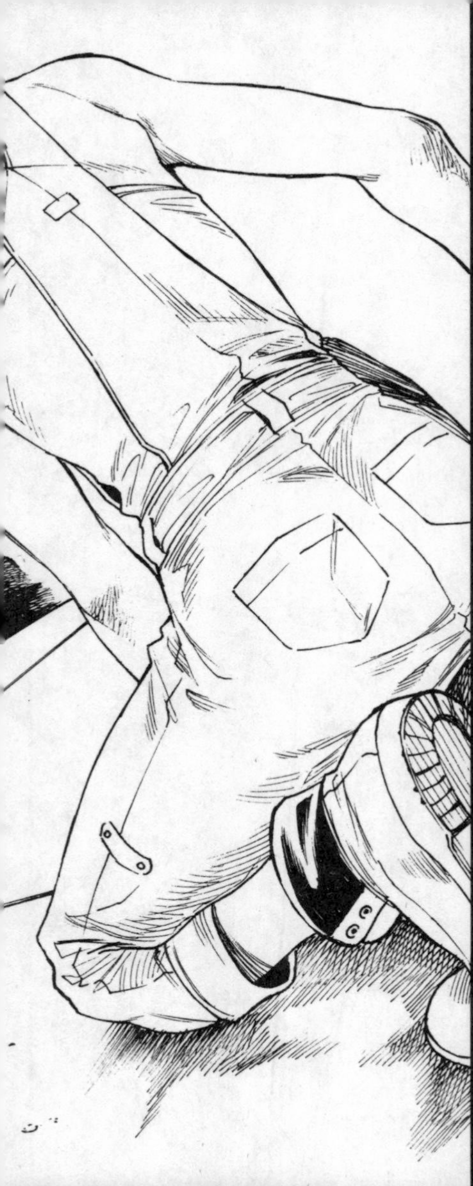

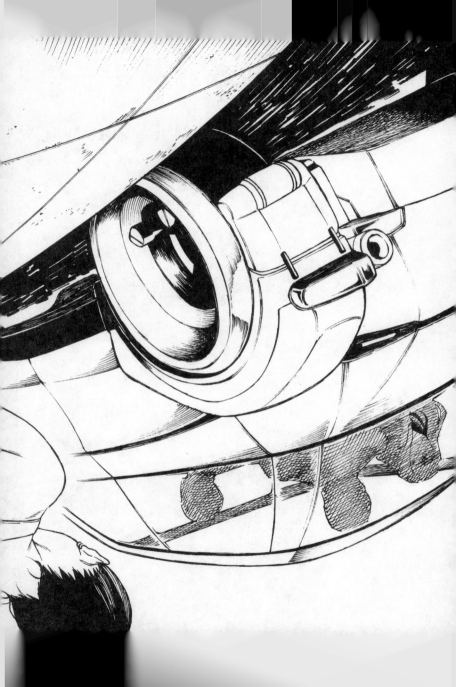

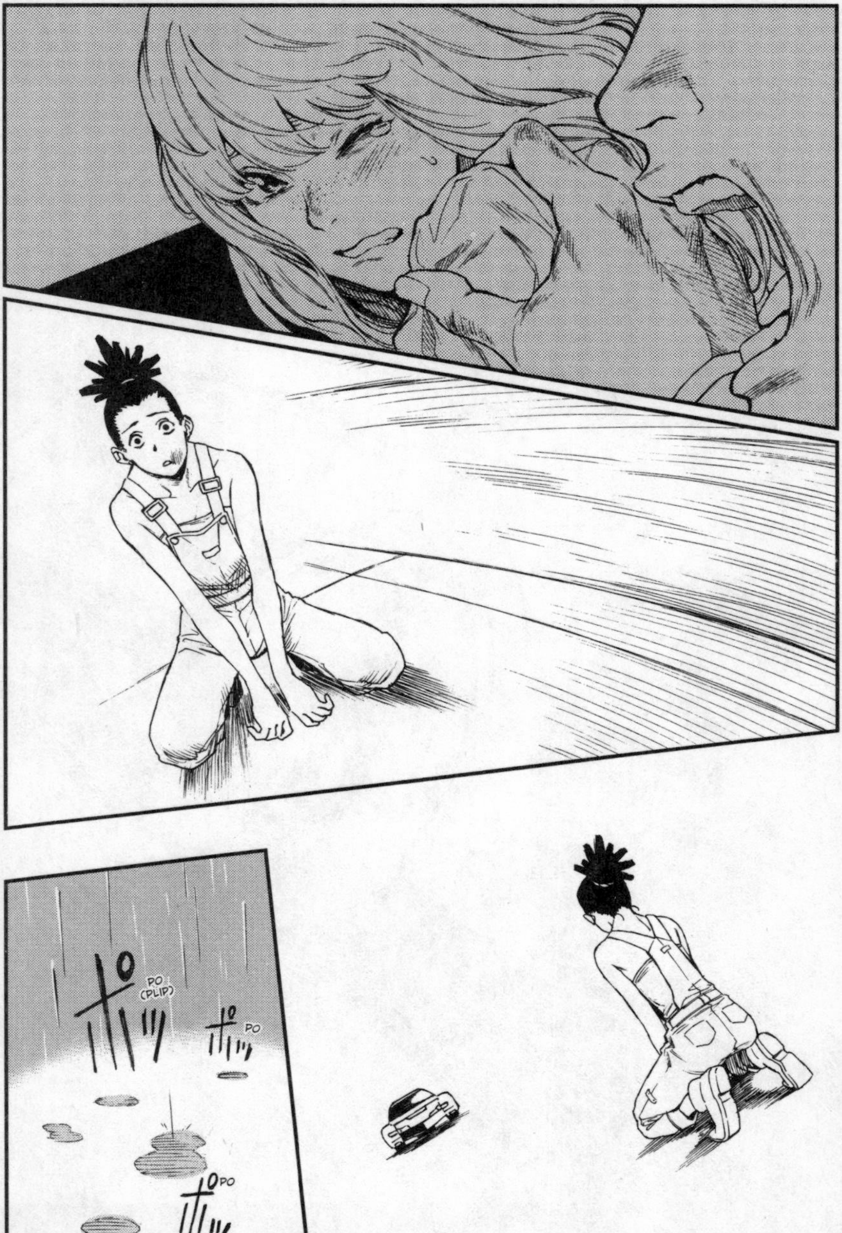
PO
(PLIP)
PO
PO

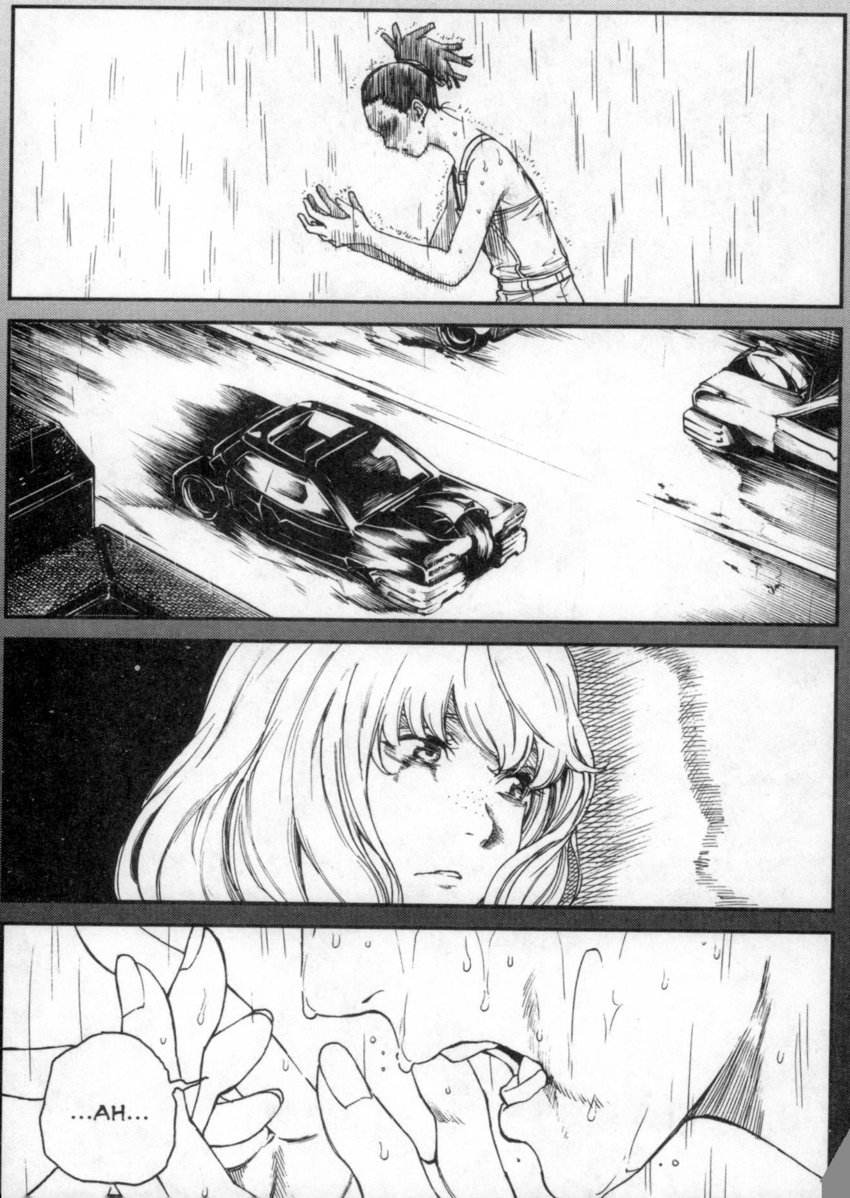
...AH...

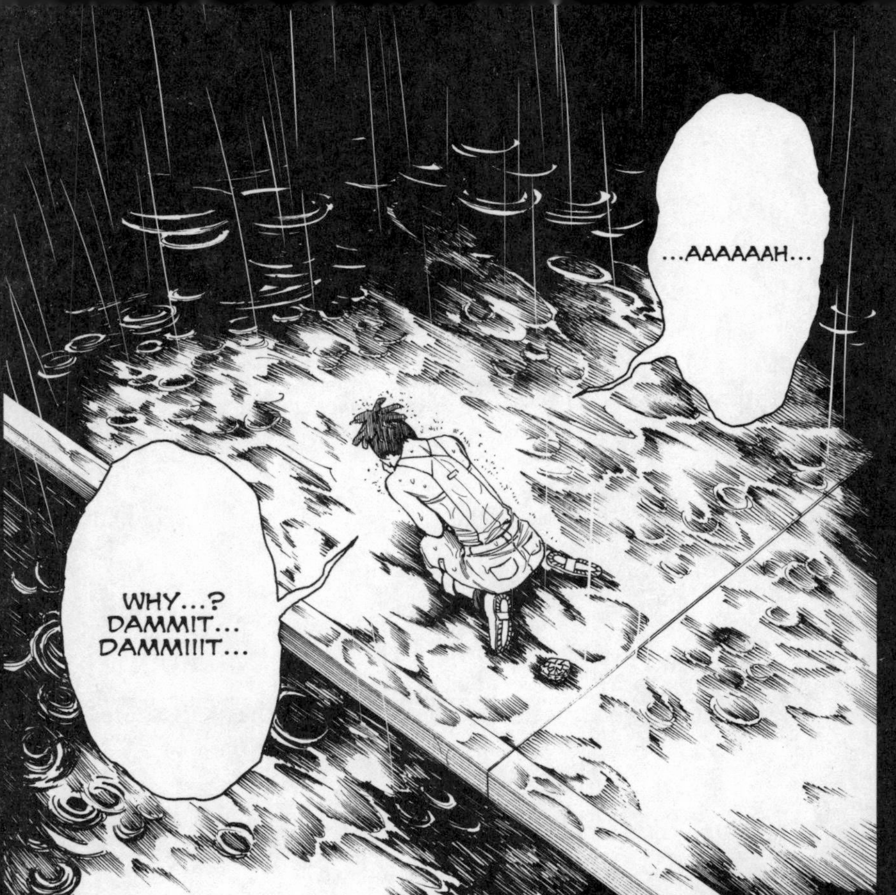
...AAAAAAH...
WHY...? DAMMIT... DAMMIIIT...

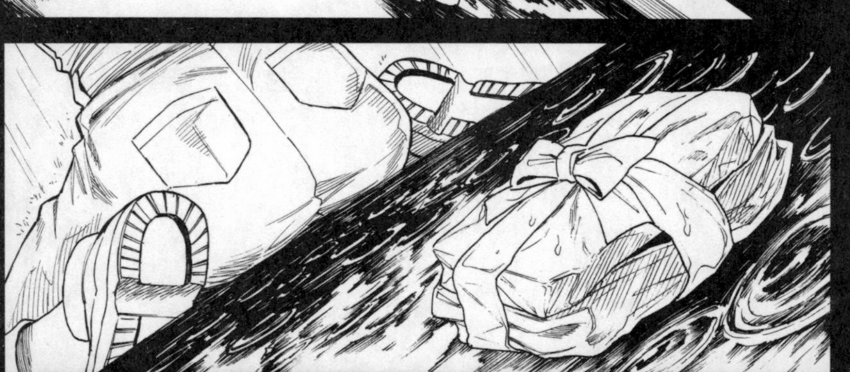

END

ep 14

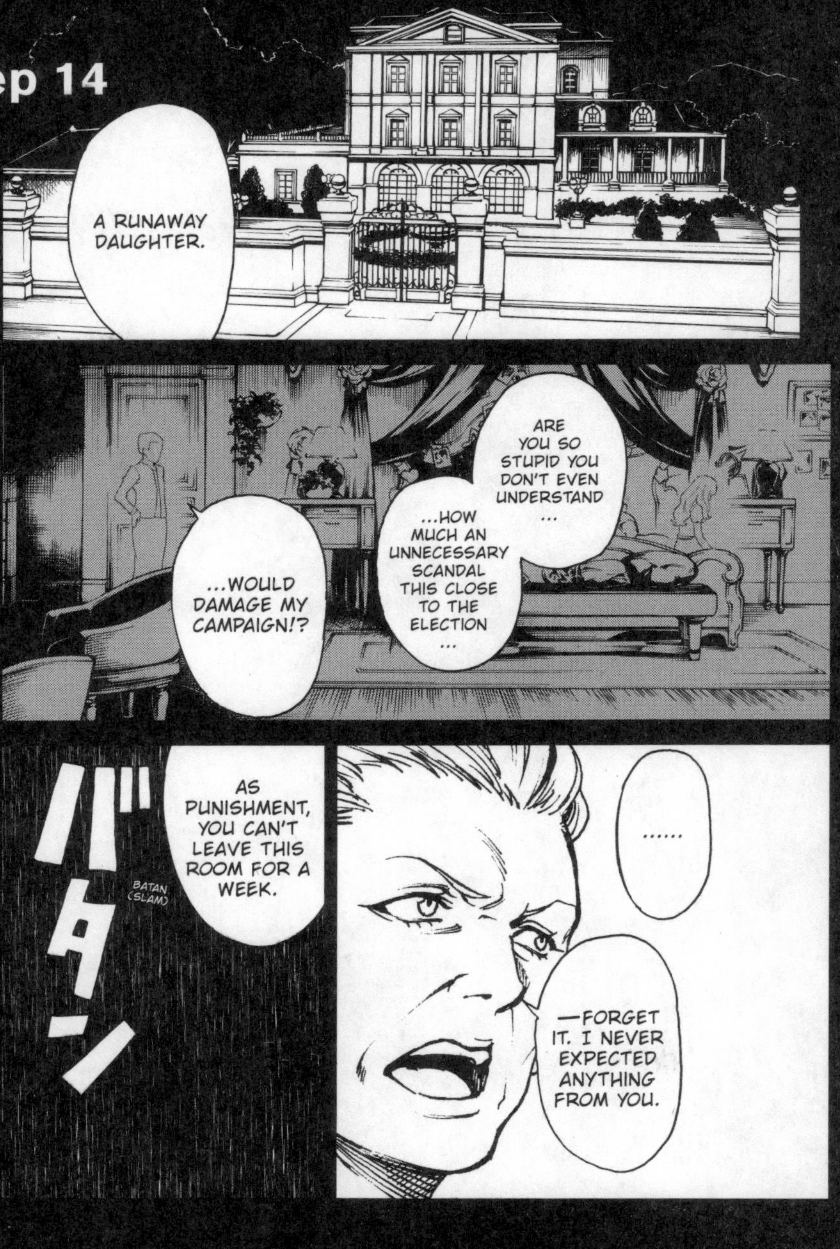
A RUNAWAY DAUGHTER.
ARE YOU SO STUPID YOU DON'T EVEN UNDERSTAND ...
...HOW MUCH AN UNNECESSARY SCANDAL THIS CLOSE TO THE ELECTION ...
...WOULD DAMAGE MY CAMPAIGN!?
......
—FORGET IT. I NEVER EXPECTED ANYTHING FROM YOU.
AS PUNISHMENT, YOU CAN'T LEAVE THIS ROOM FOR A WEEK.
バタン
BATAN (SLAM)

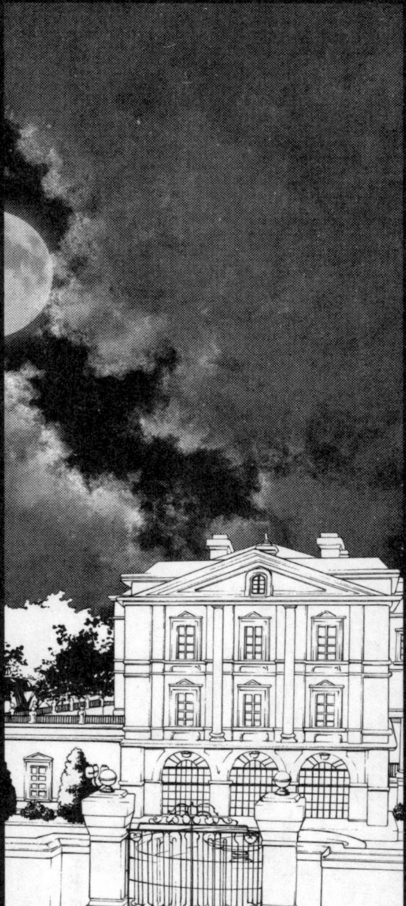

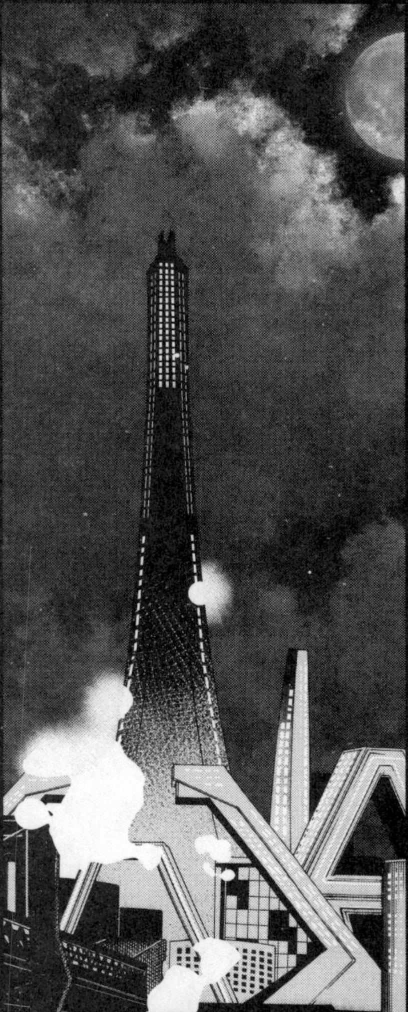

episode 14: We've Only Just Begun 2

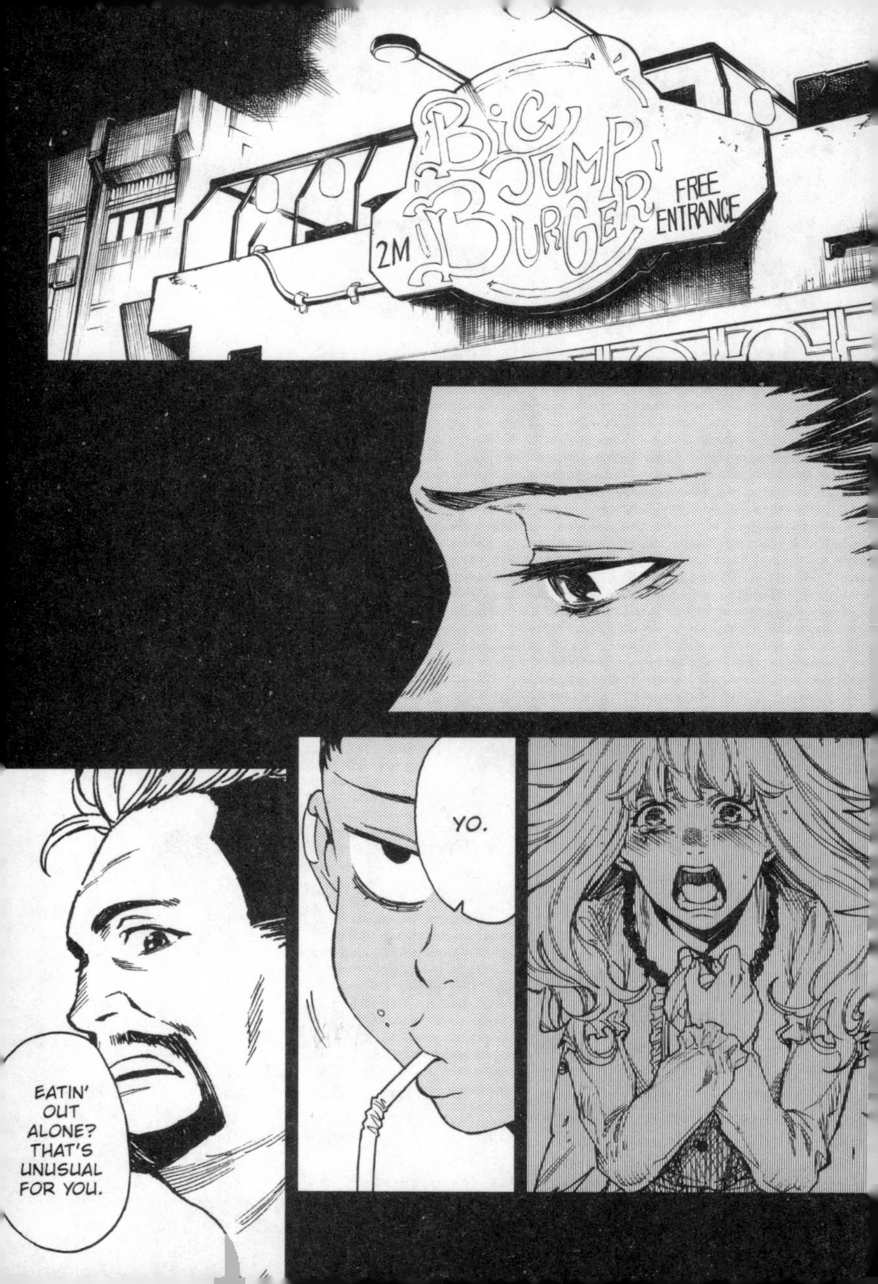
BIG JUMP BURGER
2M
FREE ENTRANCE
YO.
EATIN' OUT ALONE? THAT'S UNUSUAL FOR YOU.

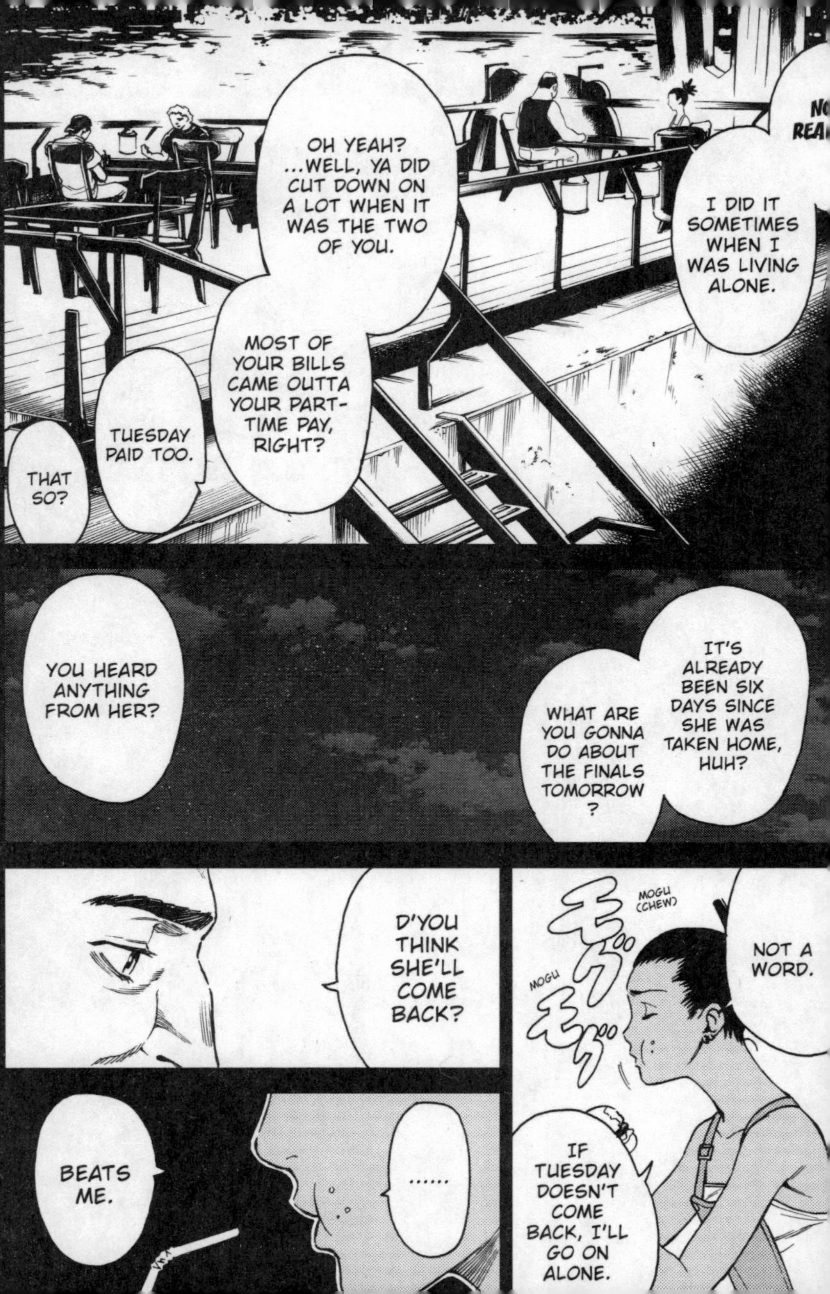
I DID IT SOMETIMES WHEN I WAS LIVING ALONE.
OH YEAH? ...WELL, YA DID CUT DOWN ON A LOT WHEN IT WAS THE TWO OF YOU.
MOST OF YOUR BILLS CAME OUTTA YOUR PART-TIME PAY, RIGHT?
TUESDAY PAID TOO.
THAT SO?
IT'S ALREADY BEEN SIX DAYS SINCE SHE WAS TAKEN HOME, HUH?
WHAT ARE YOU GONNA DO ABOUT THE FINALS TOMORROW?
YOU HEARD ANYTHING FROM HER?
NOT A WORD.
MOGU (CHEW)
MOGU
IF TUESDAY DOESN'T COME BACK, I'LL GO ON ALONE.
D'YOU THINK SHE'LL COME BACK?
......
BEATS ME.

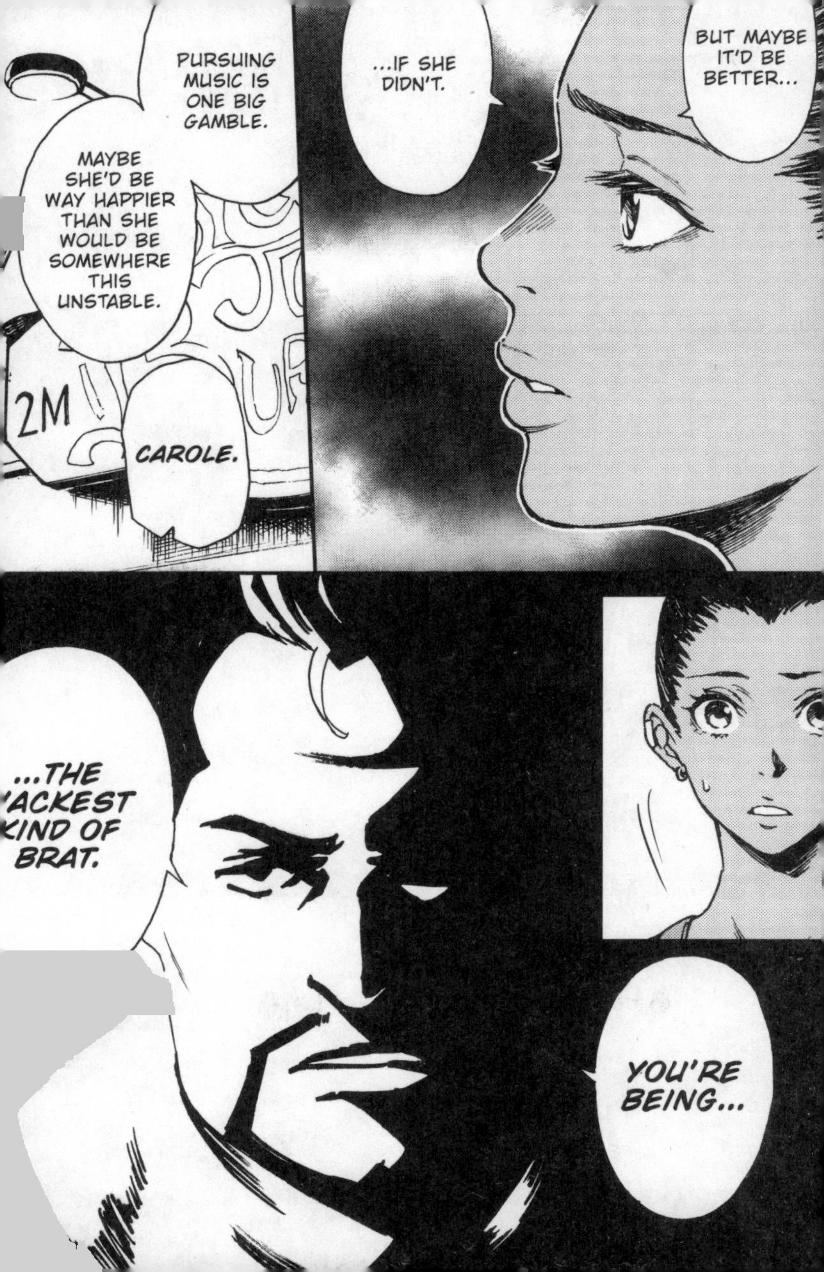
BUT MAYBE IT'D BE BETTER...
...IF SHE DIDN'T.
PURSUING MUSIC IS ONE BIG GAMBLE.
MAYBE SHE'D BE WAY HAPPIER THAN SHE WOULD BE SOMEWHERE THIS UNSTABLE.
2M
CAROLE.
YOU'RE BEING...
...THE ACKEST KIND OF BRAT.

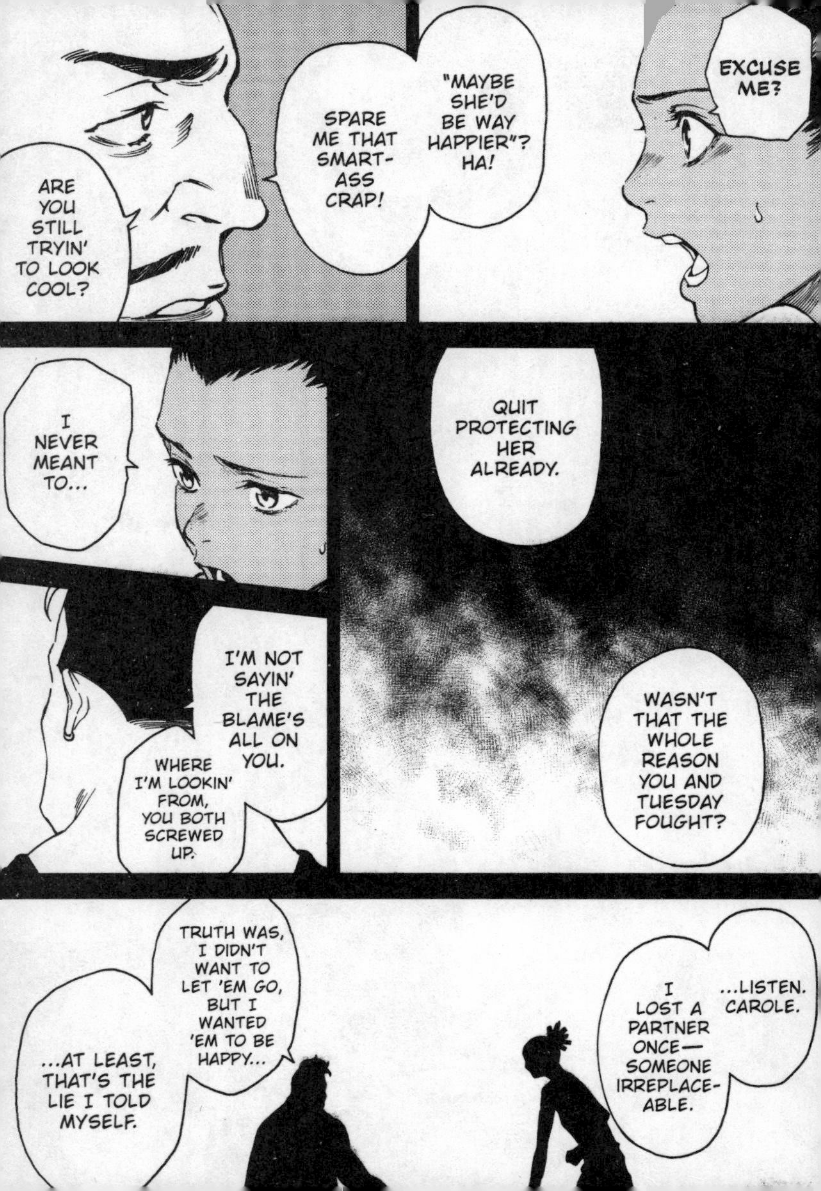
EXCUSE ME?
"MAYBE SHE'D BE WAY HAPPIER"? HA!
SPARE ME THAT SMART-ASS CRAP!
ARE YOU STILL TRYIN' TO LOOK COOL?
QUIT PROTECTING HER ALREADY.
WASN'T THAT THE WHOLE REASON YOU AND TUESDAY FOUGHT?
I NEVER MEANT TO...
I'M NOT SAYIN' THE BLAME'S ALL ON YOU.
WHERE I'M LOOKIN' FROM, YOU BOTH SCREWED UP.
...LISTEN. CAROLE.
I LOST A PARTNER ONCE—SOMEONE IRREPLACE-ABLE.
TRUTH WAS, I DIDN'T WANT TO LET 'EM GO, BUT I WANTED 'EM TO BE HAPPY...
...AT LEAST, THAT'S THE LIE I TOLD MYSELF.

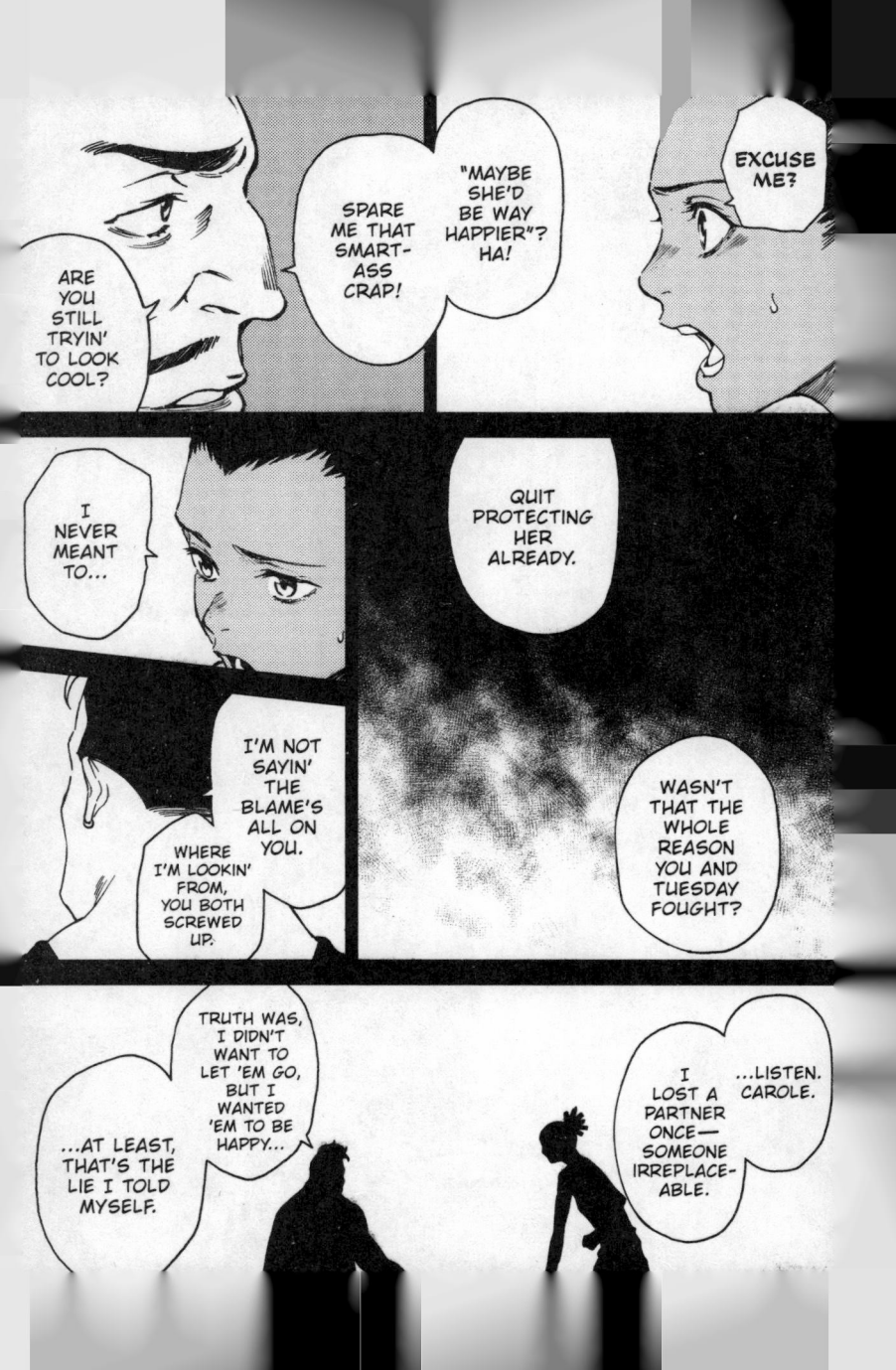

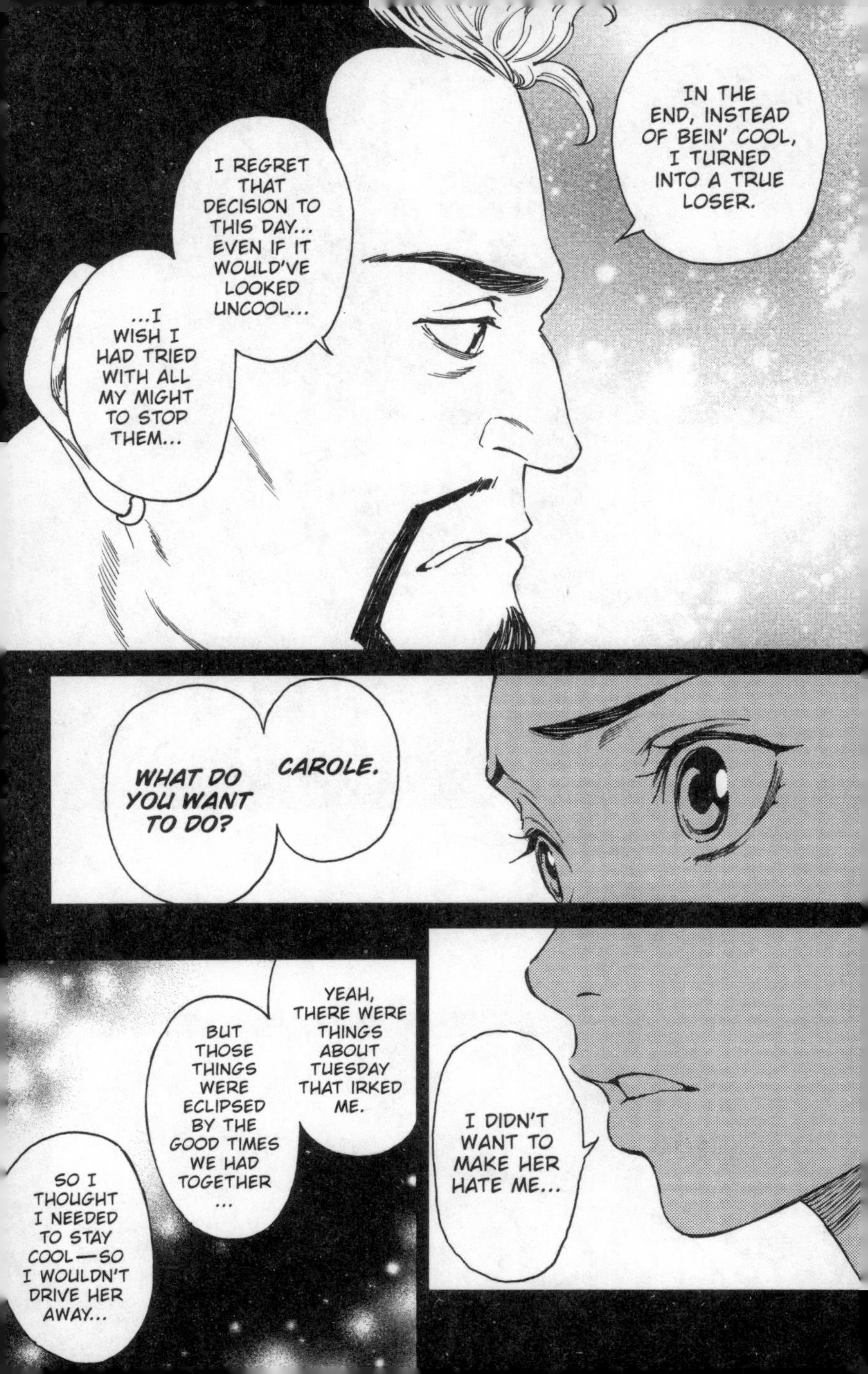
IN THE END, INSTEAD OF BEIN' COOL, I TURNED INTO A TRUE LOSER.
I REGRET THAT DECISION TO THIS DAY... EVEN IF IT WOULD'VE LOOKED UNCOOL...
...I WISH I HAD TRIED WITH ALL MY MIGHT TO STOP THEM...
CAROLE.
WHAT DO YOU WANT TO DO?
I DIDN'T WANT TO MAKE HER HATE ME...
YEAH, THERE WERE THINGS ABOUT TUESDAY THAT IRKED ME.
BUT THOSE THINGS WERE ECLIPSED BY THE GOOD TIMES WE HAD TOGETHER...
SO I THOUGHT I NEEDED TO STAY COOL—SO I WOULDN'T DRIVE HER AWAY...

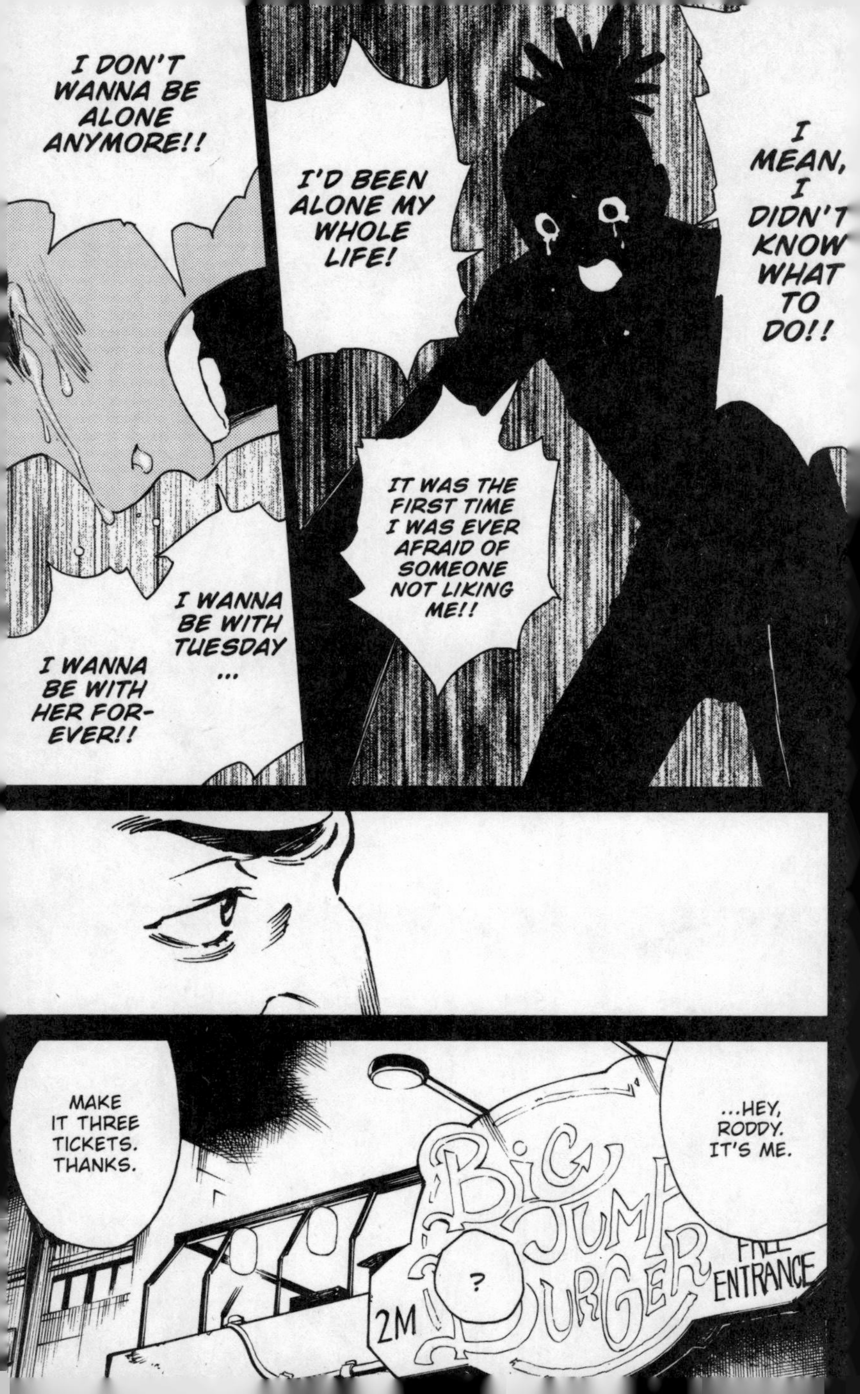
I MEAN, I DIDN'T KNOW WHAT TO DO!!
I'D BEEN ALONE MY WHOLE LIFE!
IT WAS THE FIRST TIME I WAS EVER AFRAID OF SOMEONE NOT LIKING ME!!
I DON'T WANNA BE ALONE ANYMORE!!
I WANNA BE WITH TUESDAY ...
I WANNA BE WITH HER FOR-EVER!!
...HEY, RODDY. IT'S ME.
ENTRANCE
2M
?
MAKE IT THREE TICKETS. THANKS.

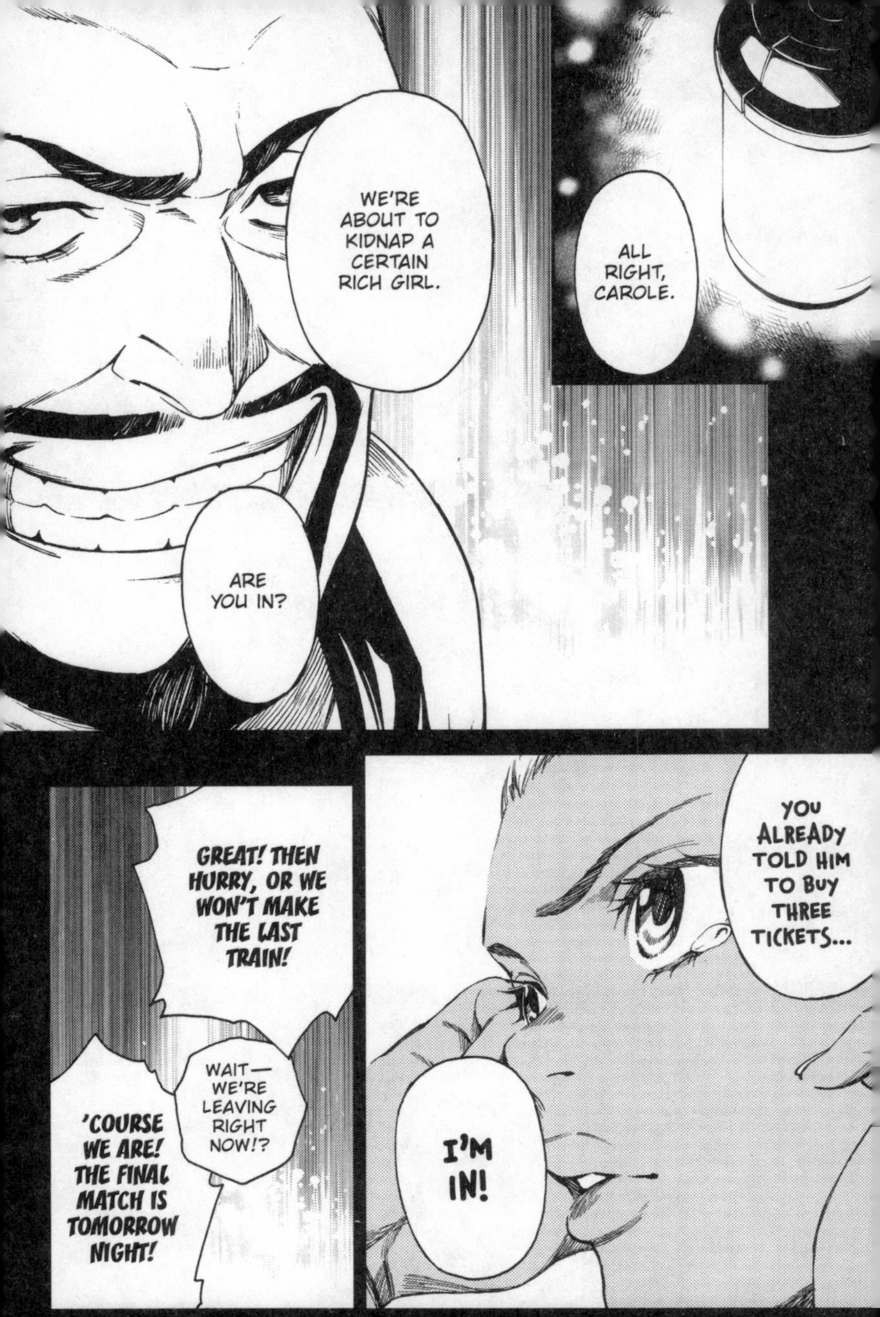
ALL RIGHT, CAROLE.
WE'RE ABOUT TO KIDNAP A CERTAIN RICH GIRL.
ARE YOU IN?
YOU ALREADY TOLD HIM TO BUY THREE TICKETS...
I'M IN!
GREAT! THEN HURRY, OR WE WON'T MAKE THE LAST TRAIN!
WAIT— WE'RE LEAVING RIGHT NOW!?
'COURSE WE ARE! THE FINAL MATCH IS TOMORROW NIGHT!

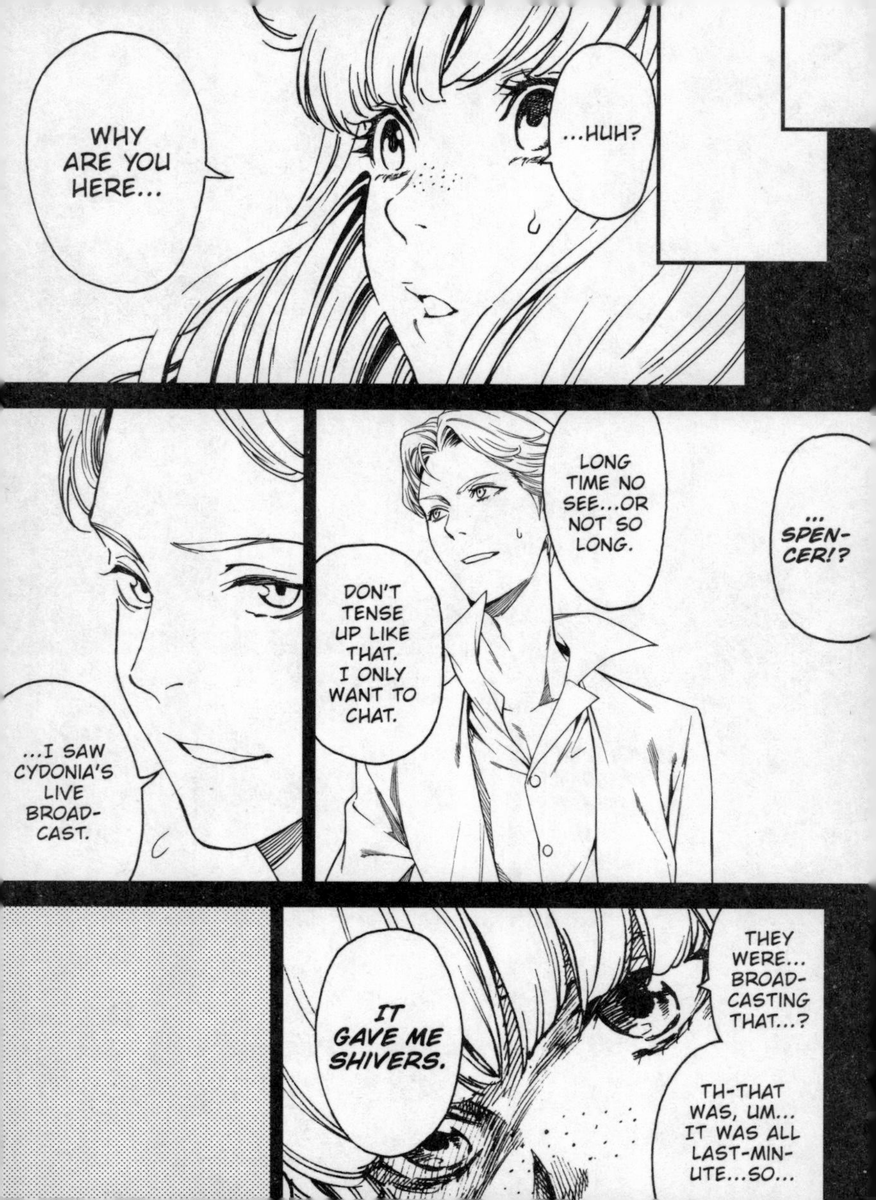
...HUH?
WHY ARE YOU HERE...
... SPEN-CER!?
LONG TIME NO SEE...OR NOT SO LONG.
DON'T TENSE UP LIKE THAT. I ONLY WANT TO CHAT.
...I SAW CYDONIA'S LIVE BROAD-CAST.
IT GAVE ME SHIVERS.
THEY WERE... BROAD-CASTING THAT...?
TH-THAT WAS, UM... IT WAS ALL LAST-MIN-UTE...SO...

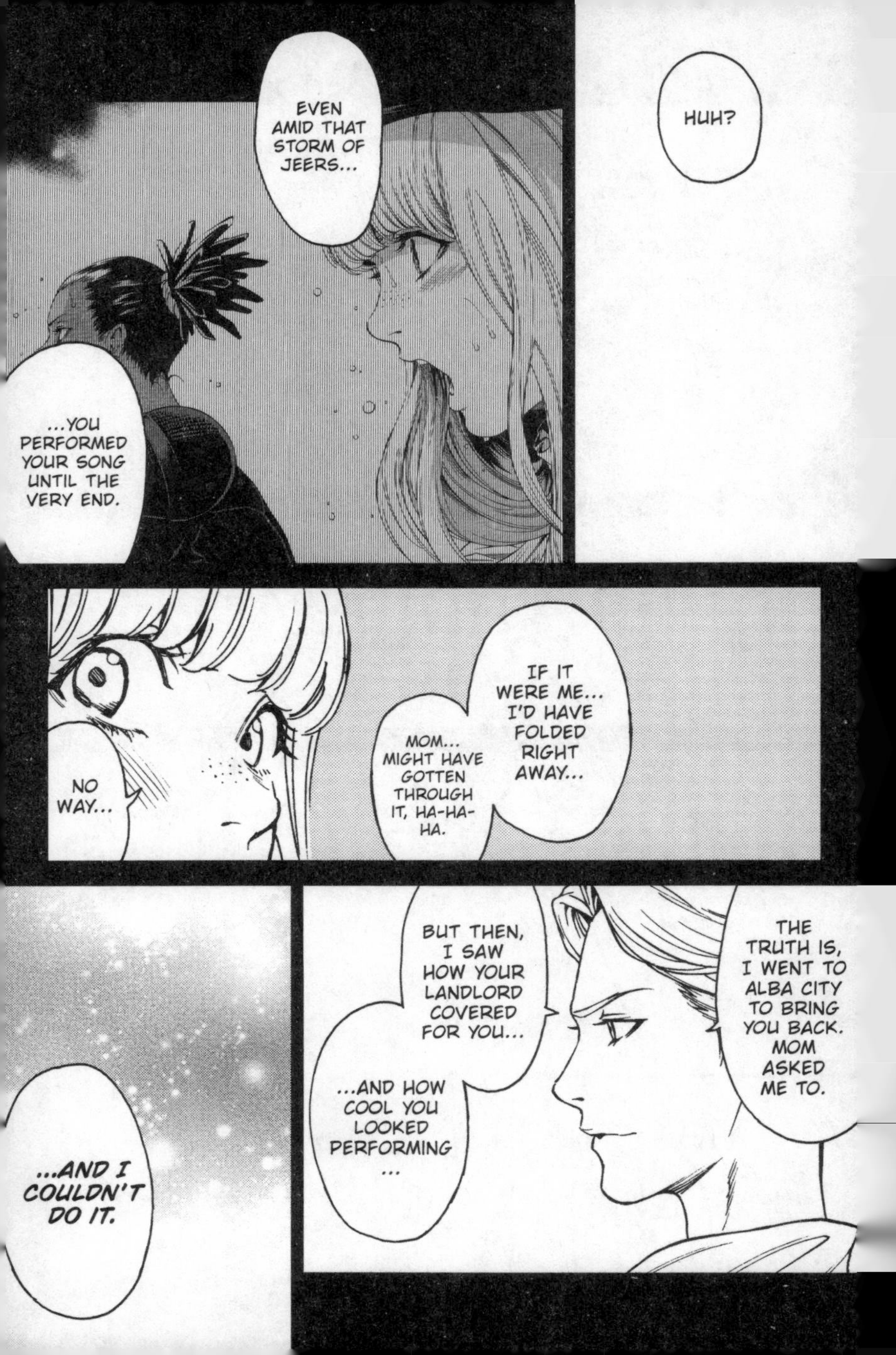
HUH?
EVEN AMID THAT STORM OF JEERS...
...YOU PERFORMED YOUR SONG UNTIL THE VERY END.
IF IT WERE ME... I'D HAVE FOLDED RIGHT AWAY...
MOM... MIGHT HAVE GOTTEN THROUGH IT, HA-HA-HA.
NO WAY...
THE TRUTH IS, I WENT TO ALBA CITY TO BRING YOU BACK. MOM ASKED ME TO.
BUT THEN, I SAW HOW YOUR LANDLORD COVERED FOR YOU...
...AND HOW COOL YOU LOOKED PERFORMING...
...AND I COULDN'T DO IT.

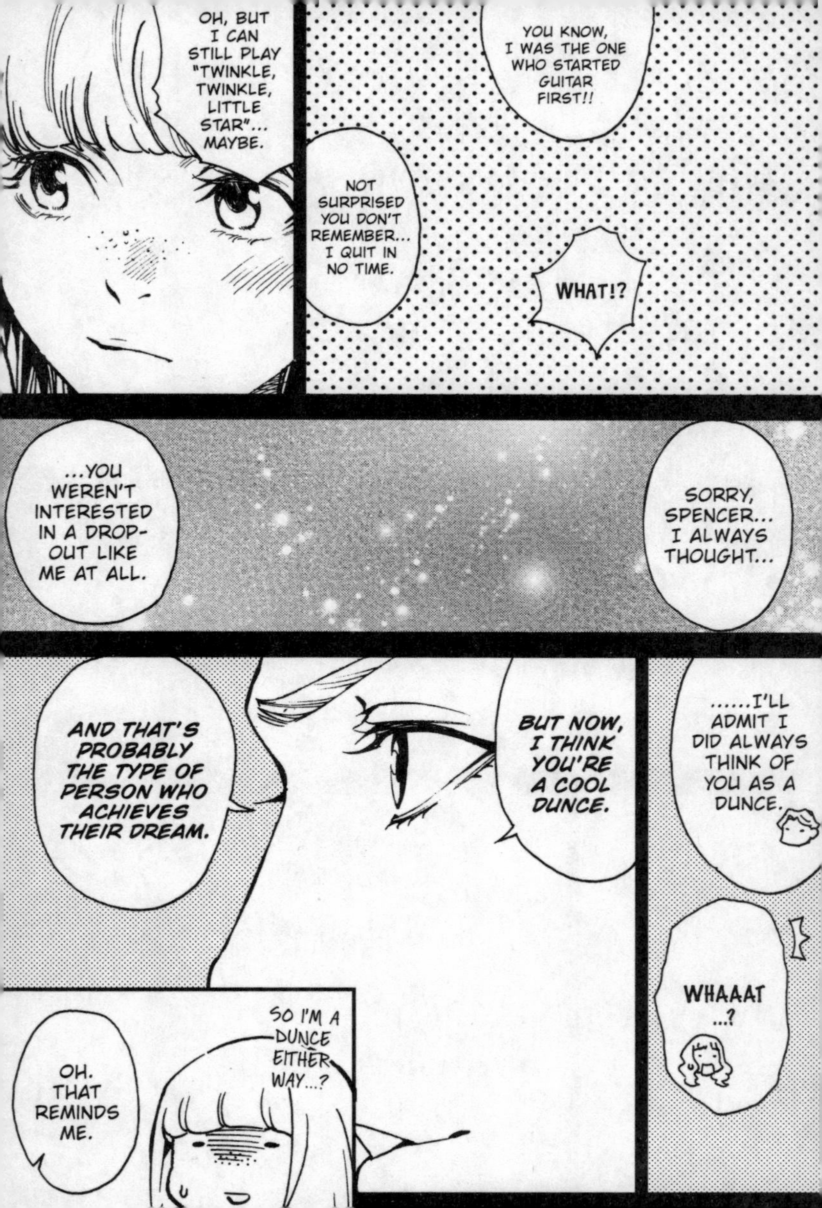
YOU KNOW, I WAS THE ONE WHO STARTED GUITAR FIRST!!
NOT SURPRISED YOU DON'T REMEMBER... I QUIT IN NO TIME.
WHAT!?
OH, BUT I CAN STILL PLAY "TWINKLE, TWINKLE, LITTLE STAR"... MAYBE.
SORRY, SPENCER... I ALWAYS THOUGHT...
...YOU WEREN'T INTERESTED IN A DROP-OUT LIKE ME AT ALL.
......I'LL ADMIT I DID ALWAYS THINK OF YOU AS A DUNCE.
WHAAAT ...?
BUT NOW, I THINK YOU'RE A COOL DUNCE.
AND THAT'S PROBABLY THE TYPE OF PERSON WHO ACHIEVES THEIR DREAM.
SO I'M A DUNCE EITHER WAY...?
OH. THAT REMINDS ME.

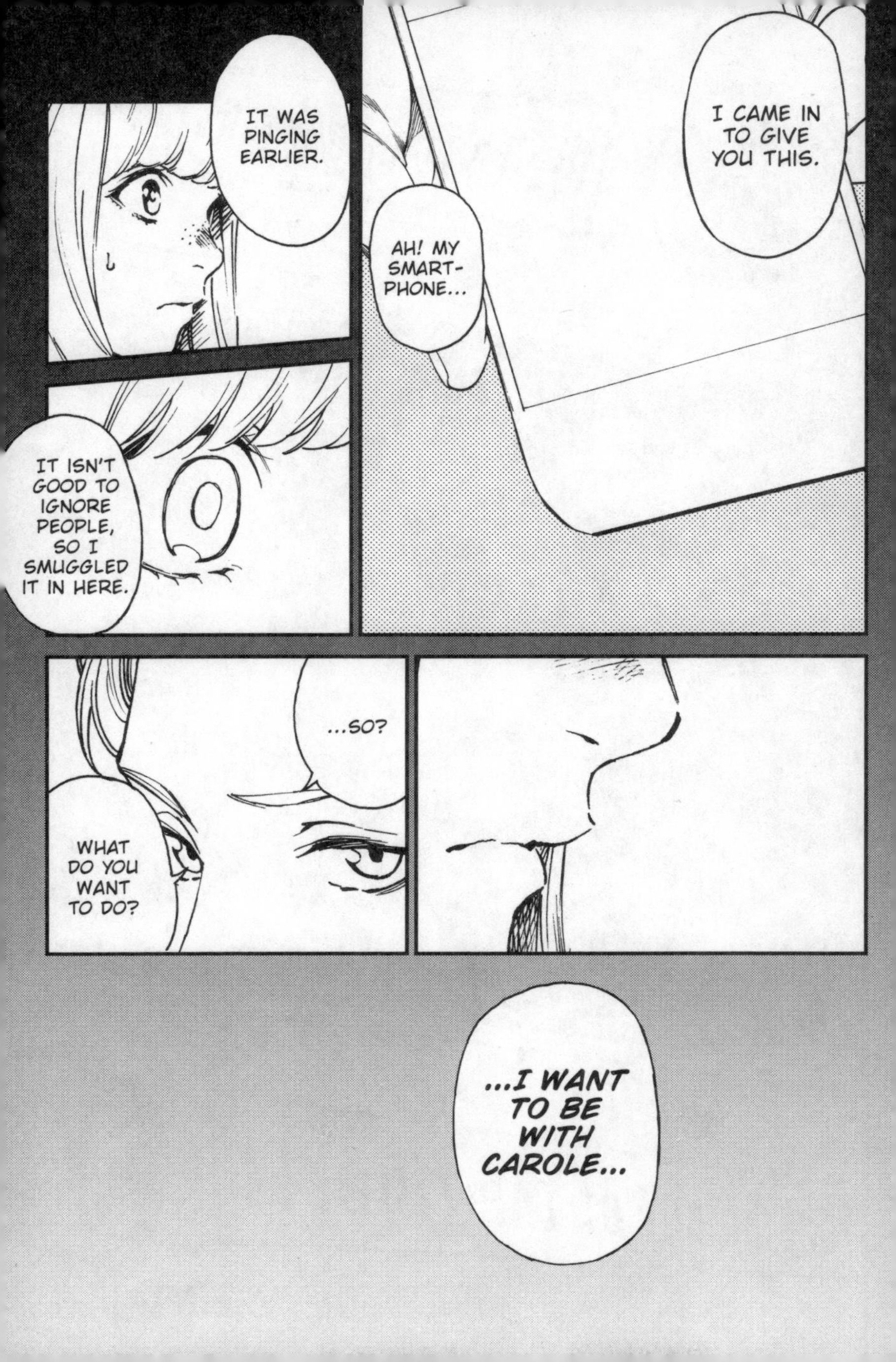
I CAME IN TO GIVE YOU THIS.
AH! MY SMART-PHONE...
IT WAS PINGING EARLIER.
IT ISN'T GOOD TO IGNORE PEOPLE, SO I SMUGGLED IT IN HERE.
...SO?
WHAT DO YOU WANT TO DO?
...I WANT TO BE WITH CAROLE...

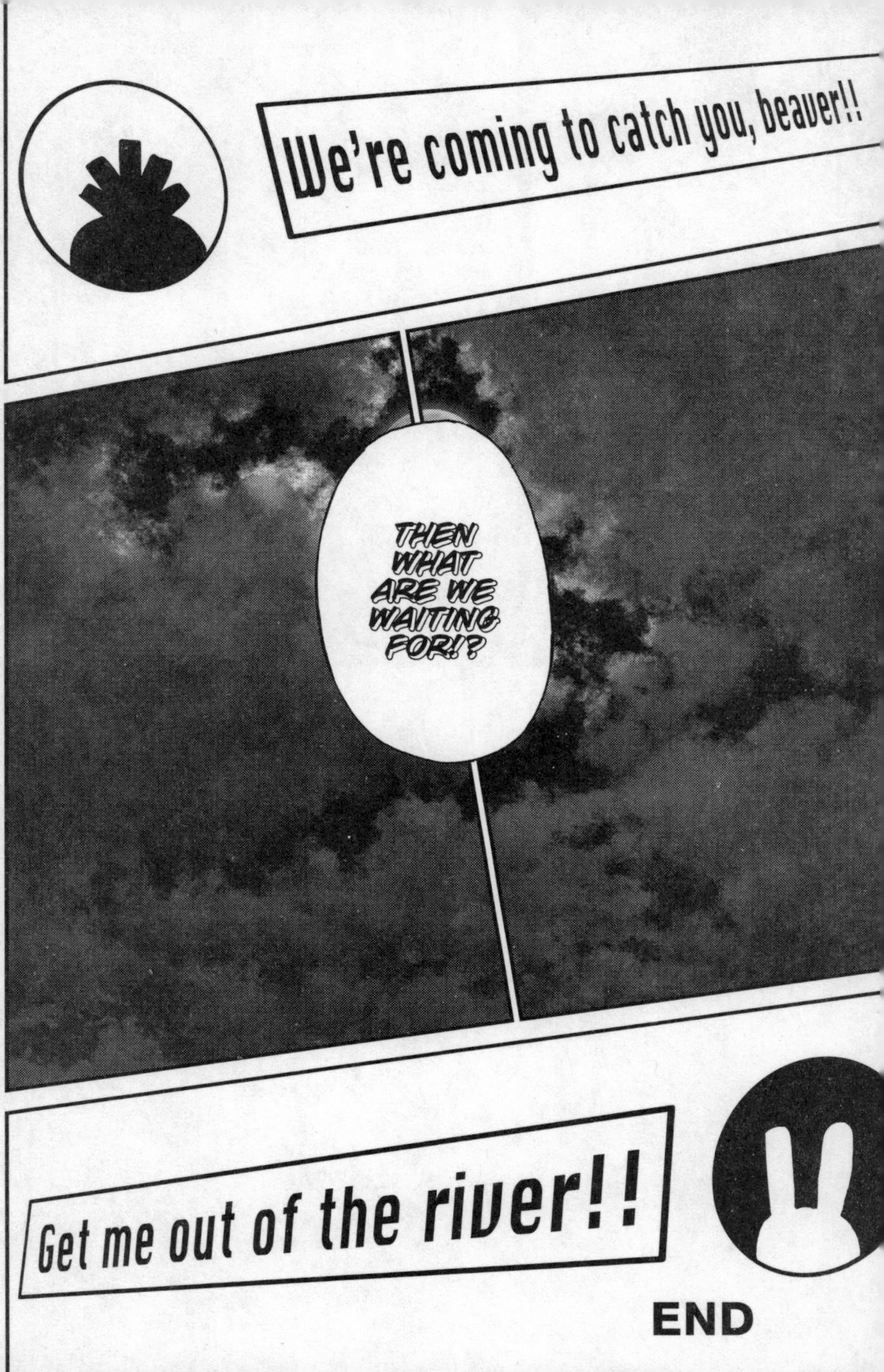
We're coming to catch you, beaver!!
THEN WHAT ARE WE WAITING FOR!?
Get me out of the river!!
END

episode 15: We've Only Just Begun 3

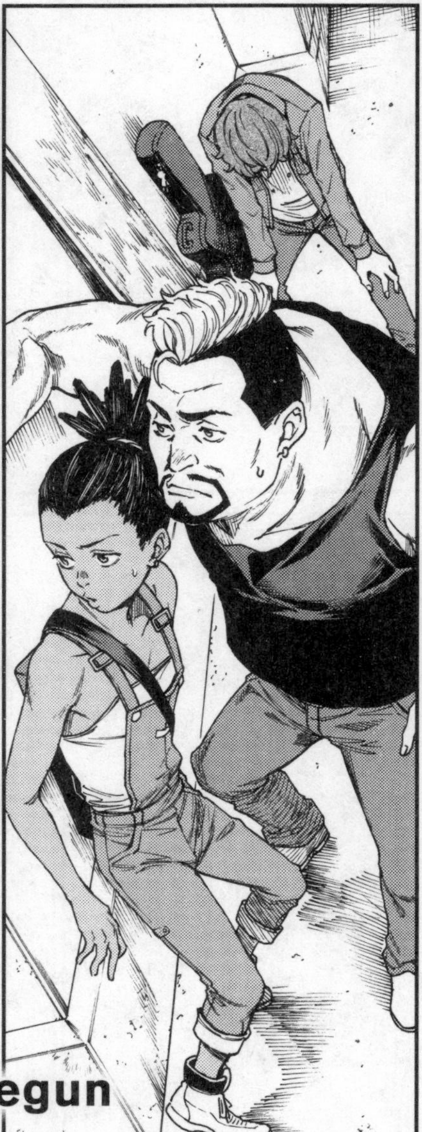

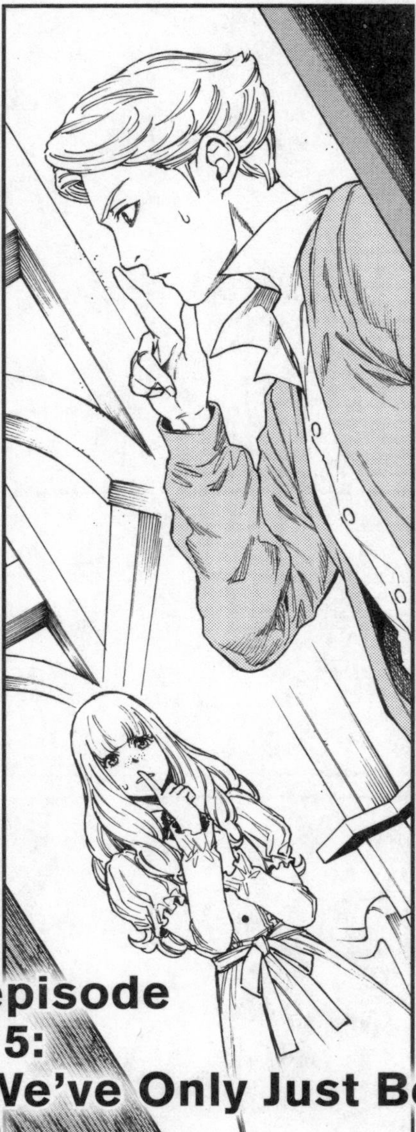

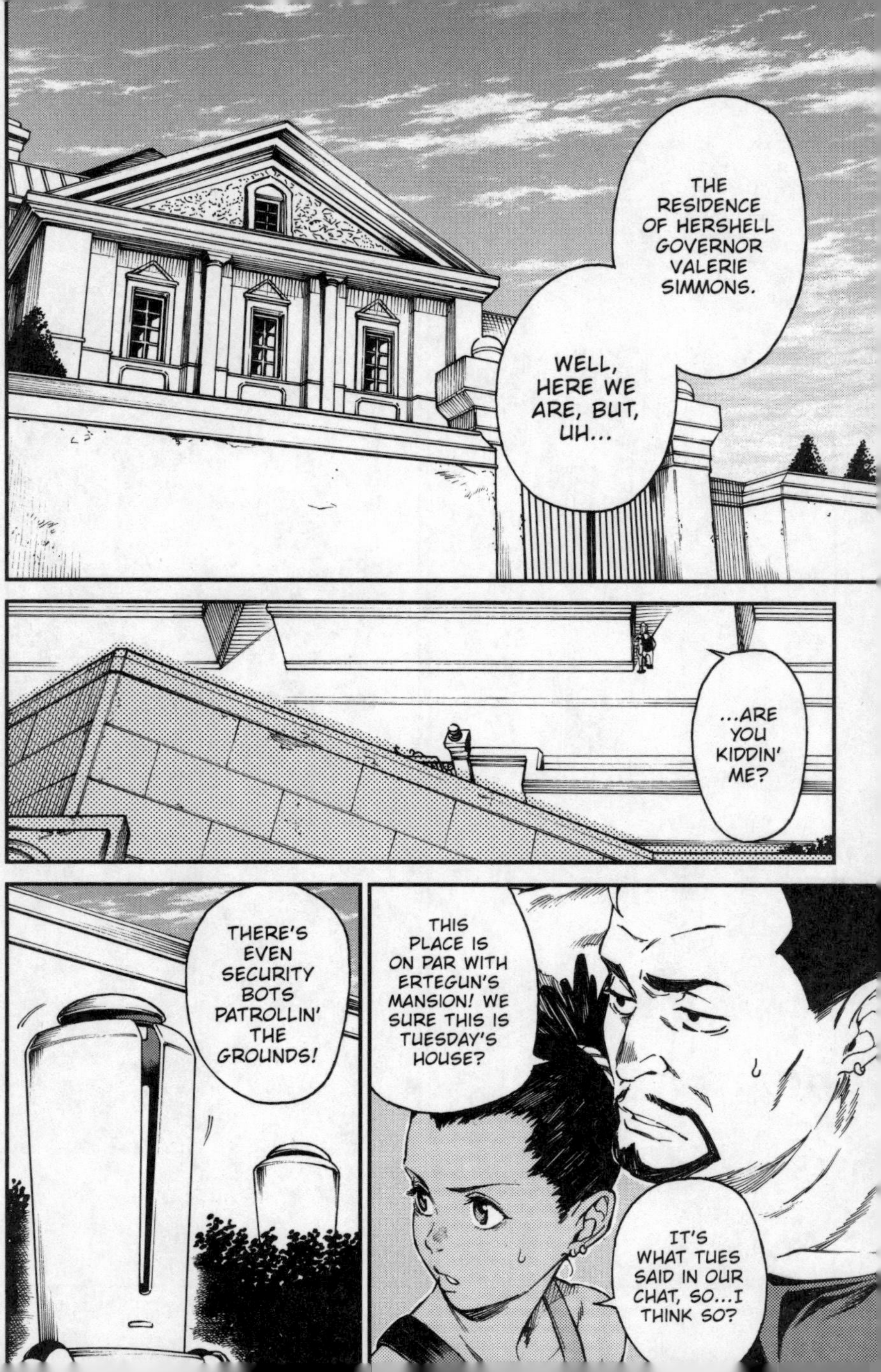
THE RESIDENCE OF HERSHELL GOVERNOR VALERIE SIMMONS.
WELL, HERE WE ARE, BUT, UH...
...ARE YOU KIDDIN' ME?
THIS PLACE IS ON PAR WITH ERTEGUN'S MANSION! WE SURE THIS IS TUESDAY'S HOUSE?
THERE'S EVEN SECURITY BOTS PATROLLIN' THE GROUNDS!
IT'S WHAT TUES SAID IN OUR CHAT, SO...I THINK SO?

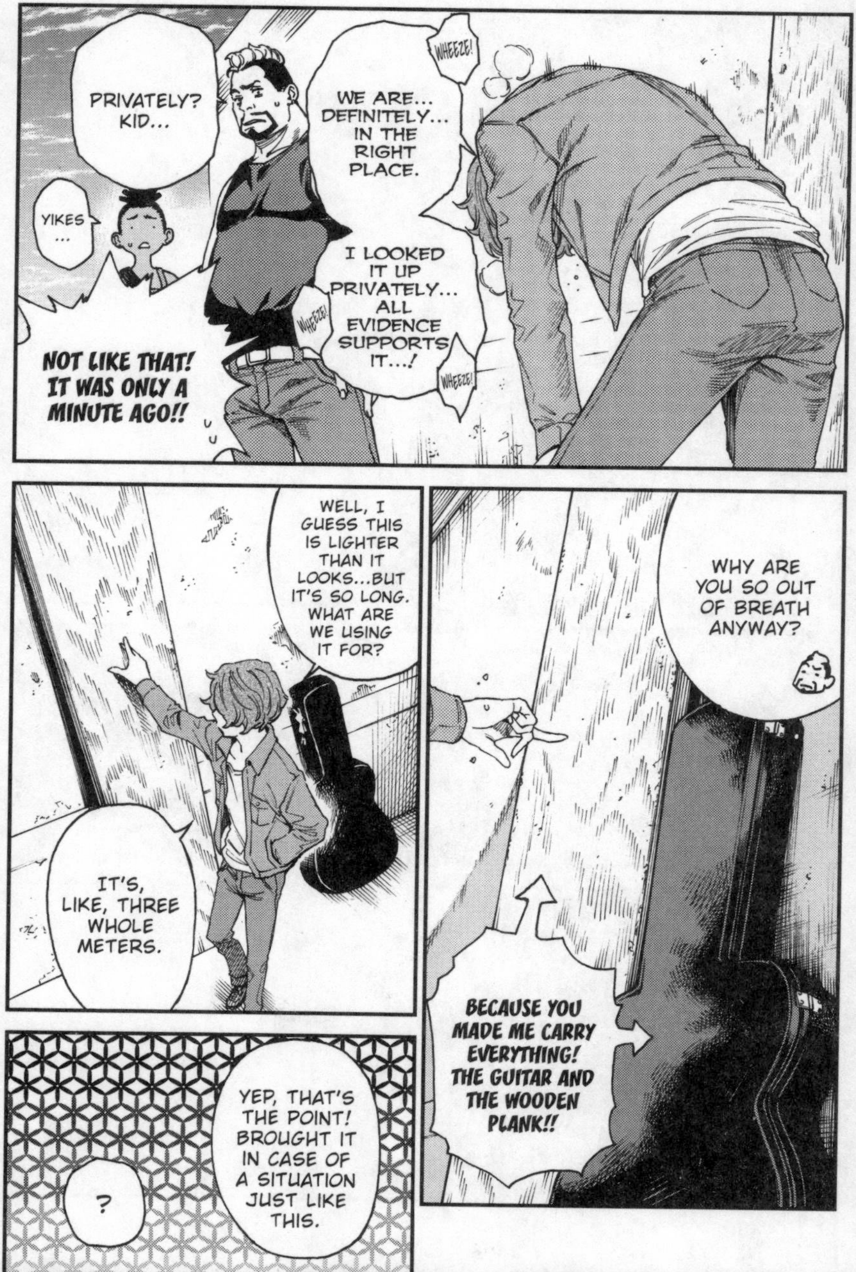
WHEEZE!
WE ARE... DEFINITELY... IN THE RIGHT PLACE.
I LOOKED IT UP PRIVATELY... ALL EVIDENCE SUPPORTS IT...!
WHEEZE!
WHEEZE!
PRIVATELY? KID...
YIKES...
NOT LIKE THAT! IT WAS ONLY A MINUTE AGO!!
WHY ARE YOU SO OUT OF BREATH ANYWAY?
BECAUSE YOU MADE ME CARRY EVERYTHING! THE GUITAR AND THE WOODEN PLANK!!
WELL, I GUESS THIS IS LIGHTER THAN IT LOOKS...BUT IT'S SO LONG. WHAT ARE WE USING IT FOR?
IT'S, LIKE, THREE WHOLE METERS.
YEP, THAT'S THE POINT! BROUGHT IT IN CASE OF A SITUATION JUST LIKE THIS.
?

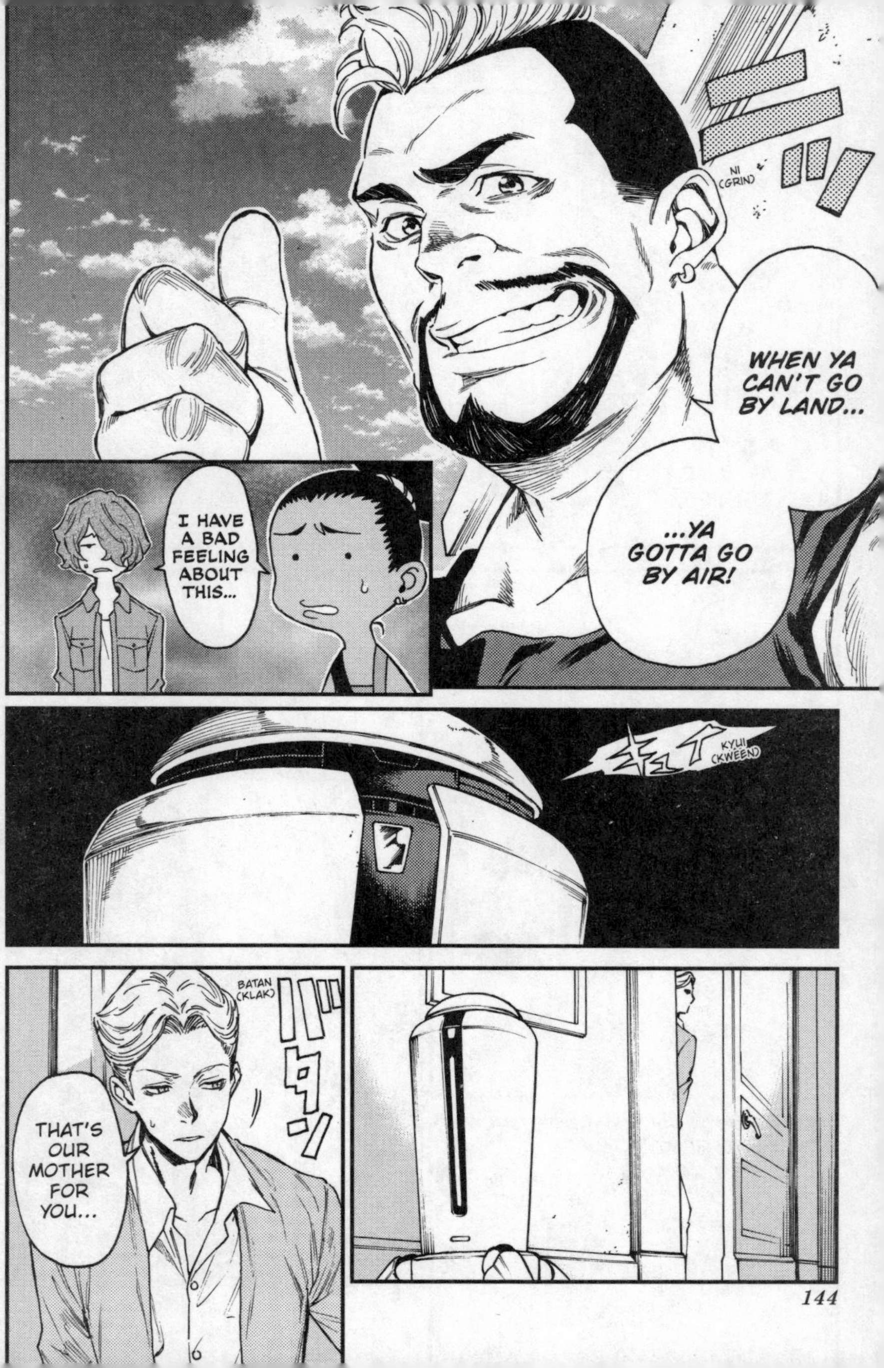
NI (GRIN)
WHEN YA CAN'T GO BY LAND...
...YA GOTTA GO BY AIR!
I HAVE A BAD FEELING ABOUT THIS...
KYUI (KWEEN)
BATAN (KLAK)
THAT'S OUR MOTHER FOR YOU...

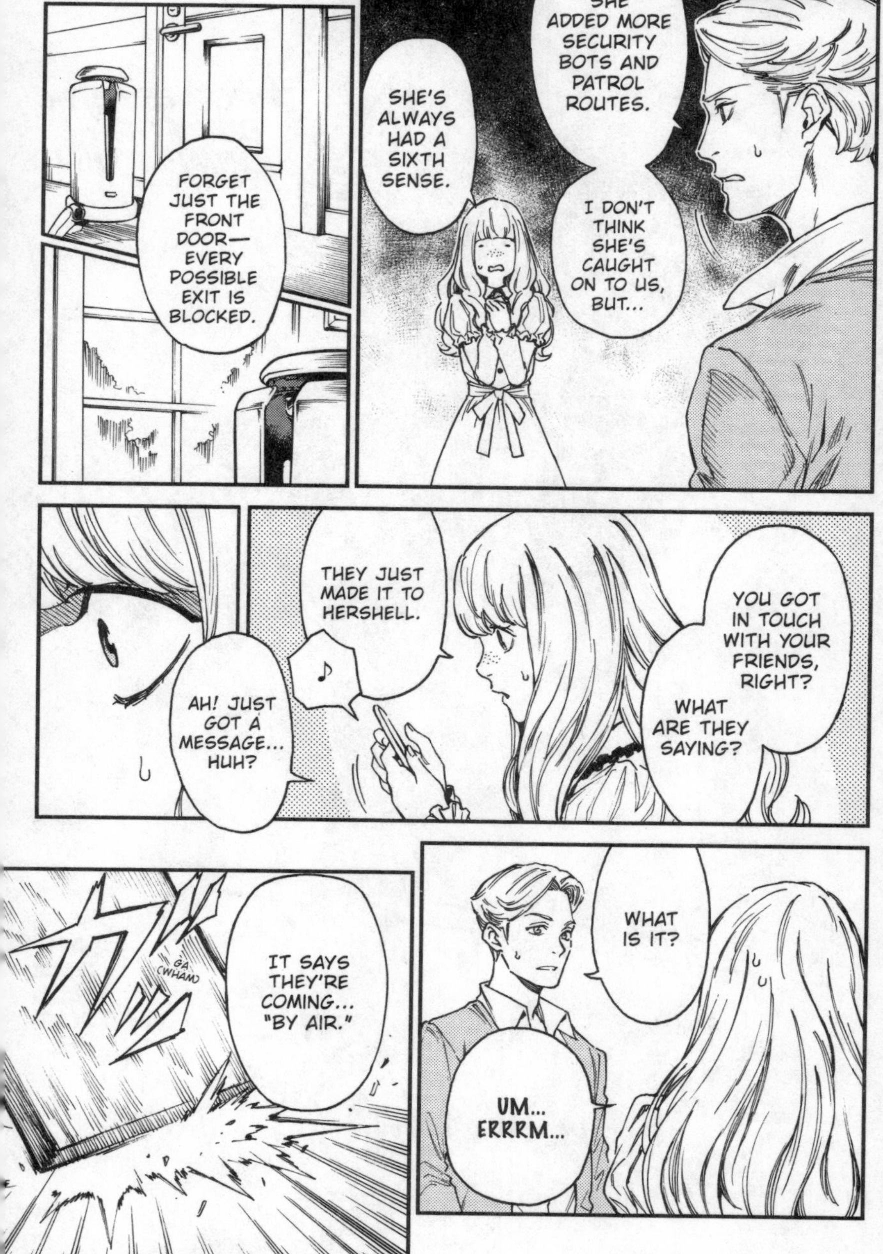
SHE ADDED MORE SECURITY BOTS AND PATROL ROUTES.
I DON'T THINK SHE'S CAUGHT ON TO US, BUT...
SHE'S ALWAYS HAD A SIXTH SENSE.
FORGET JUST THE FRONT DOOR—EVERY POSSIBLE EXIT IS BLOCKED.
YOU GOT IN TOUCH WITH YOUR FRIENDS, RIGHT?
WHAT ARE THEY SAYING?
THEY JUST MADE IT TO HERSHELL.
♪
AH! JUST GOT A MESSAGE... HUH?
WHAT IS IT?
UM... ERRRM...
IT SAYS THEY'RE COMING... "BY AIR."
GA (WHAM)

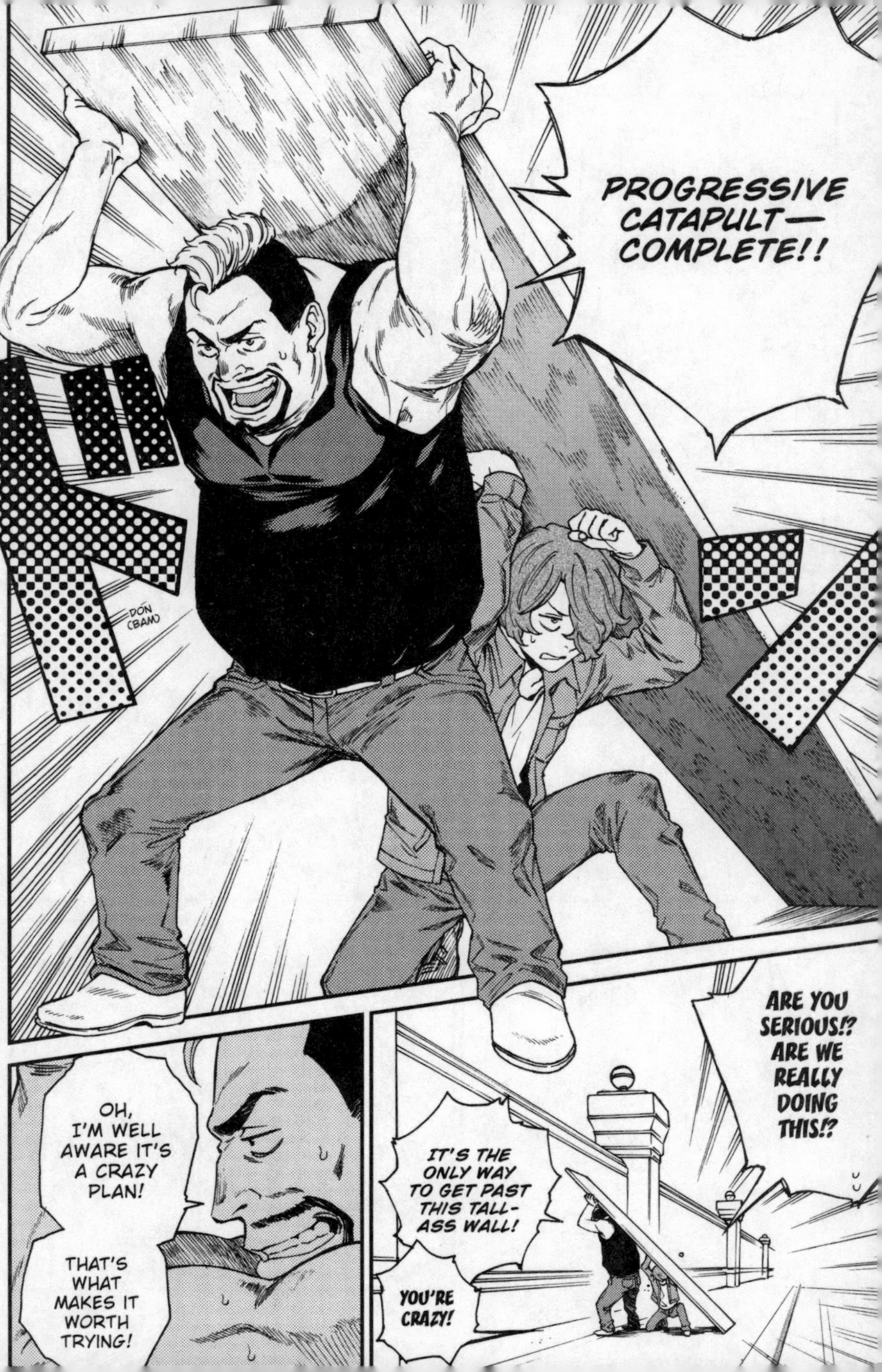
PROGRESSIVE CATAPULT— COMPLETE!!
DON (BAM)
ARE YOU SERIOUS!? ARE WE REALLY DOING THIS!?
IT'S THE ONLY WAY TO GET PAST THIS TALL-ASS WALL!
YOU'RE CRAZY!
OH, I'M WELL AWARE IT'S A CRAZY PLAN!
THAT'S WHAT MAKES IT WORTH TRYING!

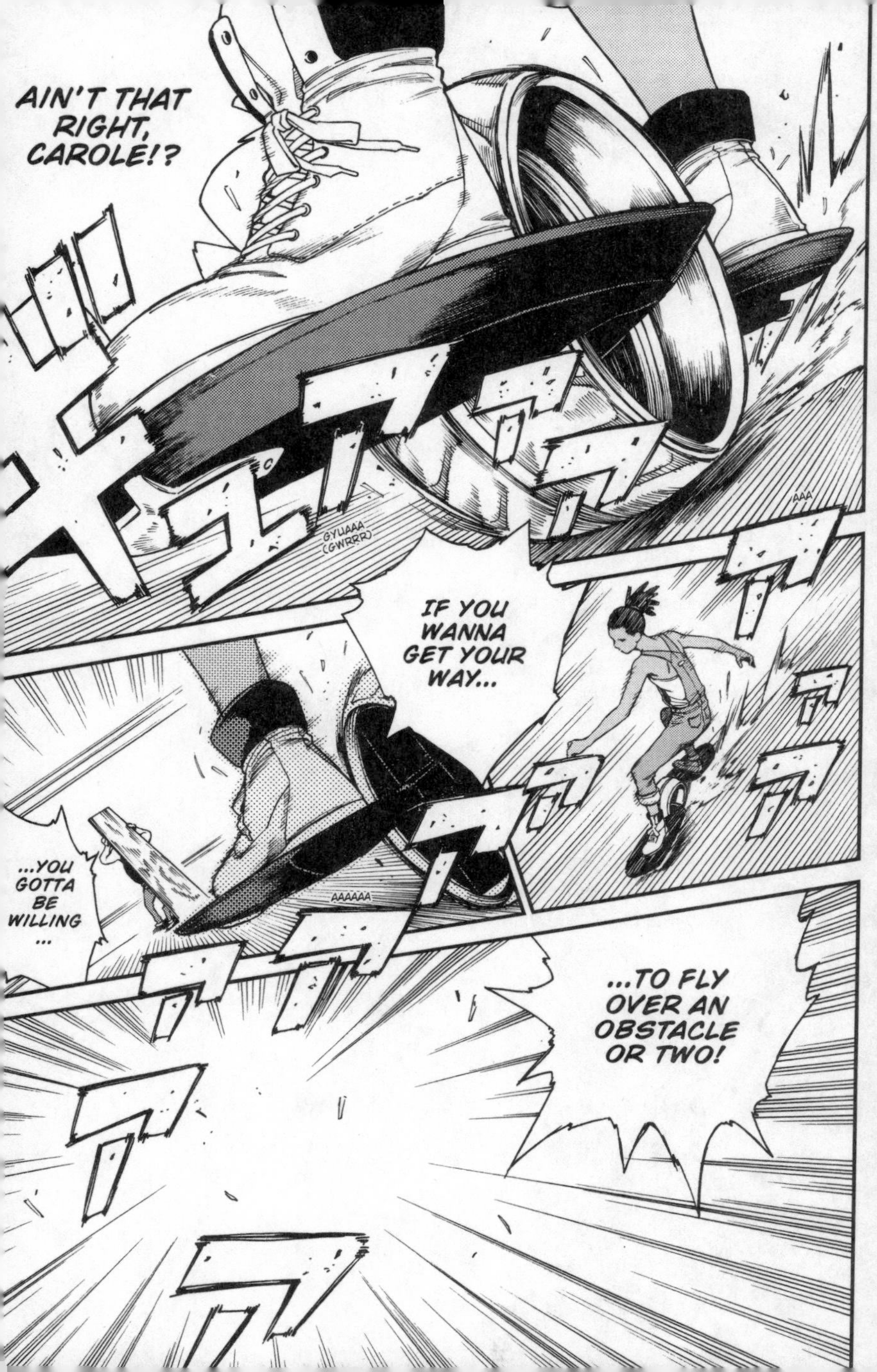
AIN'T THAT RIGHT, CAROLE!?
GYUAAA (GWRRR)
AAA
IF YOU WANNA GET YOUR WAY...
AAAAAA
...YOU GOTTA BE WILLING ...
...TO FLY OVER AN OBSTACLE OR TWO!

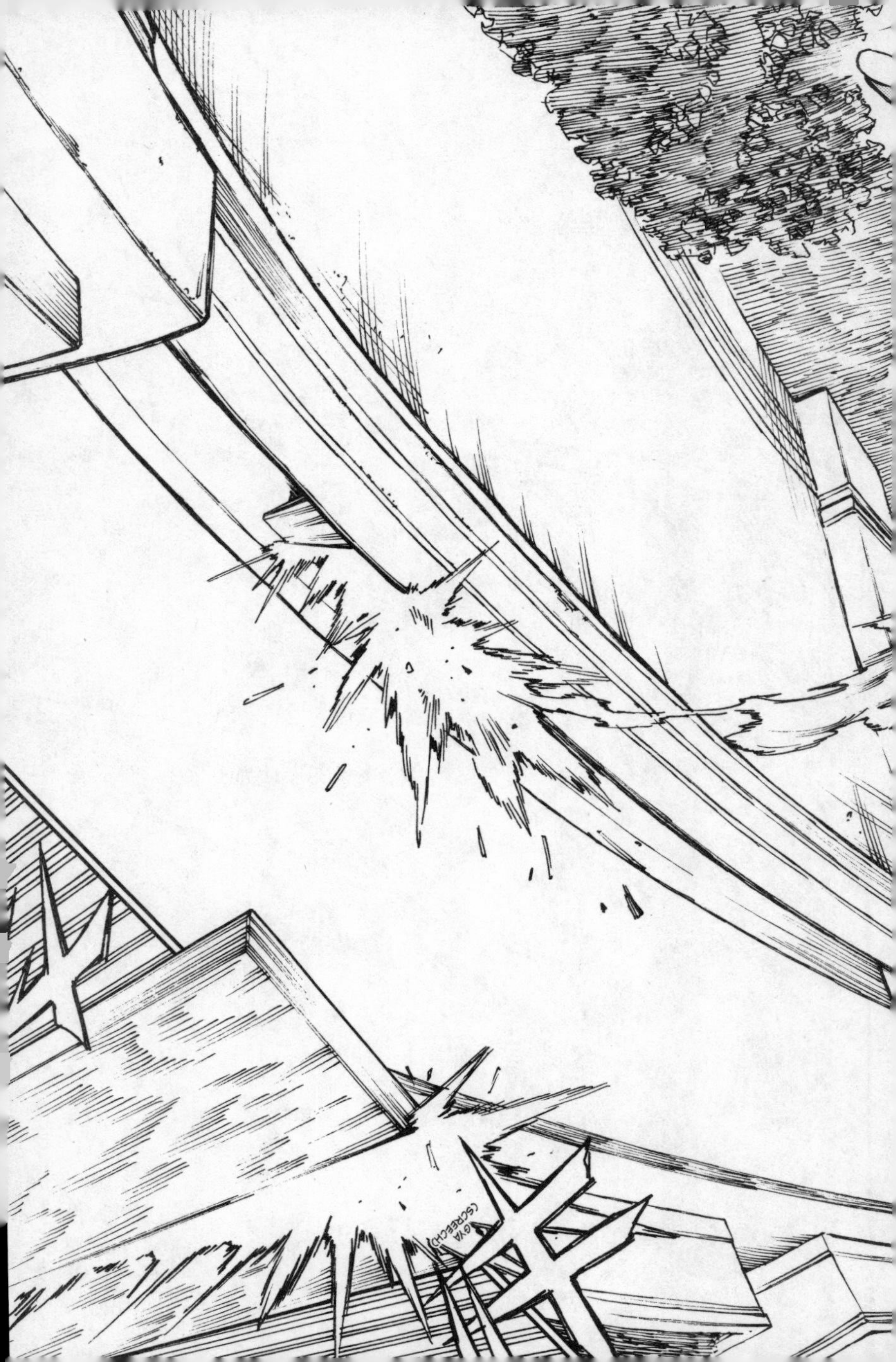
GYA
(SCREECH)

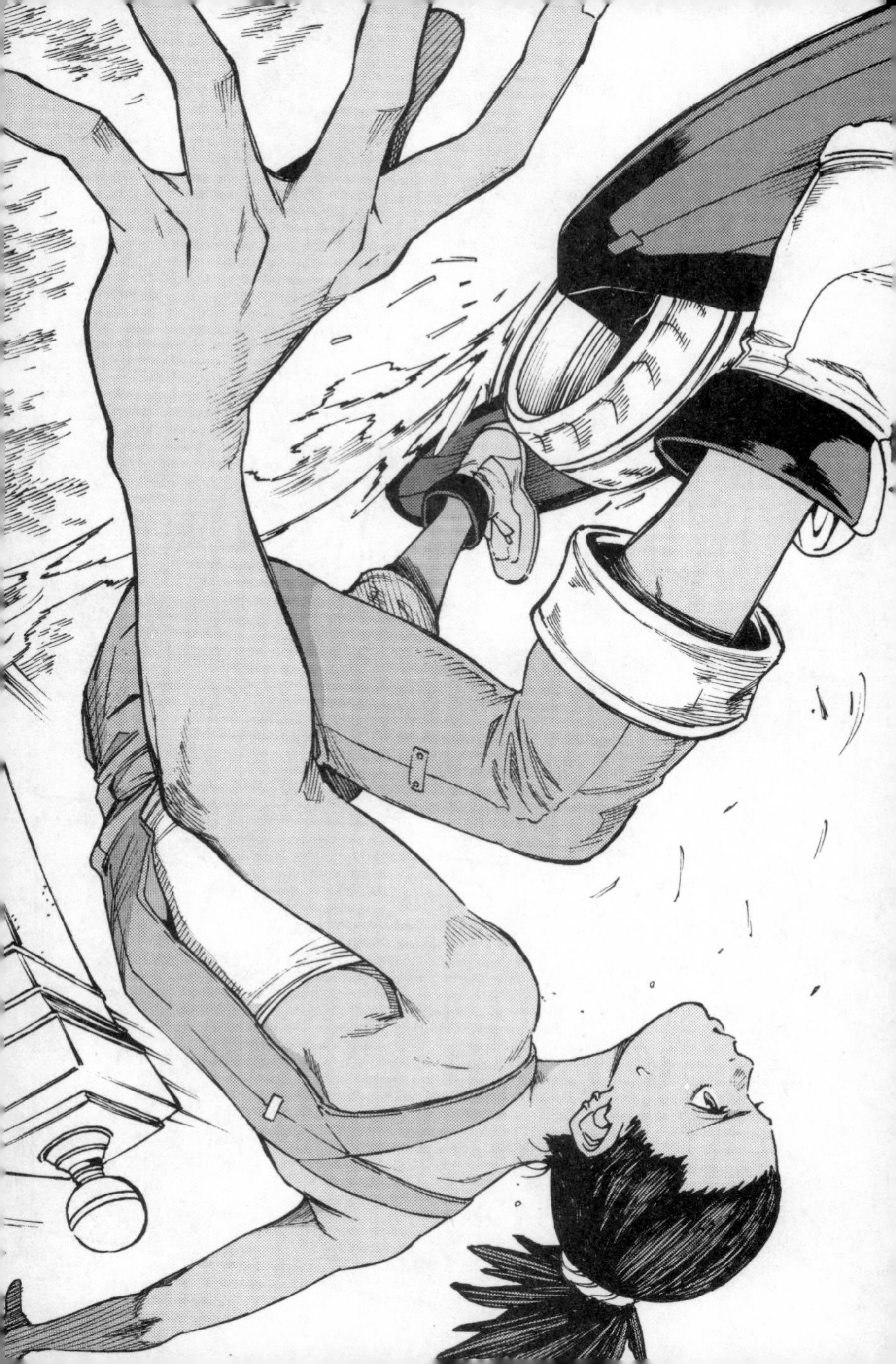

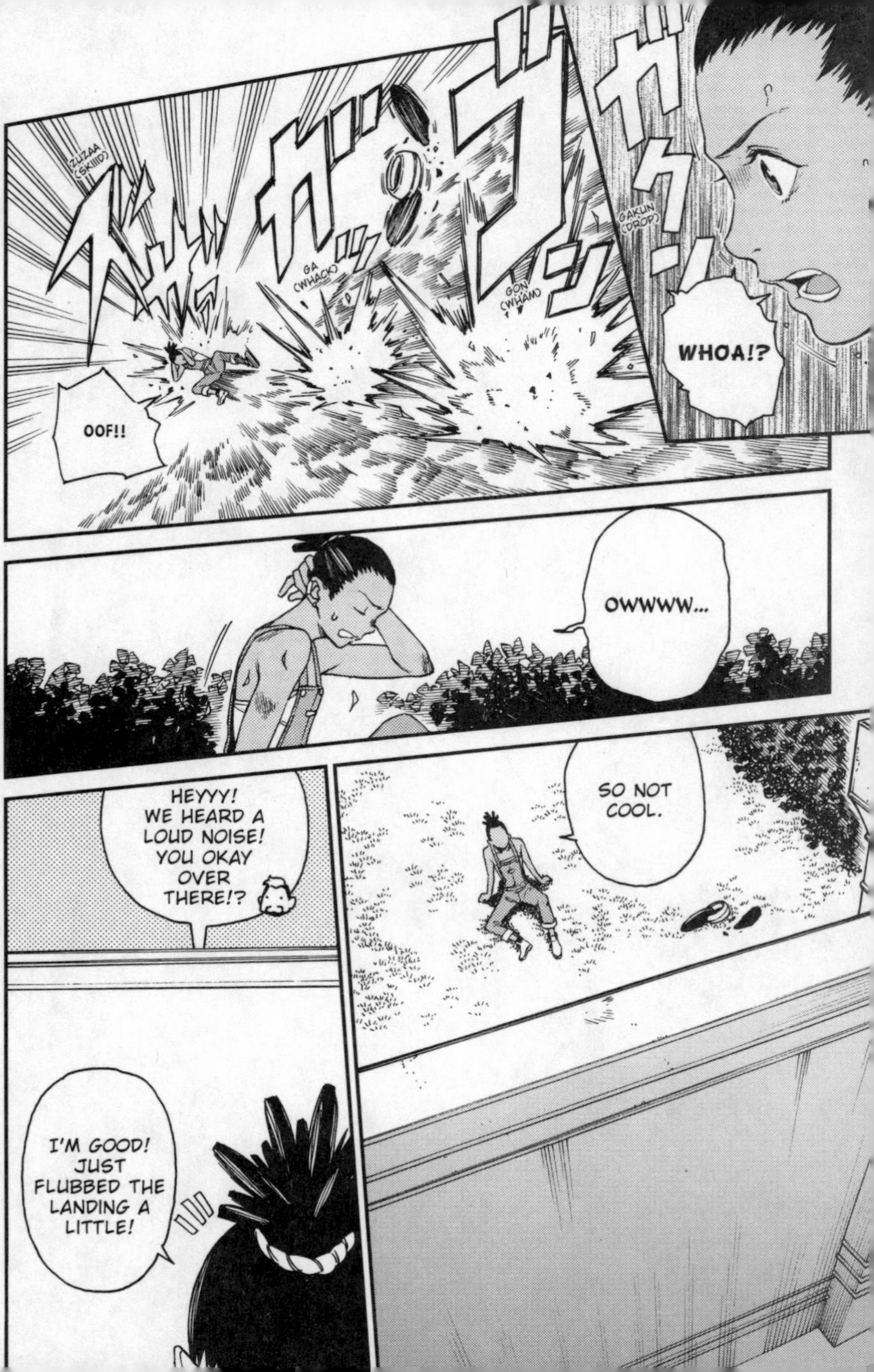
GAKUN (DROP)
WHOA!?
GON (WHAM)
GA (WHACK)
ZUZAA (SKIIID)
OOF!!
OWWWW...
SO NOT COOL.
HEYYY! WE HEARD A LOUD NOISE! YOU OKAY OVER THERE!?
I'M GOOD! JUST FLUBBED THE LANDING A LITTLE!

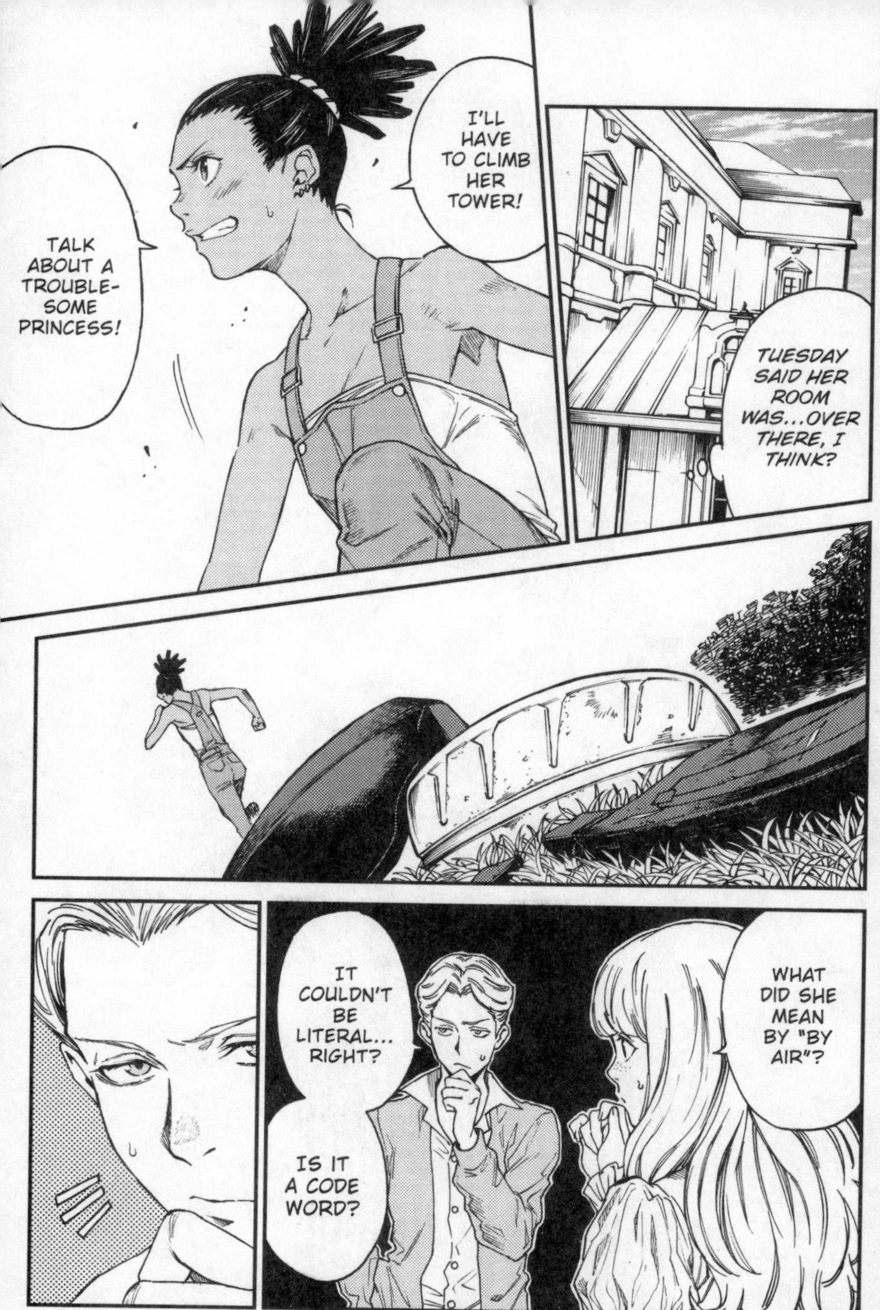
TUESDAY SAID HER ROOM WAS...OVER THERE, I THINK?
I'LL HAVE TO CLIMB HER TOWER!
TALK ABOUT A TROUBLE-SOME PRINCESS!
WHAT DID SHE MEAN BY "BY AIR"?
IT COULDN'T BE LITERAL... RIGHT?
IS IT A CODE WORD?

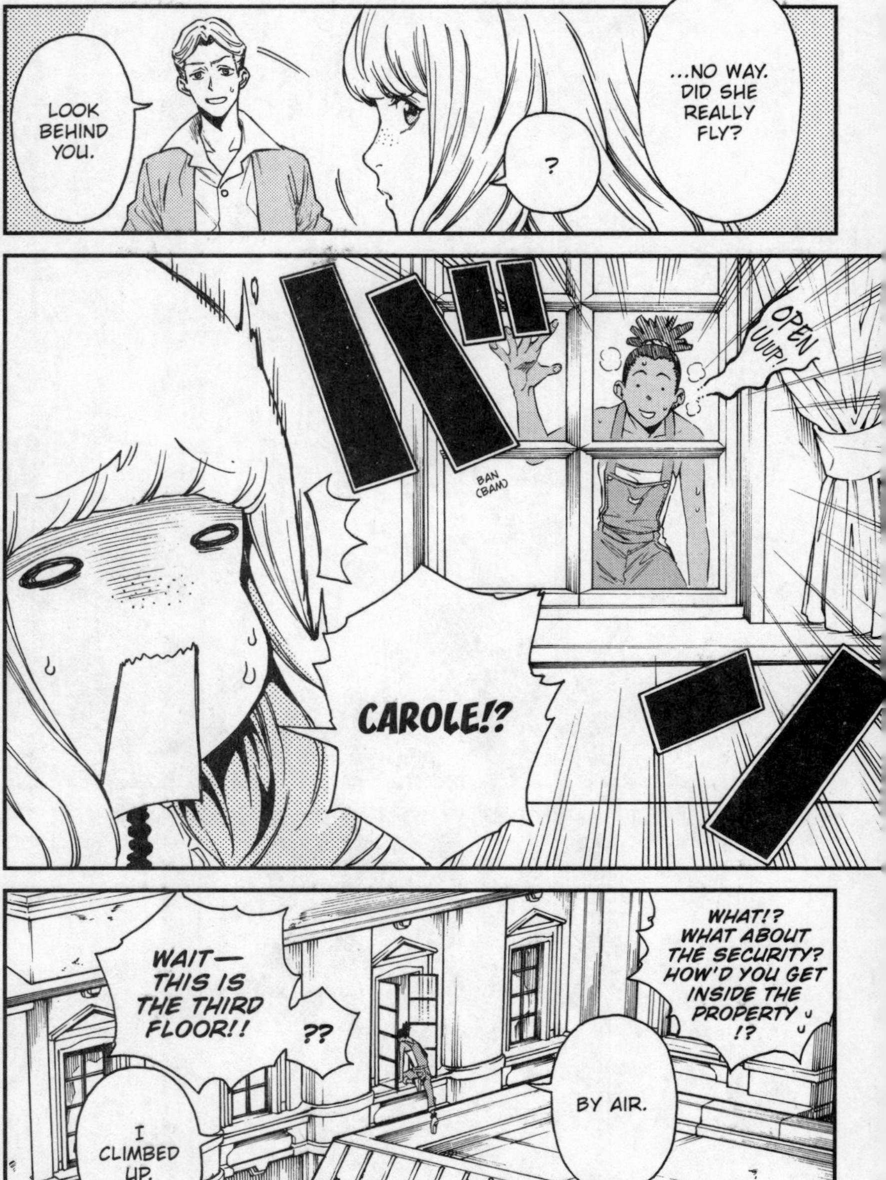
...NO WAY. DID SHE REALLY FLY?
?
LOOK BEHIND YOU.
OPEN UUUP!
BAN (BAM)
CAROLE!?
WHAT!? WHAT ABOUT THE SECURITY? HOW'D YOU GET INSIDE THE PROPERTY !?
BY AIR.
WAIT— THIS IS THE THIRD FLOOR!!
??
I CLIMBED UP.

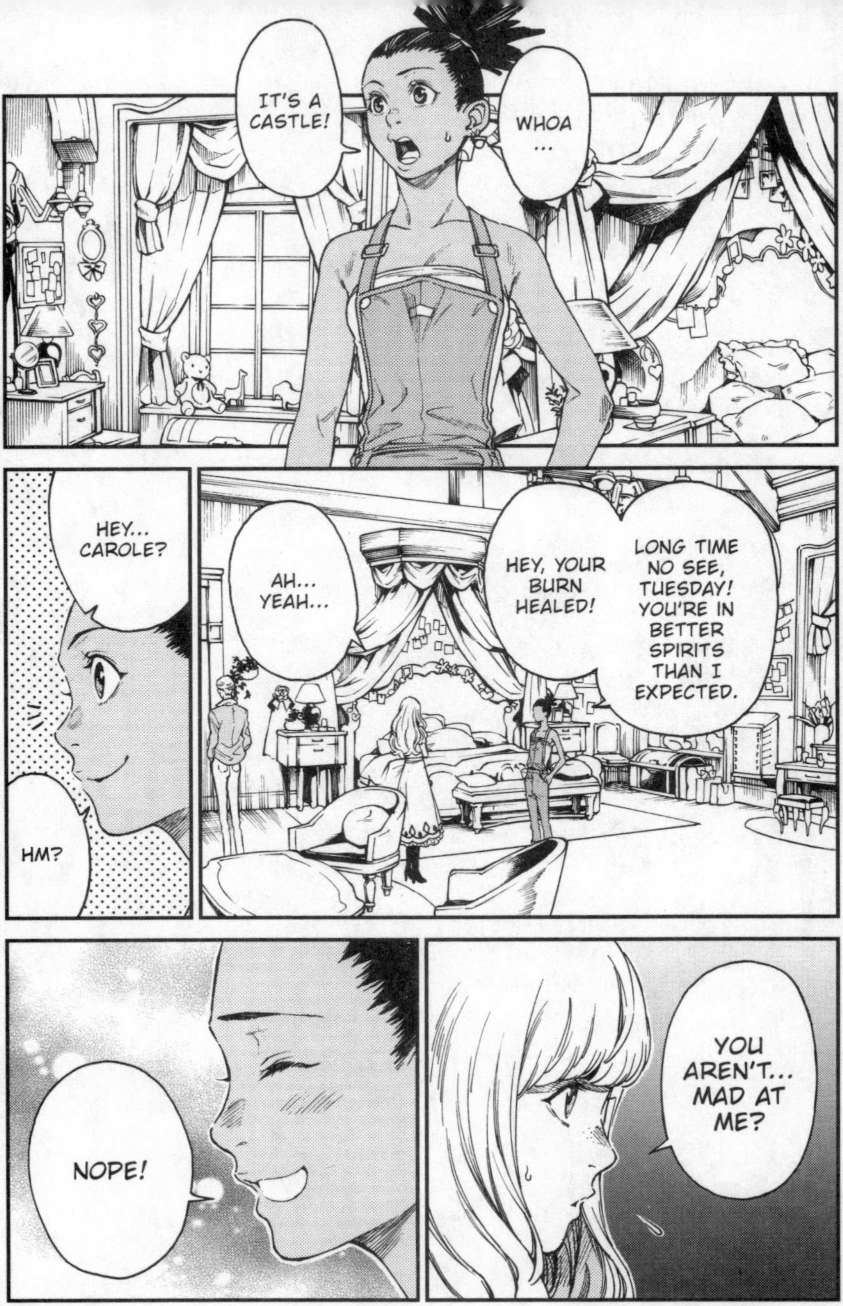
WHOA ...
IT'S A CASTLE!
LONG TIME NO SEE, TUESDAY! YOU'RE IN BETTER SPIRITS THAN I EXPECTED.
HEY, YOUR BURN HEALED!
AH... YEAH...
HEY... CAROLE?
HM?
YOU AREN'T... MAD AT ME?
NOPE!

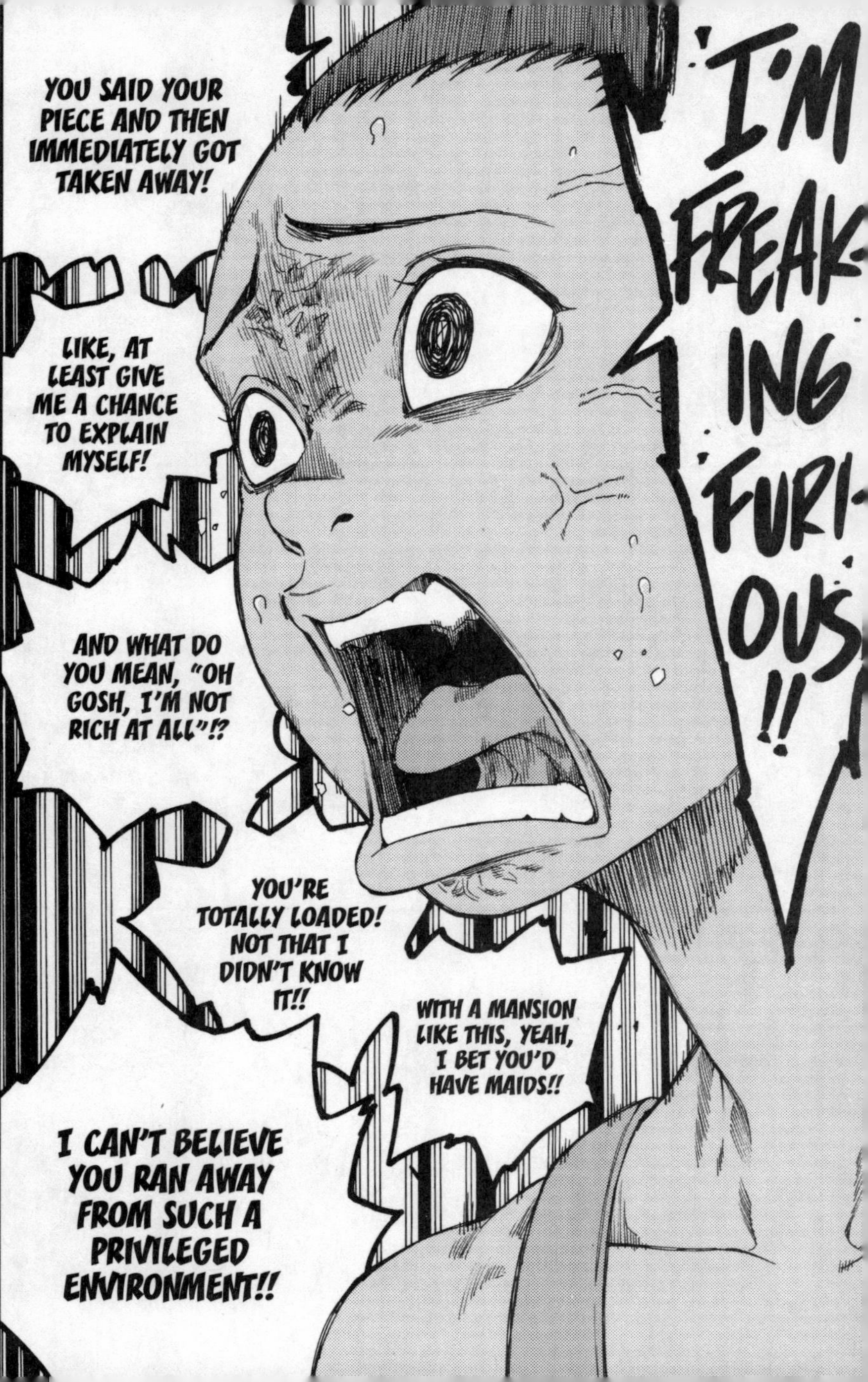
I'M FREAK-ING FURI-OUS!!
YOU SAID YOUR PIECE AND THEN IMMEDIATELY GOT TAKEN AWAY!
LIKE, AT LEAST GIVE ME A CHANCE TO EXPLAIN MYSELF!
AND WHAT DO YOU MEAN, "OH GOSH, I'M NOT RICH AT ALL"!?
YOU'RE TOTALLY LOADED! NOT THAT I DIDN'T KNOW IT!!
WITH A MANSION LIKE THIS, YEAH, I BET YOU'D HAVE MAIDS!!
I CAN'T BELIEVE YOU RAN AWAY FROM SUCH A PRIVILEGED ENVIRONMENT!!

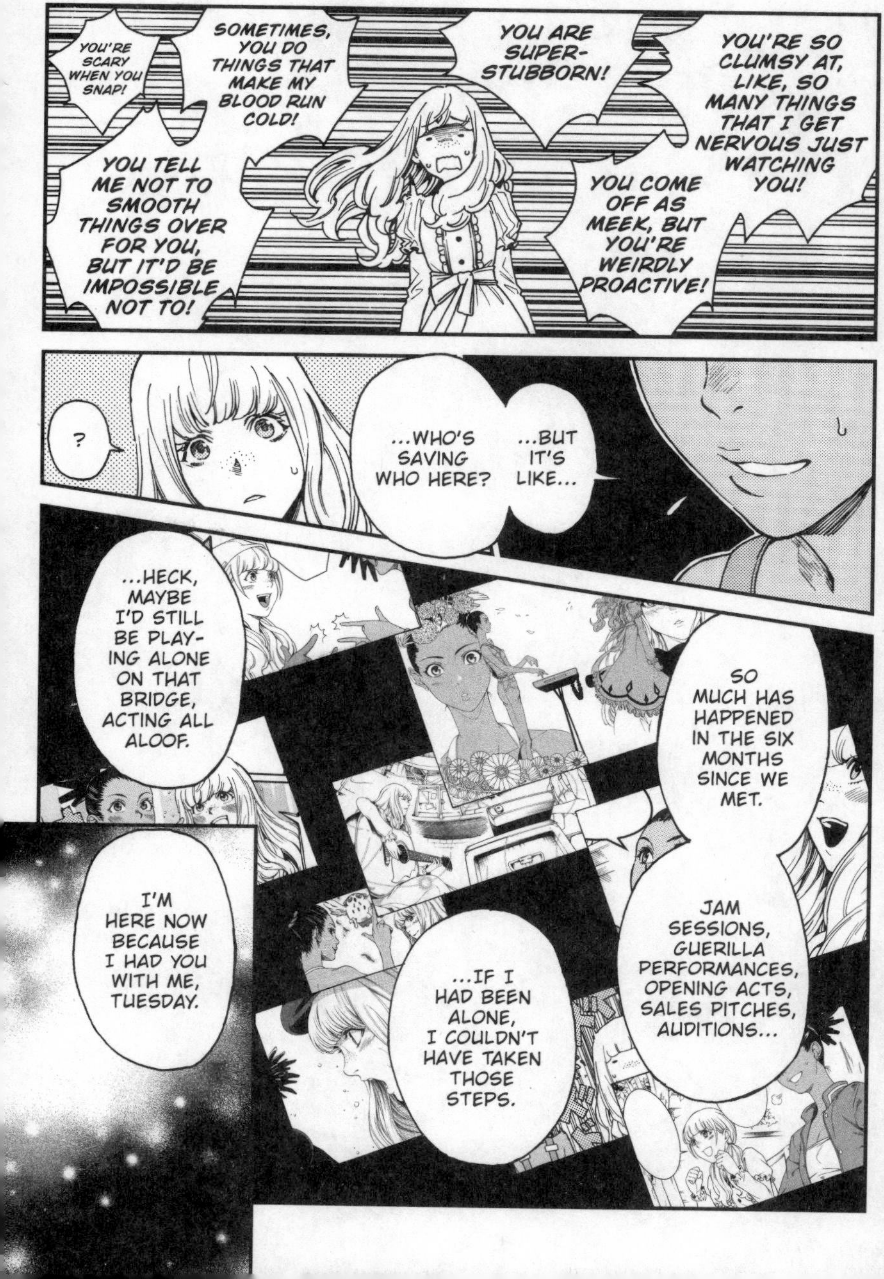
YOU'RE SO CLUMSY AT, LIKE, SO MANY THINGS THAT I GET NERVOUS JUST WATCHING YOU!
YOU ARE SUPER-STUBBORN!
YOU COME OFF AS MEEK, BUT YOU'RE WEIRDLY PROACTIVE!
SOMETIMES, YOU DO THINGS THAT MAKE MY BLOOD RUN COLD!
YOU'RE SCARY WHEN YOU SNAP!
YOU TELL ME NOT TO SMOOTH THINGS OVER FOR YOU, BUT IT'D BE IMPOSSIBLE NOT TO!
...BUT IT'S LIKE...
...WHO'S SAVING WHO HERE?
?
SO MUCH HAS HAPPENED IN THE SIX MONTHS SINCE WE MET.
JAM SESSIONS, GUERILLA PERFORMANCES, OPENING ACTS, SALES PITCHES, AUDITIONS...
...IF I HAD BEEN ALONE, I COULDN'T HAVE TAKEN THOSE STEPS.
...HECK, MAYBE I'D STILL BE PLAYING ALONE ON THAT BRIDGE, ACTING ALL ALOOF.
I'M HERE NOW BECAUSE I HAD YOU WITH ME, TUESDAY.

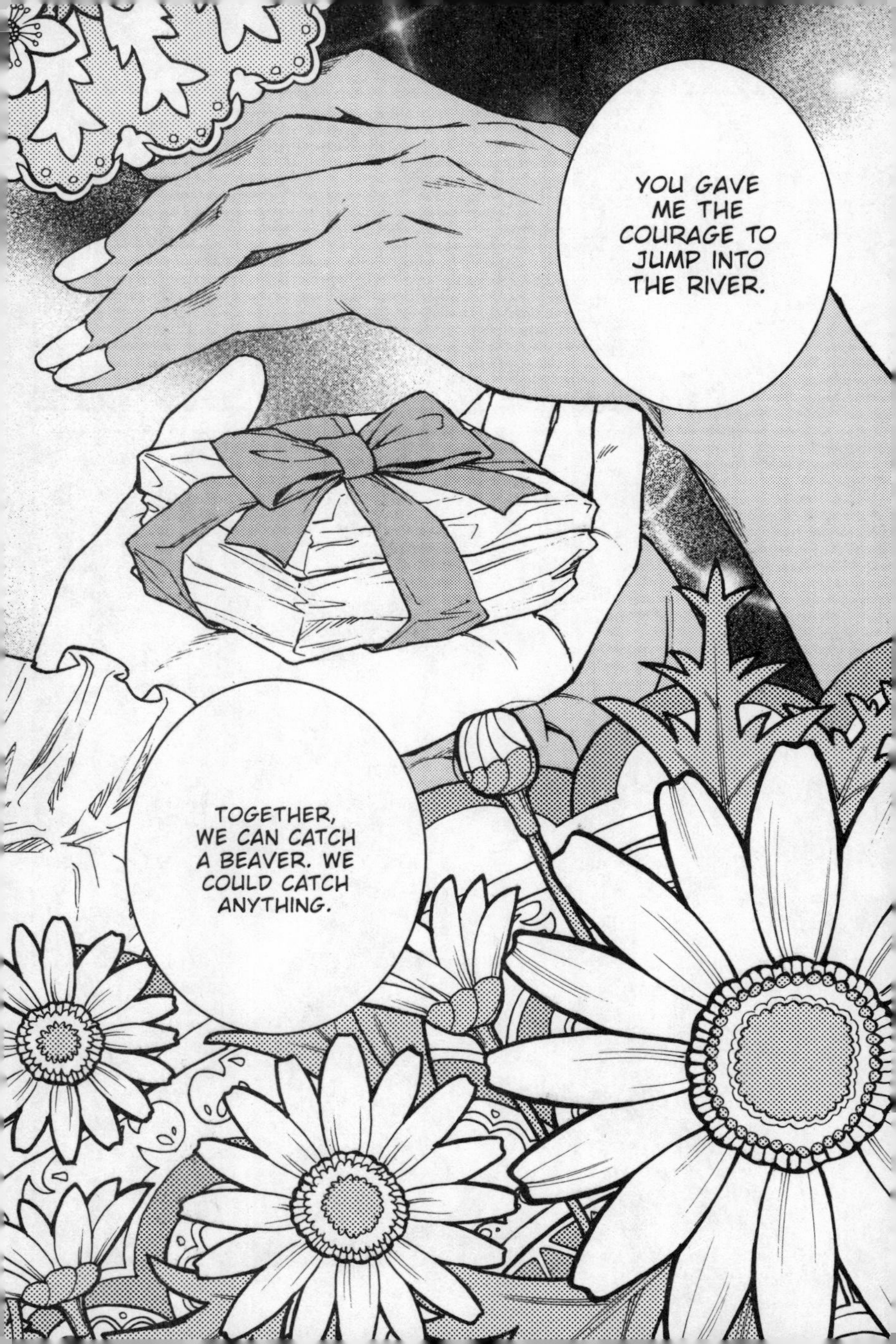
YOU GAVE ME THE COURAGE TO JUMP INTO THE RIVER.
TOGETHER, WE CAN CATCH A BEAVER. WE COULD CATCH ANYTHING.

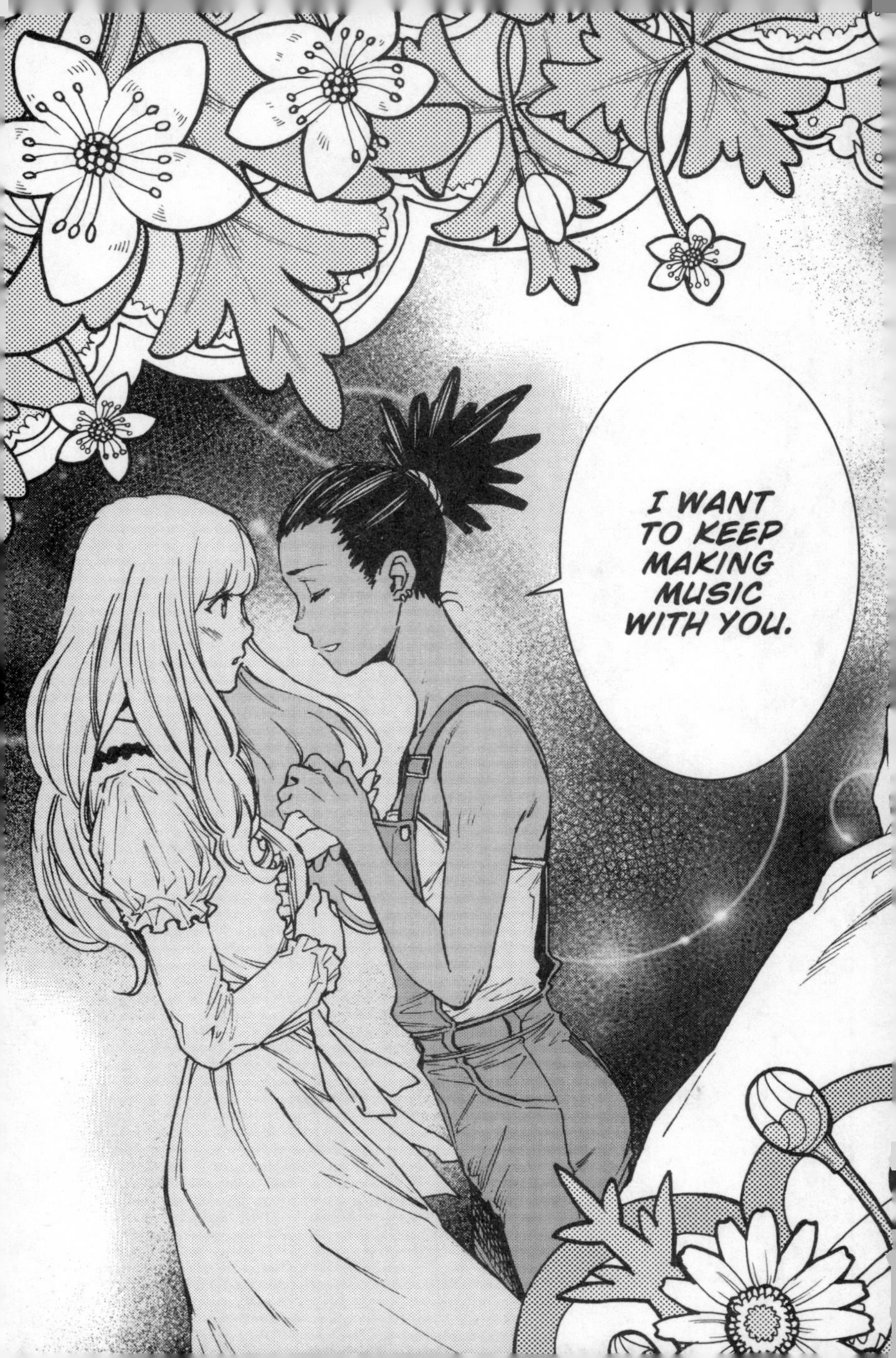
I WANT TO KEEP MAKING MUSIC WITH YOU.

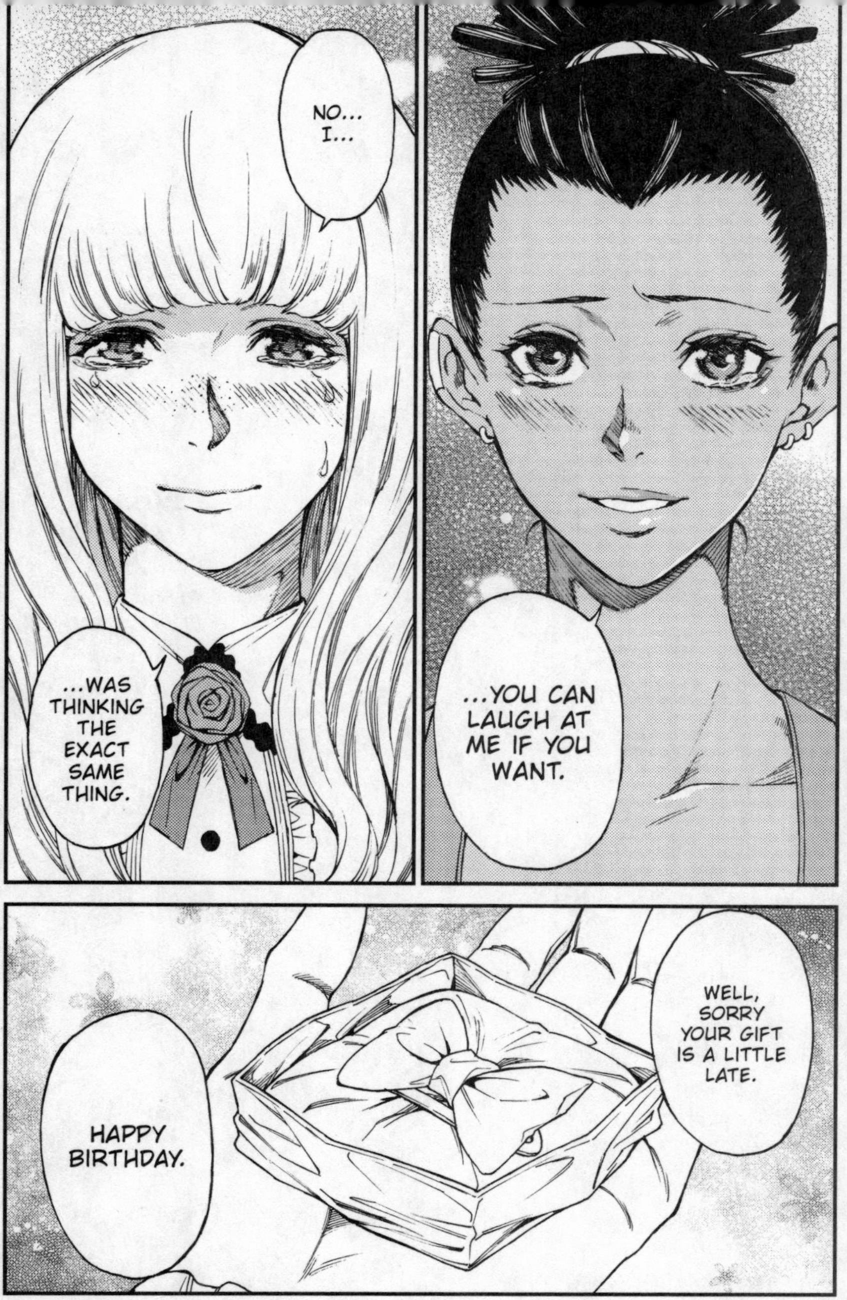
...YOU CAN LAUGH AT ME IF YOU WANT.
NO... I...
...WAS THINKING THE EXACT SAME THING.
WELL, SORRY YOUR GIFT IS A LITTLE LATE.
HAPPY BIRTHDAY.

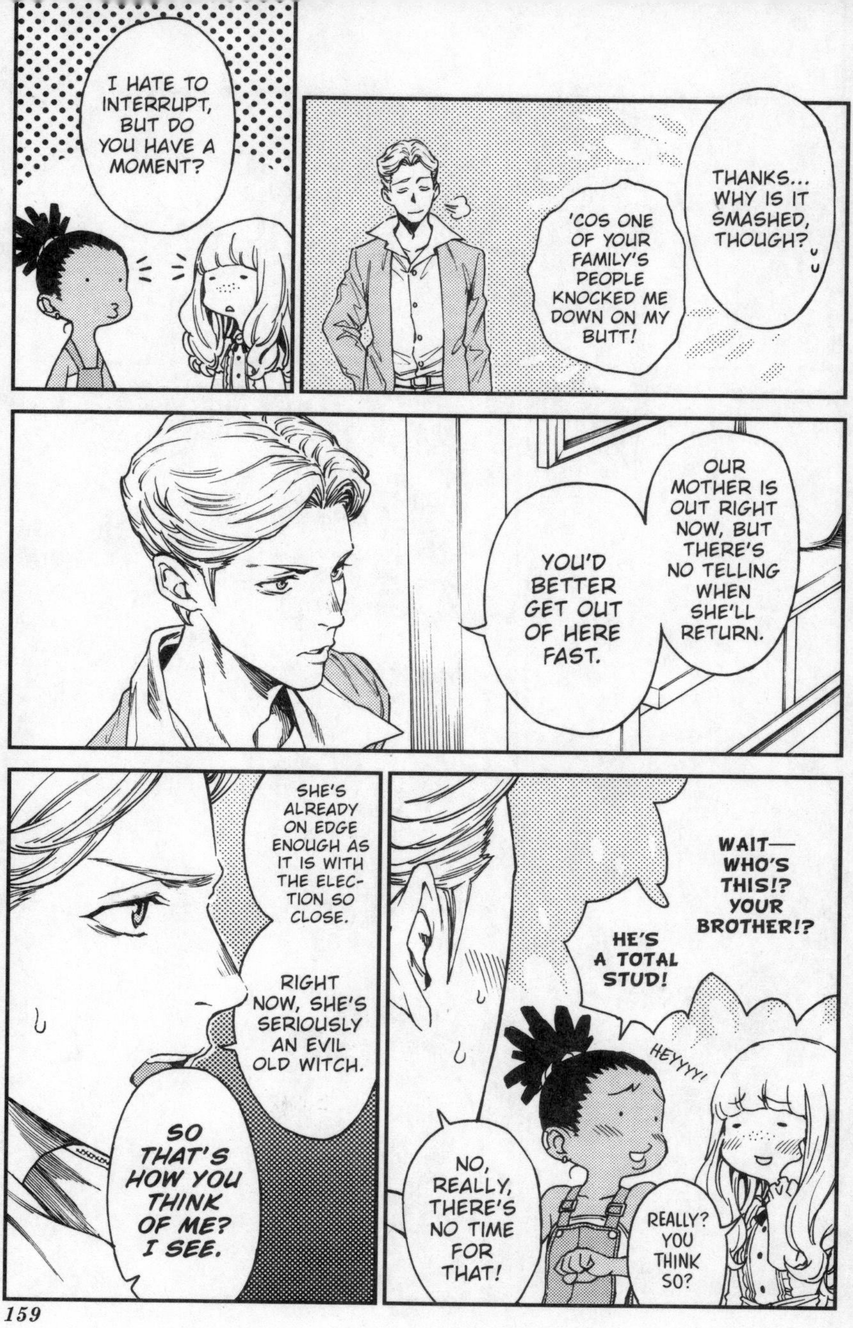
THANKS... WHY IS IT SMASHED, THOUGH?
'COS ONE OF YOUR FAMILY'S PEOPLE KNOCKED ME DOWN ON MY BUTT!
I HATE TO INTERRUPT, BUT DO YOU HAVE A MOMENT?
OUR MOTHER IS OUT RIGHT NOW, BUT THERE'S NO TELLING WHEN SHE'LL RETURN.
YOU'D BETTER GET OUT OF HERE FAST.
WAIT— WHO'S THIS!? YOUR BROTHER!?
HE'S A TOTAL STUD!
HEYYYY!
NO, REALLY, THERE'S NO TIME FOR THAT!
REALLY? YOU THINK SO?
SHE'S ALREADY ON EDGE ENOUGH AS IT IS WITH THE ELEC-TION SO CLOSE.
RIGHT NOW, SHE'S SERIOUSLY AN EVIL OLD WITCH.
SO THAT'S HOW YOU THINK OF ME? I SEE.

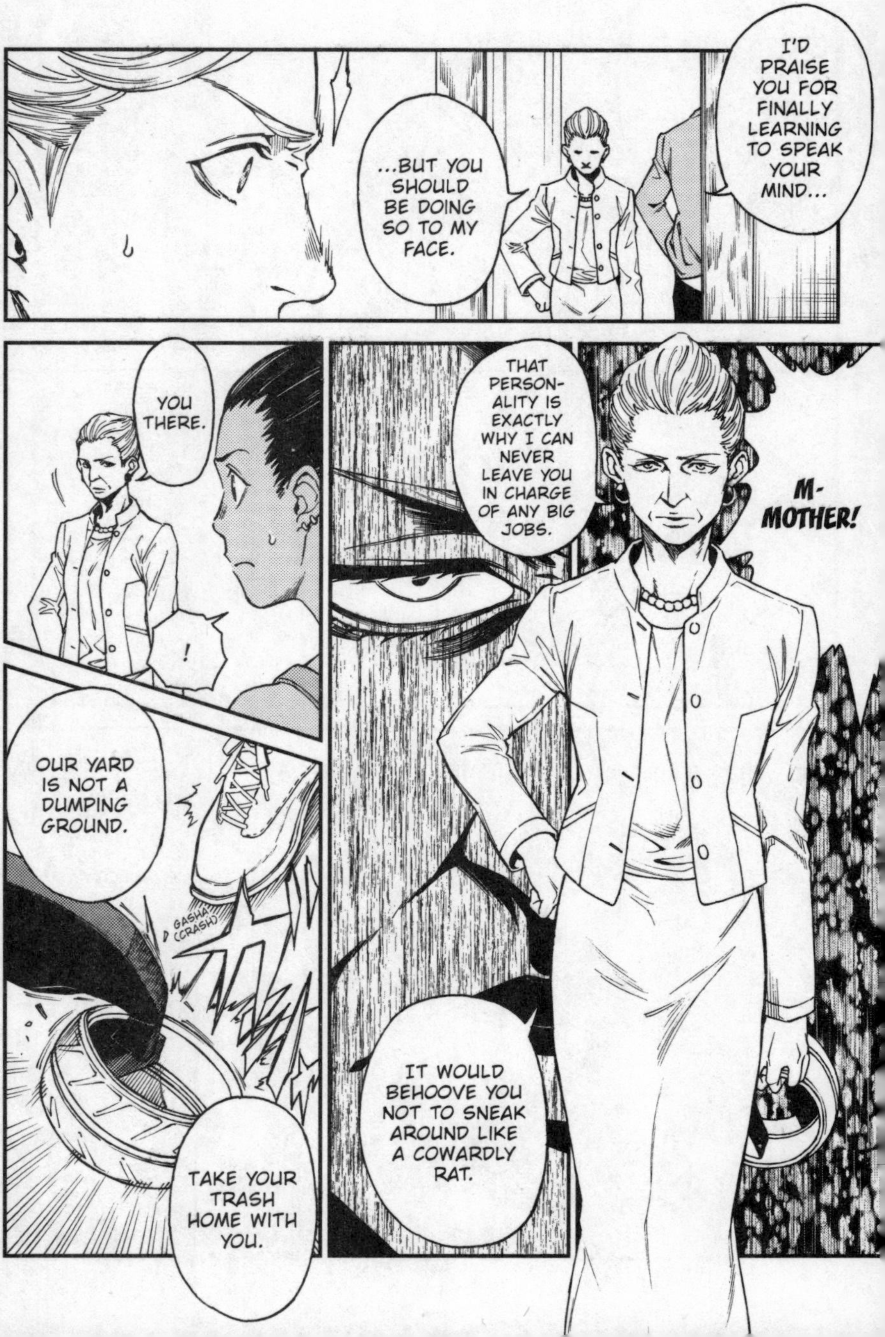
I'D PRAISE YOU FOR FINALLY LEARNING TO SPEAK YOUR MIND...
...BUT YOU SHOULD BE DOING SO TO MY FACE.
M-MOTHER!
THAT PERSON-ALITY IS EXACTLY WHY I CAN NEVER LEAVE YOU IN CHARGE OF ANY BIG JOBS.
IT WOULD BEHOOVE YOU NOT TO SNEAK AROUND LIKE A COWARDLY RAT.
YOU THERE.
!
OUR YARD IS NOT A DUMPING GROUND.
GASHA (CRASH)
TAKE YOUR TRASH HOME WITH YOU.

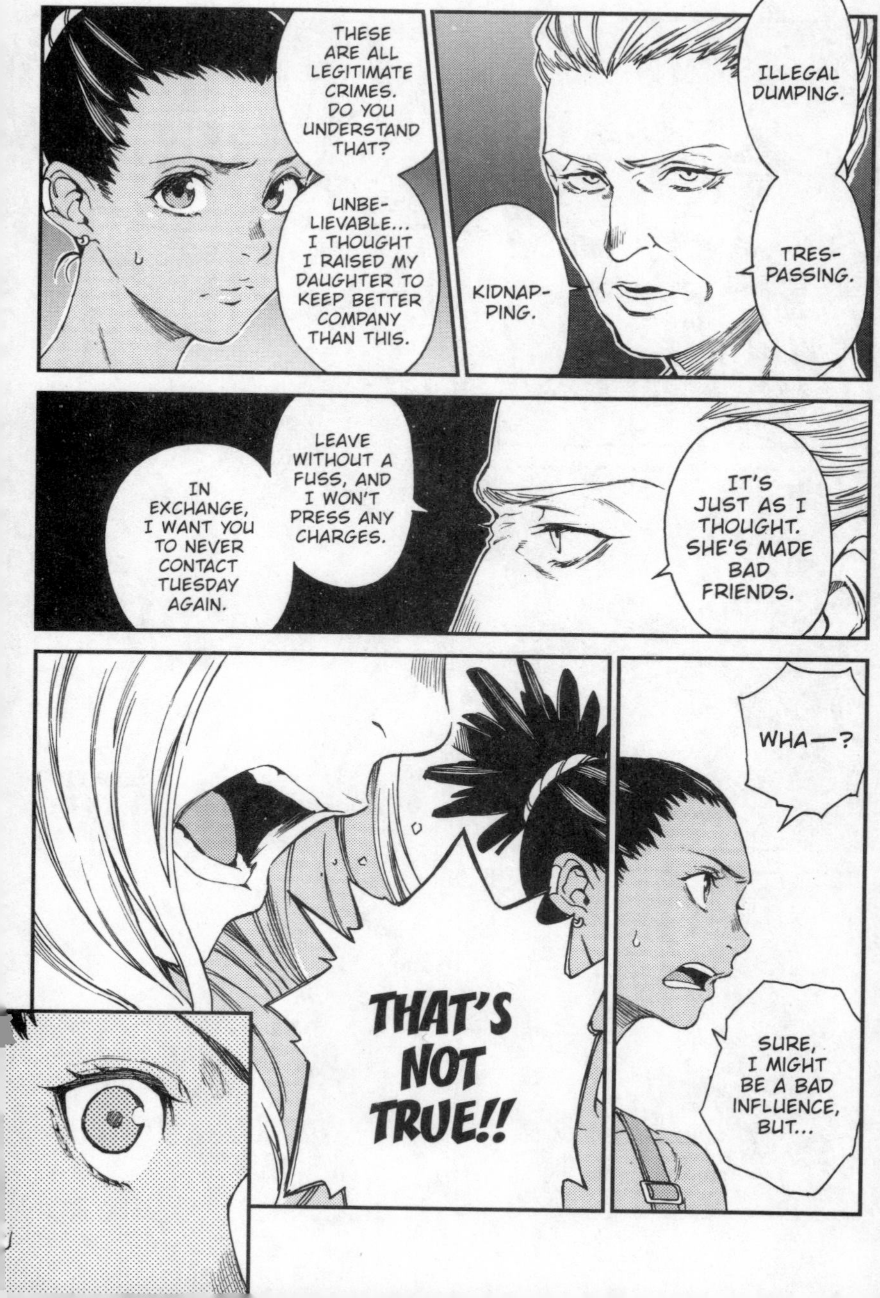
ILLEGAL DUMPING.
TRES-PASSING.
KIDNAP-PING.
THESE ARE ALL LEGITIMATE CRIMES. DO YOU UNDERSTAND THAT?
UNBE-LIEVABLE... I THOUGHT I RAISED MY DAUGHTER TO KEEP BETTER COMPANY THAN THIS.
IT'S JUST AS I THOUGHT. SHE'S MADE BAD FRIENDS.
LEAVE WITHOUT A FUSS, AND I WON'T PRESS ANY CHARGES.
IN EXCHANGE, I WANT YOU TO NEVER CONTACT TUESDAY AGAIN.
WHA—?
SURE, I MIGHT BE A BAD INFLUENCE, BUT...
THAT'S NOT TRUE!!

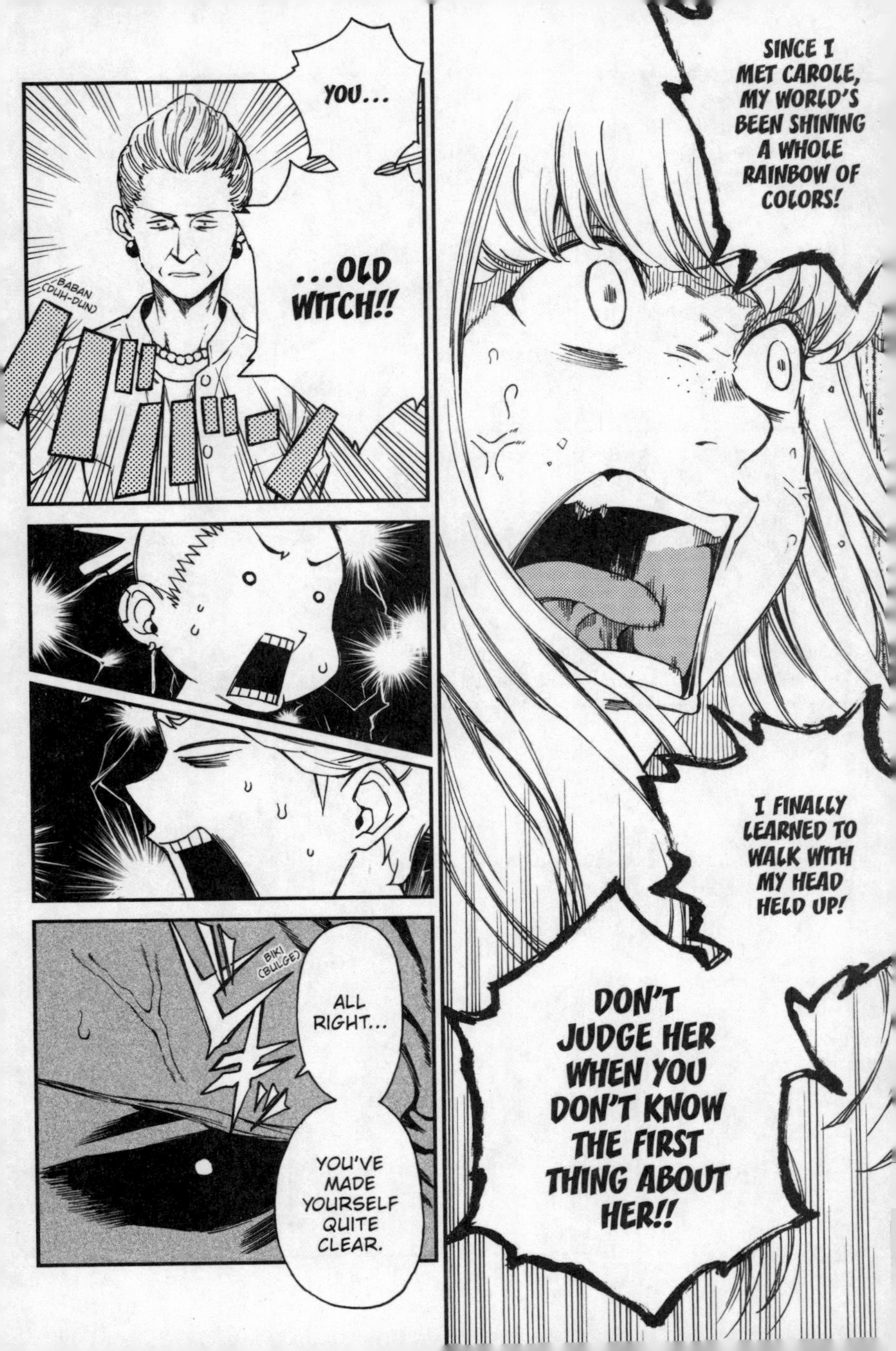
SINCE I MET CAROLE, MY WORLD'S BEEN SHINING A WHOLE RAINBOW OF COLORS!
I FINALLY LEARNED TO WALK WITH MY HEAD HELD UP!
DON'T JUDGE HER WHEN YOU DON'T KNOW THE FIRST THING ABOUT HER!!
YOU...
...OLD WITCH!!
BABAN (DUH-DUN)
BIKI (BULGE)
ALL RIGHT...
YOU'VE MADE YOURSELF QUITE CLEAR.

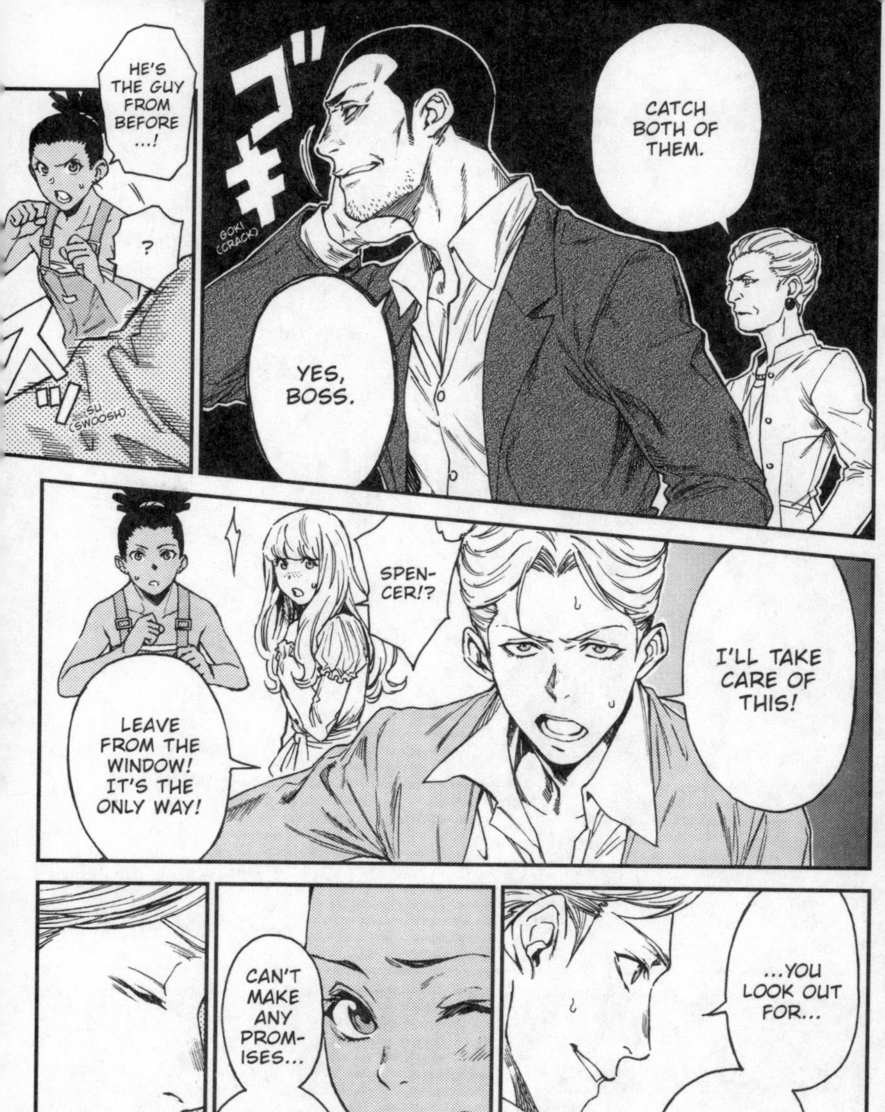
CATCH BOTH OF THEM.
GOKI (CRACK)
YES, BOSS.
HE'S THE GUY FROM BEFORE ...!
?
SU (SWOOSH)
I'LL TAKE CARE OF THIS!
SPEN-CER!?
LEAVE FROM THE WINDOW! IT'S THE ONLY WAY!
...YOU LOOK OUT FOR...
...MY CLUMSY SISTER FOR ME, ALL RIGHT?
CAN'T MAKE ANY PROM-ISES...
...'COS I HAVE HER LOOKIN' OUT FOR ME ALL THE TIME TOO!

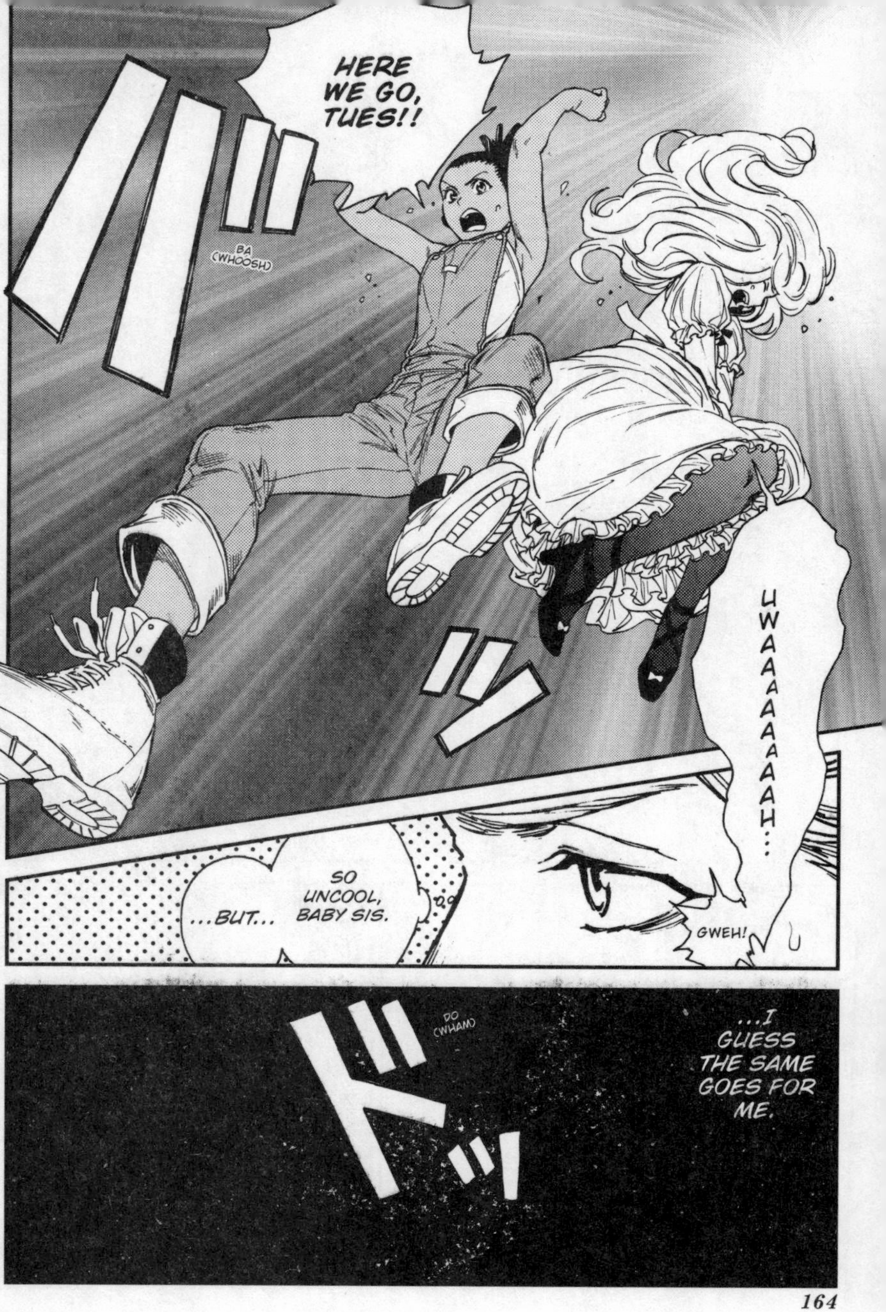
HERE WE GO, TUES!!
BA (WHOOSH)
UWAAAAAAAAAAAH...
GWEH!
SO UNCOOL, BABY SIS.
...BUT...
...I GUESS THE SAME GOES FOR ME.
DO (WHAM)

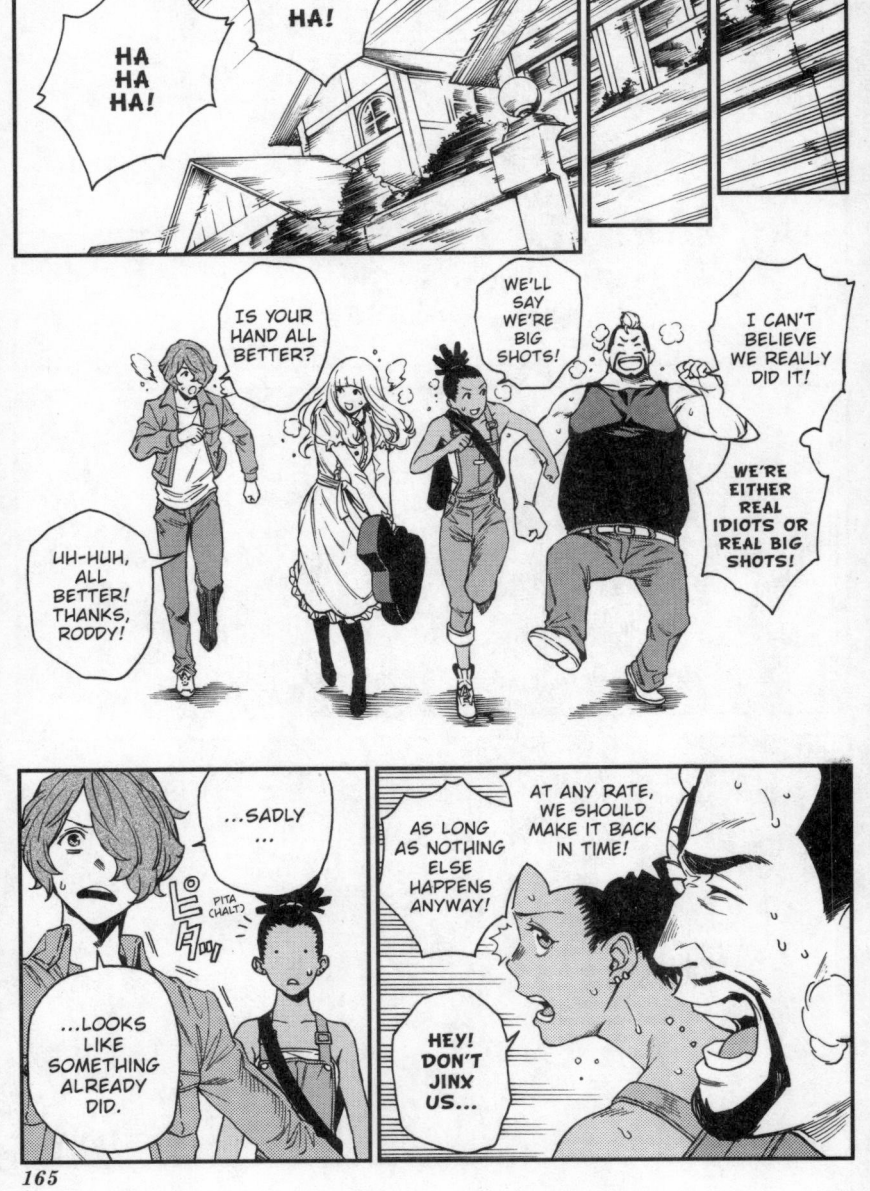

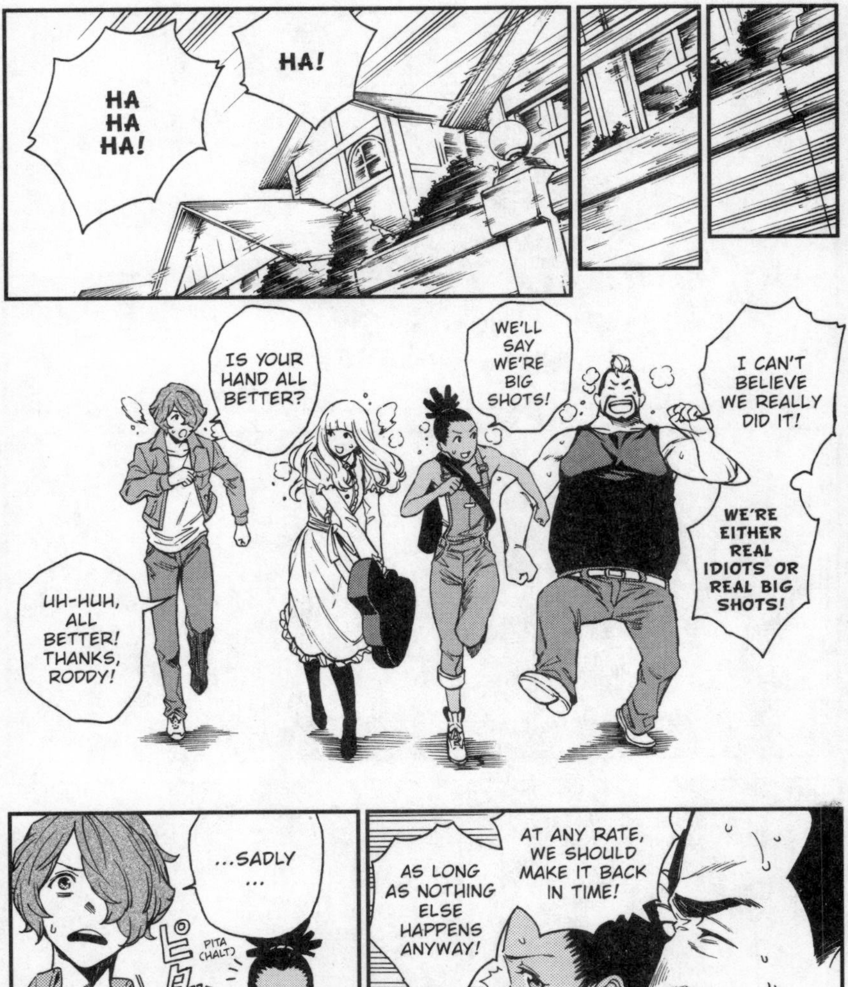
HA!
HA HA HA!
I CAN'T BELIEVE WE REALLY DID IT!
WE'RE EITHER REAL IDIOTS OR REAL BIG SHOTS!
WE'LL SAY WE'RE BIG SHOTS!
IS YOUR HAND ALL BETTER?
UH-HUH, ALL BETTER! THANKS, RODDY!
AT ANY RATE, WE SHOULD MAKE IT BACK IN TIME!
AS LONG AS NOTHING ELSE HAPPENS ANYWAY!
HEY! DON'T JINX US...
...SADLY ...
PITA (HALT)
...LOOKS LIKE SOMETHING ALREADY DID.

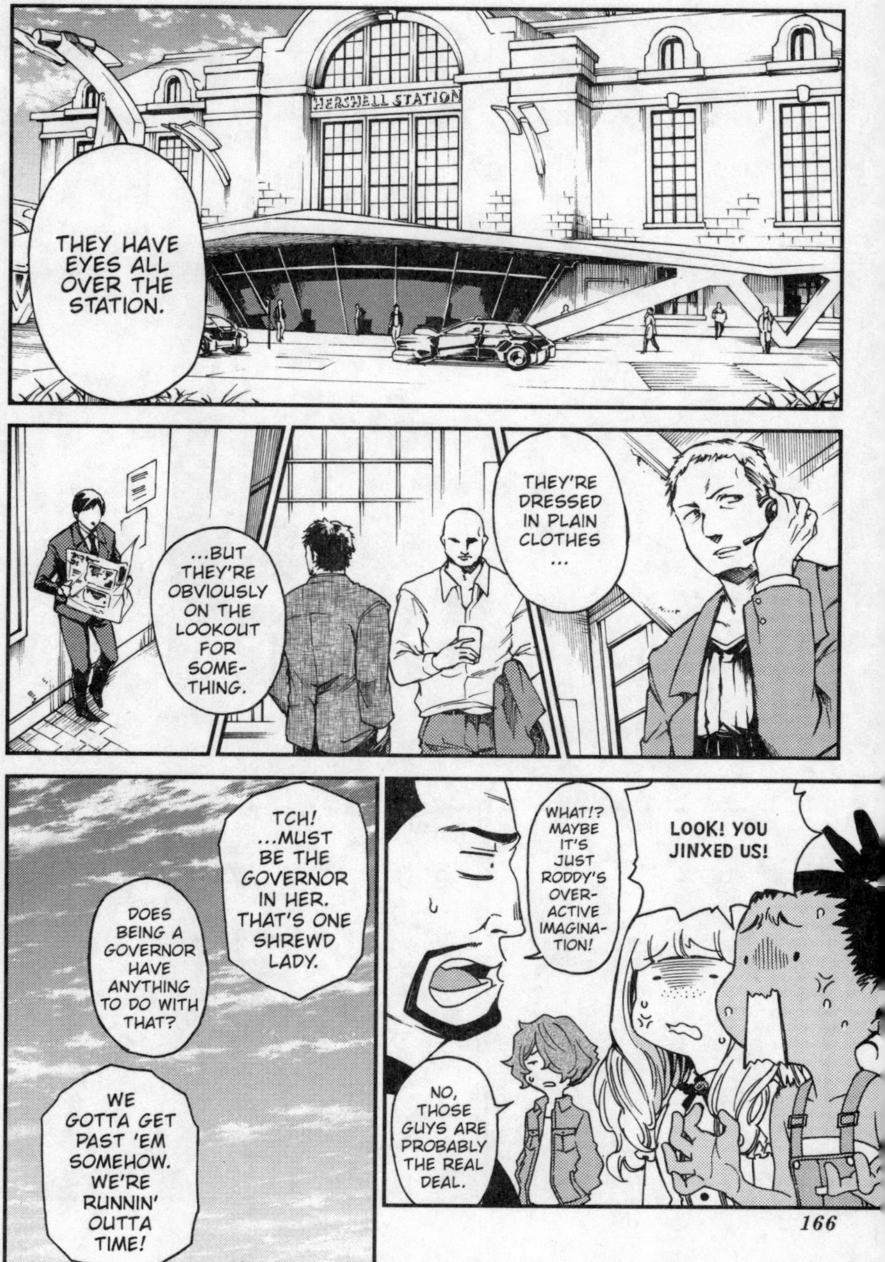
THEY HAVE EYES ALL OVER THE STATION.
HERSHELL STATION
THEY'RE DRESSED IN PLAIN CLOTHES ...
...BUT THEY'RE OBVIOUSLY ON THE LOOKOUT FOR SOME-THING.
LOOK! YOU JINXED US!
WHAT!? MAYBE IT'S JUST RODDY'S OVER-ACTIVE IMAGINA-TION!
NO, THOSE GUYS ARE PROBABLY THE REAL DEAL.
TCH! ...MUST BE THE GOVERNOR IN HER. THAT'S ONE SHREWD LADY.
DOES BEING A GOVERNOR HAVE ANYTHING TO DO WITH THAT?
WE GOTTA GET PAST 'EM SOMEHOW. WE'RE RUNNIN' OUTTA TIME!

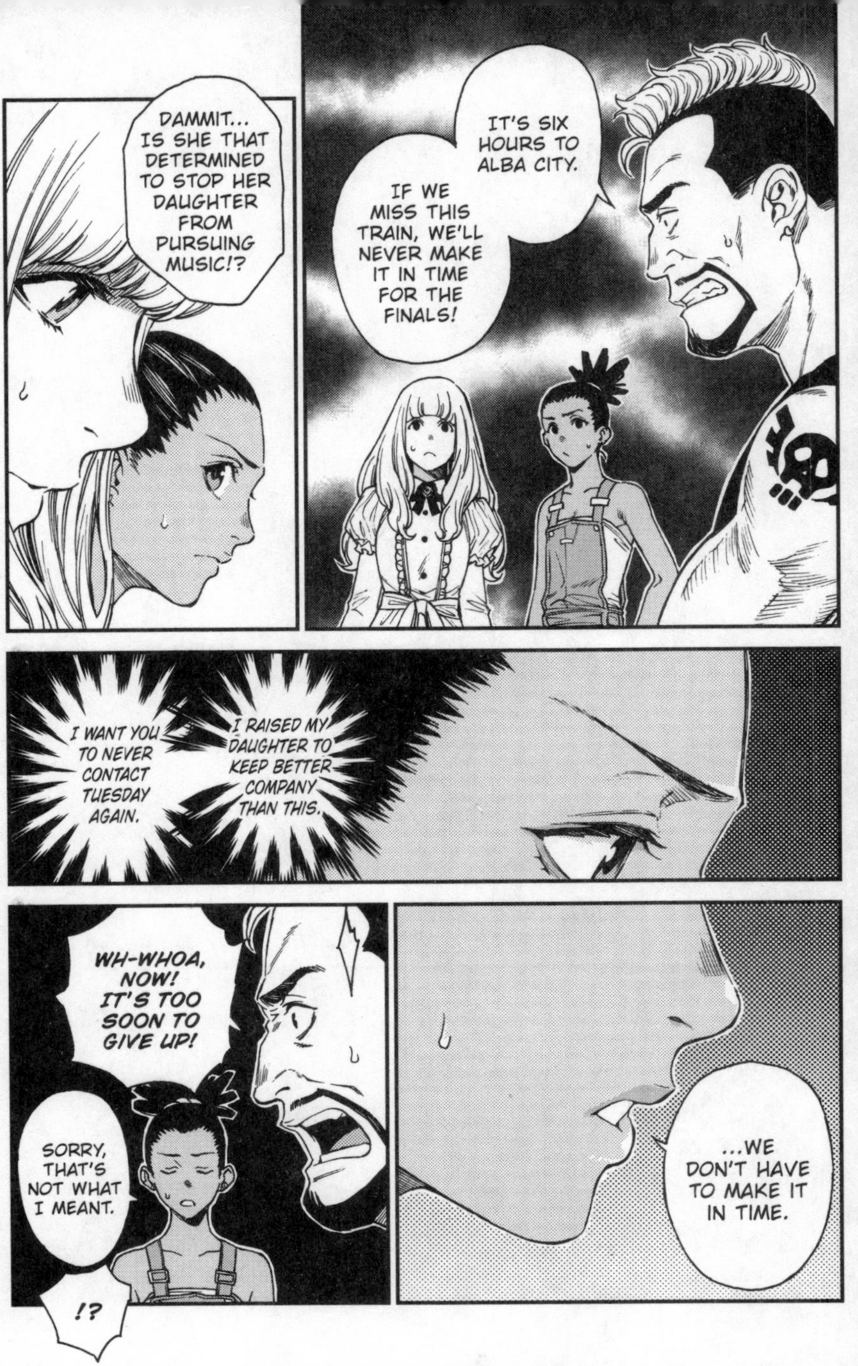
IT'S SIX HOURS TO ALBA CITY.
IF WE MISS THIS TRAIN, WE'LL NEVER MAKE IT IN TIME FOR THE FINALS!
DAMMIT... IS SHE THAT DETERMINED TO STOP HER DAUGHTER FROM PURSUING MUSIC!?
I RAISED MY DAUGHTER TO KEEP BETTER COMPANY THAN THIS.
I WANT YOU TO NEVER CONTACT TUESDAY AGAIN.
...WE DON'T HAVE TO MAKE IT IN TIME.
WH-WHOA, NOW! IT'S TOO SOON TO GIVE UP!
SORRY, THAT'S NOT WHAT I MEANT.
!?

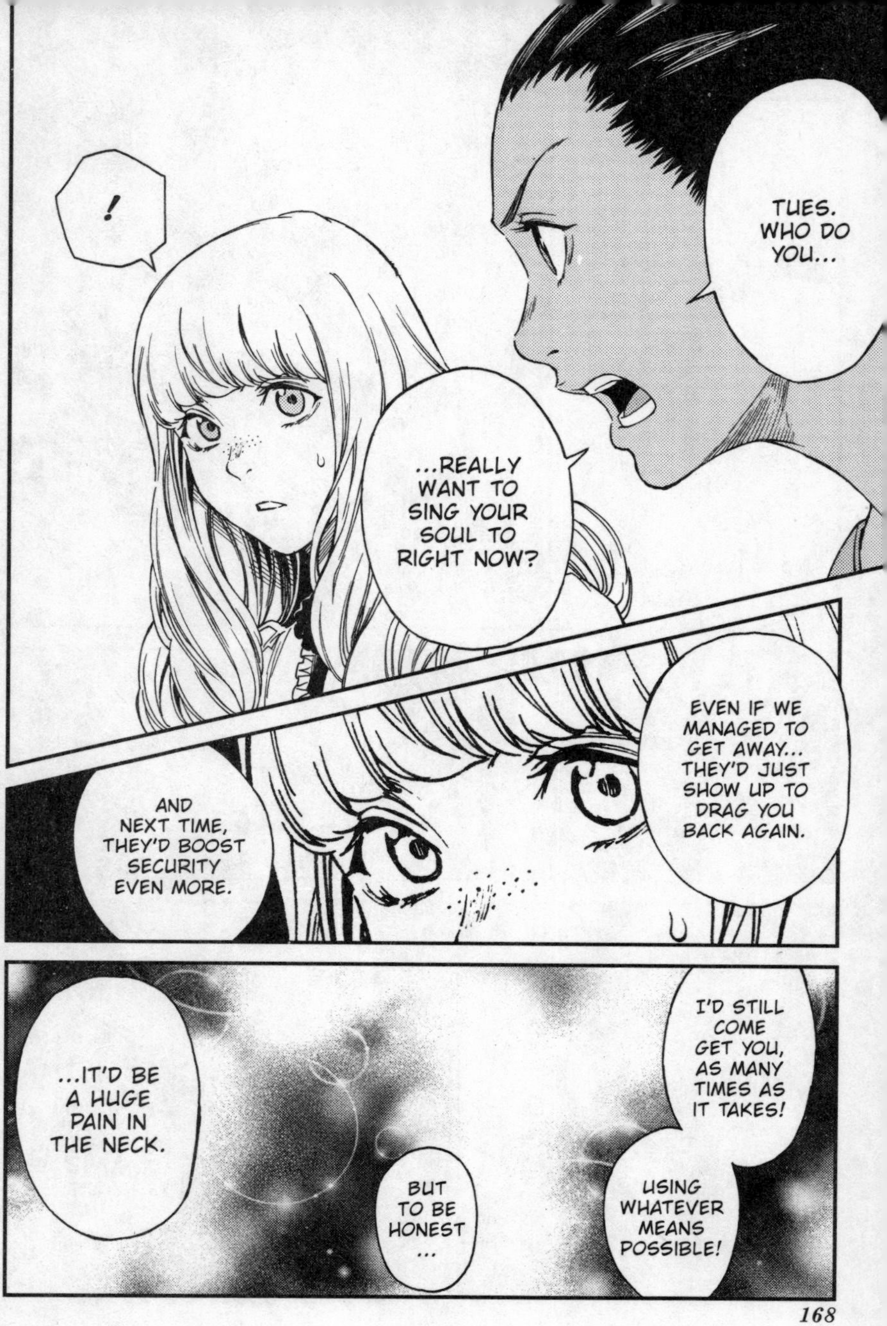
TUES. WHO DO YOU...
...REALLY WANT TO SING YOUR SOUL TO RIGHT NOW?
!
EVEN IF WE MANAGED TO GET AWAY... THEY'D JUST SHOW UP TO DRAG YOU BACK AGAIN.
AND NEXT TIME, THEY'D BOOST SECURITY EVEN MORE.
I'D STILL COME GET YOU, AS MANY TIMES AS IT TAKES!
USING WHATEVER MEANS POSSIBLE!
BUT TO BE HONEST ...
...IT'D BE A HUGE PAIN IN THE NECK.

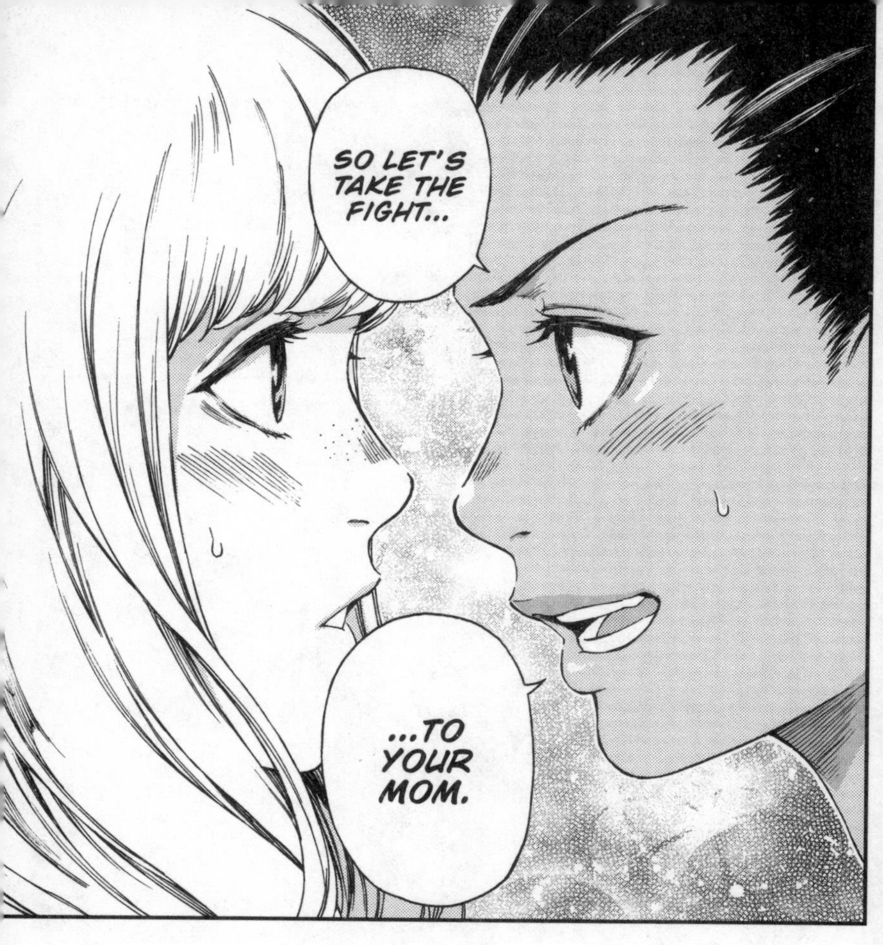
SO LET'S TAKE THE FIGHT...
...TO YOUR MOM.
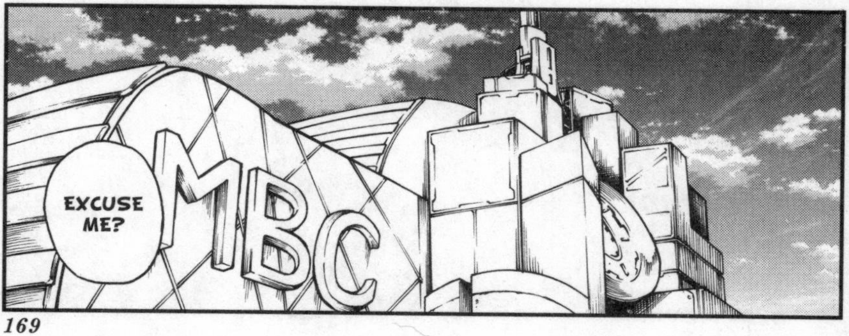
EXCUSE ME?
MBC

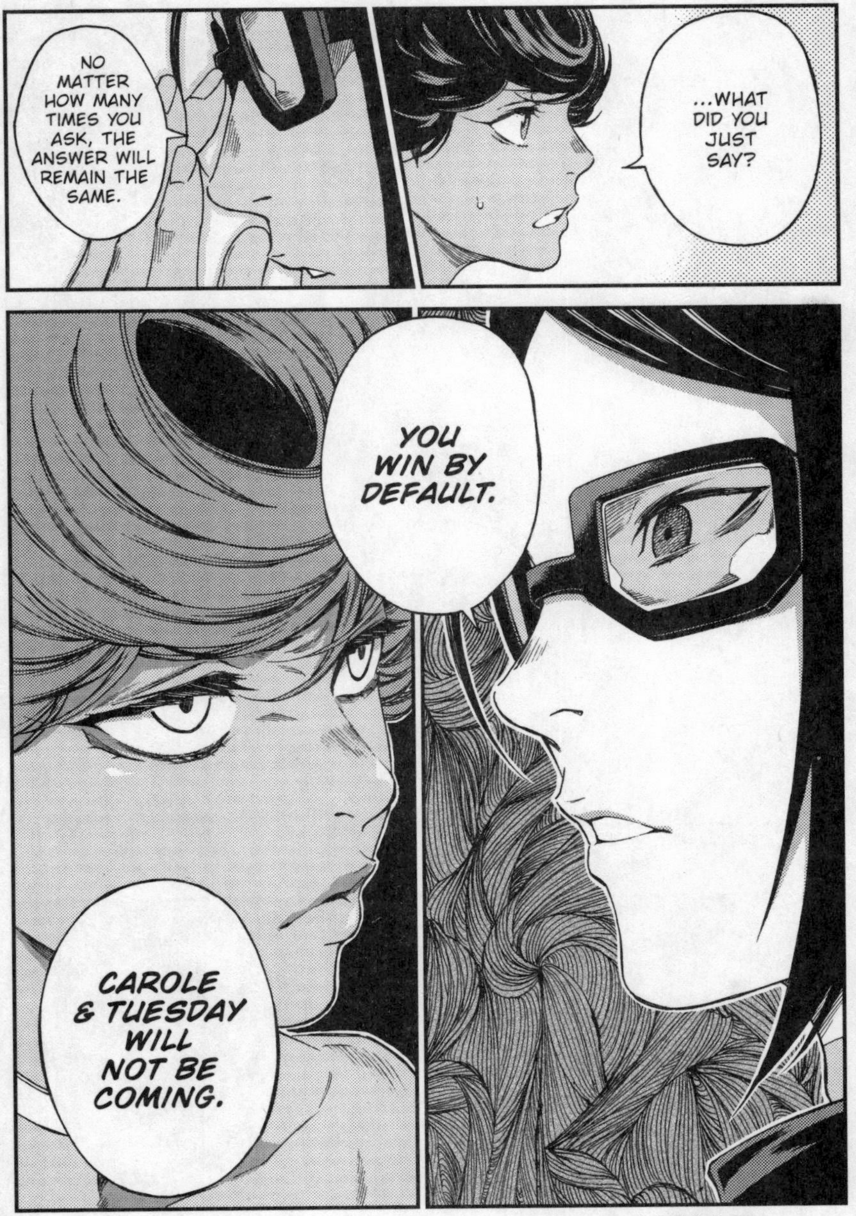
...WHAT DID YOU JUST SAY?
NO MATTER HOW MANY TIMES YOU ASK, THE ANSWER WILL REMAIN THE SAME.
YOU WIN BY DEFAULT.
CAROLE & TUESDAY WILL NOT BE COMING.

END

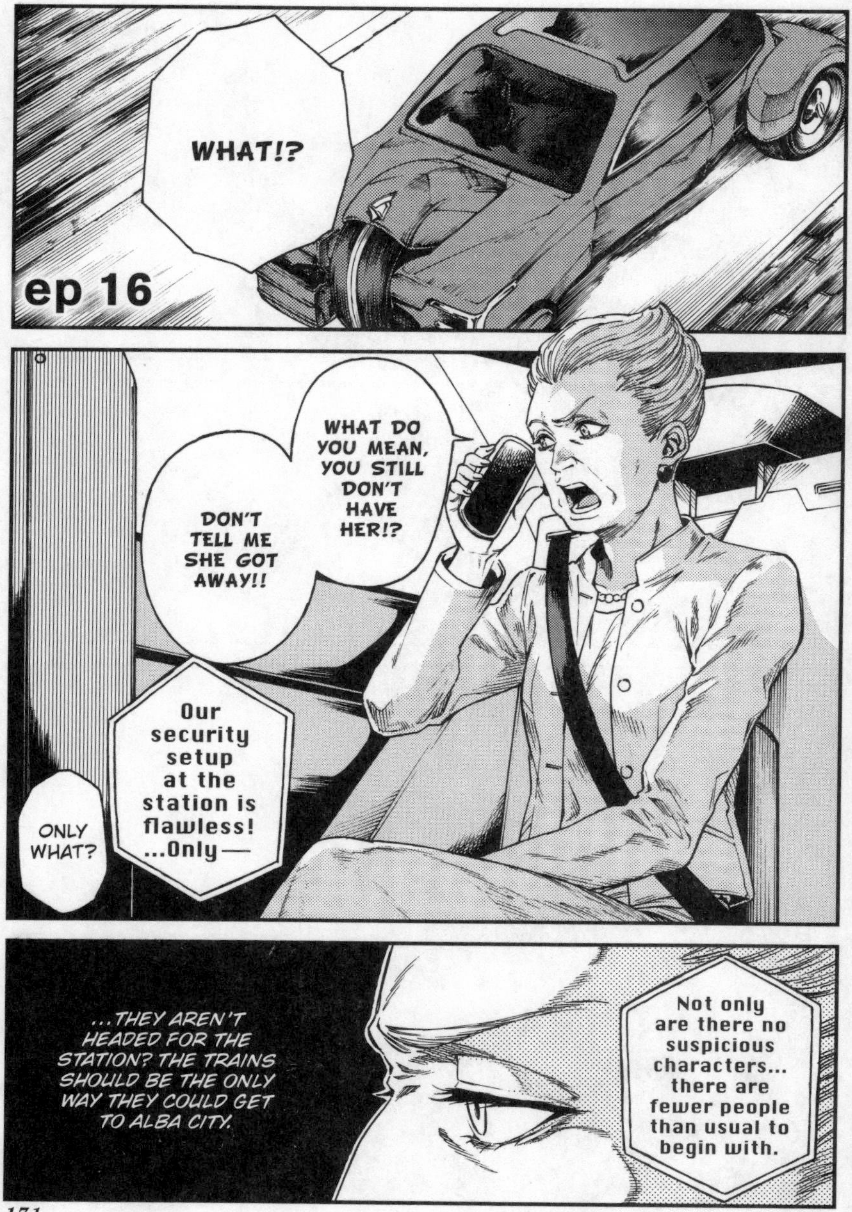
WHAT!?
ep 16
WHAT DO YOU MEAN, YOU STILL DON'T HAVE HER!?
DON'T TELL ME SHE GOT AWAY!!
Our security setup at the station is flawless! ...Only—
ONLY WHAT?
Not only are there no suspicious characters... there are fewer people than usual to begin with.
...THEY AREN'T HEADED FOR THE STATION? THE TRAINS SHOULD BE THE ONLY WAY THEY COULD GET TO ALBA CITY.

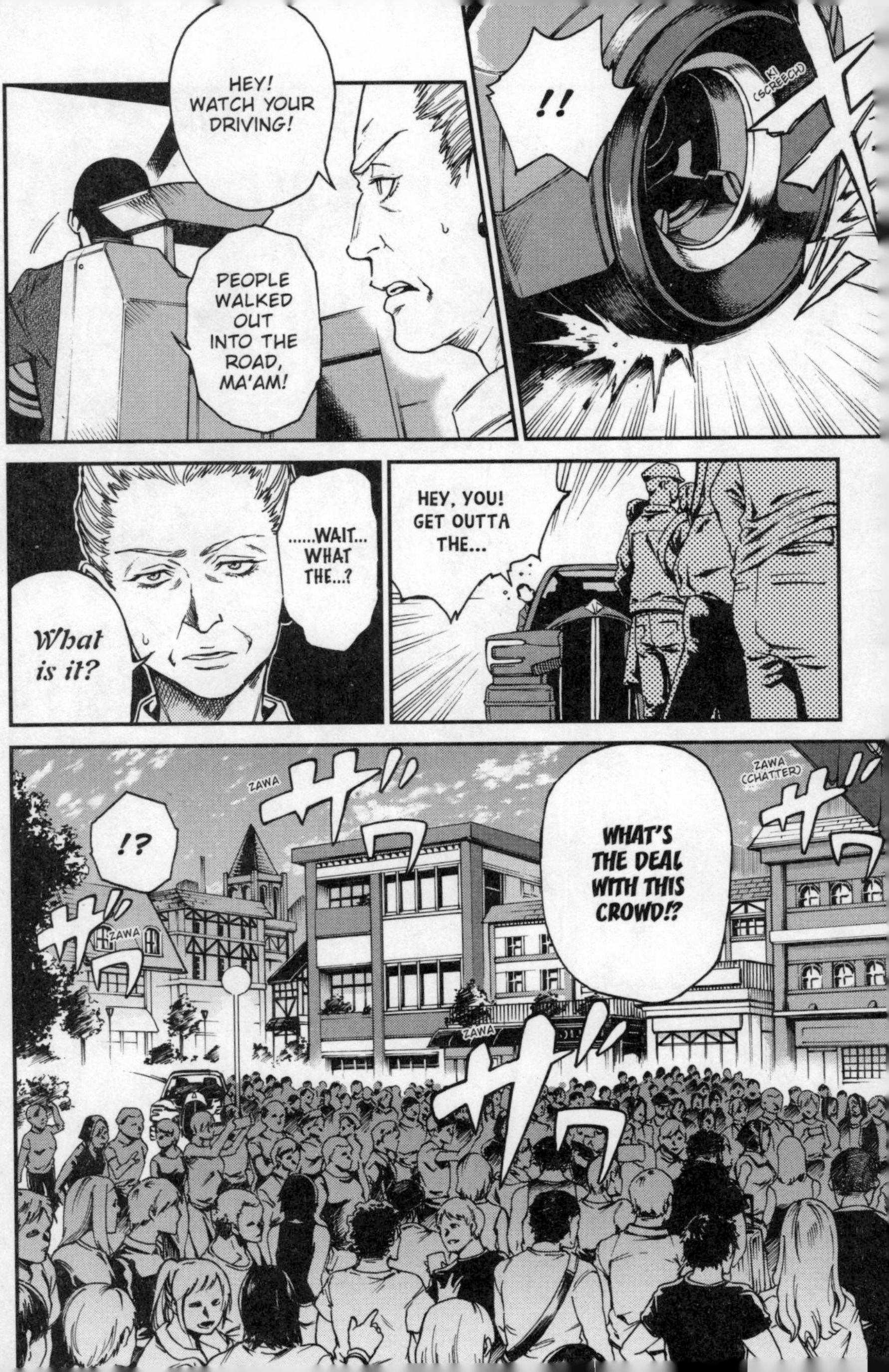
KI (SCREECH)
!!
HEY! WATCH YOUR DRIVING!
PEOPLE WALKED OUT INTO THE ROAD, MA'AM!
HEY, YOU! GET OUTTA THE...
......WAIT... WHAT THE...?
What is it?
ZAWA (CHATTER)
WHAT'S THE DEAL WITH THIS CROWD!?
ZAWA
!?
ZAWA
ZAWA

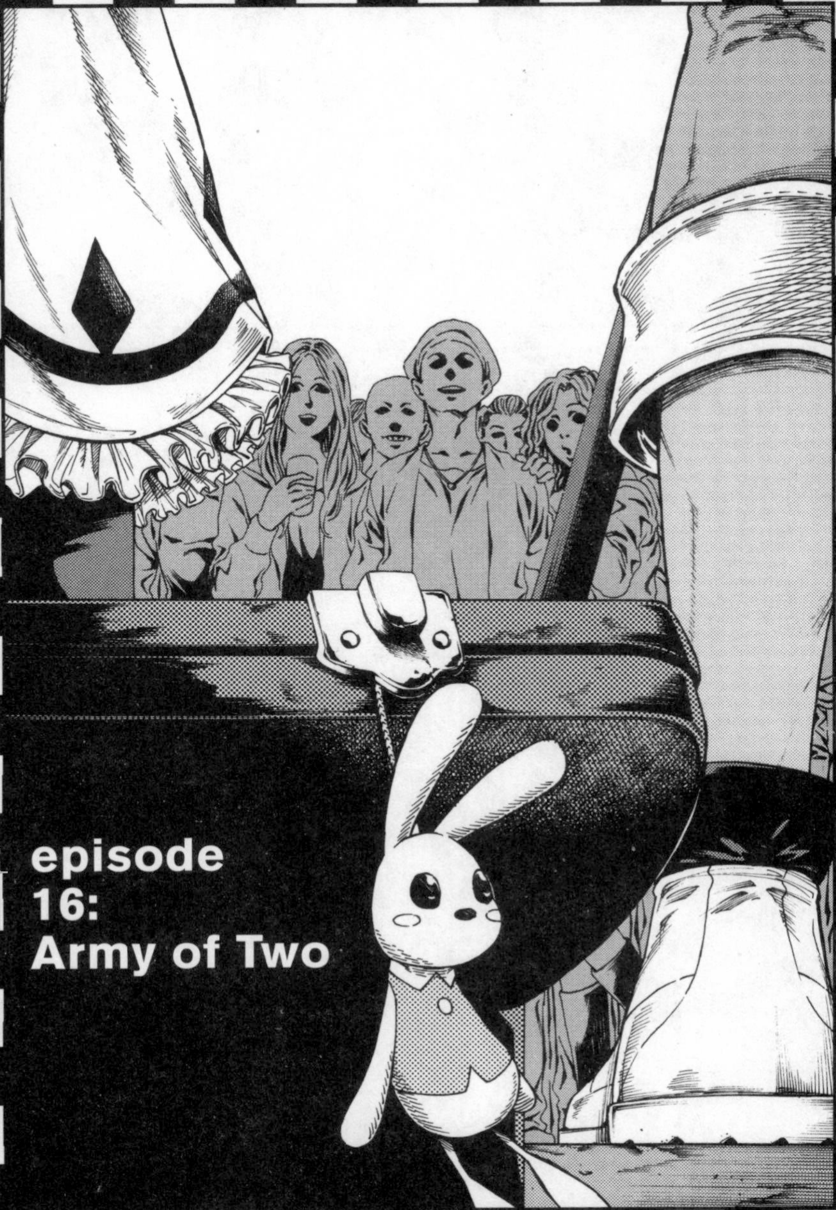
episode
16:
Army of Two

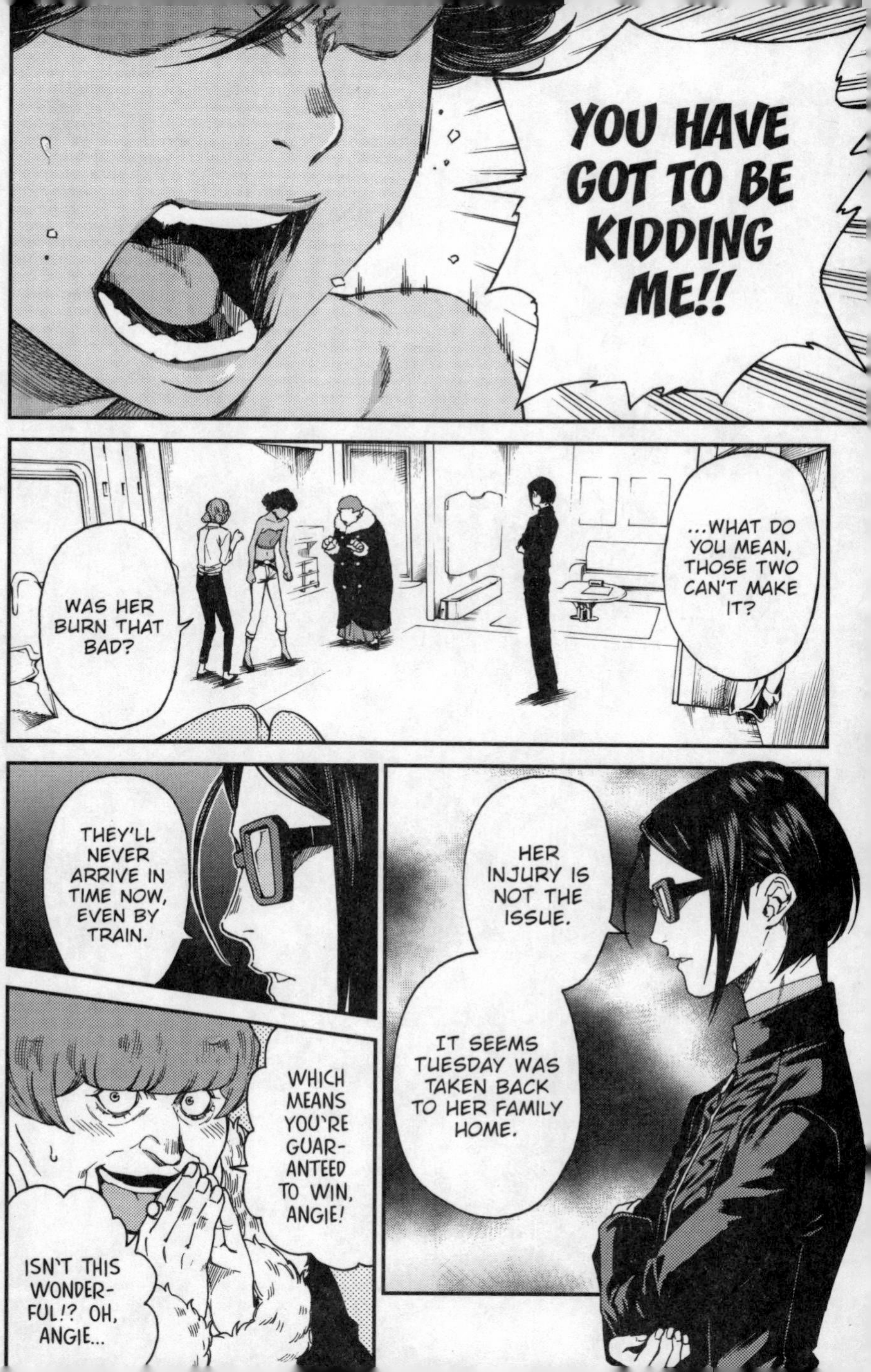
YOU HAVE GOT TO BE KIDDING ME!!
...WHAT DO YOU MEAN, THOSE TWO CAN'T MAKE IT?
WAS HER BURN THAT BAD?
HER INJURY IS NOT THE ISSUE.
IT SEEMS TUESDAY WAS TAKEN BACK TO HER FAMILY HOME.
THEY'LL NEVER ARRIVE IN TIME NOW, EVEN BY TRAIN.
WHICH MEANS YOU'RE GUARANTEED TO WIN, ANGIE!
ISN'T THIS WONDERFUL!? OH, ANGIE...

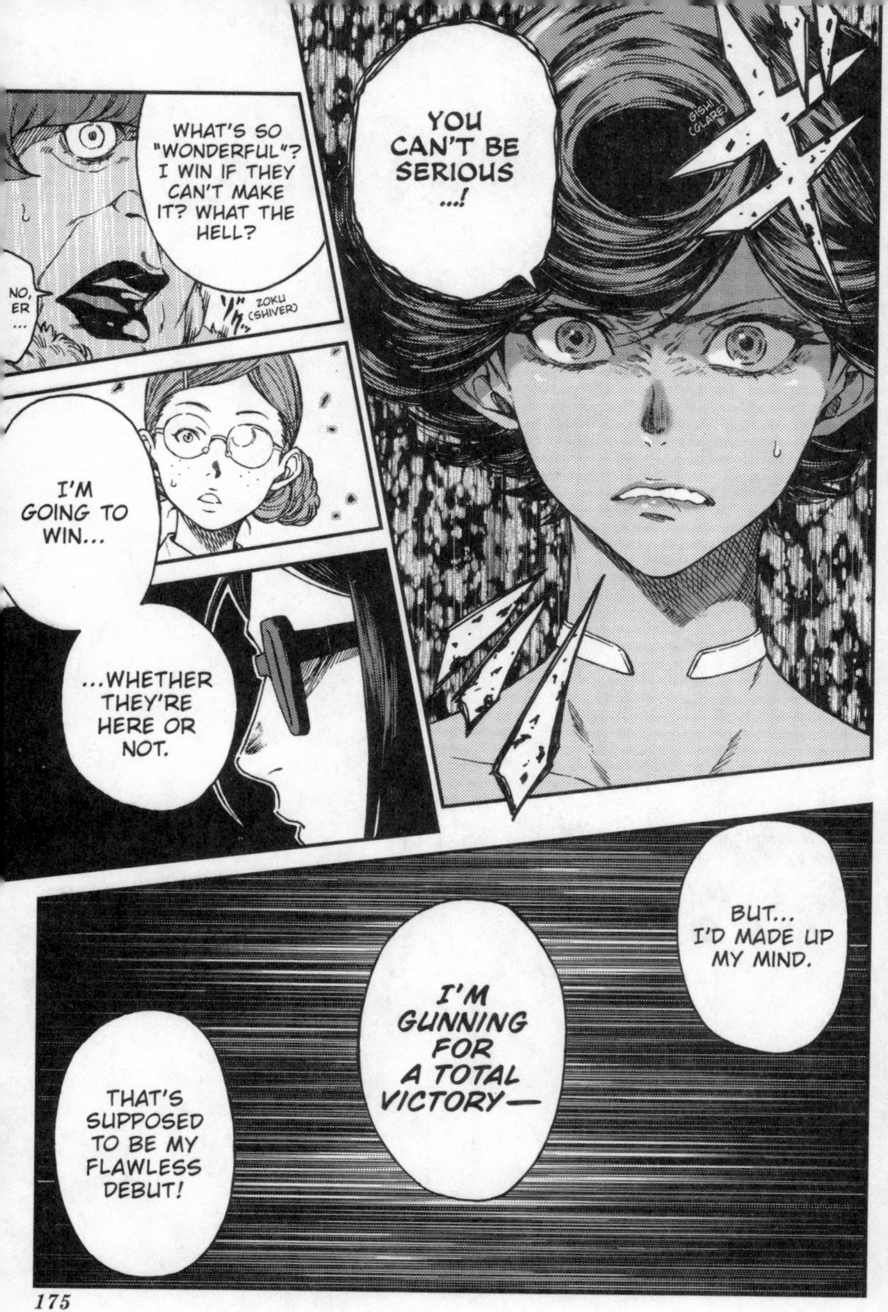
YOU CAN'T BE SERIOUS ...!
GISHI (GLARE)
WHAT'S SO "WONDERFUL"? I WIN IF THEY CAN'T MAKE IT? WHAT THE HELL?
ZOKU (SHIVER)
NO, ER ...
I'M GOING TO WIN...
...WHETHER THEY'RE HERE OR NOT.
BUT... I'D MADE UP MY MIND.
I'M GUNNING FOR A TOTAL VICTORY—
THAT'S SUPPOSED TO BE MY FLAWLESS DEBUT!

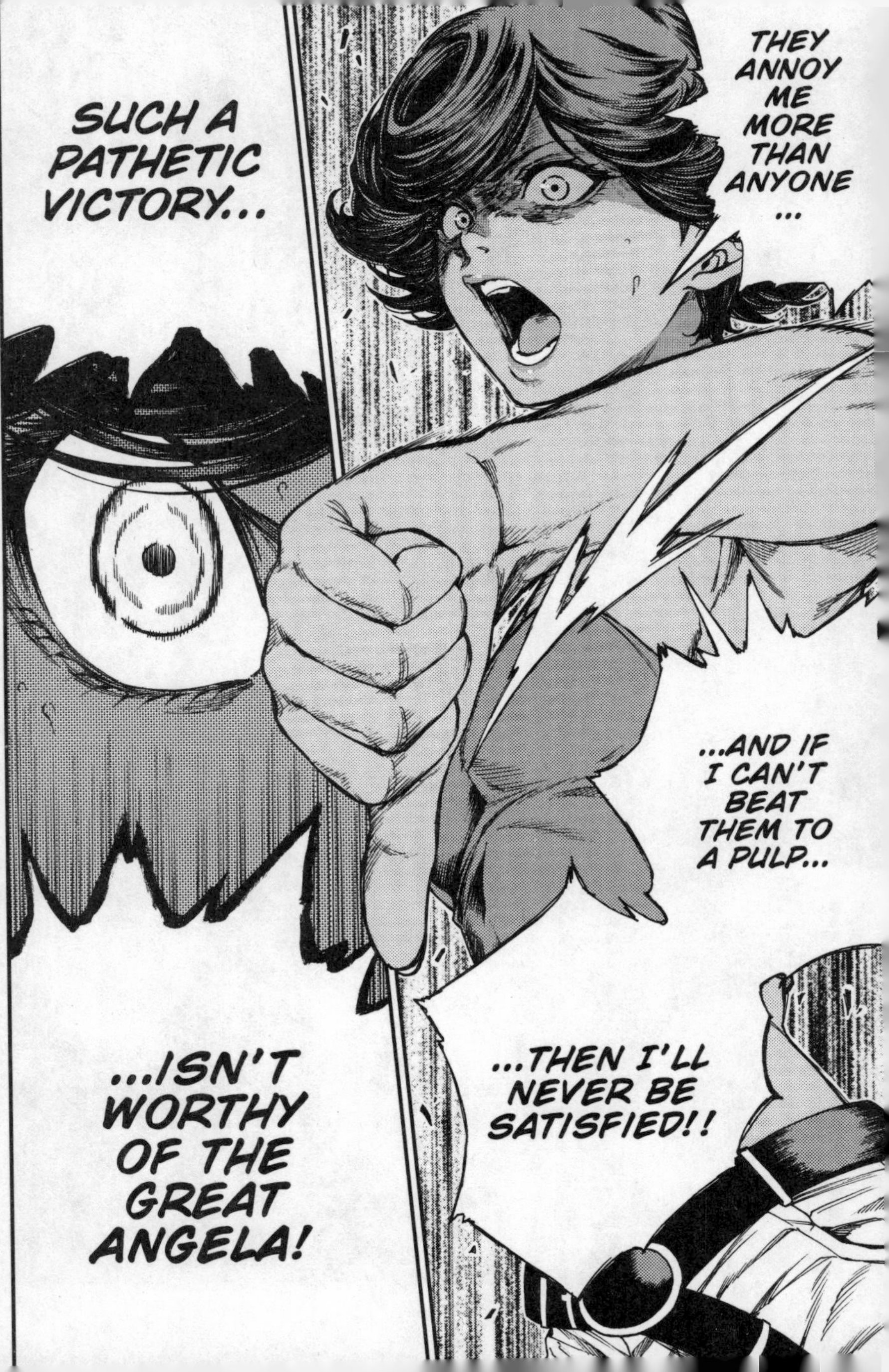
THEY ANNOY ME MORE THAN ANYONE ...
...AND IF I CAN'T BEAT THEM TO A PULP...
...THEN I'LL NEVER BE SATISFIED!!
SUCH A PATHETIC VICTORY...
...ISN'T WORTHY OF THE GREAT ANGELA!

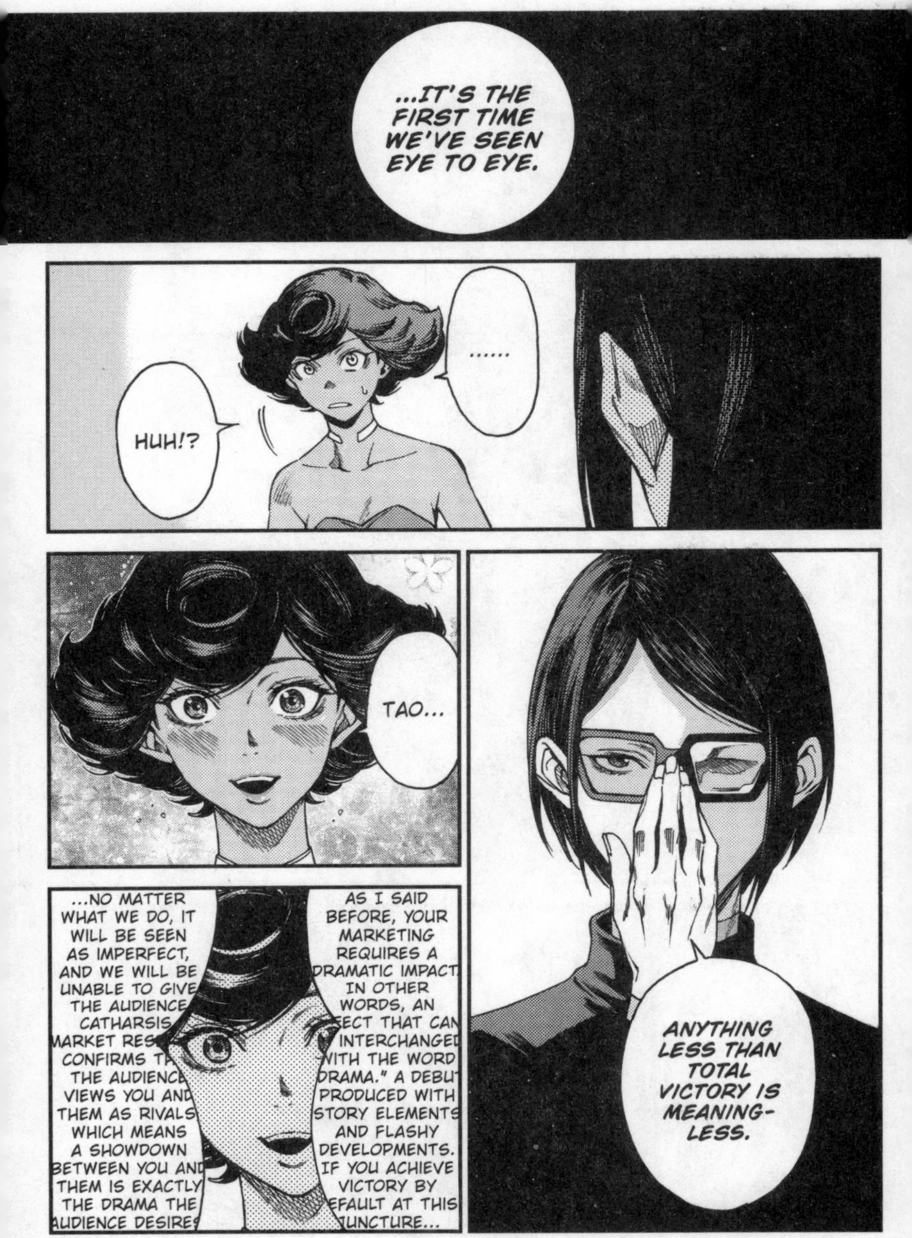
...IT'S THE FIRST TIME WE'VE SEEN EYE TO EYE.
......
HUH!?
ANYTHING LESS THAN TOTAL VICTORY IS MEANING-LESS.
TAO...
AS I SAID BEFORE, YOUR MARKETING REQUIRES A DRAMATIC IMPACT. IN OTHER WORDS, AN EFFECT THAT CAN INTERCHANGED WITH THE WORD "DRAMA." A DEBUT PRODUCED WITH STORY ELEMENTS AND FLASHY DEVELOPMENTS. IF YOU ACHIEVE VICTORY BY DEFAULT AT THIS JUNCTURE...
...NO MATTER WHAT WE DO, IT WILL BE SEEN AS IMPERFECT, AND WE WILL BE UNABLE TO GIVE THE AUDIENCE CATHARSIS. MARKET RES CONFIRMS T THE AUDIENCE VIEWS YOU AND THEM AS RIVALS WHICH MEANS A SHOWDOWN BETWEEN YOU AND THEM IS EXACTLY THE DRAMA THE AUDIENCE DESIRES

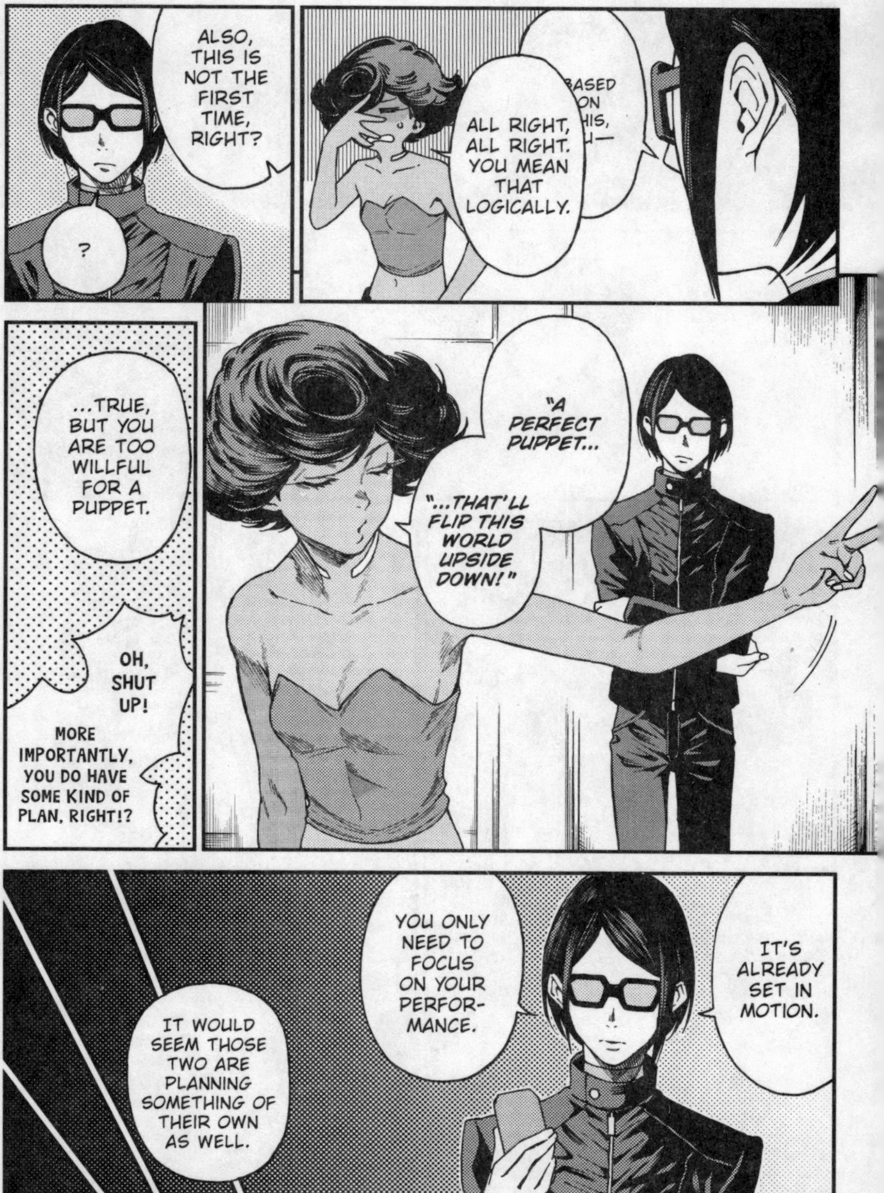
ALL RIGHT, ALL RIGHT. YOU MEAN THAT LOGICALLY.
ALSO, THIS IS NOT THE FIRST TIME, RIGHT?
?
"A PERFECT PUPPET...
"...THAT'LL FLIP THIS WORLD UPSIDE DOWN!"
...TRUE, BUT YOU ARE TOO WILLFUL FOR A PUPPET.
OH, SHUT UP!
MORE IMPORTANTLY, YOU DO HAVE SOME KIND OF PLAN, RIGHT!?
IT'S ALREADY SET IN MOTION.
YOU ONLY NEED TO FOCUS ON YOUR PERFOR-MANCE.
IT WOULD SEEM THOSE TWO ARE PLANNING SOMETHING OF THEIR OWN AS WELL.

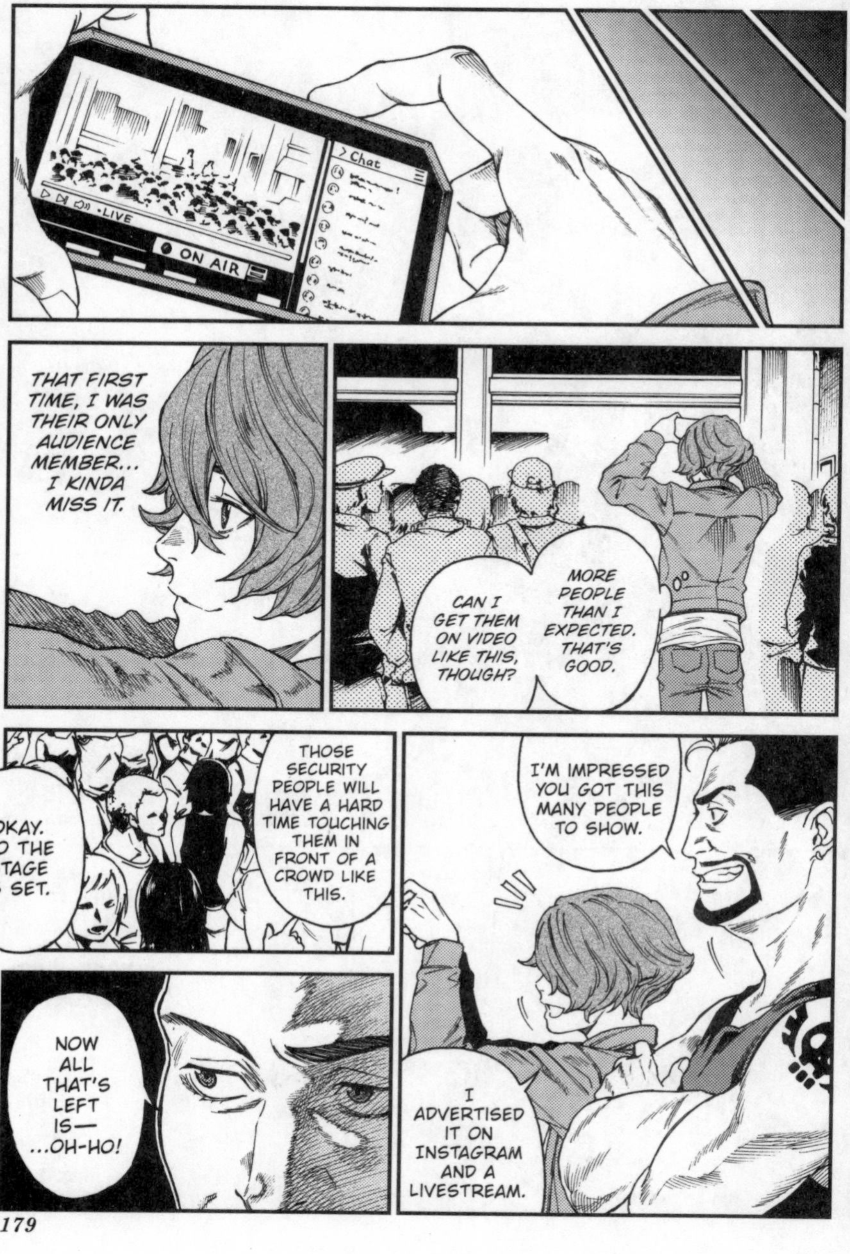

Chat
LIVE
ON AIR
MORE PEOPLE THAN I EXPECTED. THAT'S GOOD.
CAN I GET THEM ON VIDEO LIKE THIS, THOUGH?
THAT FIRST TIME, I WAS THEIR ONLY AUDIENCE MEMBER... I KINDA MISS IT.
I'M IMPRESSED YOU GOT THIS MANY PEOPLE TO SHOW.
I ADVERTISED IT ON INSTAGRAM AND A LIVESTREAM.
THOSE SECURITY PEOPLE WILL HAVE A HARD TIME TOUCHING THEM IN FRONT OF A CROWD LIKE THIS.
OKAY. SO THE STAGE IS SET.
NOW ALL THAT'S LEFT IS—
...OH-HO!

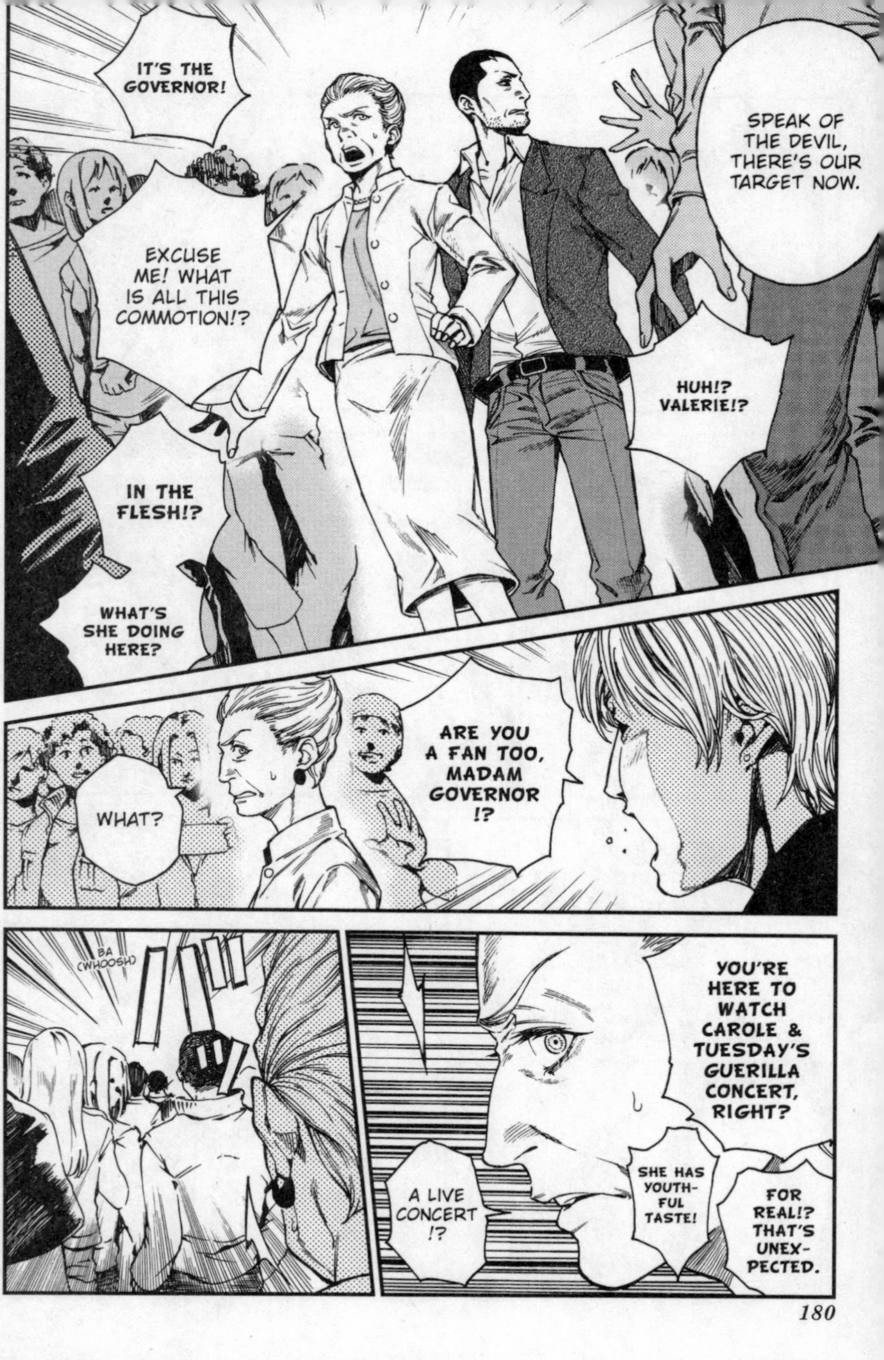
SPEAK OF THE DEVIL, THERE'S OUR TARGET NOW.
HUH!? VALERIE!?
IT'S THE GOVERNOR!
EXCUSE ME! WHAT IS ALL THIS COMMOTION!?
IN THE FLESH!?
WHAT'S SHE DOING HERE?
ARE YOU A FAN TOO, MADAM GOVERNOR!?
WHAT?
YOU'RE HERE TO WATCH CAROLE & TUESDAY'S GUERILLA CONCERT, RIGHT?
FOR REAL!? THAT'S UNEXPECTED.
SHE HAS YOUTHFUL TASTE!
A LIVE CONCERT!?
BA (WHOOSH)

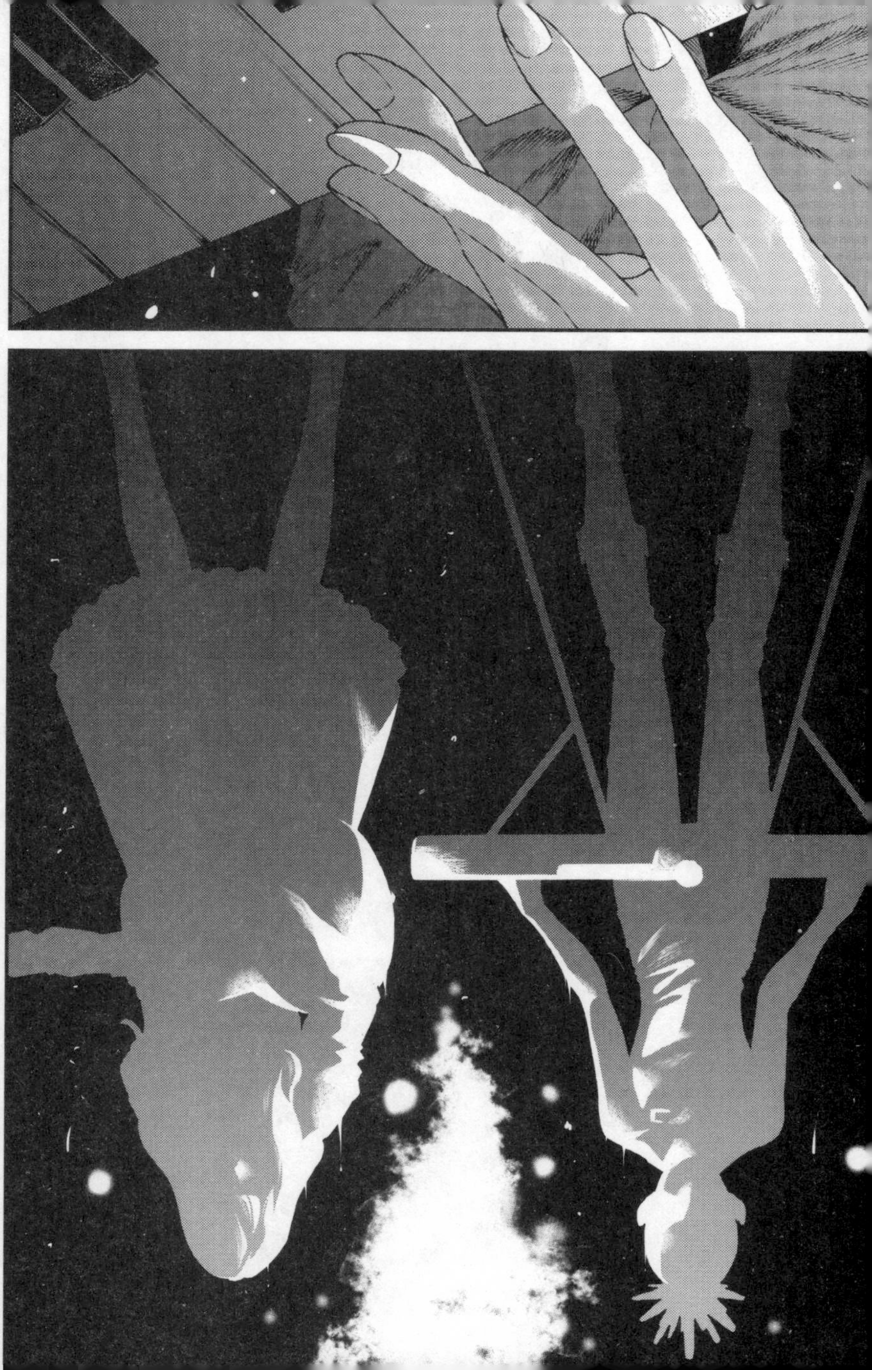

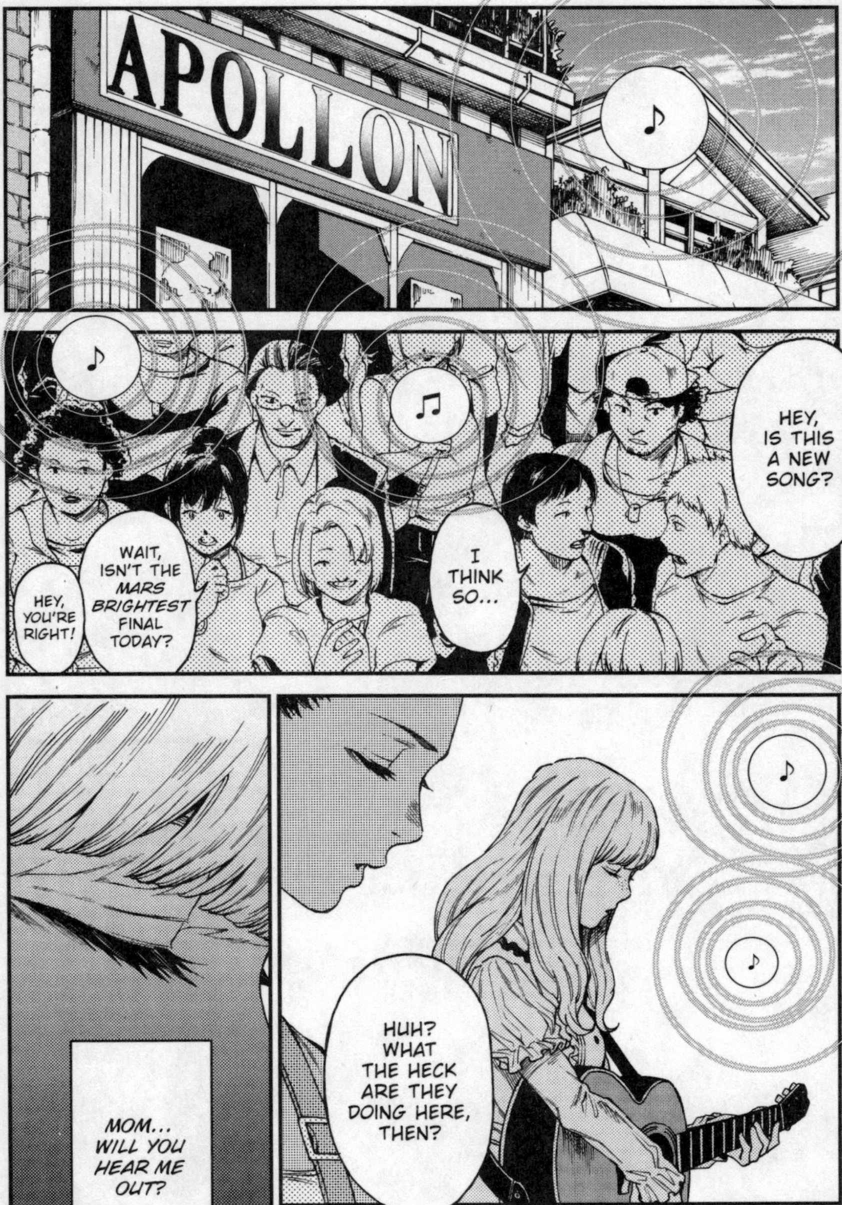
APOLLON
♪
HEY, IS THIS A NEW SONG?
♪
I THINK SO...
♪
WAIT, ISN'T THE *MARS BRIGHTEST* FINAL TODAY?
HEY, YOU'RE RIGHT!
♪
♪
HUH? WHAT THE HECK ARE THEY DOING HERE, THEN?
MOM... WILL YOU HEAR ME OUT?

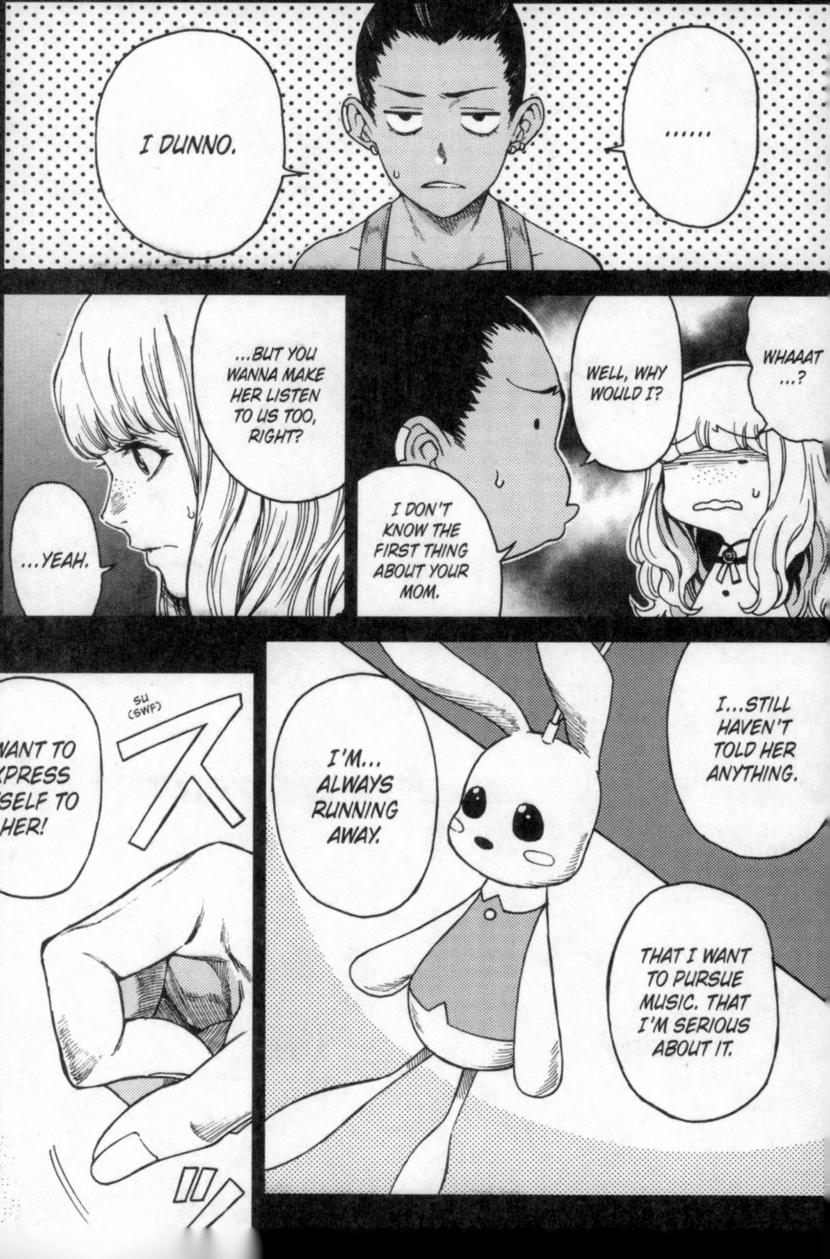
......
I DUNNO.
WHAAAT ...?
WELL, WHY WOULD I?
I DON'T KNOW THE FIRST THING ABOUT YOUR MOM.
...BUT YOU WANNA MAKE HER LISTEN TO US TOO, RIGHT?
...YEAH.
I...STILL HAVEN'T TOLD HER ANYTHING.
I'M... ALWAYS RUNNING AWAY.
THAT I WANT TO PURSUE MUSIC. THAT I'M SERIOUS ABOUT IT.
SU (SWF)
I WANT TO EXPRESS MYSELF TO HER!

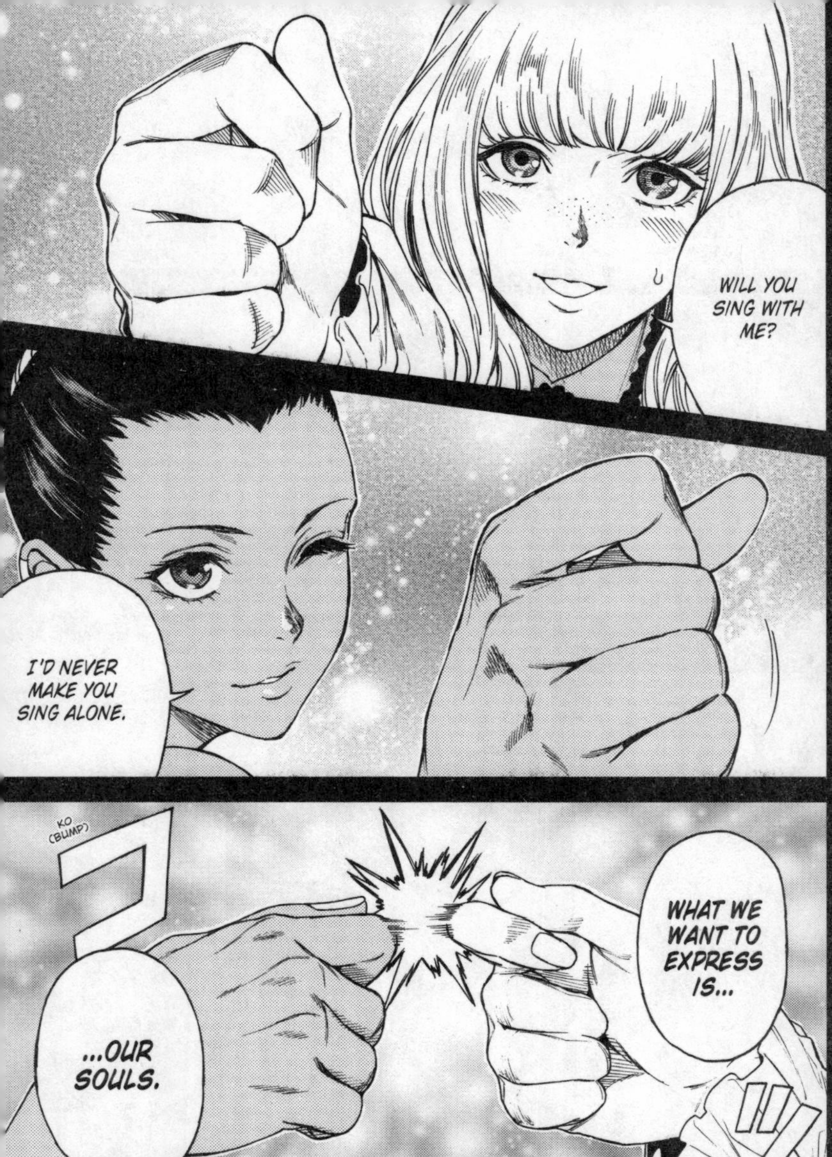
WILL YOU SING WITH ME?
I'D NEVER MAKE YOU SING ALONE.
WHAT WE WANT TO EXPRESS IS...
KO (BUMP)
...OUR SOULS.

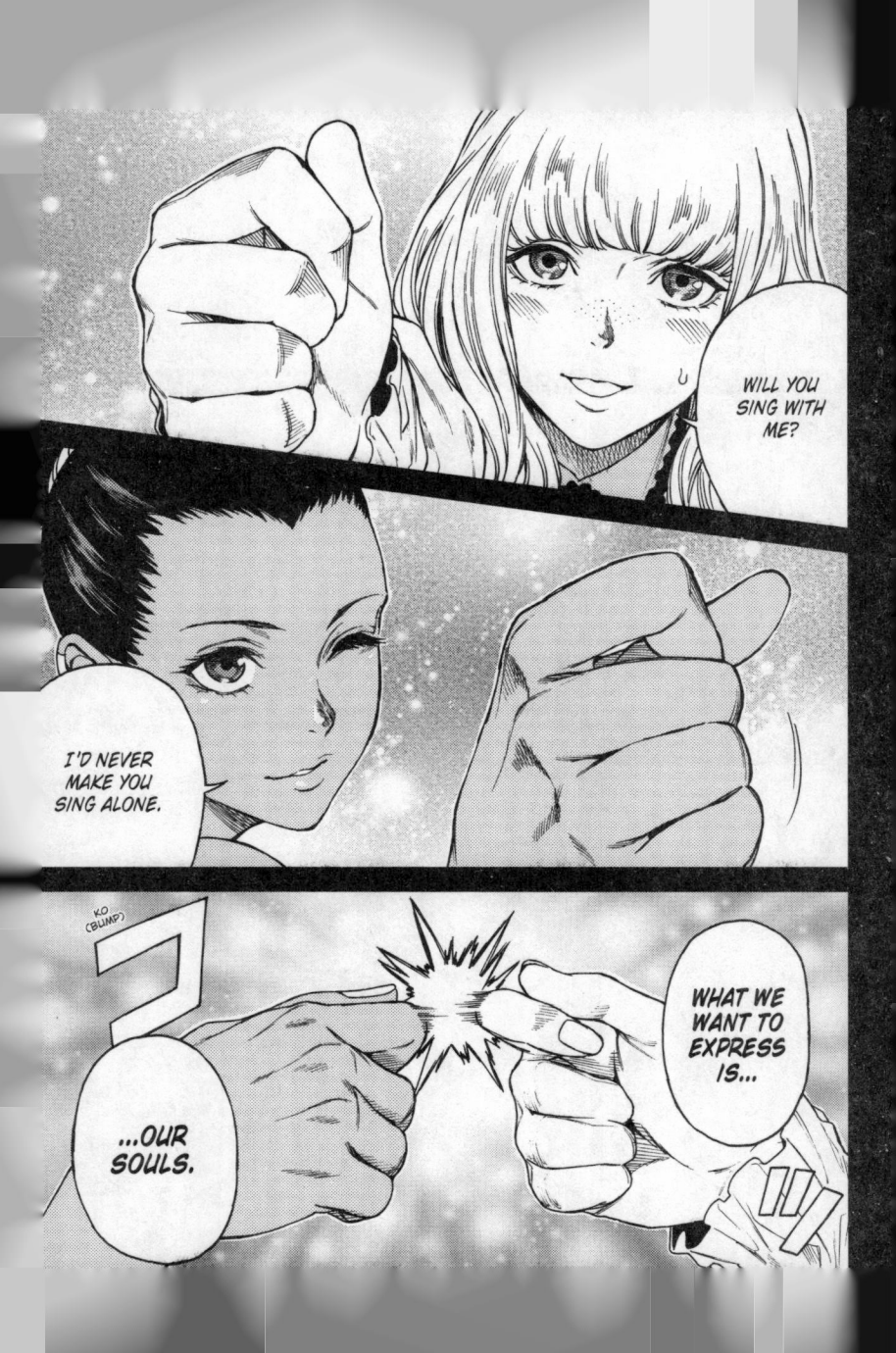

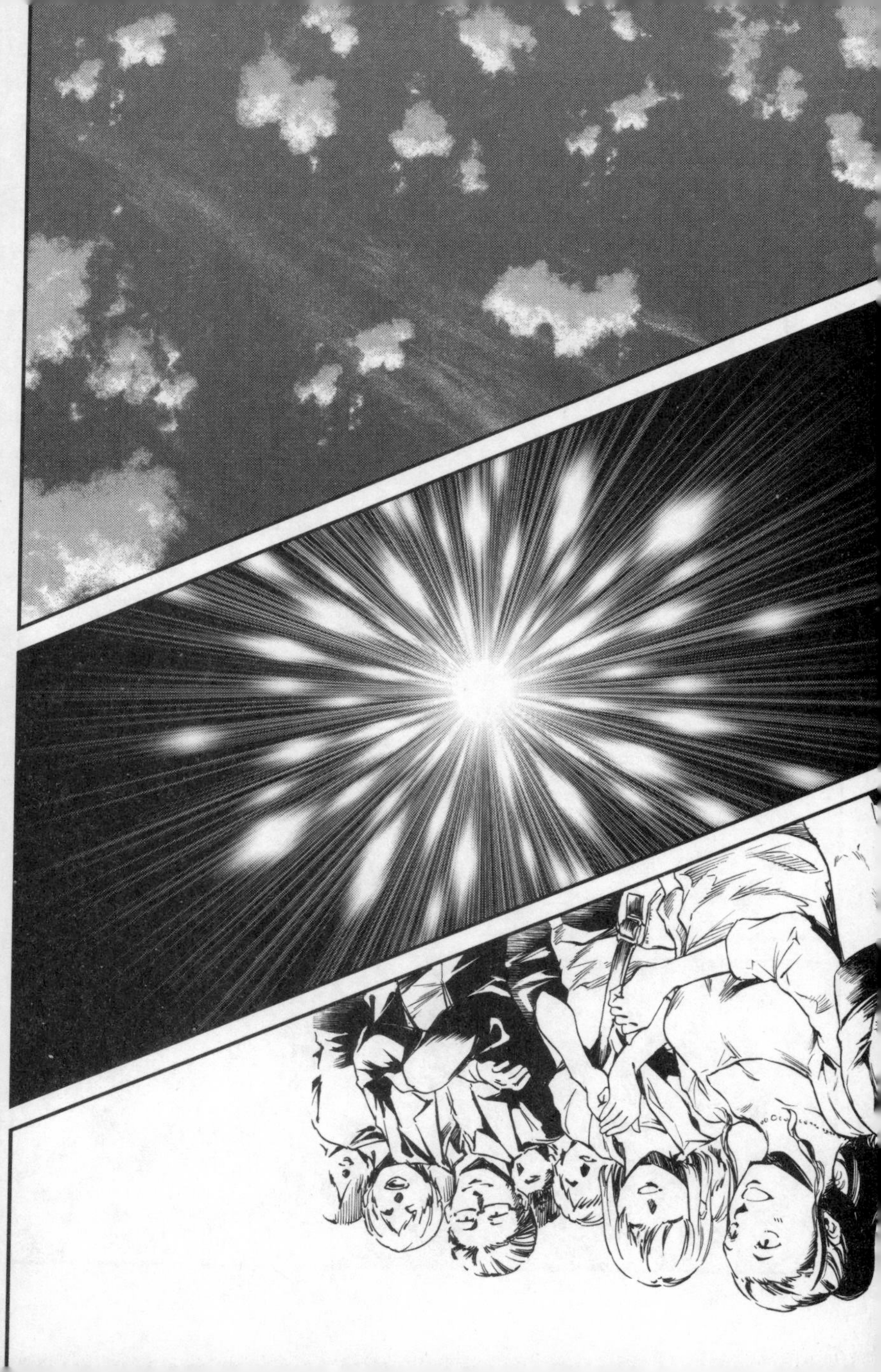

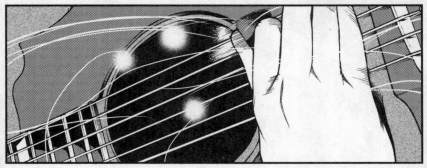

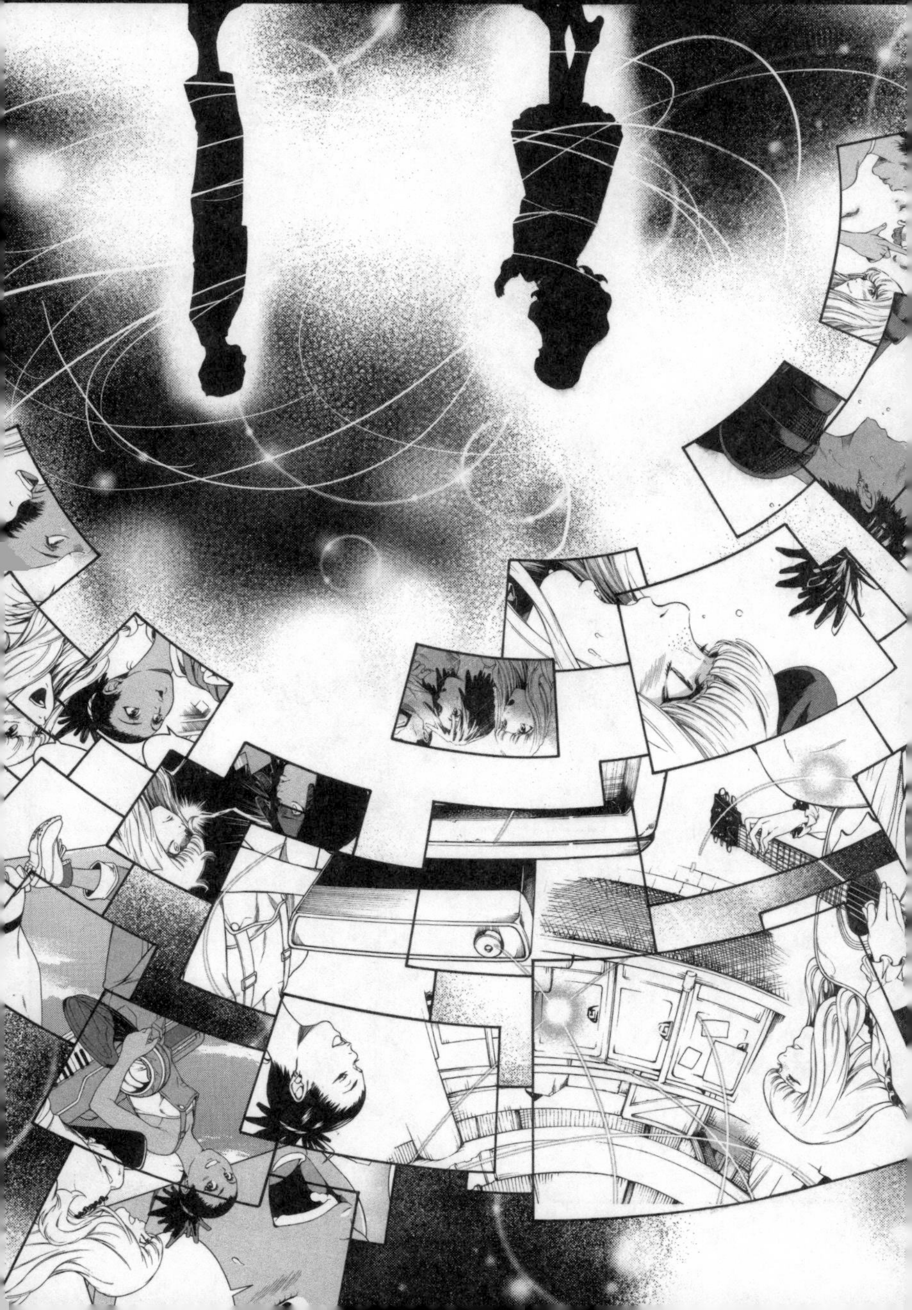

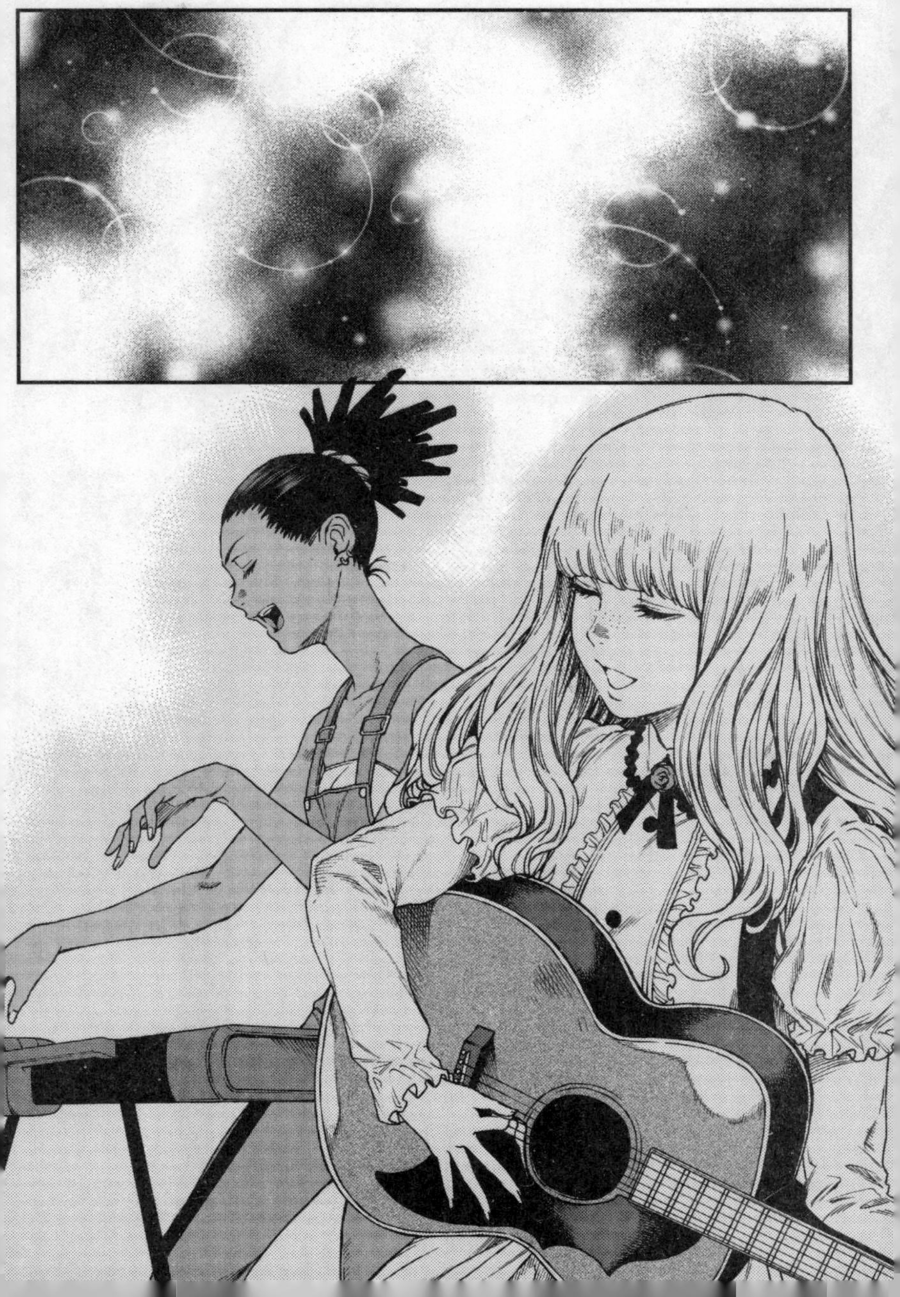

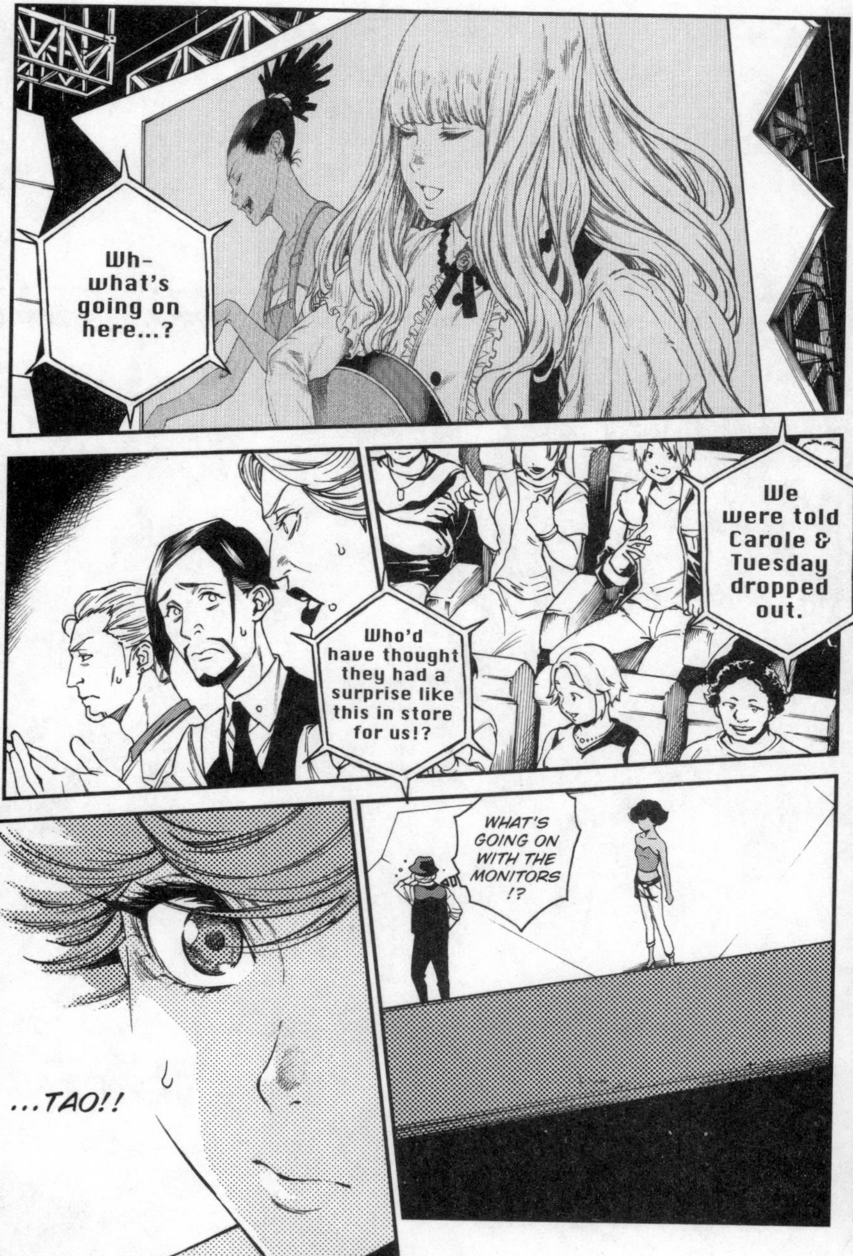
Wh-what's going on here...?
We were told Carole & Tuesday dropped out.
Who'd have thought they had a surprise like this in store for us!?
WHAT'S GOING ON WITH THE MONITORS!?
...TAO!!

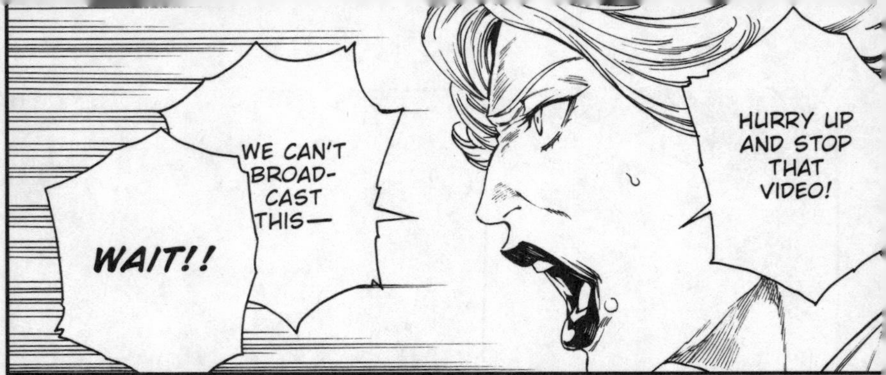
HURRY UP AND STOP THAT VIDEO!
WE CAN'T BROAD-CAST THIS—
WAIT!!

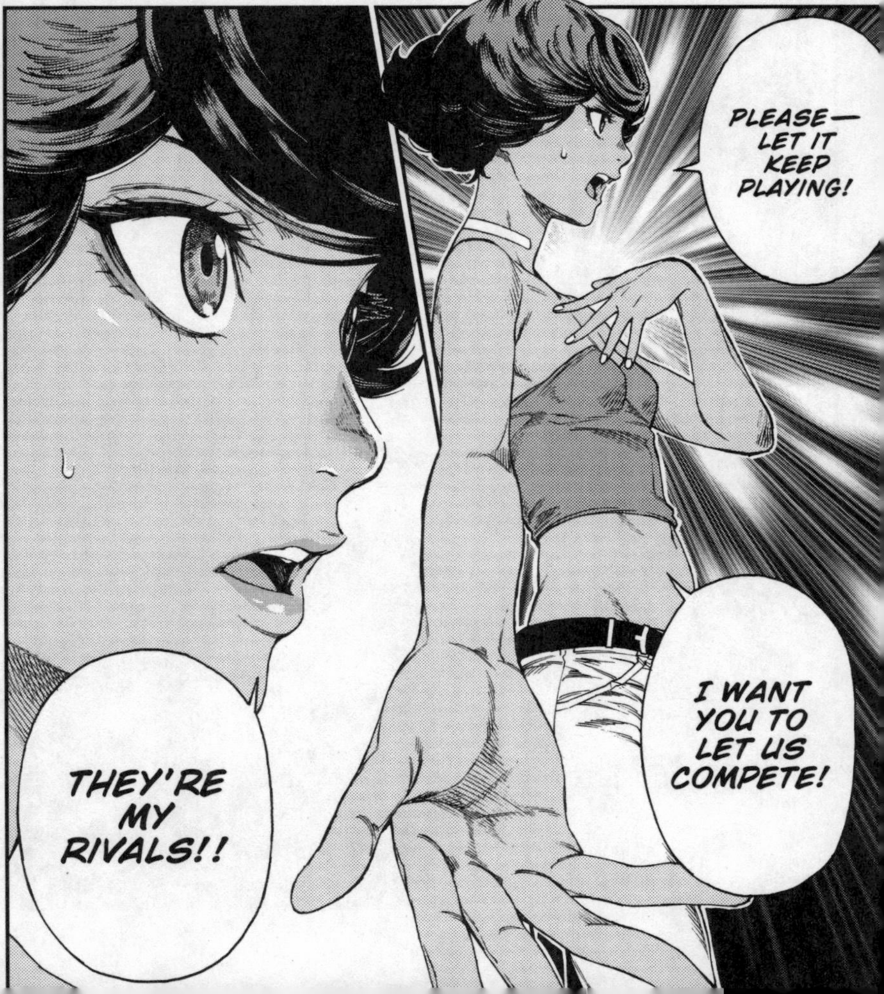
PLEASE— LET IT KEEP PLAYING!
I WANT YOU TO LET US COMPETE!
THEY'RE MY RIVALS!!

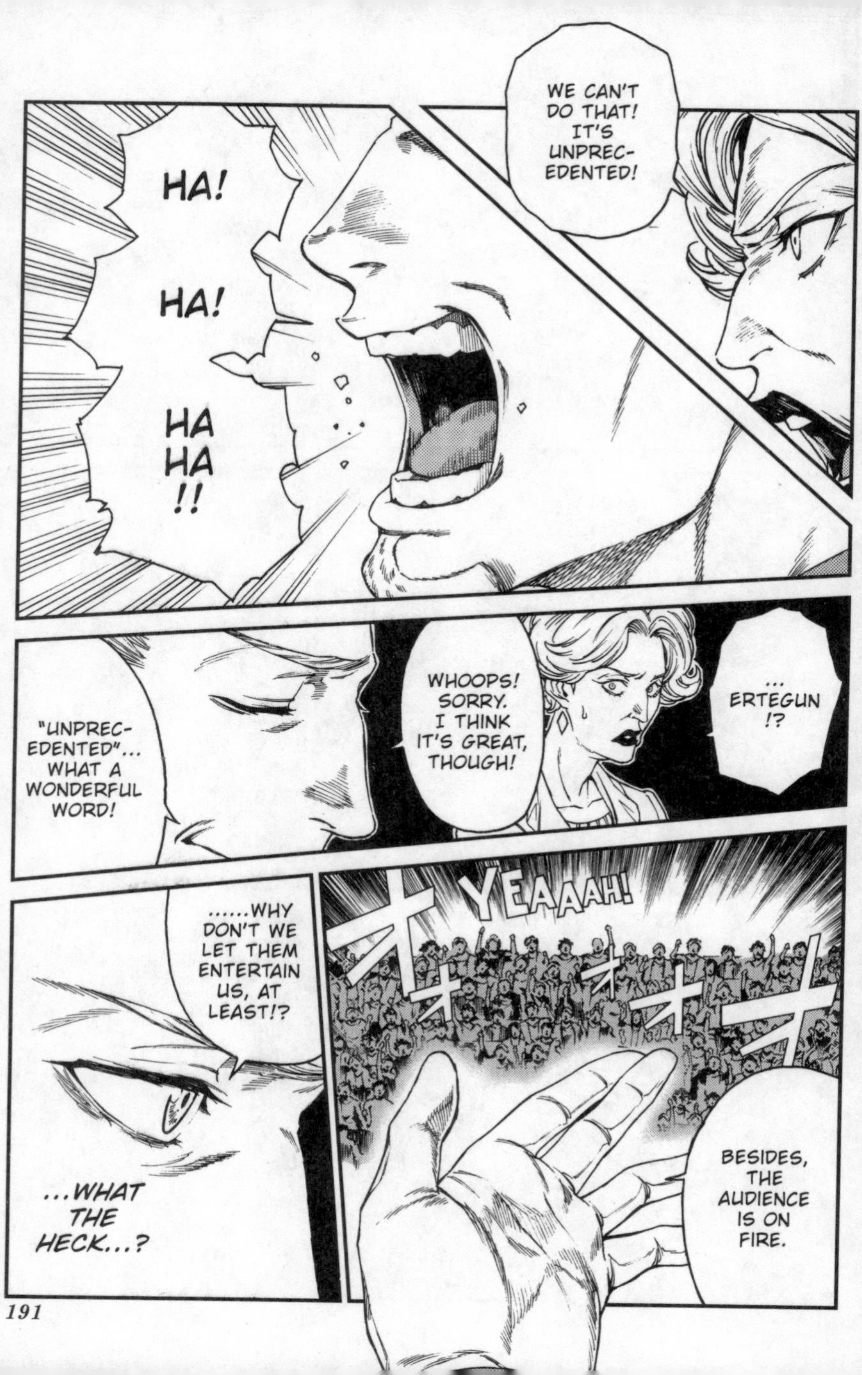
WE CAN'T DO THAT! IT'S UNPREC-EDENTED!
HA!
HA!
HA HA!!
...ERTEGUN!?
WHOOPS! SORRY. I THINK IT'S GREAT, THOUGH!
"UNPREC-EDENTED"... WHAT A WONDERFUL WORD!
YEAAAH!
BESIDES, THE AUDIENCE IS ON FIRE.
......WHY DON'T WE LET THEM ENTERTAIN US, AT LEAST!?
...WHAT THE HECK...?

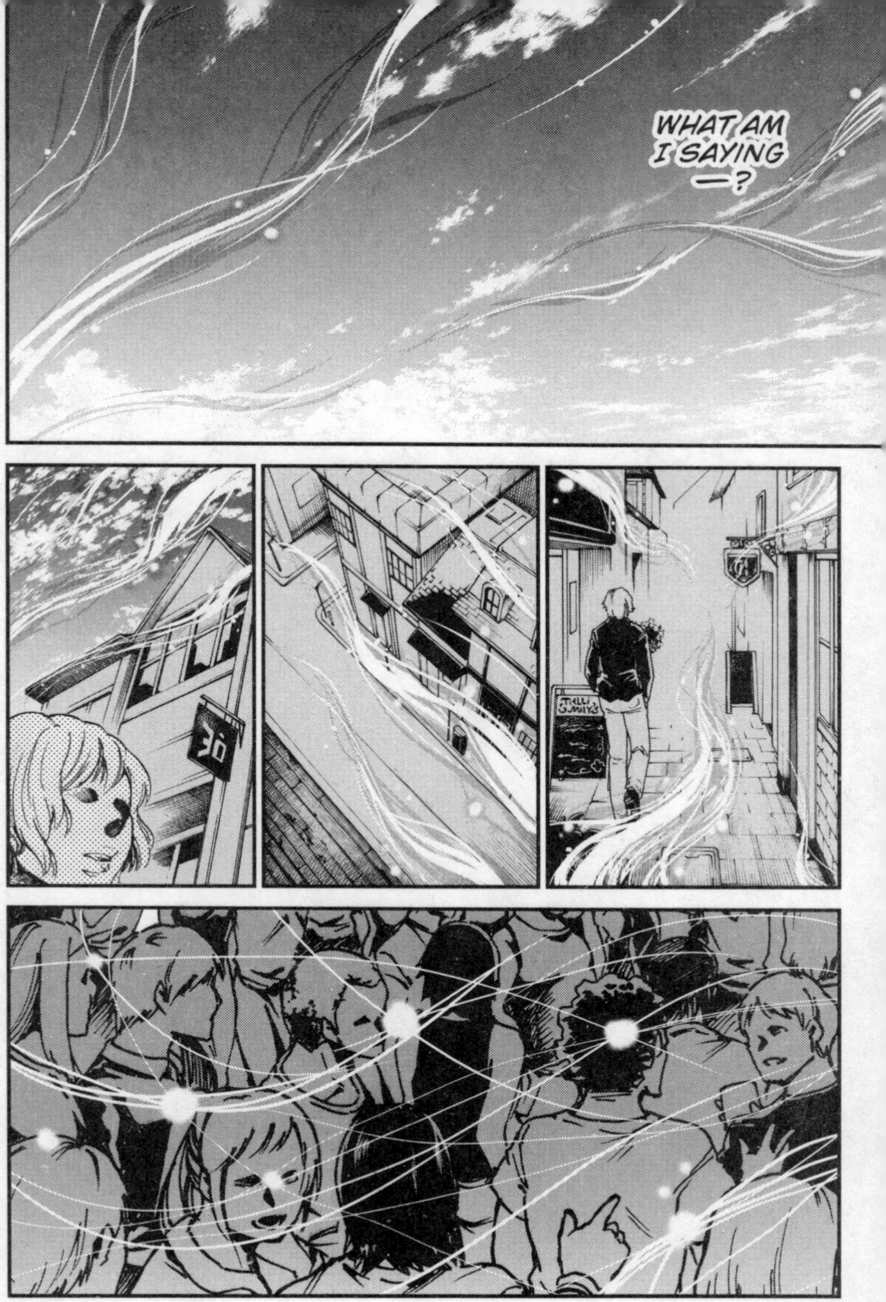
WHAT AM I SAYING —?

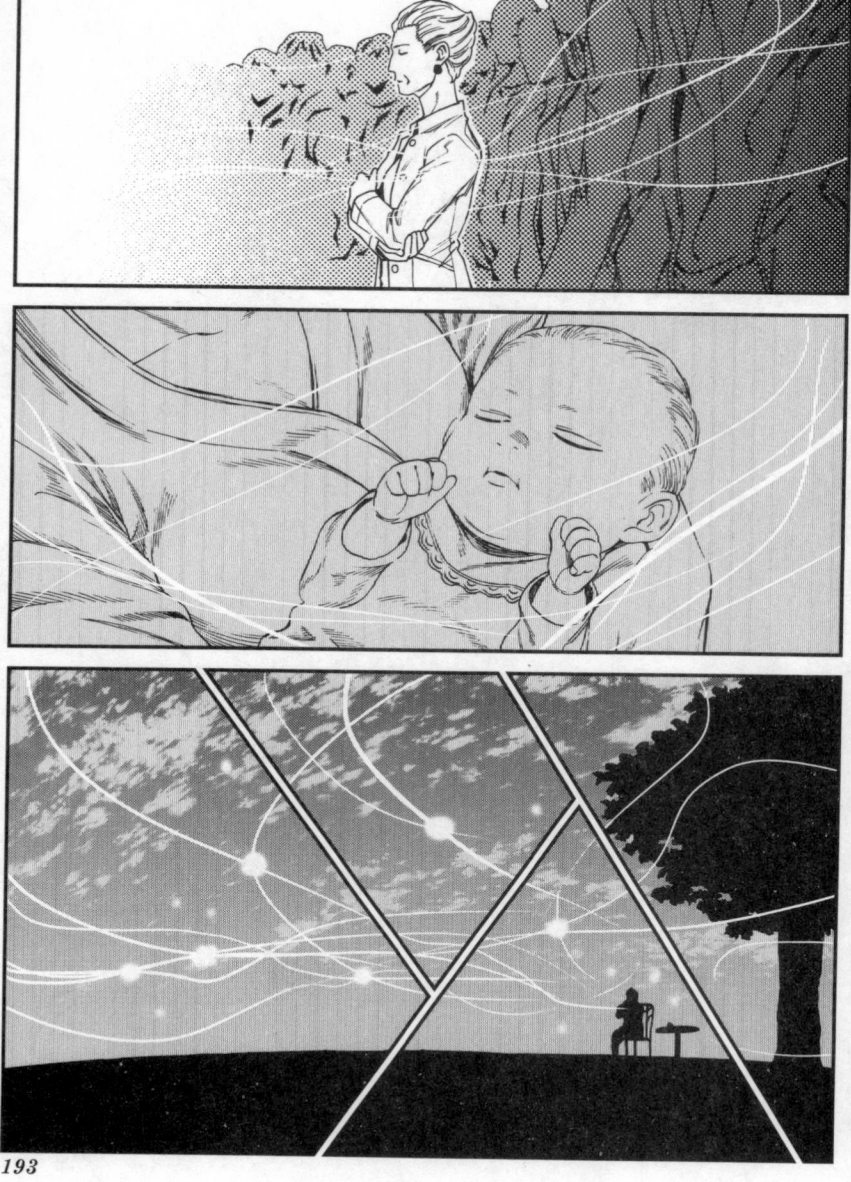

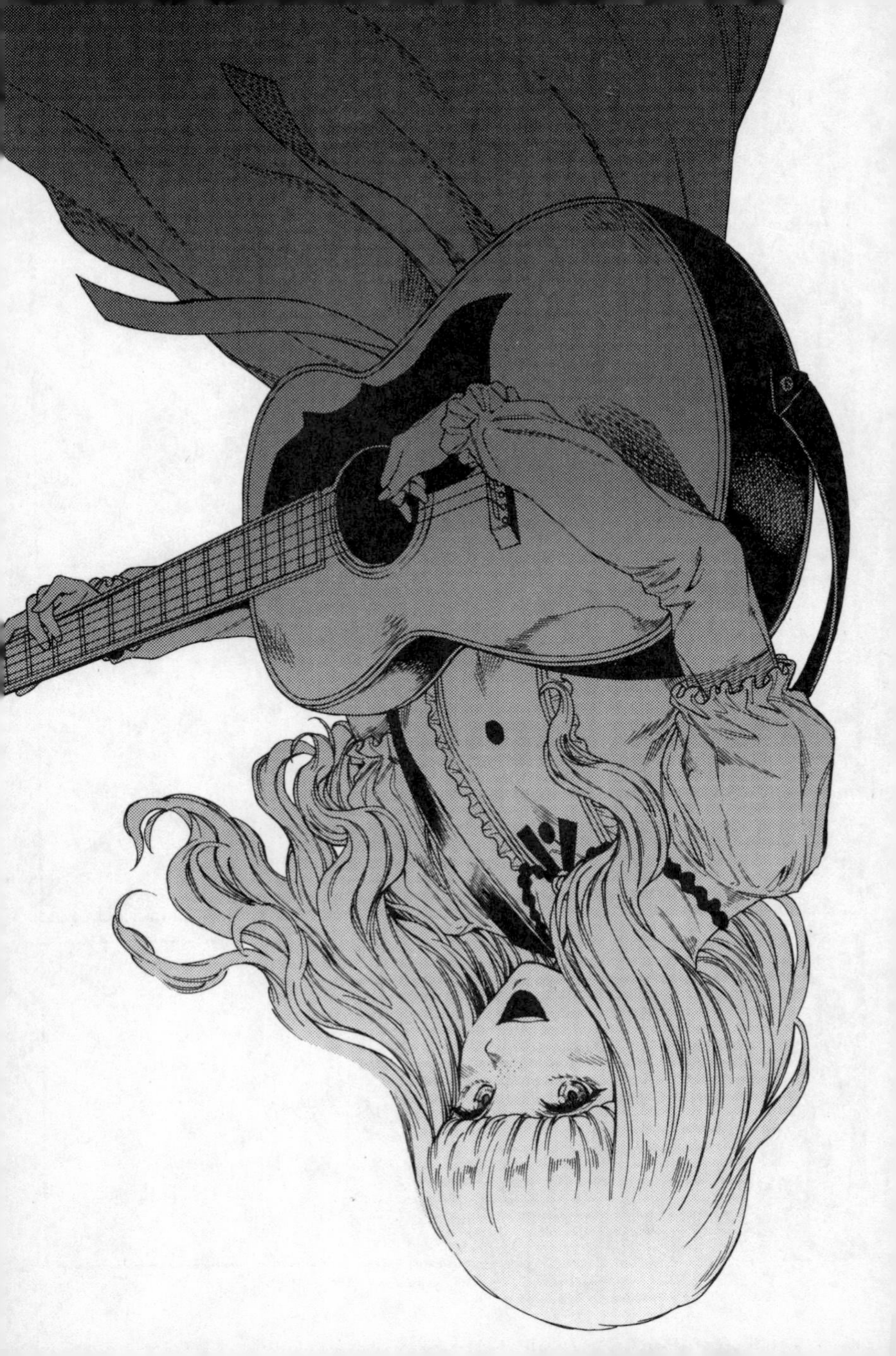

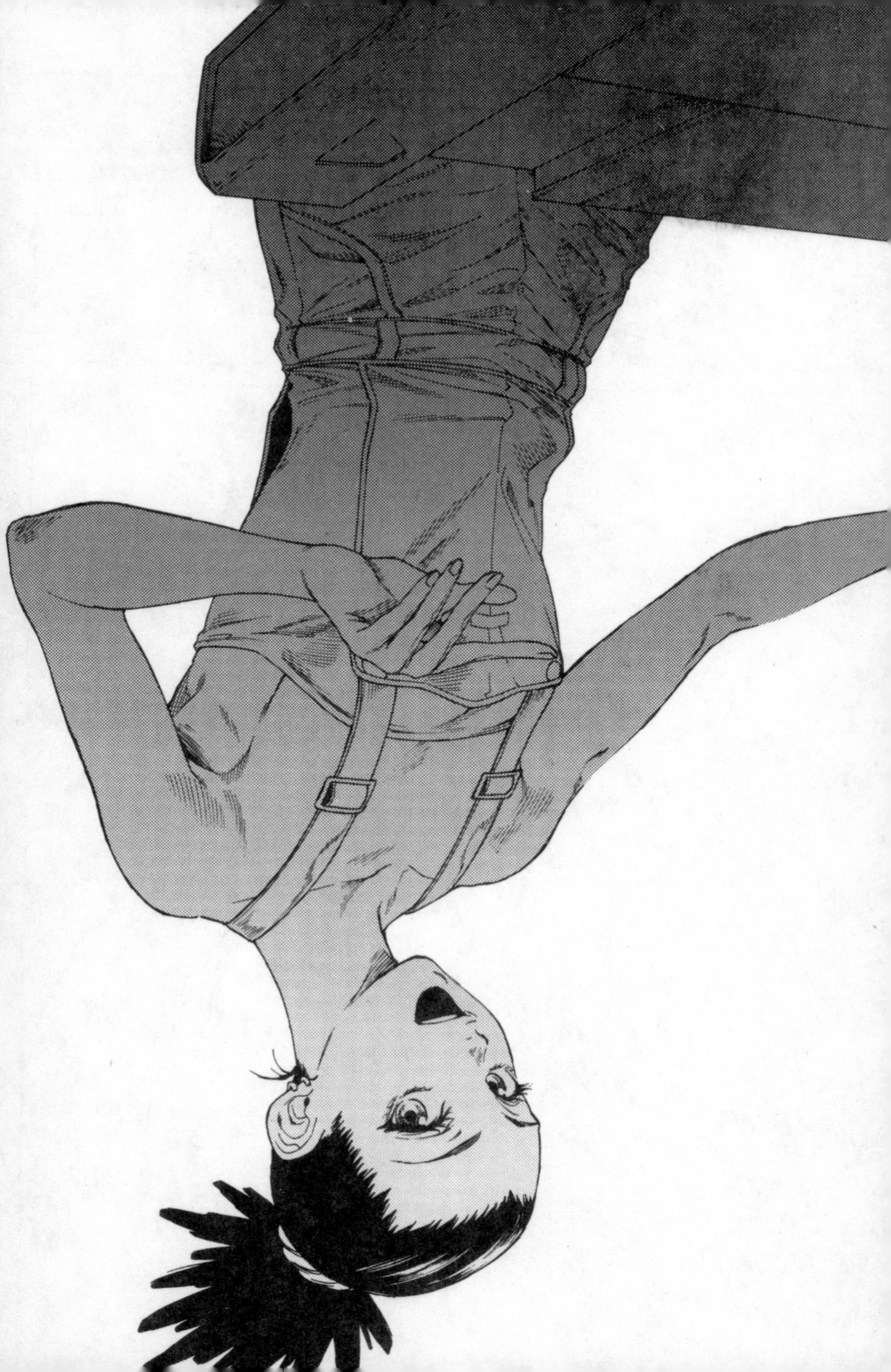

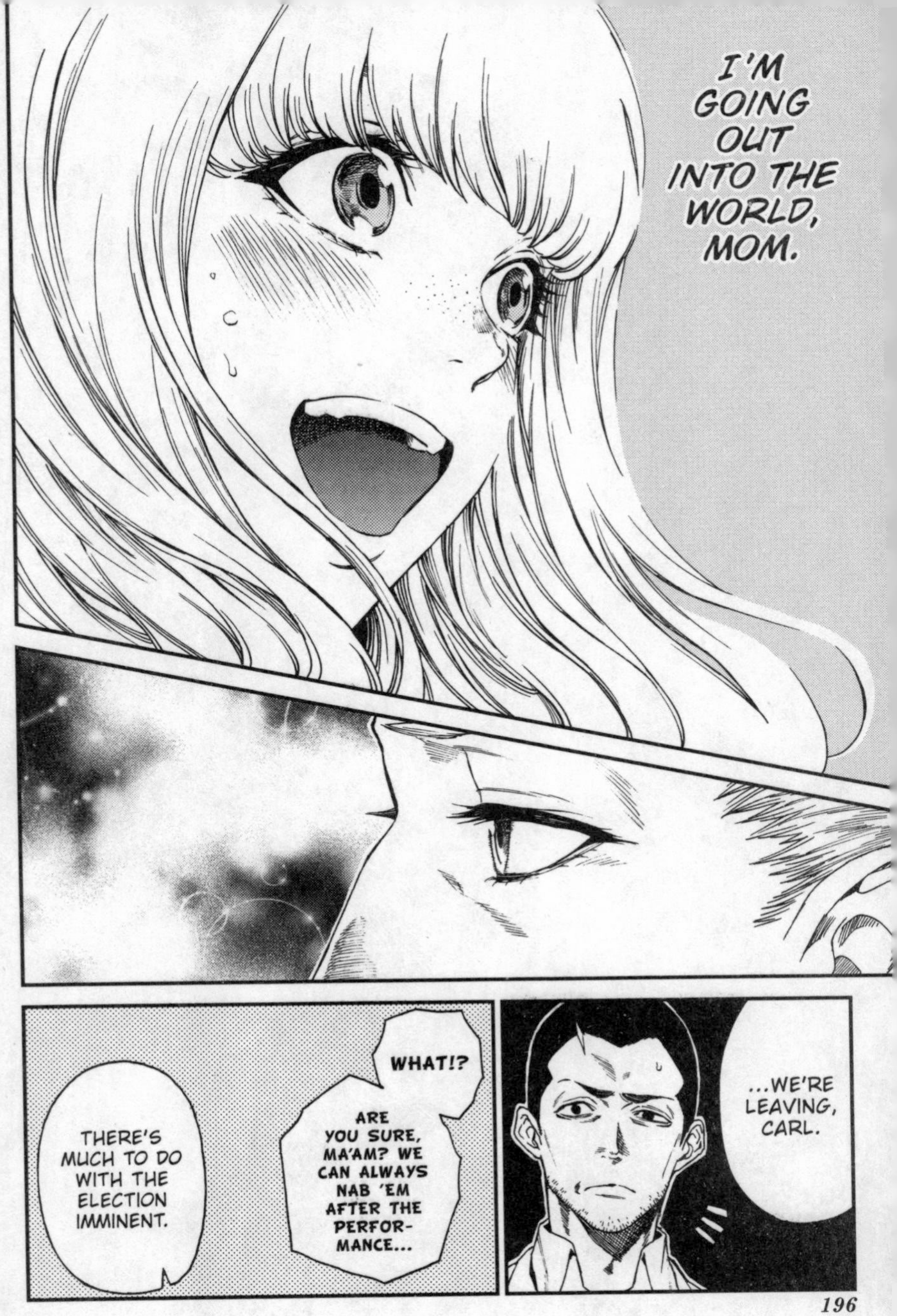
I'M GOING OUT INTO THE WORLD, MOM.
...WE'RE LEAVING, CARL.
WHAT!?
ARE YOU SURE, MA'AM? WE CAN ALWAYS NAB 'EM AFTER THE PERFORMANCE...
THERE'S MUCH TO DO WITH THE ELECTION IMMINENT.

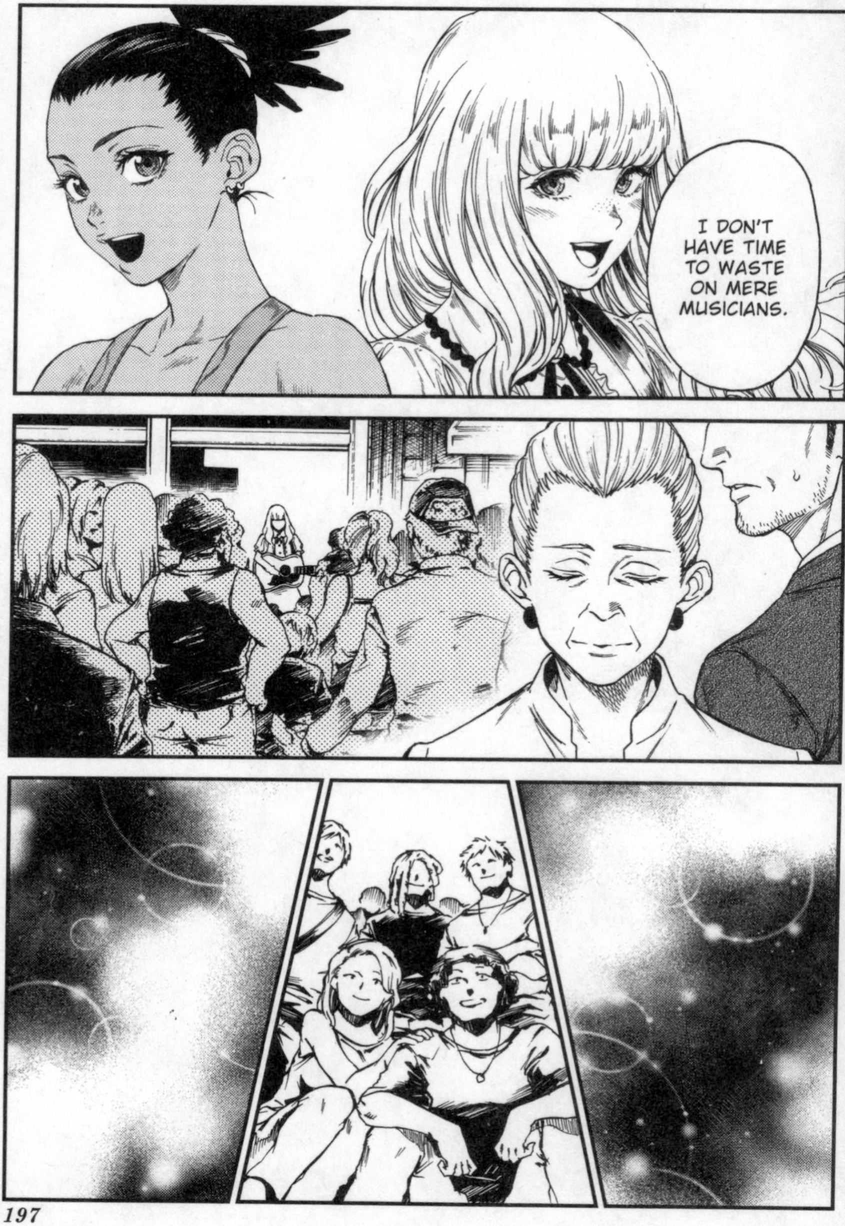
I DON'T HAVE TIME TO WASTE ON MERE MUSICIANS.

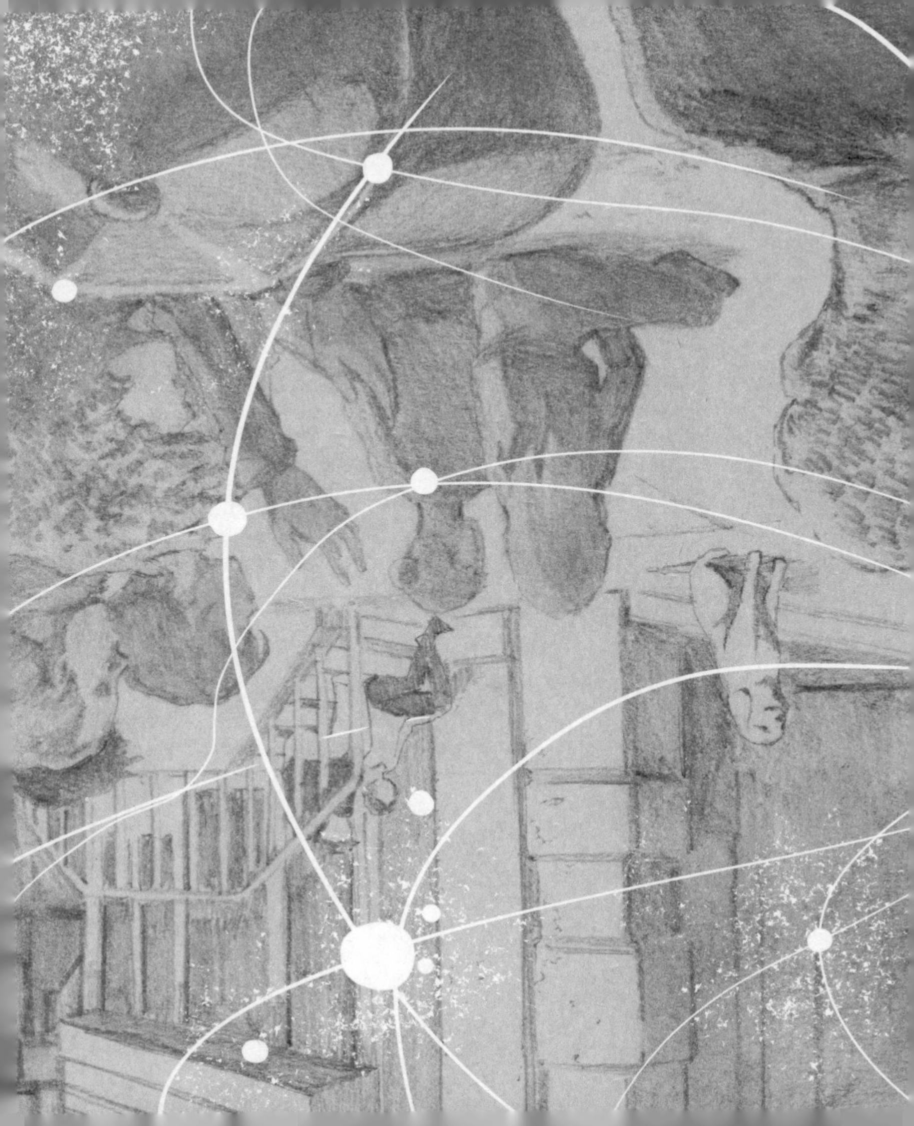

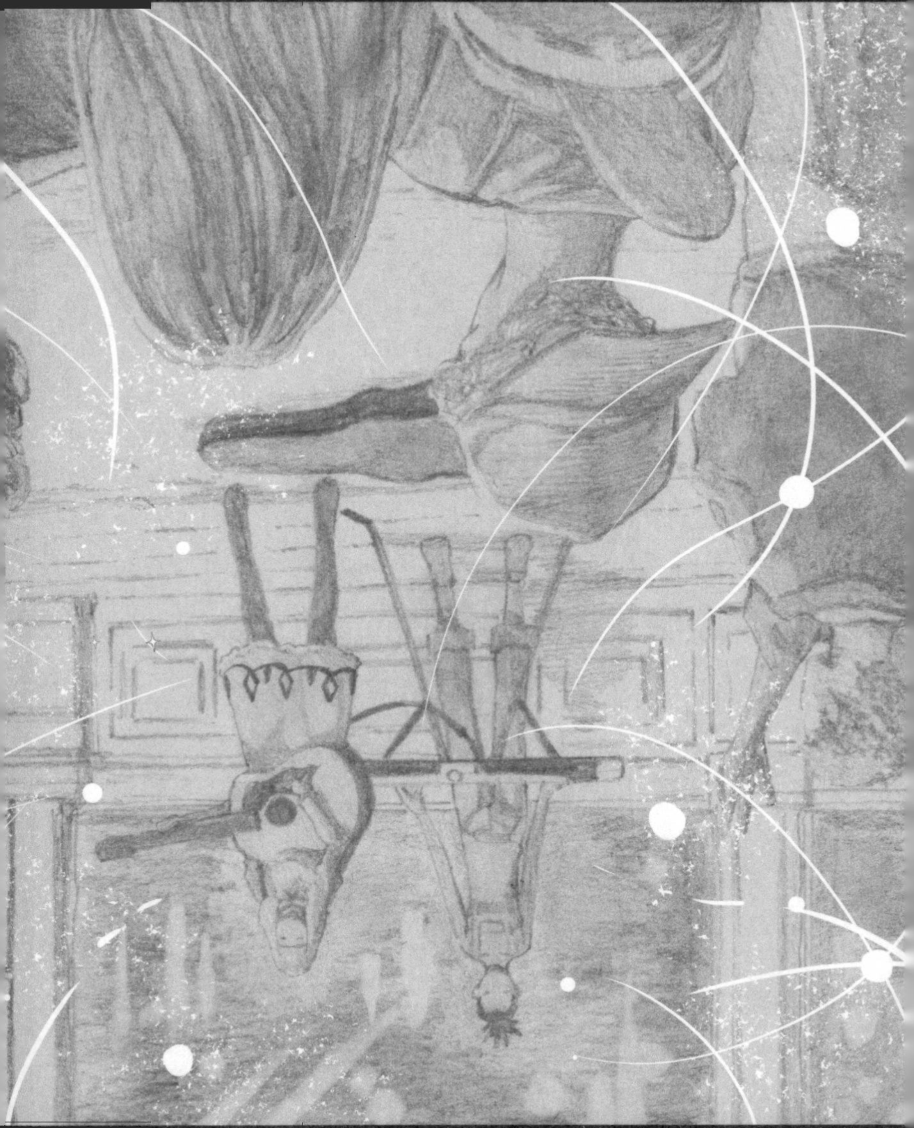

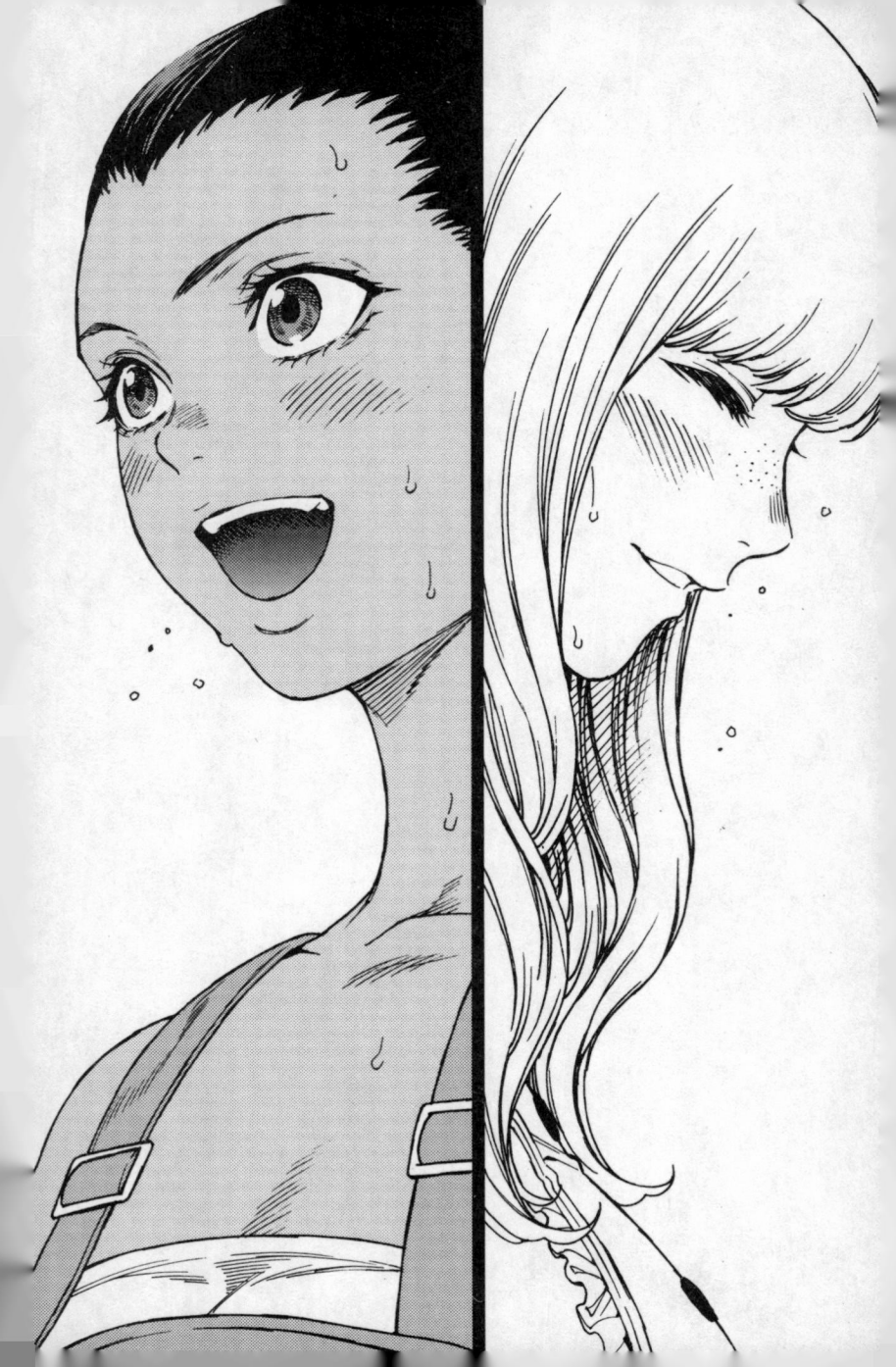

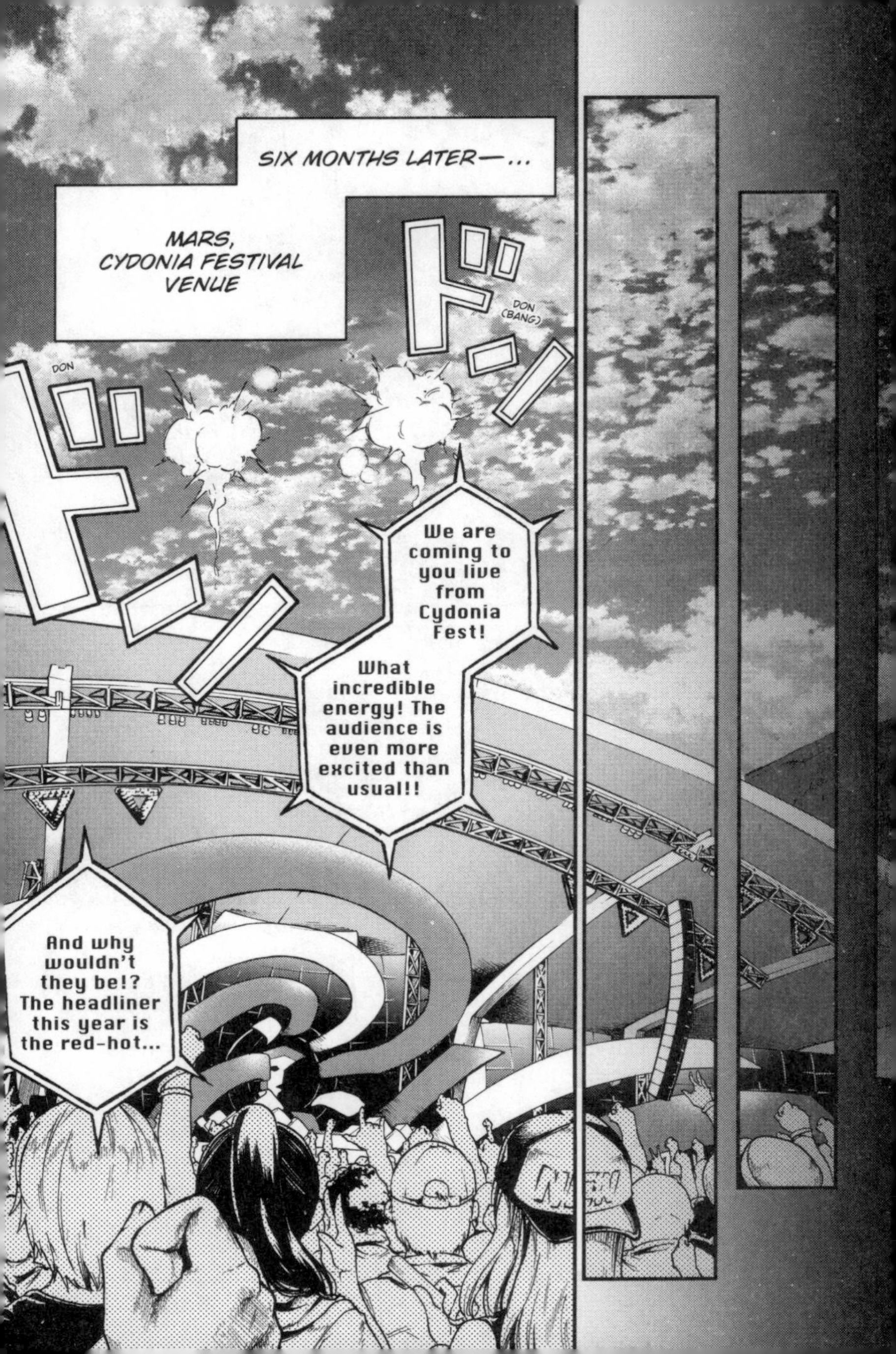
SIX MONTHS LATER—...
MARS, CYDONIA FESTIVAL VENUE
DON (BANG)
DON
We are coming to you live from Cydonia Fest!
What incredible energy! The audience is even more excited than usual!!
And why wouldn't they be!? The headliner this year is the red-hot...

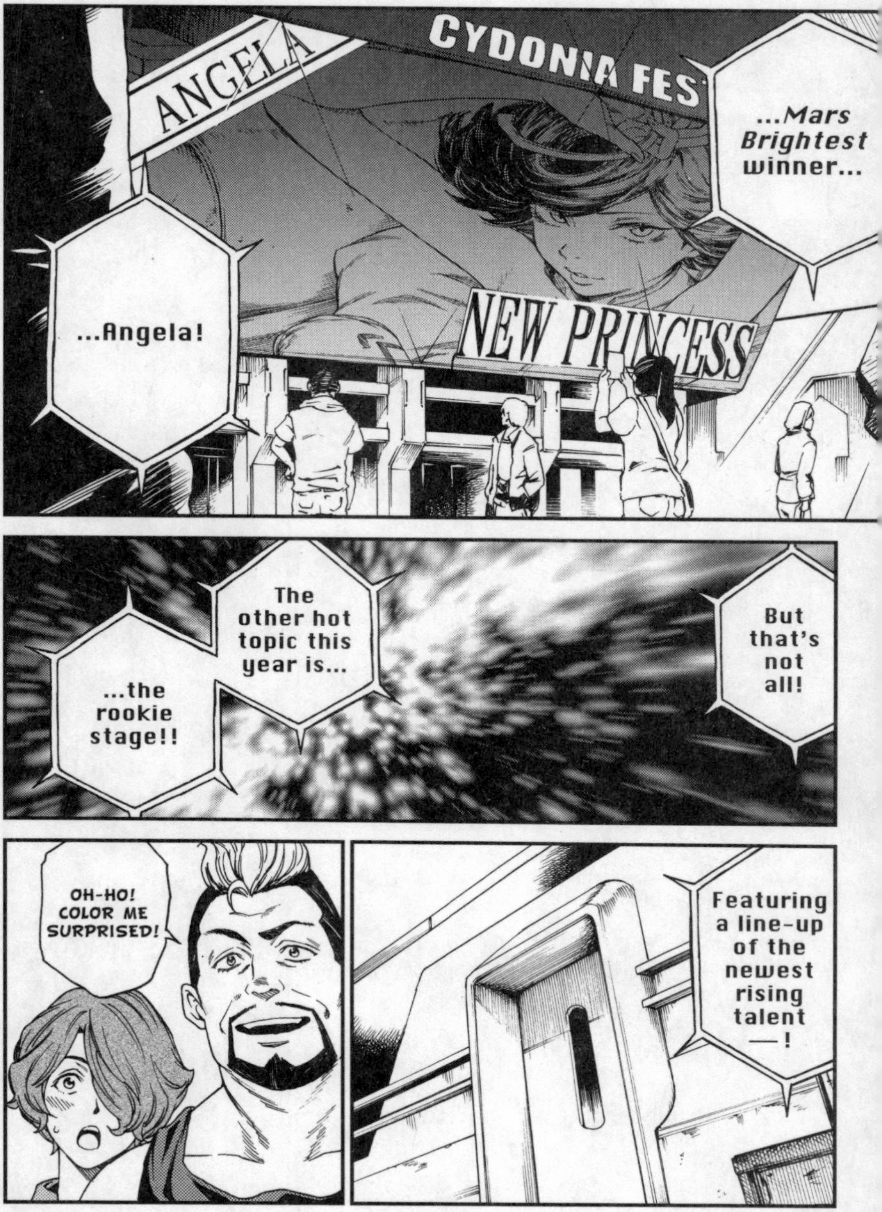
...Mars Brightest winner...
CYDONIA FEST
ANGELA
NEW PRINCESS
...Angela!
But that's not all!
The other hot topic this year is...
...the rookie stage!!
Featuring a line-up of the newest rising talent—!
OH-HO! COLOR ME SURPRISED!

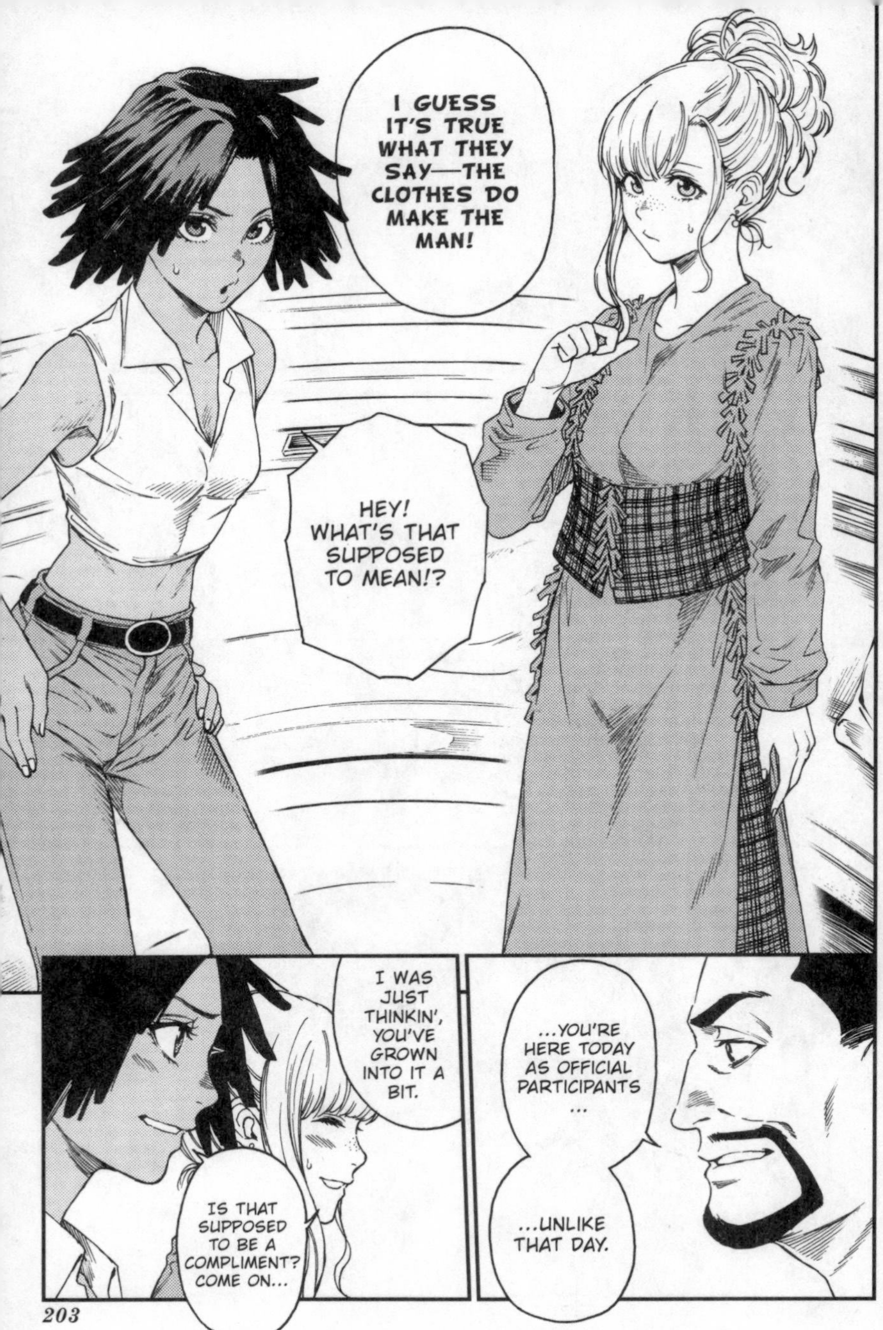
I GUESS IT'S TRUE WHAT THEY SAY—THE CLOTHES DO MAKE THE MAN!
HEY! WHAT'S THAT SUPPOSED TO MEAN!?
...YOU'RE HERE TODAY AS OFFICIAL PARTICIPANTS ...
...UNLIKE THAT DAY.
I WAS JUST THINKIN', YOU'VE GROWN INTO IT A BIT.
IS THAT SUPPOSED TO BE A COMPLIMENT? COME ON...

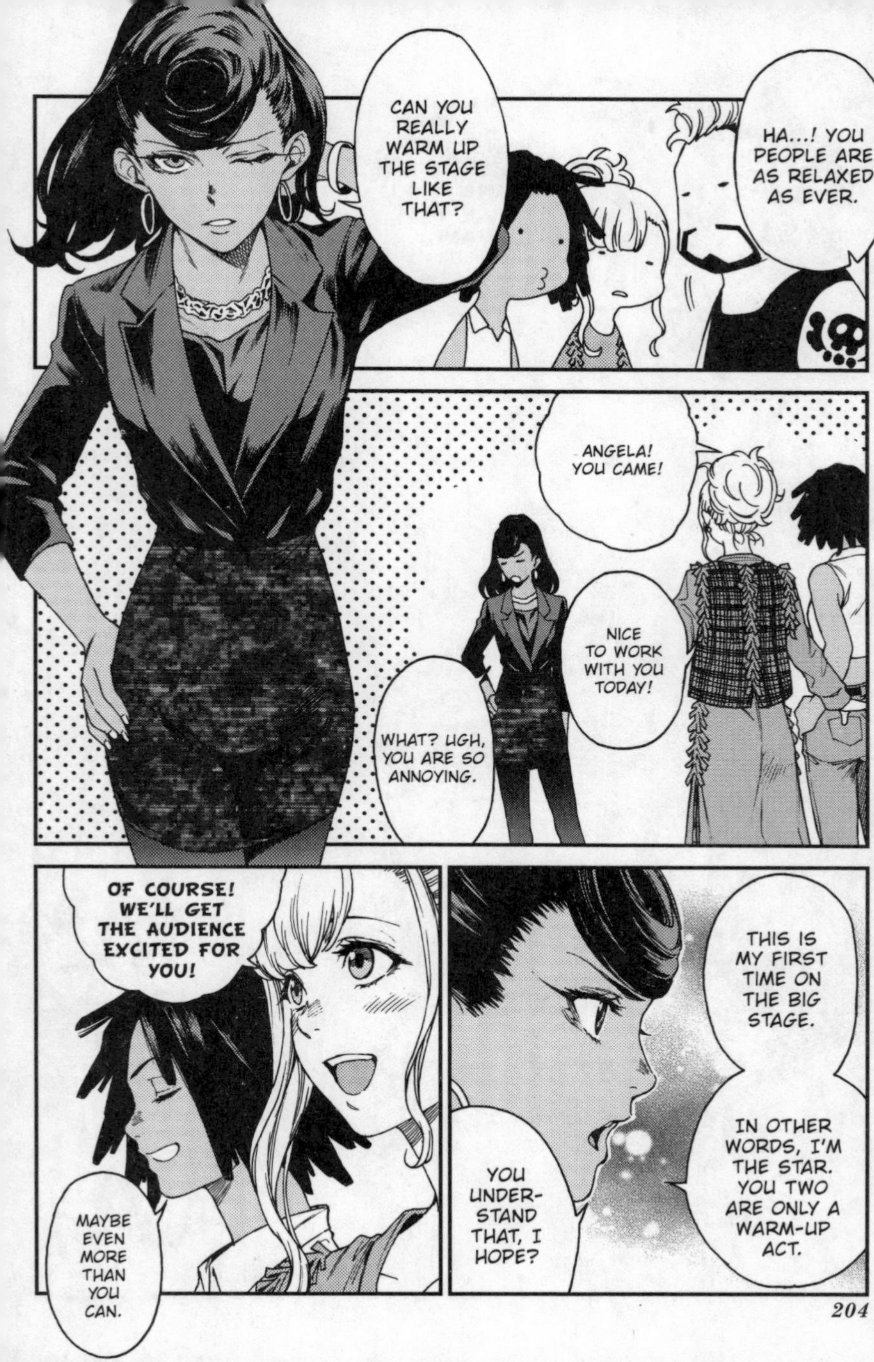
HA...! YOU PEOPLE ARE AS RELAXED AS EVER.
CAN YOU REALLY WARM UP THE STAGE LIKE THAT?
ANGELA! YOU CAME!
NICE TO WORK WITH YOU TODAY!
WHAT? UGH, YOU ARE SO ANNOYING.
THIS IS MY FIRST TIME ON THE BIG STAGE.
IN OTHER WORDS, I'M THE STAR. YOU TWO ARE ONLY A WARM-UP ACT.
YOU UNDERSTAND THAT, I HOPE?
OF COURSE! WE'LL GET THE AUDIENCE EXCITED FOR YOU!
MAYBE EVEN MORE THAN YOU CAN.

WELL, LOOK WHO'S GOT A MOUTH ON HER NOW...

TODAY, I'M FINALLY BEATING YOU IN PERSO—

AH! I FINALLY FOUND YOU!

GOOD GRIEF! MISS ANGELA, WHAT ARE YOU DOING!?

MR. TAO IS CALLING FOR YOU FOR THE FINAL MEETING!

HEY! KATY! DON'T PULL ME!

PLEASE HURRY! MR. TAO WILL LEAVE!

EXCUSE ME!? THEN YOU STOP HIM!!

HEH HEH...

......

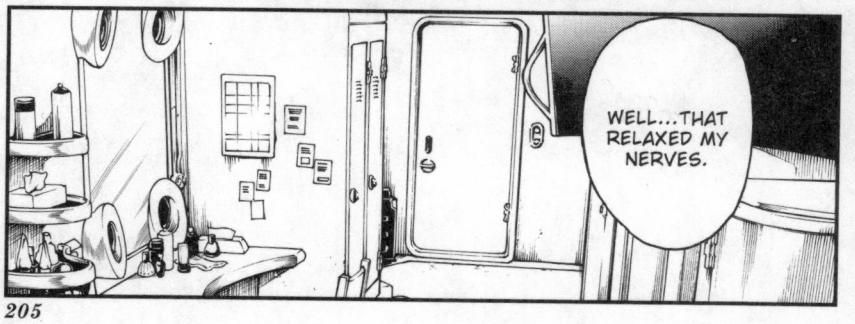

WELL...THAT RELAXED MY NERVES.

205

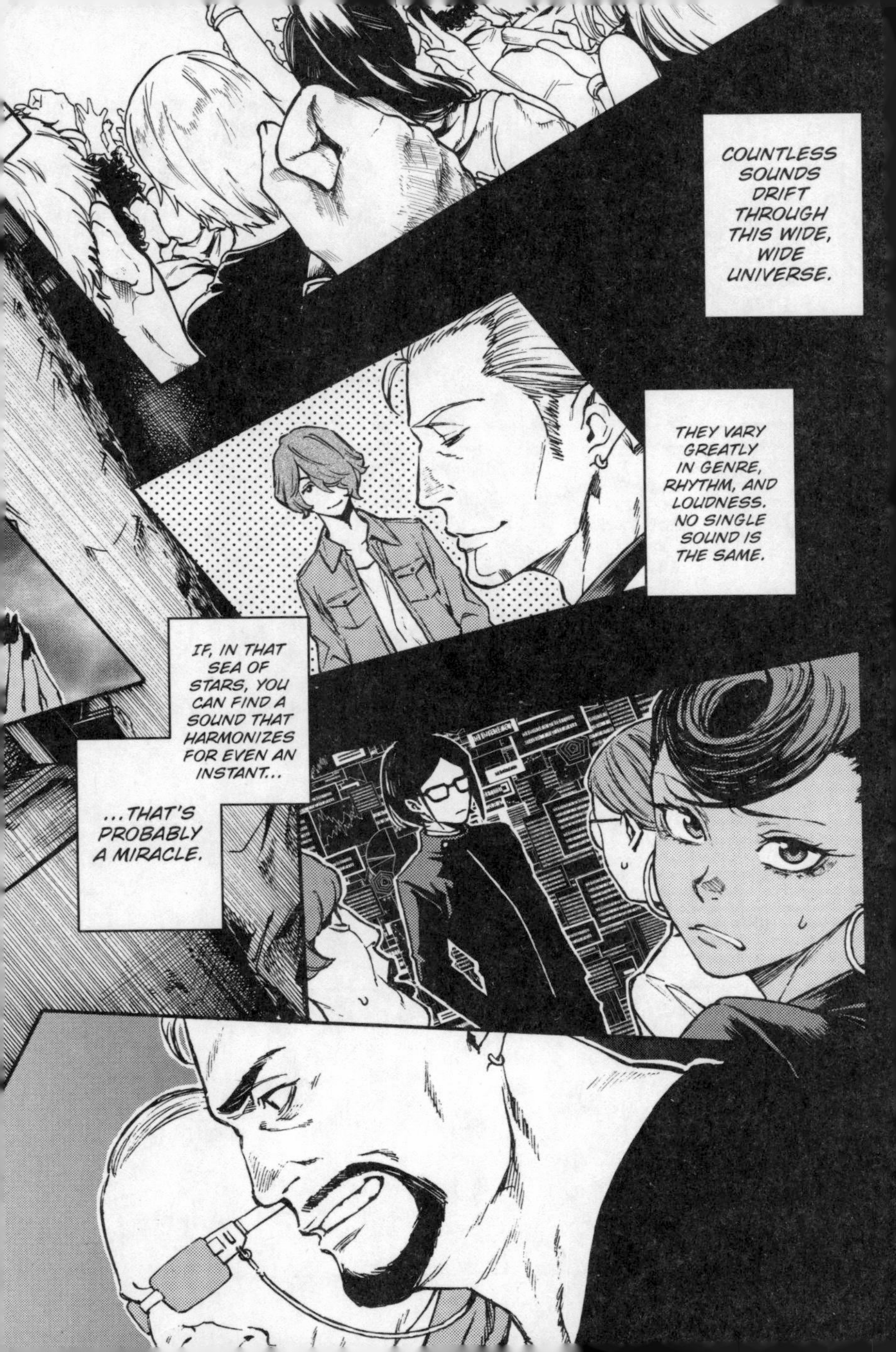
COUNTLESS SOUNDS DRIFT THROUGH THIS WIDE, WIDE UNIVERSE.
THEY VARY GREATLY IN GENRE, RHYTHM, AND LOUDNESS. NO SINGLE SOUND IS THE SAME.
IF, IN THAT SEA OF STARS, YOU CAN FIND A SOUND THAT HARMONIZES FOR EVEN AN INSTANT...
...THAT'S PROBABLY A MIRACLE.

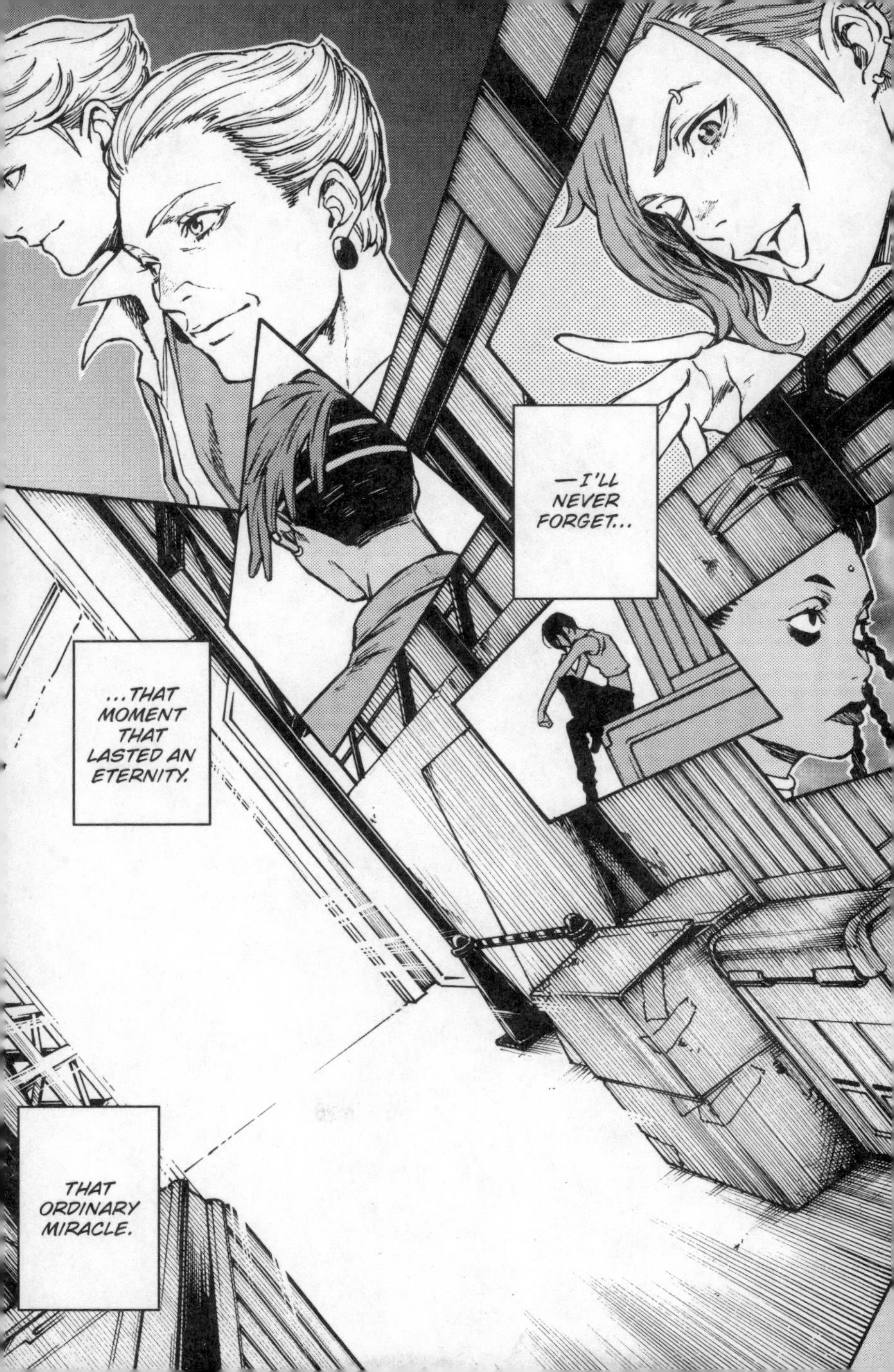
—I'LL NEVER FORGET...
...THAT MOMENT THAT LASTED AN ETERNITY.
THAT ORDINARY MIRACLE.

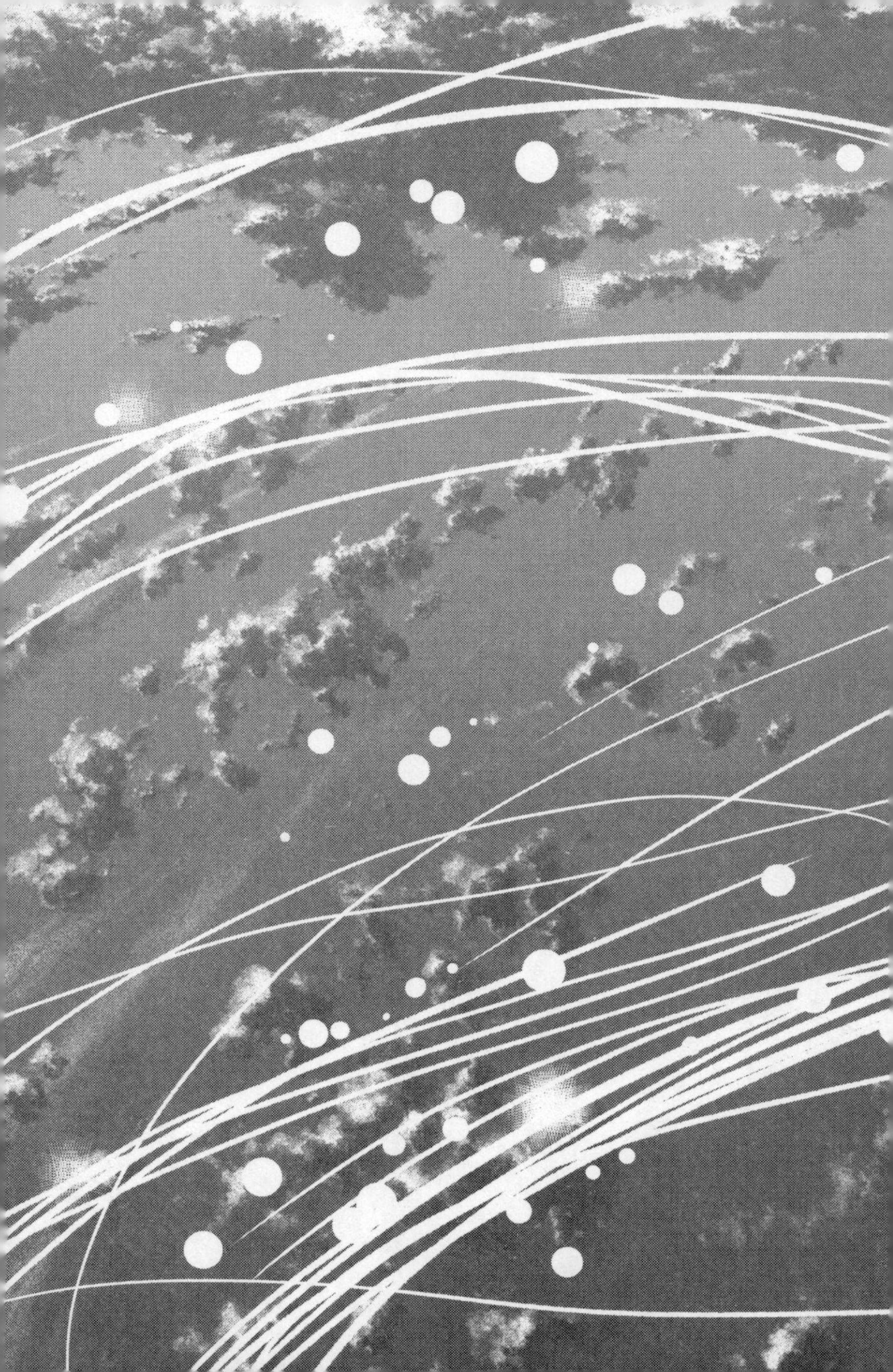

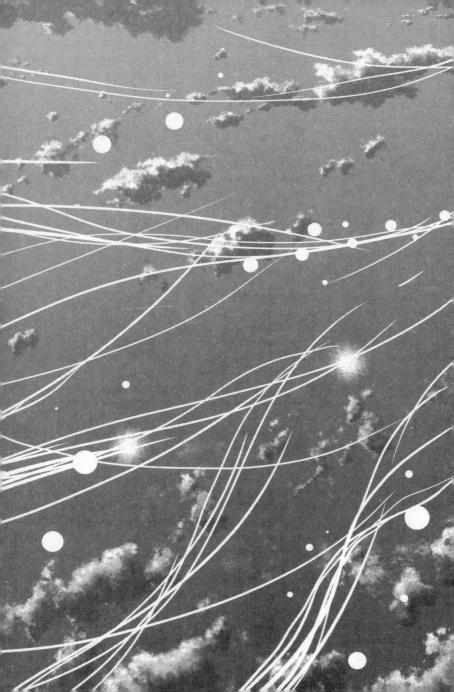

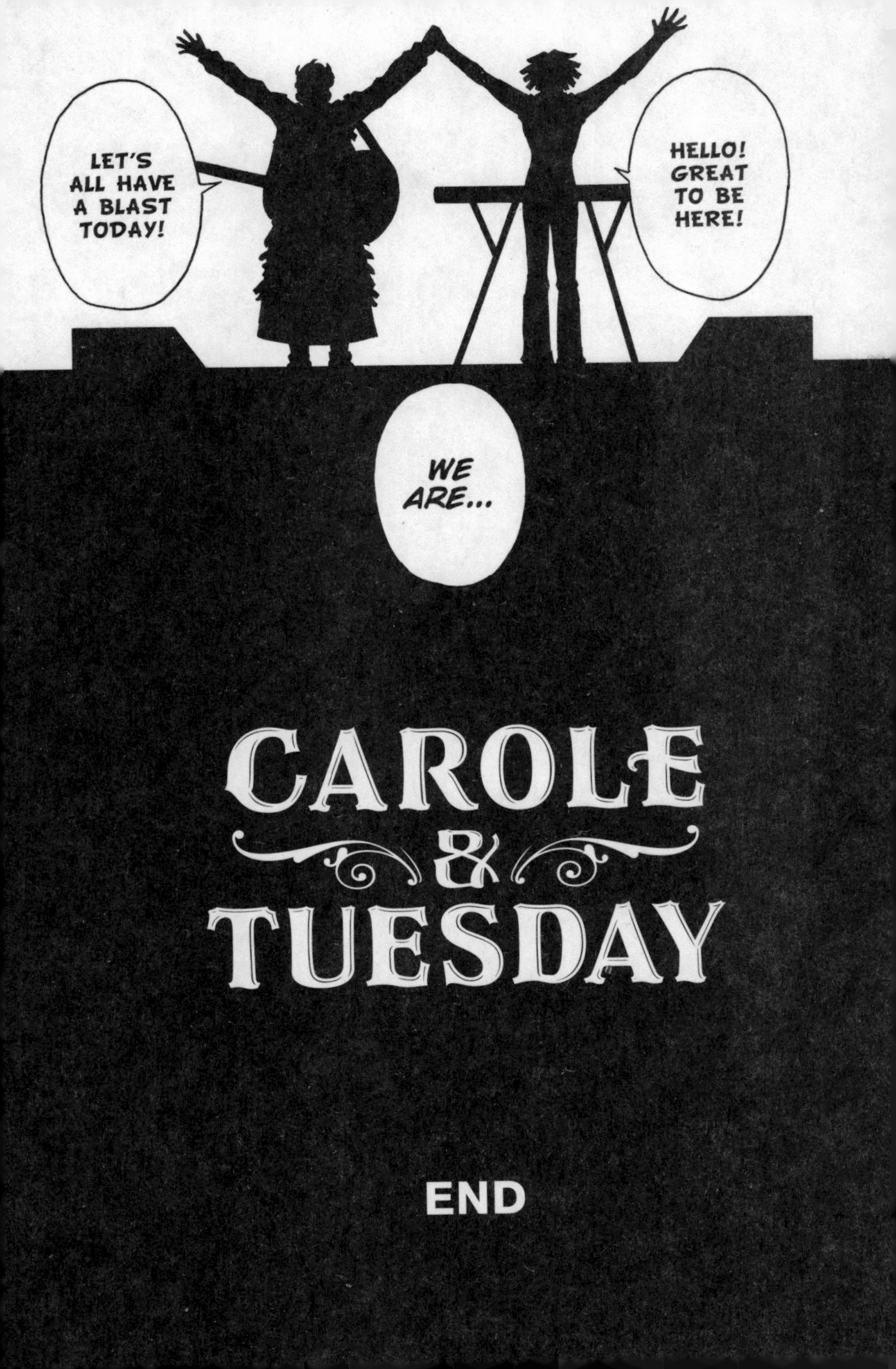
HELLO! GREAT TO BE HERE!
LET'S ALL HAVE A BLAST TODAY!
WE ARE...
CAROLE & TUESDAY
END

<SPECIAL THANKS>
Shinichiro Watanabe
The staff at BONES
Tsuyoshi Kusano
My editor

<STAFF>
Kyousuke Nishiki

CAROLE & TUESDAY

3

ART
Morito Yamataka
ORIGINAL STORY
BONES, Shinichiro Watanabe

Translation: **Amanda Haley** | Lettering: **Lys Blakeslee**

CAROLE & TUESDAY, vol. 3
© Morito Yamataka 2020
© BONES, Shinichiro Watanabe 2020
First published in Japan in 2020 by KADOKAWA CORPORATION, Tokyo.
English translation rights arranged with KADOKAWA CORPORATION, Tokyo and Yen Press, LLC through Tuttle-Mori Agency, Inc.

English translation © 2022 by Yen Press, LLC

Yen Press
150 West 30th Street, 19th Floor
New York, NY 10001

Visit us at yenpress.com ♫ facebook.com/yenpress ♫
twitter.com/yenpress ♫ yenpress.tumblr.com ♫ instagram.com/yenpress

First Yen Press Edition: January 2022

Yen Press is an imprint of Yen Press, LLC.
The Yen Press name and logo are trademarks of Yen Press, LLC.

Library of Congress Control Number: 2020933563

ISBNs: 978-1-9753-3872-5 (paperback)
       978-1-9753-3873-2 (ebook)

10 9 8 7 6 5 4 3 2 1

WOR

Printed in the United States of America